Strangers in the Land

To Mary, who shared all the hardships and joys of our long association with India

Strangers in the Land

The Rise and Decline of the British Indian Empire

Roderick Cavaliero

I.B. Tauris *Publishers*
LONDON • NEW YORK

Published in 2002 by I.B.Tauris & Co Ltd
6 Salem Road, London W2 4BU
175 Fifth Avenue, New York NY 10010
www.ibtauris.com

In the United States of America and in Canada distributed by
St Martins Press, 175 Fifth Avenue, New York NY 10010

ISBN 1 86064 797 9

A full CIP record for this book is available from the British Library
A full CIP record for this book is available from the Library of Congress

Library of Congress catalog card: available

Project management by Steve Tribe, London
Printed and bound in Great Britain by MPG Books Ltd, Bodmin

CONTENTS

Maps

ILLUSTRATIONS

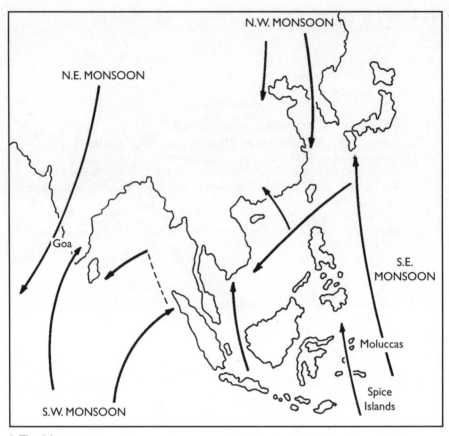

1. The Monsoons

2. India at the time of Clive

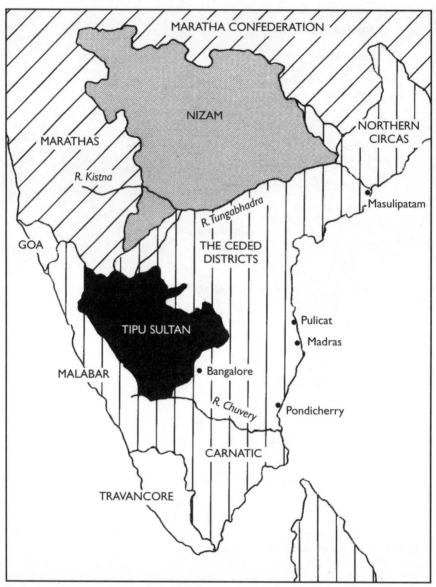

3. South India at the time of Wellesley

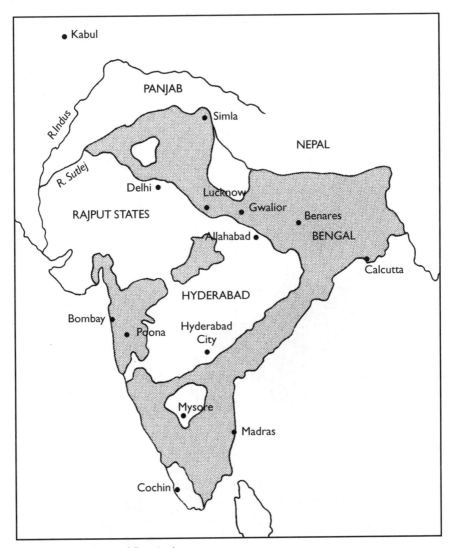

4. India at the time of Bentinck

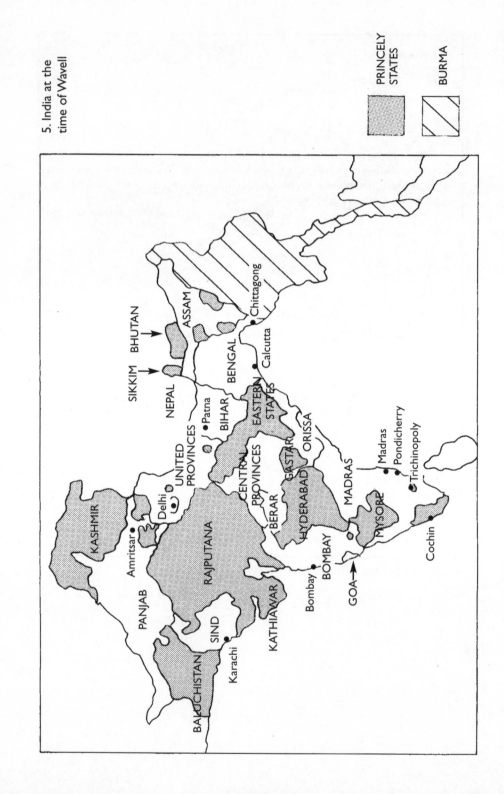

5. India at the time of Wavell

PRINCELY STATES

BURMA

We are necessarily very much confined to our houses by the heat: all our wants and businesses which could create a greater intercourse with the natives is done for us, and we are, in fact, strangers in the land.

Lord William Bentinck, 1807

PREFACE

That a small western power should come to India from a
distance of thousands of miles and subjugate this vast
continent full of martial races and illimitable resources
is an astounding phenomenon in human history.

GS Sardesai, *New History of the Marathas*
(Bombay 1948) iii, p 514

A British writer may be pardoned for the view that of all
the great imperialisms the British contained the greatest
proportion of constructive elements.

John Strachey, *The End of Empire*, p 12

For now the Empire is not a matter for wonder, only for
shame. Hardly an English child... feels a flicker of pride
or even interest today in the colossal imperial risks and
achievements.

Jan Morris, reviewing *The Oxford History of the
British Empire* in the *Spectator*, 18/25 December 1999

YEARS OF APOLOGISING FOR the Raj have encouraged Britons to want to forget
the whole experience. Though from the start it was seen as a temporary phenomenon which would eventually be at one with Nineveh and Tyre and though no
one was so vulgar as to talk of a thousand year Raj, most people thought the
British presence in India would last more than 240 years. When India left the
empire, the heart went out of Great Britain; it is hard to remember that, now
shrunken, solipsistic, offshore, she once ruled the sea and a quarter of the population of the globe. That experience was not all good and not all bad but, whatever
it was, it was 'an astounding phenomenon'. The British acquired, first, an empire
and, then, an imperial ideal. That ideal was generally paternalist, justified by a
commitment to the toiling millions rather than a ruling caste. The preservation
of that empire did, in fact, inhibit political change and social development, so
that the hindsight of history now condemns it. But the real indictment of empire
is that Britons remained strangers in the land and never really understood or
properly appreciated what they called the jewel in the crown. Thus they could
never fill the role of Platonic guardians they had assigned to themselves. Despite
the high commitment to service and the public good, they could not accept that
the ruled were fit to rule.

I have kept Indian place-names as they were known in the days of the Raj and
conform to the 1968 edition of the *Handbook to India, Pakistan and Burma*,
published by John Murray.

I have to thank the late Mr Hardwari Lal, former MP and vice-chancellor of Kurukshetra University, for encouraging me to write this account, perhaps not quite as he would have wished, since he was an unreserved admirer of the British character; Professor K Paddayya for presenting me with the entire set of novels by Meadows Taylor and his *Autobiography*, recently reprinted in India; my late colleague, David Reid, for the loan of a rare book on Syed Ahmad Khan; Professor VN Datta for the gift of his books on Sati, and on Maulana Azad, and his selection of source documents on Indian independence; Mr Jagmohan Mahajan for his books on British artists in India; Professor Sudhir Chandra for his book on *The Oppressive Present*; Mrs Markie Walker for permission to quote from her edition of the *Letters and Journals* of her grandmother, Ruby Elliot, the daughter of Lord Minto; and Professor Wallace-Hadrill for permission to quote his comment from an interview with *The Times*.

1. 'To Agra and Lahore of Great Mogul'

Whereon for different cause the Tempter set
Our second Adam, in the wilderness,
To show him all Earth's kingdoms and their glory...
... Samarchand by Oxus, Temir's throne
To Paquin, of Sinean Kings, and thence
To Agra and Lahore of Great Mogul...

Milton, *Paradise Lost*, xi, 389–91

With silke of China, with Sandols, with elephants teeth,
Velvets of Vercini, great quantity of Pannina, which
cometh from Mecca... with an infinite quantity of cloth
made of Bumbast of all sorts, as white stamped and
painted, with great quantity of Indico, dried ginger and
conserved, Myrabolans drie and condite, Boraso in
paste, great store of sugar, great quantity of Cotton,
abundance of Opium, Assa Fetida, Puchio, with many
other sorts of drugges, turbants made in Diu, great
stones like Corneolas, Granats, Diaspry, Calcidonii,
Hematists and some kinde of naturall Diamonds.

Richard Hakluyt, *The English Voyages*, iii:
'The Voyage and Travell of M Caesar Fredericke,
Merchant of Venice, at Cambaietta'

'JOHN COMPANY' (THE COMPANY of Merchants of London Trading into the East Indies) was born on the last day of 1600, two years before the United Netherlands Chartered East India Company, or the *Vereenigde Oostindische Compagnie* (VOC) was formed out of six competing municipal companies, the first of which had been set up in Amsterdam in 1594. Both were to seek markets in the extended world empire of Spain which, since 1581, had incorporated the kingdom of Portugal and its overseas possessions. For the Dutch, commercial gain at the expense of the Portuguese was part of their war of liberation from Spain. For the English it was a permanent way of singeing the King of Spain's beard. Both Portugal and Spain had originally forced their way into tropical waters to outflank the Arab and Indian Muslim traders, who controlled the supply of spices and fine quality textiles from the east. Their motive was less national enrichment than the achievement of a centuries-long crusade against Islam. In circling the Cape of Good Hope, Vasco da Gama aimed to strike a ruinous blow at the legendary wealth of Grand Cairo, Damascus and Istanbul. When Columbus stumbled upon the Americas he was searching for a route to the great Christian empire in the east which would, in a final Armageddon, crush the power of

1

Islam for ever. When Philip II inherited the throne of Portugal in 1581, Spain ruled an empire that stretched from China to Peru.

The silver of South America had enabled the new crusaders to establish themselves behind enemy lines, in Indonesia, India, Ceylon, east and south Africa. The Portuguese, however, did not have enough ships to ruin the more traditional sources of supply. Huge quantities of pepper still travelled overland from the Red Sea to the Levant, to be shipped by Venice to its consumers.[1] But they had enough to alter the trading patterns of the east. Their firepower impressed coastal princes with the dangers of their enmity and the value of their friendship. Where Portugal had pointed, Spain followed. To the Habsburg family, which was beginning to look on the Holy Roman Empire as a family fief, universal empire seemed almost within reach, with the help of trade, religion, military might and unlimited silver.

Against such a world order was ranged the spirit of Protestant Europe. It was not the Muslims who shattered the dream, but what seemed, to the astonished Pope in Rome and the puzzled Jesuits in Japan, the treason of Christians themselves. The chance to strike a profitable blow against the common enemy, in what had been, for 70 years or so, a Portuguese lake, was too tempting to both Dutch and English. They came first to loot and destroy. Riches enough to make personal fortunes could be found in galleons and carracks, which sailed in the Pacific and Indian oceans, unaware of their danger, and in the go-downs that supplied them. By the end of the sixteenth century the predators decided that the colonial wealth of Portugal and Spain might be shared with profit. First the Dutch and English, then, before a hundred years were out, Scots, French, Danes, Brandenburgers, Flemings and Swedes formed trading companies to exploit it.

Spanish silver coins, minted in New Spain, and exchanged legally or stolen by privateers, made European traders welcome from Zanzibar to Nagasaki. Silver and gold from Europe had, for centuries, financed the trade cycle into which they had now broken. When Alaric ransomed Rome in 1409, he carried away 5,000 lbs of gold, 30,000 lbs of silver and 3,000 lbs of pepper, in lieu of specie, because so much of the silver and gold of Rome had gone east to pay for the spices that made the semi-putrid meat of Europe palatable.[2] *Piper nigrum*, the pepper vine, thrived in the hot loam of the Malabar coast of India, from Goa to Cape Comorin. It needed only the rough bark of a tree for support and a mulch of leaves and cow-dung for manure. It was transplanted early in the European Middle Ages to the Indonesian islands and became the staple that exchanged in the markets of Asia for textiles, ivory, elephants, horses, salt and saltpetre. The fruit when dried and mashed releases a small blackened seed, the peppercorn. Pepper was the 'powdered gold' of the rajahs and sultans who grew it, of the Chinese who owned the junks that carried it to Canton and Nagasaki, of the Persian and Arab middlemen who brokered it in Hormuz, of the dhows that shipped it up the Red Sea to Grand Cairo and Alexandria, of the caravans which supplied Baghdad and Byzantium and of the merchants of Venice and Genoa whose fortunes it made.

The civilisations of monsoon Asia were of an ancient pedigree, grown rich by trade. The cycle of winds bound together, in its seasonal round, markets from Africa to Japan, and the climate it created had generated the world's 'culture hearths', where animals and plants were first domesticated and developed by man. They blew, moreover, at predictable times and in constant directions, ideal for ships which navigated by the stars and, though violent, they did not menace them as seriously as the tempests of the Atlantic and Pacific oceans. They blew, moreover, to convenient meeting places in Java and the Moluccas, cargoes of copper from Nagasaki, silks and porcelain from Canton, cottons from Gujerat, chintzes from the Coromandel coast, calicoes from Malabar, saltpetre and rice from Bengal. There they exchanged one for the other or for pepper, mace and nutmeg.

In the centre of this network of monsoon cultures was India. In the tenth and eleventh centuries of the Christian era, the Chola kings of south India had sent expeditions across the Bay of Bengal to Sumatra and Siam but, by 1500, an elaborate tapestry of taboos decreed defilement to any caste Hindu who crossed the 'black water' and the carrying trade had fallen into the hands of Muslim traders from Africa and the Gulf, who made their homes where they found themselves and whose faith allowed them a wife in every port. The Indian ocean was an Arab sea. There being few trees on Arabian shores suitable for the manufacture of large ships, Arab trading vessels were lightly built to catch the monsoon winds, swift sailers with capacious holds, crewed by skilful and intrepid navigators. Having no enemies with worse than cold steel, they carried no artillery and had no metal to strengthen their hulls.

When the heavily-armed Portuguese ships, built to be battered by Atlantic winds and seas, finally entered the Arabian Sea, their victims were no match for them. Within the first 15 years of the sixteenth century, the Portuguese had captured all the principal ports on the coasts of East Africa, Arabia and the East Indies.[3] Given the population of Portugal (1,250,000 souls at most) and the demands made on its shipping, this achievement was as remarkable as, if not more so than, the exploits of Hernan Cortes and Francisco Pizarro. Like the Spaniards in South America, the Portuguese arrived in the Indian ocean at a time when their victims were diverted by what they believed were more significant threats from elsewhere. The Mamelukes in Egypt had their eyes firmly fixed on the menace from Ottoman Turks and did not take much account of what was happening in their own backwater, while local rivalry among the rajahs of India and the sultans of Java and Malaya allowed the Portuguese to insert themselves in the Malabar pepper and the Malacca clove markets. There was always a chieftain who was ready to use Portuguese technology to further his short-term objectives. The arms trade from the west had begun. European captains were not usually ready to part with the secrets of their power, but individual artificers could be persuaded to share their skills by the generous gratifications Asian monarchs were able to give them. It was not long before the heavy weapons that had given the Europeans their advantage were being manufactured locally.[4]

The Portuguese grand purpose was to monopolise trade, not to build a territorial empire. They imitated Asian traders by settling in extra-territorial ghettos in the major emporia from Persia to China. When they began to build forts, as they did in Goa, to protect their factories against European rivals or discontented natives, it did not worry princes like Bahadur Shah of Gujerat, who believed that 'wars by sea are merchants' affairs and of no concern to the prestige of Kings'.[5] This royal disdain for merchants was not an affectation, even though it was trade across the water which provided the sinews of Muslim hegemony in India – the precious metals which were not found in the sub-continent, but from which the coins were minted with which the taxes were paid.[6] The north-European image of India in the sixteenth century was based on little more than a vision of riches. Dr Faustus, sublimely ignorant of the perils of the seas beyond the Cape of Good Hope, was content to let the spirits 'fly to India for gold/Ransack the ocean for orient pearl'. Othello, who owed his pearl ear-pieces directly to the India trade, confessed after he had murdered Desdemona that he had behaved like 'the base Indian (who) threw a pearl away'. The vision of pearl-fishing was that of the Master of *lo Studiolo* of Francesco I dei Medici, in the Palazzo della Signoria in Florence. There, Bronzino's pupil, Alessandro Allori, painted his naked pearl-fishers, a cross between gods and satyrs, nereids and harlots, dipping and diving for stupendous scallop shells bearing pearls the size of carbuncles.

Francis Drake, the first Englishmen to burst into the Indian ocean, in 1580, approached it from the east and was too impatient to stop and explore its wonders. He sailed across it like a defiant trespasser, inciting his countrymen to follow. Those who entered it by the Atlantic route, round the Cape, soon learned the hard way that it was not a journey lightly to be undertaken in small vessels with inadequate navigational aids. The Portuguese carracks were twice their size and had learned the perils of the passage. Had it not been for the example of the Dutch, who had, by the end of the sixteenth century, brought back their ex-peditions to the east almost intact (the voyage of 1595 showed a profit of 2,500%), and for the capture by Drake in 1587 of the *Sao Felipe* carrack, with goods worth over £100,000 from the Indies, the English may well have given up.

Englishmen had got to India, across land, and not found it a welcoming place. John Newbery and Ralph Fitch, who had sailed in 1583 with 'the husband bound for Aleppo, master of the Tiger', were carrying letters, personally inscribed by Elizabeth I to 'the most invincible and most mighty prince, Lord Zelabdim Echebar, King of Cambaya'.[7] They started off across the Arab crescent to Baghdad, shipping for Hormuz from the mouth of the Euphrates, and thence reached Goa. Arrested as commercial spies and threatened with the *strapado* they escaped, with surprising ease, and eventually reached the court of the Great Mughal at Fatehpur Sikri, whence Newbery went home to bring a ship out of England to meet Fitch in Bengal in two years time. The ship never came because Newbery died on the journey home and Fitch was only back in London in 1591, after sailing down the Ganges to Hooghly, and visiting Burma and Thailand. His return coincided with a petition to the Queen from a group of London merchants to send an expedition into the Indies.

Zelabdim Echebar was Elizabethan English for Jalal-ud-din Muhammad Akbar, fourth in a dynasty created by India's most recent invaders, whose origins lay in the vast plains of Asia. For the Portuguese, when they captured Goa from the Turkish sultan of Bijapur, had only just beaten the Mughals into India. India's invaders had always come by land, over the mountain passes from Afghanistan, or across the deserts of Baluchistan. In 1517 the king of Kabul, Babur 'the Tiger', Zahir-ud-din Muhammad, made his first of several raids into the Indian plains. Babur's blood was that of the Mongol Timur the Lame, Marlowe's Tamberlaine,

4

enriched by Uzbecki, Turkic, Persian and Afghan strains, out of which cauldron of genes emerged a prince of brilliance in war, in letters, in love, in daring, the equal of Julius Caesar or Charles XII of Sweden. Kabul was too small for a man of his universal ambition and, having entered India first as an invited mercenary, he came the second time, in 1525, as a conqueror. The pincer-like pressure, on one side, of the Safavid Shah of Persia and, on the other, of Turkic-speaking Uzbecks, both of whom had designs on his kingdom, forced Babur, who could only muster a tiny army of 12,000 men, to try his fortune on a throw. In 1526, at the battle of Panipat, a few miles north-west of Delhi, the invader, using his artillery (until the arrival of the Portuguese virtually unknown in India) with the skill of a Napoleon, overthrew the army of the sultan of Delhi. North India was at his feet. His great grandson was the Augustus to this Afghan Caesar and, in the reign of Akbar (1556–1605), the dynasty of the Mughals was firmly set in Agra.

Akbar believed that 'a monarch should be ever intent on conquest, otherwise his neighbours rise in arms against him. The army should be exercised in warfare, lest from want of training it becomes self-indulgent.'[8] His reign was seldom to see that army at peace. The fertile province of Gujerat (Cambay) was conquered in 1572 when, at Surat, the precocious monarch first met the sea. Akbar went on to subdue the Rajput principalities, a congeries of tiny states ruled by Hindu caste warriors, some tracing their ancestry to the Sun, others to the Moon, but seldom in fact reaching beyond the fifth century of the Christian era, who had spent the intervening millennium fighting each other and the Muslims from the north. Ignoring monsoon, rain and river, Akbar pursued his enemies, as far as Bengal. With that conquest the Mughal empire now covered the whole Indo-Gangetic plain from the Arabian Sea to the Bay of Bengal, from the Himalayas to the Narbada river, an empire richer than any in the world. Akbar made a number of forays into central and southern India, but expansion further south was to be the work of his son, Jahangir (1605–27) and his grandson and great grandson after him.

The steady domination of the Indian sub-continent by Islamic conquerors, since the first Muslim invasions in the last quarter of the twelfth century, had not meant the Islamisation of the land. The civil service of Muslim rulers was composed largely of Hindu subjects who managed their economies, raised their loans, carried out their foreign policy and sometimes commanded their armies. Hindu princes were ready to pledge their loyalty to an overlord, be he Hindu or Muslim, provided he left them the freedom of their religion and the effective substance of their local power. They provided wives and concubines for the overlord's bed, troops for his armies and tribute for his treasury. Akbar and his children and grandchildren had numerous Hindu wives. Hindu rajahs, particularly the Rajput chieftains who closely resembled Italian renaissance princelings in their love of splendour and intrigue, manoeuvred their allegiances adroitly between contending parties, often the Great Mughal's own children, and secured *jagirs* and titles as a reward for success. They were ready to support one Muslim ruler against another, even against a fellow Hindu ruler. Their goals were the survival of their dynasties and the preservation of their gods and, for most of the two centuries of Mughal rule from Delhi, the Rajputs proved among the staunchest of its props.

Sixteenth and seventeenth-century India resembled *quattrocento* and *cinquecento* Italy in many ways. Hindu princes were not struggling against militant Islam, and were no different from Muslim princes in their struggles for power and territory and in their resistance to the encroaching power of the Mughals, just as Italian city states and despots had resisted the armies of the Empire, of France, and of Spain. With the Indo-Gangetic plain subdued, the house of Timur turned its attentions to the great highland plateau of central India. Hindu geographers divided the Indian sub-continent into two at the river Narbada, all the lands south of which they called the Deccan (derived from the Sanskrit word for south). Later historians confined the area to the highlands between the rivers Narbada and Kistna, which is the definition now used. From the coasts, east and west, the plateau is reached by chains of mountains known as the western and eastern Ghats. At the northern end, the two ranges unite with the Vindhya mountains, together forming a protective pyramid, which cuts the peninsula off from the easily traversed riverine plains of the north. The land slopes gently from west to east and the great rivers, the Cauvery (Kavari), Godavari and Kistna flow from the western Ghats into the Bay of Bengal. Whereas the armies of Babur and Akbar could race from Kabul to Chittagong, campaigning in the Deccan was arduous, and armies were confronted by rivers in spate, fortresses on seemingly impregnable mountain tops, intractable country, perfect for guerrilla warfare, and shortages of food caused by drought and of draught cattle by murrain.

Two Muslim kingdoms shared the Deccan and looked uneasily to the north. The sultanate of Bijapur and the kingdom of Golconda were the two survivors of a confederation of five Muslim powers that had destroyed the old Hindu empire of Vijayanagar in 1565. The Bijapur sultanate was founded at the end of the fifteenth century by a Turkish adventurer who claimed to be the son of the Ottoman emperor, Murad II. Though it nursed Goa uncomfortably in its bosom, Bijapur had learned to live with the benefits as well as the perils of Portuguese trade. Golconda's splendour in part derived from the diamond mines on the river Kistna. The kingdom had been founded by another Turkish adventurer at about the same time as the Portuguese had seized Goa, and stretched from the Godavari river to the Cauvery. Its capital since 1589 was Hyderabad. Ralph Fitch had been there, 'a very faire town, with fair houses of brick and timber... Here the men and women go with a cloth bound about their middles without any more apparell'.[9] Eight days journey east lay Masulipatam on the coast of Coromandel, 'whither come many shippes out of India, Pegu and Sumatra, very richly laden with Pepper, spices and other commodities'.[10] They exchanged these for the chintzes (dye-stamped fine cotton cloths or batik) manufactured along the coast, which had become the preferred costume of the Malays in the archipelago.

The Portuguese had built up their formidable commercial empire with a necklace of fortified bases, which the Dutch were bent on destroying. In 1580 they chased them out of the Banda Islands in the south Moluccas, the central emporium for cloves, nutmeg and its derivative, mace. By 1595 they had established their factory at Bantam (Jakarta) in western Java. To the members of the Levant company, sitting in London, the overland spice trade to Europe seemed doomed, and on 10 April 1591 Sir James Lancaster was commissioned to take three ships east and test the possibility of trade in the south China sea. It was essentially a piratical venture, to be paid for by plunder, but was beset by disasters. When, on 24 May 1594, Lancaster and 24 survivors crawled into Rye, they had precious little to show for the voyage, except that it could be done. So the newly chartered Honourable East India Company in London decided to set up its first factory on the tiny volcanic island of Pulo Run in the Spice Islands. It had neither the resources nor the will to do more.[11]

The Company now constituted itself with a general Court of Proprietors, each holding upwards of £200 stock, with a Court of Committees elected by the proprietors, which did the work. Its early membership made it look like an appanage of the Levant Company, and its tiny staff was responsible only for raising the stock to finance each voyage. Quick profits were what they looked for, but the first voyage of 1600–1 brought back so much pepper that the domestic market was glutted. It was all paid for by Spanish silver coins; the piece of eight rials, being particularly pure, was very acceptable for re-minting into local coinage. Many of these coins were originally privateer's loot, but peace with Spain was being negotiated and Company vessels were instructed to treat both Spanish and Portuguese with respect. The amalgamated Dutch companies, on the other hand, were under no such constraint; they had been given power to make alliances and wage war, and were virtually 'a state within a state'.[12] They freebooted themselves into Ambon (Amboina), the principal emporium of the Moluccas, and seized control of the production of spices from the Portuguese factors. As they were determined to enforce their monopoly in the archipelago, the English, only timid allies in their war of independence, were not exactly welcome.[13] Even so, the quick profits the Company merchants expected were delivered: 95% cumulative on the first two voyages, 234% on the third and fourth. In 1609 the founding charter was renewed.

The Company was not intended merely to meet an appetite for the rich products of the orient. It was also expected to export the principal national products, woollen broadcloth and linen cloths, bound to be in demand in the realm of Ahasuerus, who, according to the Book of Esther, 'reigned from India even unto Ethiopia'.[14] They would be sold to merchants from the cold north, China and Japan, for silver, with which to buy spices in Indonesia, on which, while the Company had the import monopoly, great profits were to be made in London. But the Chinese and Japanese merchants they met at Bantam were not interested in woollen or linen goods, and there was clearly no market for them in the tropics. With the end of the Spanish war silver, too, became scarce. What exchanged well for spices were the chintzes and silks from India, which were beginning to clothe the people of south Asia. These were shipped from Surat on the Gujerati coast, from Hooghly in the Bengal estuary and from Masulipatam on the Coromandel coast, and to these centres both Dutch and English turned their attention. The first Dutch factory in India opened in 1609 at Pulicat on the Coromandel coast (the name that so seduced the pen of Edward Lear was a corruption of Cholamandalam, the realm of the great Chola kings, *floreant* 907 to 1310 AD). Two years later the English settled at Armagaum, near Pulicat, but, finding the Hollanders too aggressive, they decamped in 1611 to Masulipatam. The Dutch followed them there in 1619 but, as the city was firmly under the control of the local monarch, neither party was allowed to molest the other.

Masulipatam was the principal mart for the cotton piece goods which were to be 'the left arm' of the Dutch company's trade in the Moluccas, and which exchanged for the spices which formed 'its right arm'. 'Arse-clouts' for slaves and 'light fabrics for light women' had a ready sale in monsoon Asia and Africa, as well as in Europe.[15] Both the English and the Dutch had also marked the only ocean port of the Mughal empire at Surat as the place from which Portuguese control of the Arabian Sea might most easily be challenged. The Portuguese had no exclusive privileges in Mughal lands and no power to exclude rivals. Surat was where the Mughals satisfied their appetite for the 'splendid and trifling' with which they bedizened their persons and their courts: ivory, coral, amber, silks, velvets, brocades, perfumes, drugs, wines and brandies, horses, African slaves, gold, silver and spices. No precious metals were mined in India, but by creating an entrepôt trade in all the products of India and the east, the Mughals could satisfy the ostentatious needs of a warrior aristocracy. They believed, like the Sultan of Bijapur, that trade was not a matter for them, but they would profit from it.[16] In Surat merchants could buy pepper from Malabar, indigo from Ahmedabad and Agra, musk from Patna, cinnamon from Ceylon, cowries from the Maldives, silk from Bengal, as well as all the spices of the Moluccas more easily than from Bantam. From Surat, pilgrims made the *haj* to Mecca and traders penetrated the Red Sea, where Indian middlemen supplied the overland caravans from Suez, Mocha and Aden. In 1606, the Company directors turned their attention once more to the lands of Zelabdim Echebar. Akbar, however, was dead and his son, Jahangir, was emperor and Mukarrab Khan the governor of Surat.

The Third Voyage carried both a plentiful cargo of broadcloth and William Hawkins, a Turkish-speaking merchant and self-styled ambassador. On 28 August 1608 he was the first Company commander to set foot on Indian soil, even if it was only the oozy and fetid swampland at the mouth of the Tapti river. Despite the letter from James I to the emperor Akbar, he was treated with contumely by both the Mughal governor and the Portuguese, neither of whom wanted the English (whom they could not tell apart from the Dutch) in those parts. The Portuguese agent in the city gave 'not a fart for [Hawkins'] commission' and called King James a king of fishermen, a mere tributary to his king in Lisbon.[17]

In Agra, however, the emperor Jahangir, 'Conqueror of the World', who liked anyone ready to drink with him, found Hawkins a good potman, and promised him, but never delivered, an imperial *firman*, permitting the establishment of an English factory at Surat. But as the two men supped and drank together until they were stupefied, the courtiers plotted the removal of Hawkins. They were assisted by the drunken and lecherous behaviour of the English crewmen he left behind at Surat. By 1611, Jahangir had been persuaded to dismiss the English 'ambassador' from Agra. Hawkins' return to Surat coincided with the arrival of the Sixth Voyage, carrying, ever hopefully, a cargo of English broadcloth and woollens. Though it did some trade, Jahangir and the Portuguese overrode any favours that the governor may have been disposed to show the English, and on 9 February 1612 the fleet was forced to sail. The Portuguese in India knew that, if they were not to suffer in their Indian and Arabian trade the defeats they had suffered from the Dutch in Indonesia, all Protestant interlopers must be expelled from India.

A new 'embassy' was soon on its way to Jahangir, with the Twelfth Voyage, accompanied by a painting of naked Venus toying with her son, for the emperor's amorous moments, together with two musicians, one to play the virginals and the other the cornet whenever he wanted music. The merchants of Surat relaxed enough to take some of the broadcloth as horse-blankets and what they gave in exchange was, in due course, to bring about a revolution in England. The light Indian cottons were cheaper and more versatile than heavy German or Lincolnshire linen. It was not long before a respectable citizen of London insisted on cotton sheets for his bed and his wife on tablecloths and napkins for his table, dress lengths for her own back and, eventually, underwear for her hitherto unprotected pudenda. 'A new vocabulary of chintzes and calicoes, taffetas, muslins, ginghams and cashmeres entered into everyday use'.[18]

Informal embassies having failed to secure the much-wanted firman, it was time to flatter the Mughal emperor with a real ambassador. No matter how much he dressed himself up in titles, everyone knew that Hawkins was a mere merchant, and the descendants of Genghis Khan held merchants in low esteem. In October 1614, Sir Thomas Roe was duly selected to be James I's envoy to the Great Mughal. On 2 February 1615 the embassy rowed out from Tilbury for the ships that were to carry it to India, with an elaborate baroque coach and two more musicians for Jahangir. Its reception in September by the governor of Surat, the future emperor Shahjahan, was too casual for Roe, prickly with the pride of a puissant power, and only five weeks of diplomatic sulks finally convinced him that this ambassador was not going to behave like a merchant and bribe his way. At last, with the help as interpreter of an Italian Protestant employed as a jeweller in imperial service, he delivered his credentials. His conversations at court with the Jesuit, Francesco Corsi, convinced him that the Portuguese were 'in their wane and might, while they are swimming for life, easily be sunk'. If the Company were to be more aggressive, 'it would strike such a terror and give such reputation to our cause as would almost decide the contention for this [Indian] trade at once'.[19]

Though the ambassador always met with 'a free and noble jollity' from the 'affable and courteous' Jahangir,[20] he found it almost impossible to concentrate the emperor's mind on trade. Mughal emperors were above considerations of merchandise and this one was drunk by the late afternoon. Indeed Sir Thomas complained that he had not enough decent wine (unlike the Jesuits) to proffer the Conqueror of the World and thus advance his cause. He had to deal with venal and dilatory officials, who were not impressed by the embassy's gifts so far and who waited to see the value of his bribes before doing anything. What Roe wanted was an agreement that English merchants could have access to all ports under Mughal control, pay a non-discriminatory customs duty, trade freely, rent factories and enjoy the right to own property. In return the English would sell the emperor arms at a fair price and assist him in his just wars.

What he got was authority for the English to reside in Surat and travel inland, not to mention the other gifts of the court: 'hog's flesh, deer, a thief and a whore'.[21] He dutifully warned the emperor that the Dutch, unlike the English, would 'build forts for defense of themselves, whereby little by little they would become masters of the port'. They would also be 'disorderly, especially by drink... and gain more by stealing in one year than by trading in many'.[22] But to the

Mughals there was nothing to choose between Dutch and English and Shahjahan gave them equal rights. There was no going against Mughal authority, which was quite strong enough to keep Portuguese, English and Dutch in check.

Roe thought that factories at Surat, Burhanpur, Ahmedabad and Agra would be plenty. Why go to the trouble of setting up in Bengal when its silks, musk and civet could be bought as cheaply in Agra? Yet by 1618, when it was time for him to go, he had still not signed a treaty with the emperor to formalise the English right to trade, and the Dutch were still in Surat. The volume of business was modest, but the return to the shareholders who subscribed to Company stock for each voyage continued to be attractive. From 1615 to 1629 only 27 ships sailed from Surat for London, a very small proportion of the whole trade, and nothing to compare with the fleets of vessels sailing from the east into Dutch ports. Though Queen Elizabeth thought that the Dutch 'prosecute their voyages with a more honourable resolution', James I had been persuaded in 1609 to extend the Company's 15-year monopoly of the East Indies trade indefinitely, but the guarantee of indefinite monopoly stirred the directors to turn themselves into a joint stock company.[23] Instead of raising subscriptions for voyages as they were planned, investors were invited to underwrite a series of voyages and receive dividends from profits. These proved not to be as high as in the early voyages, but the return on money was still good. The profit on pepper, however, was overtaken by that on silks and cottons, and its price fell from 26 pence a pound in 1613–16 to 17 pence in 1627.

In the Brazils, there being no civil society with which the traders could deal, the Portuguese controlled the manufacture and warehousing of the produce they marketed in a *feitoria*, a term adopted by both British and Dutch. In the East Indies, Europeans dealt with their suppliers through the local prince or Mughal governor, who levied tribute, or taxes or both. A firman was always necessary and, as the Mughals did not want permanent colonies of traders in Indian ports and would only agree to what were in effect residence permits, they refused extra-territorial status. Factories, therefore, became collectives of traders, with go-downs or warehouses, dealing locally on their own account and with the home country through their Company. Nominally, factories were controlled by the Court of Directors in Lisbon, Amsterdam or London, but they were two years away from India, this being the average time for a return voyage, including that spent in port waiting for a cargo and for the seasonal monsoon wind by which one was blown part of the way home. Effective control was in the hands, therefore, of a chief agent, usually the longest-serving merchant, and his council. In due course factories sprouted branches, each with its own chief agent. The council of chief agents and merchants then elected a president. Some factories grew into virtually independent enclaves, of which the president became the governor, but as he had no casting vote he often presided helplessly over a divided and hostile council. Gain was the principal motor in their lives. In a climate in which disease could strike without warning and fatally in a matter of hours, merchants needed to make their pile as quickly as possible if they were ever to return home to enjoy it.

Disease was not the only enemy. Despite an agreement in 1619 that the Dutch would share the trade of the Indonesian archipelago with the English, in February

1622 a Japanese spy implicated the English factors in a wholly fictitious plot to seize the Dutch factory at Amboina in the Moluccas. They were arrested, submitted to the water torture and, on improbable confessions, sentenced to death. The Massacre of Amboina put paid to any hopes that the two peoples could deal as friendly rivals in that rich market. The president of Bantam was, himself, soon to preside over the withdrawal of all English factors from Bantam itself, and from Makassar in Sulawesi. The English capture in 1621 of Hormuz, emporium of the trade 'in all spices, drugges, silke, cloth of silk, brocardo' out of Persia, and India's principal source of Arab steeds for breeding for both war and pleasure, was a coup which partly compensated for humiliation in Indonesia and worried the Dutch enough for them to establish a factory at Surat.[24]

A branch factory at Patna withered because but the distance was too great from Surat, but in 1634 the English made a more durable arrangement at Balasore (Baleswar) in Orissa, at the westernmost mouth of the Ganges. In 1639 the chief agent at Armagaum, Francis Day, responsible to the Company's president at Bantam, and anxious, it was said, to be closer to his Indian mistress at Mylapore near the tomb of the Apostle Thomas, negotiated with the local *nayak* permission to fortify a settlement and factory close by. He also secured the right to collect customs duties, on payment of an annual quit-rent. By 1641, Fort St George housed all the go-downs and merchants' houses, while a thriving 'black town' of cotton spinners and their looms, grew round it. Despite the danger and discomfort of coming ashore through the rolling surf, despite the absence of protection from monsoon winds which might be afforded by a serviceable creek, despite its total dependence on the hinterland for food and water, Fort St George was little by little to grow into the great city and presidency of Madras.[25]

The Company had its own fleet of 30 to 40 East Indiamen, brand new vessels which were sufficiently well armed to beat off the assaults of Muslim pirates and Christian rivals but too large to sail further up the Thames than Deptford. To its own dockyard there, it added another in 1614 at Blackwall, which was to grow into the great East India dock, incorporating in 1806 the Brunswick dock. The Company became one of the major employers of skilled labour in London and, as a mercantile giant, needed to raise capital. The London money market was another child of the Voyages. The Company also attracted envy. For in 1635, the Convention of Goa at last concluded the long war of attrition with the Portuguese in the east. Five years later they were to throw off the yoke of Spain and return to their historic friendship with England. The prospect of Anglo-Portuguese amity suggested at court that the embattled Company trading to the East Indies no longer needed a monopoly to make trade profitable. The Crown's interests, they argued, were not best served by factories dependent on the whims of local rulers. The English should imitate the Dutch who, by creating virtual colonies in Indonesia, had beaten off all competition, controlled the production of the spices they wished to export, and now enjoyed the sole profit. The King, seeing a source of money which might enable him to continue ruling without Parliament, chartered a rival company. Named after its principal stakeholder, Sir William Courteen, it was established in 1635 to trade with Goa, Malabar, China and Japan and the duty on its merchandise was personal to the King.

11

The ensuing years were not good for either Company. Courteen's Association established factories on the Malabar coast to import pepper direct from India and ruined its rival's factories in Indonesia, but otherwise it did not prosper. It spent much of its energy and resources trying to settle a colony in Madagascar, and when the civil war in England dried up investment, its traders became increasingly desperate. Their methods were so close to buccaneering that they called down the wrath of Mughal governors who could not distinguish between the two companies. Only with the greatest difficulty did they survive the Anglo-Dutch war of 1652–4. So close did they come to voluntary liquidation that, in 1657, the Lord Protector Cromwell amalgamated the two rivals into a single company based on a new issue of joint-stock, sufficient, it was hoped, to give it a permanent source of capital. Of the £786,000 subscribed, only half was called up, but it was enough to give the New Company enough to buy up all the existing factories, forts and privileges of the Old.

In 1651 the English moved from Balasore to Hooghly with permission, they claimed, from Shahjahan's son, in gratitude to a ship's surgeon of the Company, who healed his daughter of dreadful burns. In 1658 Hooghly opened a branch at Kasimbazar which gave the English direct access to Bengal rice, saltpetre, muslins and raw silk. The silk production of Bengal was third in size to that of Persia and China and, owing to the demand from both the English and the Dutch, it was to overtake them both. The austere habits of the Puritans had now given way to luxury and the Dutch were experiencing their golden age. More profitable still was saltpetre. 'But for the supplies of India,' wrote Macaulay, 'the English government would be unable to equip a fleet without digging up the cellars of London in order to collect the nitrous particles from the walls'.[26] So rapidly did the demand expand that the emperor Aurangzeb tried to restrict its export in case it was used against Muslims.

Charles II reissued Cromwell's charter on condition that the Company's trade was limited to India. Between 1662 and 1664 it paid a dividend of 20%, reduced subsequently by renewed Dutch wars. In 1669 it could boast that it put to sea 25 to 30 'of the most warlike ships in England, with 60 to 100 men in each ship', supplying 'the nation with pepper, indigo, calicoes and several useful drugs, near the value of £150,000 to £180,000 per annum'. It also re-exported 'to Italy, Spain, Turkey and Guinea to the amount of £200,000 or £300,000 per annum… And these goods exported do produce in foreign parts, to be returned to England, six times the measure in specie that the Company exports from hence… Were it not for the East India Company we should be at the mercy of the Dutch traders, … and we should lose the protection secured for the country by the employment of so many stout ships and mariners'.[27]

In 1682, the dividend paid was 50% and John Evelyn sold the 'adventure he had bought in 1657 for £250 to the Royal Society for £750, it having been 'extra-ordinary advantageous, by the blessing of God'.[28] Charles's charter permitted the Company, wherever it could, to fortify its factories. Forbidden by the Mughal governor to do so in Surat, the merchants had already cast their eyes on the Portuguese enclave on Mumbai island. It was one of only four fair-weather ports on the western coast sufficiently land-locked to shelter ships during the south-west monsoon. As the largest island of an archipelago in an estuarine swamp, it

12

was virtually impregnable from the land. In 1654 Cromwell had been advised to buy it, but in 1661 it was transferred to the British crown as dowry for a Portuguese bride. In 1665 British troops finally took possession, but over 300 of the 400 men sent to occupy the enclave died before the English flag was finally raised from Bombay fort.

Charles II, deeply in debt to the Company which was now the richest corporation in the realm, leased it his fever-ridden dowry in perpetuity at a rent of £10 a year, paid punctually until 1730, when it seemed hardly worth collecting. The directors may have wondered what they had acquired. Difficult to assail by land, it was wide open to attack by sea, and pathetically vulnerable to the depredation of both Dutch and Indian pirates. Worst of all, between the mosquitoes, the rotten arrack and the foul women, a man's life there was measured at two seasons. But there was no local governor or monarch powerful enough to enforce tribute or constrain trade. Within 20 years Bombay had become a thriving mart, with a settlement of 60,000 souls, the 'seat of power and trade in the East Indies'.[29] From 1669 to 1677, it was governed by the Surat president, Gerald Aungier, whose enlightened and tolerant rule attracted Hindu, Parsi and Armenian capitalists, money-lenders and traders, all subjected to an equitable tax system. He drained the swamp and linked the islands of the archipelago by a network of causeways. He set up three courts of justice and a tribunal for non-English causes, converted the old Portuguese law court into an infirmary, built an Anglican church, established a mint to convert English silver to *sicca* (newly-minted) rupees and constructed a ring of protective towers. These were manned by German mercenaries, more reliable than the London riffraff recruited by the Company's crimps, and were enough to deter the Dutch from attack in 1673. In 1687 the directors ordered the chief agent in Surat to transfer himself and his presidency to Bombay.

Plague and cholera, caused by the silting of the creeks after Aungier's death in 1677, delayed the move until 1708, but Bombay was now the chief of all the Company's factories in India. Aungier believed that trade could only securely be carried 'sword in hand' and the directors were converted to sovereign enclaves on the Dutch and Portuguese model.[30] But there was no suggestion that this should include territorial conquest. In 1683, Fort St George was created a Presidency independent of Bantam, and incorporated as a municipality with a mayor, aldermen and burgesses. The Company now had another sovereign possession to be defended against all comers, even the legitimate sovereign of the Carnatic within whose domain it was located. Seven years later, on 24 August, Job Charnock ordered Captain Brooke to 'come up with his Vessell to Chutanutte (Sutanati) where we arrived about noon, but found ye place in a deplorable condition, nothing being left for our present accommodation and ye Rains falling day and night. We are forced to take ourselves to boats which considering the season of the year is very unhealthy'.[31] There was little in these bleak words to presage either the city of palaces or the city of dreadful night, but it proved to be the birthday of Calcutta.

Job Charnock had first come to Bengal in either 1655 or 1656. He joined the Company there and served first in the Patna factory, revived as a branch of Balasore in 1658. There, legend reported, he snatched a young widow from her husband's funeral pyre and made her his wife without benefit of clergy. From there he moved to Kasimbazar, the licensed residence for foreign traders near the silk city of Maksudabad. In 1686, Charnock was promoted to chief agent and president of the Council of the Bay of Bengal at Hooghly. He took over at a moment of crisis. Bengal, to her Mughal conquerors, was 'a paradise on earth'.[32] The vast plain between the Ganges and Brahmaputra rivers was fruitful to the point of prodigality and, though regularly flagellated by tempest and flood, produced readily marketable surpluses of grain, mainly rice, cotton, sugar and salt. Bengal cotton pieces and raw silk found their way to central Asia and the Middle East, and a growing amount of Bengali opium was already exported to south-east Asia. The trade attracted Gujerati and Marwari *banians*, merchants from the west and north of India, and Armenians, on the perpetual quest for wealth and security, who settled in the bazaar towns on the Hooghly river. By the end of the seventeenth century they had been joined by Portuguese, Dutch, English, French and Danes, and even by traders from the Imperial and Royal Prussian Companies based in Ostend and Danzig. The Mughal nawab or viceroy lived in a style that was almost imperial and the great merchants competed as builders and patrons of the arts. Though tribute money still made its way to the emperor in Delhi, the nawab was virtually an independent ruler, and for nearly half a century the stability and general benevolence of rule from Dacca created optimum conditions for trade. Bengal had good communications, labour was cheap, skills, especially in textiles, were advanced, the currency was sound and credit extensive.[33]

The nawab tolerated European traders so far from the coast so long as they behaved themselves. In 1656, he exempted the English company from import and export duties traded in its name, for a payment of 3,000 rupees a year. It was a good deal at the time and within 25 years 60% of all English imports from Asia came from Bengal. Even before it was due to be reviewed in 1678, the Mughal authorities knew that the annual payment was too low, and began to levy duties equal to those levied in Surat. To the directors in London this was oppression. 'Since those governors' (principally of Hooghly and Maksudabad) 'have... got the knack of trampling upon us, and extorting what they please of our estate from us, by the besieging of our Factorys and stopping of our Boats upon the Ganges, they will never forbear doing so till we have made them sensible of our Power.'[34] That the Company would do by waging war on their shipping in the Bay of Bengal. The result was disastrous. The Company's action had the effect of a mosquito on the hide of an elephant, but in 1690, the new nawab, anxious to bring the disturbance to foreign trade to an end, offered the Company a new deal. For ten times the former annual quit-rent, he would compensate the Company for its goods lost at Hooghly and allow it to start a settlement at Sutanati.[35] There Charnock arrived, disconsolately, on 24 August.[36]

There was no point in regretting the sybaritic life in Hooghly. Job Charnock rapidly cleared a site in the jungle and started to fortify it. There was something about the place that appealed to his black spirit – he liked to have refractory slaves whipped as he took his meals, so that their shrieks added relish to his food – but it is unlikely that he ever thought of Sutanati as more than a temporary halt. There was a vast salt-water lake to the north-east which periodically flooded, leaving dead animals and fish to putrefy in temperatures that never fell below

80°F. There was thick jungle to the south, surrounding the temple where, according to legend, the little toe of Kali, the eponymous deity of Calcutta and the wife of Shiva the Destroyer, came to land when her husband attacked her in heaven with an axe. Unlike all other trading posts in Bengal, it was on the east bank of the river, away from the direction of any Mughal attack from the west, while the salt lake and jungle protected it from an assault from the direction of Dacca. Company ships could effectively prevent any river crossing, so that it was defensible, if it could ever be made habitable. But Charnock died in 1693 before he could lay the foundation of the factory that was to become Calcutta, and lies with his Indian wife in a simple Mughal-style mausoleum where St John's church and cemetery now stand. His burial slab, of a foliated igneous rock at that time unnamed, gave the world his other memorial – charnockite. Saint or sinner, the directors thought well of him; he did not ostentatiously enrich himself and, though he was not always honest, he was more interested in success than fortune. That was to come to his successors.

2. 'A FIELD LEFT OPEN FOR ADVENTURERS'

Organised power having broken down, the field was left
open to adventurers and new claimants for dominion.
Among these... the British, and the British alone at the
time, possessed many of the qualities necessary for
success. Their main advantage was that they were
foreigners coming from a far country. Yet that very
disadvantage worked in their favour, for no one took
them very seriously or considered them as possible
contestants for the sovereignty of India.

Jawaharlal Nehru, *The Discovery of India*, 1946, p 324

When the French came ashore the citizens of Goa,
seeing them smart, clean and well-dressed, with
moustaches held high and swords by their side... took
them for French nobles, being unable to imagine that
soldiers and sailors could ever wear such beautiful
shirts, stockings well tucked up and pretty shoes.

The Abbé Carré, *Le Courier de l'Orient*, p 273

Thus the midday halt of Charnock – more's the pity!
Grew a city
As the fungus sprouts chaotic from its bed
So it spread
Chance-directed, chance-erected, paid and built
On the silt.

Rudyard Kipling

JAHANGIR'S GRANDSON, AURANGZEB (1658–1707), was the last of the brilliant
quartet of Mughal emperors which started with Humayun, and his reign was to
be the apogee of the Mughal empire, which foreign traders had the power to
annoy but not to dismay. There were other, more serious threats to Mughal power,
and at his death in 1707, at the great age of 97, the treasury was bankrupted, his
wives and children faced starvation, and Marathas followed his shambling armies
like vultures, while their outfliers ravaged Gujerat and the Carnatic. Rajputs,
Jats and Sikhs boiled with rebellion and the mighty edifice that Babur had started
to build was beginning to crumble. The imperial court hid behind the walls of
Shahjahanabad in a Versailles-like trance, riven by factional squabbles. So sudden
was death at court that nobles going there would pay a formal farewell to their
families.[1] Central rule of so vast a country as India, with its dissonant religions,
castes and tribes, had from the start depended on the delegation of power. The

great emperors from Babur to Aurangzeb spent most of their reigns on the march. Their sons, acting as viceroys and governors, often showed less loyalty to their fathers than to their own pursuit of power, and many of the campaigns in the seventeenth century were of son against father and brother against brother. The rule of an independent-minded viceroy, often an imperial heir, did not mean that Mughal rule locally was either weak or deficient but Aurangzeb 'had constantly to warn his nobles against the consequences of a tendency among them to flout Mughal norms and royal prerogatives'.[2] He knew that once the emperor lost the loyalty and respect of his own creatures, the empire would either break up into a loose federation of virtually independent states or balkanise into mutually hostile ones.

The restless campaigns of the emperor 'whose might still shook the world', only masked the weakness already apparent in his empire.[3] After his death, power seeped to Muslim warrior states in Oudh (Awadh), Bengal and the Deccan which took over the empire's experienced corps of revenue farmers, local aristocrats and *zamindars*. The *subahdar* of a totalitarian emperor, experienced in managing an army of occupation and a prosperous commercial economy, needed little instruction in how to become an absolute ruler himself. Though the emperor in Delhi remained the source of all titles and legitimacy, even to rebels like the Marathas, and though he continued to receive their tribute, the *nawabis* were soon autonomous provinces, trading profitably with each other and with the foreign companies in their midst. The central power of India was replaced by many different Delhis, in Lucknow, Dacca, Murshidabad, Hyderabad, Poona and Seringapatam.

Within this *tessitura* of Mughal successor states were the princes, Hindu as well as Muslim, often little more than village bosses, who had resisted the collection of taxes by the imperial revenue farmer, overrun their neighbours, and engrossed enough power and wealth to secure title and status, upon which they struck a deal with their overlords. Some grew rich from an efficient agriculture, blessed by a never-failing monsoon, grain surpluses and the produce of craftsmen. Others were little more than soldiers of fortune, chieftains of small armies of retainers at the service of greater princes. Some claimed descent from Vedic heroes or Constantinopolitan sultans, even from the sun and moon, but they gave service for land. The source of wealth was the village, each with its headman, its immutable cycle of sowing, monsoon and harvest, changing little as cities rose and fell and palaces crumbled.[4] Though India numbered about a fifth part of the world's population, she produced overall an agricultural surplus, interrupted by the occasional failure of the monsoon, or by its over-prodigality which caused famine and flood. For centuries she had had a sophisticated network of jurists, bankers and money-changers, who stimulated and protected the flow of capital and investment. This network ensured that Mughal rule did not disintegrate after 1707, and its different parts 'were economically integrated by inter-regional trade along the coastal as well as inland routes... Distant credit markets remained connected despite political turmoil'.[5]

Aurangzeb's conquest of both Bijapur and Golconda seemed to put Mughal rule in India beyond challenge, but for the defection of his Maratha mercenaries. By throwing off the yoke of Bijapur just as it was itself threatened by Aurangzeb, their chieftain of chiefs, Shivaji, born in 1627, and believed by many to be a divine incarnation sent to rescue Brahmanism from its Muslim oppressors, created in his twentieth year an independent Hindu *raj* in his family estate or jagir at Poona. The English factors at Surat were twice to experience daring and destructive raids from the 'sheevagees', in 1664 and 1670, trembling within their factory walls while the Mughals fled. The Marathas were a mountain people of low-caste farmers, devoted to their Brahman chiefs, locked in the inhospitable terrain of the western Ghats, from which they emerged to pillage the rich lands on either side of the range, and to turn north-west India into a playground of flying armies. They moved in 'an overwhelming mass, like a cloud of locusts' yet, despite their loose formation which resembled disorder, they seldom ran out of control.[6] Their cavalry rode light and lived off the land, acquiring a fearsome reputation for looting and scavenging. Only rivers seemed to hold them up. They were to be the last empire builders before the British, carrying 'their banners to the banks of the Indus, while their cavalry scoured the country from Lahore to Murshidabad, from Delhi to Seringapatam'.[7]

The house of Shivaji was never to throw up another leader of his quality so that, in the absence of a strong central power, local chiefs became princes who established personal rule over vast territories: the Bhosles over the plains round Nagpur, extending at one time into Bengal, the Gaekwads over the plateau round Baroda, the Holkars over the uplands of Malwa north of the Narbada river and the Scindias in the central highlands at Gwalior. In Shivaji's heartland round Poona, power was vested in the elected leader of this confederacy of princes, the *peshwa*, which office in 1713 was vested hereditarily in the house of Balaji Vishwanath. There were to be four great peshwas of the Vishwanath line, and even the mighty head of the house of Scindia, whose pride was that of the twice-born, boasted of being only their slipper bearer.

The Maratha commonwealth subsisted principally on *chauth*, tribute paid by all rulers whom they could coerce. The search for chauth established their reputation as ruthless predators and was behind the ceaseless wars that wracked the Deccan in the first half of the eighteenth century, leading to a Maratha attack on Delhi itself in 1719. The Great Mughal could no longer protect foreign factories. They had to look to their own defence. In distant London, the directors were never quite sure what was happening in India and what they did know was always many months out of date. What they least wanted was trouble with local rulers. When the factors in Rajapur, north of Goa, assisted the Muslim viceroy of Karnool to fight off a Maratha attack, Shivaji imprisoned them for two years and confiscated their goods. The president of Surat could only give them cold comfort. 'How you came in prison, you know very well. It was not for defending Company goods. It was going to the siege of Panhalla and tossing balls with a flag that was known to be English. For merchants... if meddling, must looke for a requitall of their deserts.'[8] For another century this was the received wisdom of the Company.

The Company in India faced Dutch rivals, Maratha raiders, greedy subahdars and slippery nawabs, but behind the directors in London were men jealous of its monopoly and wealth, who wished to open up the rich pickings of the east to independent traders. 'The enormous gains of the Indian Trade,' which amounted to half the trade of the nation, 'might perhaps have excited little murmuring if they had been distributed among numerous proprietors.'[9] They were not. By keeping the number down, it was possible for Sir Josiah Child to buy stock so skilfully that his income equalled the greatest of the land. In 1665, all business in London being suspended during the plague, Child wrote his *Brief Observations concerning Trade and the Interest of Money*. It was a tribute to the 'wise Dutch'. Quality control, encouragement of new invention and discovery, frugal living, a thorough education, sound banking, and their use of bills of credit as cash, these were the secrets of their trading success. He was in no doubt that it was time 'to lay the foundation of a large, well-grounded sure English dominion in India for all time to come'.[10] His entry to the Court in 1677 coincided with the appearance of a treatise almost certainly from his own pen, demonstrating 'that the East India Company is the Most National of all Foreign Trades'. Its ships exported goods and bullion worth £430,000, and imported commodities worth twice that sum. Its actual capital was £370,000, but it could borrow more on short-term interest of 6% and clear profits of 30% in a year. By 1681, when Child became governor of the Court, shares bought for £100 sold for £300 and continued to rise. It had resources enough 'to corrupt half a cabinet'.[11]

It was Child who had Fort St George created a municipal corporation on the Dutch model, in which junior merchants were called writers after the Dutch *schruyvers*, who encouraged the Company to strengthen its position at home and abroad. In this he was supported by the newly-elected president of the Surat factory in 1682. Sir John Child of Surat was no relation, though popularly supposed to be Sir Josiah's brother, but they behaved as if they were kin. In India since his tenth year, John Child had risen to his present position by assiduous ambition and forceful trading. In 1687 he secured the title of Captain-General and Admiral of the Company's forces in India, Persia and Arabia, at which 'the French and Dutch could not put themselves in a posture enough of laughing at it'.[12] He was at one with Josiah on the need for Company settlements to enjoy territorial sovereignty. Josiah, convinced that any withdrawal of Company trade would bring starvation and death to thousands of the Mughal's subjects, wanted the Company to frighten the emperor. John thought it did.

What the Mughals expected of the Company in return for its privileges was to rid the Indian ocean of pirates and police the haj. It was an impossible condition. Pirates came in all colours: British free traders, not above seizing cargoes they were denied the opportunity of buying, privateers like Captain Kidd, Marathas commanded by admirals of the house of Angria, and Ethiopian Siddis from pirate lairs on the west coast. The Company could barely police its own ships. In 1688, the Mughal governor of Surat, angry at acts of piracy which he thought the Company should have prevented, arrested the Surat factors. Sir John sequestered all Mughal ships in the western seas. The Company now learned that, while it could defy an Indian power by sea, it had no capacity to protect its settlements on land. The ensuing war caused no starvation and few deaths, Bombay town was overrun and by the end of 1689 the Company begged for peace. Aurangzeb imposed an indemnity of £150,000. Chagrin and mosquitoes carried off John Child whose removal from India was another condition of the peace. Meanwhile Sir Josiah had a battle on his hands at home. For his insistence on sustaining the Company's monopoly of trade with India, he was compared

19

for tyranny to Louis XIV, to Goliath of Gad and to the devil.[13] Against those who argued that Indian silks and calicoes were ruining the English textile industry and that commerce should be free to traders in any port in the world, he used the example of the Dutch. Their eastern trade was so prosperous because there was a Company capable of making treaties, waging war, policing the sea routes, standing up to local rulers when they became too greedy. 'The increase of our revenue is the subject of our care as much as our trade. 'Tis that must maintain our force when twenty accidents may interrupt our trade. 'Tis this must make us a nation in India. Without that we are but as a great number of interlopers, fit only to trade where nobody of power thinks it their interest to prevent us.'[14] A rival company, born in 1698 at Skinners Hall in Dowgate, soon foundered. The Mughals simply could not see any difference between one company and another; nor could William III who, wishing to concentrate on the war that was about to break out in Europe over the succession to the Spanish throne, took the bull by the horns. He forced the rival companies to merge into the United Company of Merchants Trading to the East Indies, in which the shareholders of both had equal equity, and gave them seven years to synchronise their corporate affairs.

By 1702, the Company's stake in India was the principal source of its wealth, but it was still very precarious. Neither Bombay nor Madras was sufficiently strong to resist a determined attack and Charnock's settlement at Sutanati was only just taking shape. The Dutch had proved a deadly foe to British trade in the far-flung Spice Islands, but India was of secondary importance and they had decided to concentrate on their possessions in Indonesia. But now another mortal enemy appeared on the sub-continent. As the eldest child of the Italian Renaissance, France had shown more interest in the new world than England, but continental ambitions, especially in Italy, the need to break Habsburg encirclement and religious strife at home had all delayed her colonial adventures. In 1601 the city of St Malo had its own *Compagnie des Indes Orientales*, a municipal, not national, venture, on the early Dutch model. Henry IV granted it a monopoly of eastern trade in 1604, but civil war prevented advantage being taken of royal generosity. 'Their temper being so hasty as to wish accomplishment of their desires in the moment of their conception', Richelieu did not think long voyages would be right for Frenchmen, but he was not ready to leave the East Indies and Persia to the Dutch and English.[15] In 1642 he founded *La Compagnie d'Orient* and, in 1664, Colbert, seduced by the argument that French colonies would stimulate French trade while keeping French wealth in France, extended its range. Colonies abroad, he reasoned, ready to buy French goods from French ships, protected by a strong French navy, would launch the motherland along an exponentially rising curve of wealth, and spread her *mission civilisatrice* to all the world. By saddling the Compagnie with colonisation as well as commerce, Colbert very nearly sank it from the outset. Its eastern arm was to be a federative corporation of trading companies, like the Dutch East India Company, with the power to send and receive ambassadors, make treaties and alliances, administer justice and declare war. La Compagnie des Indes Orientales was chartered with a massive injection of royal and 'forced' loans. From the start it had trouble raising capital and its dependence on the state of Louis XIV (the King had advanced three fifths of the initial capital, and in 1668 had to promise a further two million livres to clear it of debt) made it an instrument of government far more firmly than either the Dutch company which provided the model, or the British which was to prove its principal rival.

Merchants were sent to accompany the Sun King's first embassy to Persia and the Mughal courts and, in Agra, owing to the good offices of a French physician at the court of Aurangzeb, the Compagnie obtained a firman permitting the establishment of a French factory at Surat.[16] For the Mughal viceroys, dependent on external trade to furnish their lifestyle of splendour, the more foreign traders the merrier and, as they had already discerned that they had a propensity to quarrel among themselves, they could, by keeping them divided, ride their mettlesome and arrogant tempers. The French chief at Surat, an ambitious Frenchman called François Caron, who had risen in an earlier career to be director-general of one of the constituent Dutch companies, had learned that the security of factories flowed from the barrel of a gun. Before he despatched his merchants to establish factories in the major trading centres of the east, he asked Paris for a naval force to back him up. Sparing 'neither powder nor bullets to abase the pride of the Dutch',[17] the nine ships of this 'squadron of Persia', commanded by Lieutenant-General Jacob Blanquet de la Haye, was the most powerful yet seen in Indian waters. To find a base for it without incurring hostility from either the Dutch or the English, with neither of whom France was at war, Caron decided on St Thomé, or Mylapore, a centre for fine cloths and quality dyes, a few miles south of Fort St George. No sooner had he taken it than France was at war with the Dutch who overwhelmed the garrison, sacked the small French factory at Masulipatam and appeared to put paid to French hopes of sovereign territory in India. Fire was, however, breathed into the embers by an experienced watcher of the Indian scene from the French factory at Pondicherry. The former consul at Aleppo, Baron, knew that the patchwork of monarchies in the south was crumbling before expanding Mughal power and Maratha raids, but he believed the future for France in India was not in colonies, but in finding the right leader to support, and then, under his protection, promoting trade without the expense and danger of conquest. The seeds of the policy pursued by Dupleix and his disciples, the English, germinated in the court of Sher Khan Lodi, governor of the province of Valikandapuram in the ailing kingdom of Bijapur, who had invited the French to settle at Pondicherry and suggested the capture of San Thomé. What could he not do with a corps of French soldiers and a squadron of French ships?

Caron, in Surat, was not going to be involved in country wars, and had Baron recalled, but Sher Khan still offered the French the sovereignty of Pondicherry: 'as in Europe the Dutch were the neighbours of the French, so must they be in India, and for that purpose he gave us the place of Pondicherry in order to establish the nation there'.[18] No one else seemed interested in this little town of fisherman and weavers, though it had an estuarine anchorage, protected from the monsoon winds, and could be easily fortified. The Danes had deserted it for Tranquebar and Negapatam, further up the coast. The small community of 80 Frenchmen which took possession of the town in 1672 repaid Sher Khan by becoming a part of his war machine. It was the first tentative step the French took in their venture to become the surrogate ruler of India.

21

From Surat, French merchants had also established factories on the Malabar coast, in Orissa at Balasore and in Bengal at Chandernagore (Chandranagar) and Kasimbazar. With the accession to the English throne of William of Orange, they were expelled, but Pondicherry was restored at the Treaty of Ryswick in 1697, and the French entered the eighteenth century with two other settlements besides, at Chandernagore and Surat. The constant wars of Louis XIV's last years meant that he was too short of cash to bale out the company he had once so generously funded. The miracle was that it survived, not only war but the Scottish financial prestidigitator, John Law. In 1717 he rolled the Company of the East into the Company of the West to form one trading company and extended its privileges for 50 years. As he had merely created it a state 'farm', it collapsed with the rest of his system. The *Compagnie des Indes* rose from the ashes, however, recovered its factory at Masulipatam and set up new ones at Calicut and Mahé on the Malabar coast. The factors kept their heads down and were content with modest returns. The mercenary role they had filled for Sher Khan Lodi was not repeated, so that when it became propitious for France again to intervene in the ambitions of the country powers, the bases were there and were used with brilliant if ultimately futile address. The capacity for endurance of contradiction within the Indian body politic was shown by the fact that Pondicherry was only ceded to the Indian state in 1962, and still preserves the French language and the Code Napoléon.

Fort St George had played no part in the French adventure. It faced the sea, being built right on the strand facing the huge ocean, within earshot of the thunderous breakers that crashed unceasingly on its yellow sands. It looked outwards from, not inwards to India. It was a filial of Bantam until 1683, when the Dutch overran the English factory, and its eyes were set on those countries on the further shores of the Bay of Bengal, Siam, Burma, and onwards to China and Japan. It was also responsible for the Bengal trade, succouring Job Charnock in his hour of trouble and assisting his return to Sutanati. When Siam closed its borders to foreigners in 1688, Madras merchants turned to the possibilities of the Pearl river trade with Macau and Canton. Meanwhile Madras served as the entrepôt port for trade goods from the archipelago and China.

Its governor from 1687 to 1692 was the Boston-born Elihu Yale, the onomastic founder of the great university at Newhaven, Connecticut. High-handed and despotic enough to nourish the legend that he hanged his groom for a misdemeanour, he was suspended after five years, only to become a director of the Company in 1699. He is credited with the invention of the auction sale to dispose of his immense number of personal possessions, from which £500 went to endow a collegiate school which, when it applied for its charter as a university in 1745, took his name. The Yale brothers did well out of and for Madras, but its real fortunes were set on course by a reformed 'interloper', one of the Company's most pronounced bugbears at the time of the 'New' Company, founder of a political dynasty and owner of one of the greatest diamonds to dazzle European eyes before the Queen's necklace bought for Marie Antoinette. Thomas Pitt (1655–1726) was at 21 'interloping' at Balasore, 'a desperate fellow' who defied the Company with impunity. In 1690 he was elected member of Parliament for New Sarum. Five years later he bought the pocket borough of Old Sarum which he was to bequeath to his son, and his son to his son William, 'the terrible cornet of horse'. The Company, observing Pitt's commercial acumen – and his fabulous wealth – at last made the wise decision that as it could not beat him it would live with him, admitted him to membership and, in defiance of Josiah Child, appointed him governor of Fort St George in 1697. Thomas Pitt was as resolute in defence of the Company's privileges as he had once been in undermining them. He bought off the nawab of the Carnatic, ordered by the emperor to destroy Fort St George during his war with the Company. He extended the limits of the city and guided its destinies with a firm and decisive hand for 12 years, resigning in 1709 after a bitter conflict in Council. 'Diamond' Pitt returned to London to become the first 'Nabob', a legend and a source of inspiration to other fortune-hunters. The diamond that gave him his sobriquet was a huge rough stone of 400 carats weight, found in the river Kistna. In 1701 he bought it from a dealer at the height of the siege by the nawab, for the knock-down price of £20,400.[19] He sold it, polished and cut, to John Law for £135,000 as a present for the French regent. It was ensconced in the crown of all French monarchs from Louis XV to Charles X. Diamonds from the Golconda mines were a popular way of sending wealth home, shipping light and selling heavy!

Fort St George had, for south India, a relatively mild climate and the ocean airs rendered it almost healthy. Its municipal council was responsible for a city area not exceeding ten miles from the fort. But it had no harbour and everything had to be brought ashore over the ceaseless surf. Passengers seldom completed the transfer from ship to shore without a ducking. There were navigable estuaries and creeks everywhere else along the coast, at Masulipatam, Pondicherry, Cuddalore, Tranquebar and at Negapatam. Yet Madraspatanam was to rise superior to all these and to shape the fortunes of south India. This was partly due to the physical strength of Fort St George, and to the weakness of south Indian armies, but more to the fact that Madras posed no threat to its Indian neighbours, occupied in changing dynasties and allegiances. Only when these neighbours looked to it for help did Fort St George find itself threatened, and then by the French in Pondicherry.

In Bengal, once the imperial firman arrived, permitting the Company to return, the midday halt of Charnock, a damp settlement of tents, huts and boats, in which the merchants and 100 soldiers had squatted since August 1900, began to take more permanent shape. Sir John Goldsborough, chief governor of all the settlements in India, came up from Madras, marked out the site of a recently built Roman Catholic church in the tiny village of Kalikatta, between Gobindpore and Sutanati, bundled the priests off it, and had the church pulled down so that Charnock's son in law, Charles Eyre, could build a house there. Other Company servants followed his example and, in 1696, Eyre, now president of the council, started to fortify the area. A low, irregular tetragon, like a starfish, built of blocks composed of brick dust, quicklime, molasses and hemp, which made a composition stronger than stone, rose slowly between 1696 and 1712, with walls 40 feet thick and 18 feet high with diamond-shaped bastions at the four corners, mounted with ten guns each. It ran 700 feet along the river front but was not protected by a ditch or fosse on the landward side, an oversight that was to prove nearly fatal in 1756. Fort William, called after 'King Billie', became the name of the new presidency in 1700.

In 1698 the nawab agreed to sell the lease of the three villages of 'Calcutta, Chutanutte and Gobinpore' for 16,000 rupees. The Company, which did not understand the intricacies of Mughal land-holding, had not acquired a title to the land, only the zamindar's rights to collect rent from what was inalienable royal property, and by its purchase had become a tenant of the nawab. The stability and prosperity of the Bengal *nizamat* was based on the institution of the *zamindari*. The zamindars were trustees of Mughal estates, who held them under various titles, none permanently. They were in effect, large proprietors, sometimes merchants trading in staples, or capitalists who acted as the unpaid agents of the central power, farming the taxes, which the Mughals expected to be paid in cash not kind, and enforcing local security. They could levy tolls on goods passing through their often extensive estates, so that they could meet the costs of policing them. When the central power was strong, the zamindari was an effective instrument of delegated power and, throughout the seventeenth and early eighteenth centuries, people, goods and cash could move safely, virtually unprotected, around the province. The meteoric growth of Calcutta in this benign climate was in stark contrast to the fate of Surat, whose trade was hindered by the awkward tides in the Bay of Cambay, and by attacks from pirates and Marathas.

The ambiguities of this position did not prevent the Court in Fort William from exploiting its zamindari rights, by renting out plots for buildings and collecting the tax on them. By 1700 it had appointed the first collector and magistrate in 'British' India, for the plots were quickly taken up by tenants, many of them Bengalis. Calcutta was a British creation, but it was an Indian city. Company servants could not have built it on their own for, in 1712, the council numbered nine, with the president, and two of its members were the chiefs of the factories at Kasimbazar and Dacca. They presided over 51 writers and merchants – the number had nearly doubled since 1707. In 1717, the emperor Farrukhsiyar granted the Company exemption from customs duties and a concession of 38 villages. This generosity was attributed to the successful intervention of the Company surgeon, William Hamilton, in the emperor's malignant distemper, but it was more probably due to extravagant gifts worth £30,000 and a veiled threat to disturb Mughal shipping from Surat if the concession were refused. The nawab, Murshid Quli Khan, moved his capital from Dacca to Muxadabad (renamed Murshidabad in his honour) to keep a closer eye on the European factories on the Hooghly. 'If they should quarrel with the Mughal, prohibiting his subjects to trade with the Company would soon end their quarrel'.[20]

The leased villages were soon incorporated into what were dubbed Town Calcutta and Bazaar Calcutta. The English gathered round the fort, with the Portuguese and Armenians to the north of them in the Town, and the Indian population concentrated in the *burra* or great bazaar which sprawled between the Christian area and Sutanati. By 1707, this population had risen to 20,000, and the revenue cash balance to 10,000 rupees. The latter doubled in four years and then doubled again in 1712, largely from more efficient collection. The English soon objected to the judicial system in the nawab's courts, whose powers were usurped in a lordly way when in 1727 a mayor's court with aldermen was created for civil suits and a court of quarter sessions (the governor in council) for criminal cases involving Europeans. The aldermen were merchants and were not above protecting their interests by bending the law. Yet the court was popular, even with non-Company merchants, who felt that the man in the judgement seat did at least understand the niceties and naughtiness of trade. Though it received short shrift from legal purists, it was missed when, in 1774, Parliament appointed judges to a Calcutta Supreme Court to dispense a purer justice at far greater cost.[21] Within the *nawabi* of Bengal, a virtually autonomous state was growing like a cancer.

Even before Charnock was forced to leave Bengal, the volume of British trade with Bengal had outpaced that with Surat as well as that of Madras. It was not only due to the Puritan demand for saltpetre, which made Cromwell's army and navy feared in Europe, and to the Restoration demand for silks and other luxuries, but to the readiness of Hindu and Armenian banians, to advance the money to the Company to buy cargoes. Bengal was still the centre of an intricate and extensive system of credit that only an Indian could tap. By 1668 writing cargo lists in the Bengal factories had become the task of the most junior member, who might be a teenager as young as thirteen, like the future governor Vansittart (1759–64), expelled from Winchester and sent to India in 1745 'to be trayned up in our business, for wee (the directors) have observed the advantages, that others have by this way, in the knowing and well management of affairs, by encouraging young men, in hopes of preferment to be sober, industrious and faithful'.[22] Success depended on the factor's skill in dealing with the banians, who understood perfectly how important it was to load a cargo in time to catch the sailing dates before the monsoons, but whose sources of supply, farmers, weavers and miners, worked at their own speed.

After an apprenticeship of some five years, a writer could aspire to being a factor. After three years factors became junior merchants; after another three years, junior merchants became senior merchants and, finally, the most senior merchant (seniority being determined from the date of arrival in India) was the chief agent or president of the council of senior merchants. His tasks were principally to maintain order in the factory, and negotiate with the local governor. Otherwise he was busy receiving and inspecting his own goods, assembling his cargoes and adding to his meagre salary and allowances, which by no means matched his responsibilities. This hierarchy was observed in all social business in India as strictly as in a public school. Only the direct intervention of the directors could give a merchant 'added years' of seniority to bring him on faster than his colleagues, a fruitful cause of jobbery back in London, for nothing could be done about it in the factory.

In fact promotion was accelerated by nature. Between 1707 and 1775 death at post accounted for 358 out of 645 Company servants from Britain, and there may have been more, shipped home mortally ill to an early death. The percentage was highest among those joining between 1747 and 1756 when 74 per cent died in India. Only between 1767 and 1775 did the percentage drop below 50 per cent to 44 per cent, when young men had learned to live more sensibly and to profit from the experience of those who had survived. Throughout the same period, a quarter of all European soldiers died annually.[23] Sometimes it was only ten years before a writer found himself on the factory council. His object was to return to Britain as soon as he had made enough money to live for the rest of his life in peace and quiet. He was often not fit for much more. As Company merchants enjoyed absolute preference over all other British subjects in the factory, they could ensure their personal enrichment before that of others. The position of writer was, therefore, seen by the industrious sons of clergy, by the idle sons of lawyers and by educated and indigent Scotsmen as a first step to riches, which could be taken by anyone who had been through 'a regular course of arithmetick and merchant's accounts'.[24] But 'a very few years will reduce a man from opulence to beggary should he meet with misfortune.'[25]

Originally the factory was home to writers, factors, merchants and senior merchants, an implanted oasis of European order amid the roving chaos of Indian life. It combined the features of a monastery, an Oxford college and a large country house. In the seventeenth century its occupants were never numerous – nine or ten of all grades at Hooghly in 1679, and only 29 in all Bengal in 1707, all of whom lived on the premises. They sat at meals in order of seniority, but the fare was common to all, frequently gargantuan in quantity, washed down by rice-toddy, or arrack, and wine from Madeira and Shiraz. The chief agent was entitled to be carried in a palanquin and, in 1674, Governor Longhorn of Madras never went out 'without fifes, drums, trumpets and flageolet', accompanied by the members of his Council and other factors on horseback.[26] Ordinarily members of Council and the chaplain walked abroad with a native servant carrying a parasol. Even the humblest writer would have a servant to carry his pen-box and writing stand, while every physical task beyond simple motion, even dressing and undressing, was performed by body servants, little different from slaves, some of whom were indeed slaves imported from Africa. Decrees of the Court of Directors to control expenditure on unnecessary luxuries like chaises, horses and palanquins fell on deaf ears.

The humblest writer, once admitted as a covenanted servant – the civilian or civil servant, covenanted to the Company gave his name in due course to those in the service of the Crown at home and abroad – could be on the first step to a good marriage, a knighthood, a town and country house in Britain and a seat in Parliament. Company service was a career open to gentlemen and conferred that status on those of its servants who were not. Leonard Woolf, two centuries later, observed how colonial service bestowed class on its members.[27] They acquired gentility in a single generation.[28] As the seventeenth century progressed, merchants' families intermarried and recommended their sprigs to directors, many of whom were friends if not relations, so that writers often arrived in India protected by a patron. As the factories grew, young men preferred to escape from communal living and its internal discipline. The enforcement of good behaviour was the responsibility of the chaplain who, apart from conducting divine service, had at least twice a year to admonish all Company servants on their duty to live a Christian life and abandon 'lying, swearing, Curseing, drunkenness, uncleanness, profanation of the Lord's Day'. Adultery and fornication, quarrelling and disturbing the peace of the factory could be punished by fines or confinement in the stocks, and persistent offenders risked being expelled. The recurrent emphasis on good behaviour argues the only too common lack of it. From embarking in a Company ship for India, to living in a factory and exercising the functions of a merchant, there was a decalogue of don'ts.

Chaplains were not the only enemies of the evil one. Company ships captains were enjoined to enforce good morals aboard ship, and chief merchants in the factory. But observance was fitful. In 1682 the chief agent at Malda (a silk and cotton bazaar) had no trouble in enjoying 'his little seraglio of six strumpets', and newly arrived writers were introduced to the local brothel where they were immediately 'clapped'. Job Charnock lived openly with his 'Gentoo' widow for 29 years.[29] Commercial morality was left to the merchant's good sense. The Company's military service offered a separate career, and it was possible to transfer in and out of the two services. Clive did it twice. That genial rake, William Hickey, enrolled in 1769 as a cadet in Madras. His sole qualifications were his father's acquaintance with a number of directors and his assurance to 'the three old dons' who interviewed him that he could learn the manual exercises.[30] Uncertain what corps he would be joining on arrival he ordered a uniform suit for each one known to be in Madras, and an old friend of his father gave him a beautiful cut and thrust sword, with instructions to cut off the heads of half a dozen rich fellows with it.[31] Military service did not suit young William, who was eventually to make his name and fortune in Calcutta by the law.

No amount of moralising by occasional chaplains and straight-laced chief merchants could stop the writers and cadets from their pleasures and, as the annual salary was £5 with an allowance for board and lodging, most of them were soon heavily in debt. They might strut along the streets of the city that rose, like an exhalation, from the slime, but everything they wore, bought and lived in belonged to their creditors. The directors, in an avuncular way, directed that they be sent up the country to learn their trade and the language, away from the fleshpots. Robert Clive blamed the banians for encouraging young merchants to live beyond their means.

> A Banyan, worth perhaps one hundred thousand pounds, desires he may have the honour of serving his young gentleman at four shillings a week. The Company has provided chambers for him, but they are not good enough; – the Banyan finds better. The young man takes a walk about town; he observes other writers, arrived only a year before him, live in splendid apartments or houses of their own, ride upon fine prancing Arabian horses, and in palanqueens and chaises, that they keep seraglios, make entertainments, and treat with champagne and claret. When he returns he tells the Banyan what he has observed. The Banyan assures him he may soon arrive at the same good fortune; he furnishes him with money; he is then at his mercy.[32]

Despite the small margins, the uncertainty of suppliers, the hazards of catching the seasonal winds with a full cargo written up, prospects were attractive enough to tempt a growing number of young men to India, some to live well, some to die young, all in the hope of shaking the pagoda tree.[33] Until they had shaken that tree, matrimony on £5 a year was out of the question. Both Robert Clive and William Hickey drank and whored and were 'clapped' on credit, and when not 'clapped' were often struck down with sudden and unaccountable fevers.

They were the lucky ones whose robust constitutions helped them to build up some resistance to strains that could kill a man overnight. For the dinner guest you entertained today was frequently the corpse you carried to his grave tomorrow.

Trade, like life itself, was also subject to hazard. Insects, parasites, rain and damp could, in no time, reduce trade goods from Britain to ruin. Only sicca rupees were beyond the corruption of nature. Bullion, as British textiles had no market, was the principal export to India, and in 1748, of exports valued at £1,121,000, bullion accounted for £816,000. Merchants therefore had to make a profit on cargoes bought with specie. Private trade could only be practised by those with money, and most covenanted servants did not go to India furnished with much of that. Credit and trust had to underpin everything; the weaver had to be pre-paid for his materials almost a year before delivery date of the finished article, while the farmer would not plant a seed without a cash advance. Within that year, natural or man-made disaster could destroy the investment and, while Muslim rule frowned on trying to outwit the will of Allah by setting a watch on the supplier, merchants would additionally buy protection for their primary supplier, another mortgage on an uncertain future. If and when the merchandise, for which he had borrowed so expensively to buy in advance, was delivered, the merchant had then to find an investor in the cargo, so that he could hire space in a vessel. Even when he had found a ship, pirates in Asian waters and rapacious officials in Asian ports could seize his cargo. The successful, or lucky, merchant could, it was true, make a profit two to three times what British traders could make with Spain and her dominions. The indispensable cash for all this came from the banian.

The greatest of these in Bengal, 'the bankers of the world', were the Jagat Seths, Marwaris from central Rajasthan, who had established themselves at Maxudabad and who farmed the nawab's debts, and those of many other big merchants, and who owned the mint. Nearly two thirds of the revenue of Bengal passed through their hands. Judging correctly that the British were going to prosper in Bengal, they were the principal bankers of the Company and were instrumental in preserving its credit during the dispute with the nawab that ended with the battle of Plassey. At one time the directors thought that the Seths were too high and mighty and that their commissions amounted to cheating, but they could not find more amenable brokers to replace them. Then there were the Das family bank at the pilgrimage centre of Benares, and the corner-house *shroffs* and *mahajans*, who kept the young blades of Calcutta in sword-knots and champagne. Like the Jews of central Europe, they could remit money by bill of exchange and discount foreign currency, all based on the sicca rupee, the dollar of the sub-continent. Rates of interest were high, anything from 12 to 18 per cent being normal in the early eighteenth century for a Company servant, higher for an Indian. At one time virtually every European in India was in debt to an Indian, who usually hedged his loans by lending to a large number of debtors in the hope that they would not all fail together. Some Britons made fortunes quickly, some not at all, but enough was accumulated in the first half of the eighteenth century to cause the balance between the Indian and British merchant to swing in the latter's favour, and the Indian independent capitalist became increasingly, as the century progressed, the agent of a British entrepreneur.

28

The Company jealously preserved its monopoly of all trade to and from Britain, but the country trade, from India to Asian and African ports and within India itself, was open to any servant of the Company and, increasingly, to others, like 'Diamond' Pitt, who were not servants of the Company, but who were allowed to live in Company settlements provided they behaved, unlike Pitt, respectfully, and paid customs and consulage fees. By 1727 Madras had ceded primacy to Calcutta, Surat was in decline, Bombay had not yet developed the facilities of her unrivalled harbour. So badly did the Gujerati manufacturers in Ahmedabad want Bengal raw silk for their looms that they lobbied the nawab not to hinder the European traders who were so efficient at delivering it.[34] By the third quarter of the century Calcutta was the foremost port in India. The Bengal trade was increasingly carried by ships built of Burmese teak at Pegu, crewed by lascars and officered by Europeans, who offered speed and punctuality and whose threats of reprisals for harassment or delay carried force. Even so numbers were small. Between 1708 and 1713, about 11 ships were annually loaded in Bengal for Britain, a number which by the '40s had risen to some 20, generally of larger tonnage. Ships engaged in the country trade were smaller and more numerous. The Dutch preserved their factory up-river from Calcutta at Chinsura but shipped in foreign bottoms. Most of the country trade was in the hands of private merchants, not the Company which controlled inter-continental trade and charged high commissions on the export of Company goods. By 1772 Clive could tell the House of Commons that trading by sea was 'not worth the attention of Company servants' as there was no money in it.[35] Ships were expensive to build, expensive to arm and expensive to sail, and owners expected big profits, which were not always easy to earn. If all went well a freighter might clear 25% of the value of the cargo, though it was difficult not to overtrade and create a glut, whereupon prices fell. But the survival rate of British-owned shipping from the hazards of storm, piracy and erratic navigation was high enough for an increasing number of Indian banians to ship in them, so that they kept the Calcutta freighter fleet in being. Despite 30 comparatively lean years from 1740 to 1770, the fortunes of Calcutta were made. Trade with China, the Malayan archipelago and India herself had replaced the Surat trade to the Red Sea and Gulf. No other factory in India could compete.

The city by 1750 may have numbered 10,000 souls of whom only 1000 at most were Europeans. 'Most gentlemen and ladies in Bengal,' wrote Captain Alexander Hamilton in 1727, 'live both splendidly and pleasantly, the forenoons being dedicated to business, and after dinner to rest, the evenings to recreate themselves in chaises and palankins in the fields or gardens, or by water in the budgeroes (oar-driven barges)'. Over this sybaritic existence, a dark angel hovered perpetually. Many went into the hospital to undergo 'the penance of physick but few came out to give an account of its operation'.[36] The Company's income came from ground rents and consulage fees and, to encourage settlement, residents were not otherwise taxed. As early as 1703, the British merchants were building imposing homes. By 1730, the brackish tank to the east of Fort William had become a freshwater lake and the great *maidan* was a fashionable promenade for carriage and palanquin. A stylish neo-Palladian church stood in the centre of four ways, along which the chief merchant, alias the president, alias the governor, drove with his escort of red-coated cavalry and silk tunicked *chobdars*, bearing silver-plated staffs, the necessary symbol of any Indian or British dignitary until the end of empire. Warehouses crowded up to the south of the fort, gravely imperilling its defence, and stretched along the river to the creek which formed a natural boundary. Portuguese and their descendants and the Armenian community lived round their churches to the north.[37]

The defence of Calcutta had been left to nature, but in 1742 Maratha armies ravaged Bengal and put the Company in mind of the fate of Surat. Hastily, with money raised by frightened residents, a great ditch was begun, to connect the river north of the black city or burra bazaar to the salt lake. It was never finished, partly because it was too expensive, partly because the Marathas did not reappear. It became a cross between a storm drain and a cloaca, and eventually was filled in with builders' rubble. In 1747, the residential area was surrounded instead by a palisade at a cost of 70,000 rupees. When it was put to the test in 1756, it proved quite inadequate. That test was soon to come.

3. 'THAT MAN NOT BORN FOR A DESK'

> Clive – that man not born for a desk – that heaven-born general.
>
> William Pitt, December 1757

> I know not which to admire most, his folly or his treachery.
>
> Luke Scrafton on Mir Jafar Khan

> In short, I will pronounce Calcutta to be one of the most wicked Places in the Universe.
>
> Clive to Francis Sykes, July 1765

> We have granted them the *diwani* of the provinces of Bengal, Bihar and Orissa.
>
> Firman of Shah Alam II, 12 August 1765

THE EIGHTEENTH CENTURY WAS marked by two almost continuous wars, punctuated by periodic truces, between France and Britain, and between Mughal and Maratha. The victor in both conflicts in India was to be the British, but when hostilities began they scarcely figured in the reckoning. The ambition of both *nizam* and peshwa to create dynasties south of the Narbada river was handed on from father to son and dominated the sub-continent for nearly a century. The principal Mughal protagonist was the viceroy of the Deccan since 1713, the nizam Asaf Jah. While he never renounced his allegiance to the emperor, for whom he prayed every day – 'may thrones and umbrellas bring good to him who has them,' he sniffed[1] – he consolidated his independent grip on Aurangabad and Hyderabad, and by 1742 he had swallowed up most of Bijapur and Golconda, and his rule extended from the central plateau to the Coromandel coast. The Marathas, at the same time, had broken out of their ancestral lands and controlled the territory round his vice-regal capital at Aurangabad, and had raided sufficiently far south to create fiefdoms near Madras, at Vellore, Gingee and Tanjore, formerly part of Golconda. 'The Marathas have permanently planted their claws in all the imperial territory,' the nizam snarled, 'and their strength and power have increased beyond limit... I have challenged them.'[2] In 1739, an event of almost divinely prompted calamity had struck the Mughal empire a mortal blow. An Afghan bandit turned generalissimo, Nadir Shah, who had seized the throne of Isfahan, marched at the head of an army through Afghanistan into the Panjab, where he defeated the imperial army at Karnal. It was a victory without point, for Nadir Shah had no intention of occupying the throne of Delhi; instead he removed it. A fracas in the captured city led to a terrible sequel. The ex-bandit sat silent in the golden mosque for nine hours while his soldiers indiscriminately massacred the population. Then the sack complete, he returned to Persia with the peacock throne of the Mughals, which was to serve thereafter as the seat of Persian shahs.

The next year, 1740, Balaji Rao became the third peshwa. He was only 18 but he already showed more capacity than his father and grandfather, a politician to his finger tips, who knew that the secret of power in India was to be constantly on the move, not hidden behind impregnable walls. He finally established Maratha power in Poona, confronted and worsted the nizam, subdued those angry bees that plagued the western coasts, the Siddi and the Angria pirates, not to mention the most unpredictable bees of all, the merchants of Bombay. Like the great Mughal emperors, he was seldom still, appearing at sieges, negotiating after battle, inspecting accounts, adjudicating disputes, tirelessly writing and recording. No district officer was more assiduous at showing himself frequently to his people, no viceroy more preoccupied with the extension and consolidation of his people's rule. He allowed Maratha eyes to roam beyond Benares and Bhubaneswar into the heart of Bengal itself.

The nawabi had since 1740 been ruled by a Turkish adventurer, Alivardi Khan, who had, from the abundant treasury at Murshidabad, sent two crores of rupees to Delhi to secure his nomination as nawab. The British found him ready to sustain the conditions in which business flourished, but he was no match for the Marathas, who swept into Bengal in April 1742 and plundered Murshidabad. Their outfliers caused panic in Calcutta where the Company began to dig the Maratha ditch to keep them out. For the next seven years the golden province of Bengal was afflicted by roving armies, until Alivardi Khan bought off the Marathas by paying chauth of 12 lakhs of rupees a year. The merchants of Calcutta trembled, but one merchant in Bengal saw only advantage in the weakness of formerly powerful Mughal princes in the face of Maratha attack. The *surintendant* of the French factory of Chandernagore, several miles upriver from Calcutta, Joseph François, Marquis Dupleix, was the son of a rich tax farmer who had bought him a place, aged 23, on the *conseil supérieur* of Pondicherry. Dupleix had a penchant for splendour, both in his ideas and in his dress. At 33, in 1770, he was put in charge of Chandernagore and converted it from a small outpost to a thriving mart. In 1742 he was transferred to Pondicherry and pro-moted to be governor-general of all French outposts in India, a post he held until 1754.

The Carnatic (Karnatak) was, like the Deccan, a geographical name for the lowlands that flanked the Bay of Bengal for 600 miles or so from the Guntur Circar (Sarkar) to Cape Comorin. The 'black country', which was what the Carnatic signified, was estuarine soil round a number of criss-crossing rivers which formed natural boundaries to small states that struggled for some kind of independence. The nawabi, established by Aurangzeb, with its capital at Arcot, bordered on both Madras and Pondicherry. In 1743, the nizam, in his capacity as imperial viceroy, moved into the Carnatic at the head of a huge army to remove Maratha intruders and to appoint his *wazir*, Anwar-ud-din, as nawab. The factors at Madras and Pondicherry sent to Arcot to felicitate him and he promised them the hand of friendship and protection.

In 1743, too, war had broken out in Europe over the Austrian Succession. Normally, war in Europe did not affect the behaviour of factors in India. Social contact might be suspended but there were no hostilities. This time it was different. After British privateers had plundered cargoes in which Dupleix had a substantial stake, the French *gouverneur-général* resolved on local action. Mahé de la Bourdonnais, governor of Île de France (Mauritius), had put together a scratch squadron of Compagnie ships which arrived off the Coromandel coast when the British squadron was absent and found itself, unexpectedly, mistress of the seas. In a swift campaign, Dupleix occupied Fort St George in September 1746, after a week's siege. Surprisingly he was unable to master the much smaller fort St David, only a few miles from Pondicherry itself, and when the British squadron swept back into the Bay of Bengal, Dupleix's own base of Pondicherry was threatened. The French triumph was short-lived – Fort St George was restored to the British at the peace three years later – but Dupleix, thwarted by politicians in Europe, had seen a way of using the politicians of India to secure advantages for France by procuring the gratitude and dependency of Indian princes.

During the war Dupleix had built up an army of 3000 *sepoys* and 1800 European and semi-European soldiers (mainly *topasses*, or Indo-Portuguese Christians, from their distinctive headgear or *topi*). The Madras presidency, in response, had 4000 Europeans and topasses and 2000 sepoys under arms. The two armies existed to fight one another, not protect their factories from Mughal or Maratha attack. They were not large enough to do each other lasting damage, as witness the sorry attempts by both sides to master weak fortresses like Fort St David and Pondicherry, but what the war had demonstrated was the powerlessness of the nizam's new viceroy, who had twice tried to take Madras from the French with what was considered a powerful native army. Neither side wanted to disband its army, but neither could afford it. They became, therefore, available as mercenaries to native princes to fight their succession wars. Dupleix shrewdly reckoned that a monarch who owed his throne to French support would have a debt to pay. If Dupleix then were to become his subahdar, the French could live on revenue earned in India rather than on remittances from France.

His opportunity came just as the European war was ending in stalemate and status quo. In May 1748, the nizam Asaf Jah died, leaving his nizamat, as was so often the case with dying monarchs, to a disputed succession. Dupleix decided to play the part of king-maker, from which he could expect substantial rewards. In return for the cession by his preferred candidate of 42 villages which boxed in the tiny British fort at St David, and for his appointment as the new nizam's governor of all India south of the Kistna, he despatched the 30-year old Charles Joseph Patissier, Marquis de Bussy, to install him in his capital at Hyderabad. Bussy was very nearly France's Clive. A brilliant and opportunistic commander, he had that rare capacity, shared with Clive, to engage the loyalty of Indian troops and to secure victory against fearful odds. He set up his camp at Aurangabad and took the affairs of 'his' nizam in hand. He recruited, trained and regularly paid his sepoys, so that Bussy's *gardis* were soon the envy and terror of Maratha and Mughal alike, for their uniformed discipline, their firmness under fire, and their devastating use of artillery. Even the Marathas' spoiling tactics of hit and run failed to break their cohesion, and the peshwa ordered his commanders to avoid them and learn from their example. To meet his costs the nizam assigned him a stretch of land on the eastern coast between the Carnatic and Orissa, known as the Northern Circars, which he managed and milked with French rigour. Bussy, moreover, was a consummate politician and never exceeded his powers, always appearing to sustain native administration while slowly replacing it with French models. His readiness to 'observe Asiatic customs' meant that he held the balance of power in south-central India.[3] Bussy was, moreover, unwaveringly loyal to this French chief, and his presence in the Deccan meant that Dupleix's influence extended over the fortunes of some 30 million people. It was a threat the British could not ignore.

The nawabi of the Carnatic was again under dispute, and the two pretenders turned to both sides for help. Muhammad Ali's appeal to Fort St George did not fall on deaf ears. If he could be brought by British support into his inheritance, he would control the rich rice fields of the south which fed Madras and, linked in friendly embrace with the Company, provide a buffer against sudden attack, which had succeeded so easily in 1746. The instrument to achieve this was a young writer who had already shown he was not born for a desk. Robert Clive had volunteered for military service, attracting the attention of the regular army veteran, Colonel Stringer Lawrence, who commanded the Presidency troops. Lawrence recognised, behind what seemed to others reckless bravado, a brain naturally quick to size up a situation and use it to advantage. Bussy's removal to Hyderabad was to prove providential for, against a professional soldier of genius, Clive's career might have ended at its beginning. He was matched against the less competent mercenaries of France. South Indian armies, divided by treachery and intrigue, and dedicated to causes of no possible interest to the rank and file, were more often than not factions bound together for the hour by the interests of the commanders who paid them. Clive's success against inferior, often suborned, opponents with minimal loss of life and material, created that reputation for invincibility which he never really deserved.

Clive also had the luck of the bold. His dash for Arcot in August 1751 left the Forts St George and St David virtually undefended. Marching his 400-odd troops, rather less than half Europeans, through a thunderstorm of epic violence, he seemed the very avatar of a Pandava warrior in the Máhabhárata, so that the unnerved garrison in the city fled. Clive instantly raised the colours of the Mughal emperor in Delhi and of his rightful viceroy, Muhammad Ali, thus preserving the fiction that the Company acted in the interests of Mughal legitimacy. A relieving force was scattered by a typical Clive manoeuvre, a night attack, and the 50-day siege that followed proved a more near-run thing than Clive had expected. But he defended the crumbling fortifications against a vastly superior force by speed and bluff. Dupleix could not believe that so paltry a force of 'contemptible riff-raff' had defied one commanded by a Frenchman.[4] His principals in France, however, wanted peace. They had only supported him so far because they believed he would live off Indian rents, so they had stopped his remittances from France. The result was that he never had enough money to back his plans, and when the Compagnie recognised this, he was recalled in 1754.

Muhammad Ali was now *de facto* nawab of the Carnatic and a client of the British. The Carnatic had become their sphere of interest, while the Deccan remained French. With Dupleix's departure, the nizam tried unsuccessfully to rid himself of his overmighty subject, but Bussy was too strong for him. He continued to rule the roost in Hyderabad, a virtually independent satrap, but there was no Dupleix in Pondicherry to exploit him. Had he had a Bussy in the Carnatic as well as the Deccan, Dupleix's triumph could have been stupendous. In Paris, however, his superiors did not understand what he was trying to do, but they were impressed by Bussy's achievements enough, 30 years later, to send him back to India to repeat them. Bussy apart, the French mercenaries in India were second-rate, relying more on gasconades and the legendary French reputation for brilliance in war. They were defeated by a *blageur* more dextrous than they.

Not only had the two Companies embarked on a dangerous policy of intervening in the affairs of their neighbours, they had also, in south India at least, changed the rules of war. There is much in Indian warfare in the seventeenth and eighteenth centuries reminiscent of mediaeval Italy. Princes put their wealth into the appearances of a considerable army. The cavalry glinted in its livery and tempered steel, while elephants in elaborate head and body armour hauled or pushed field-pieces, either expensively purchased or more expensively cast with foreign help, and could be used as battering rams in battle itself. The foot-soldiers or peons, hastily impressed and poorly trained, were massed in phalanxes to look formidable. Generals, who commanded only the loyalty of their own retainers, could bring about victory or defeat by committing them to or withholding them from battle, and the death of a general in combat usually meant the immediate withdrawal of his men. The cause of a petty dynast in southern India, especially if he were a northern Muslim, reliant on alien mercenaries from Afghanistan or Turkestan, was hardly worth dying for. Native armies disintegrated rapidly if there was the danger of a slaughter.[5]

The worst thing to happen to an Indian army was to battle with an enemy determined to win, like Babur at Panipat, Nadir Shah at Karnal and Clive at Kaveripak. More often, combinations, concessions and outright bribery made a battle, like Plassey, more a transaction than a conflict.[6] Impregnable fortresses were usually captured by treachery or barter. The ceaseless campaigning of Mughal emperors and viceroys, the engrossment of weaker neighbours, the customary conflict between heirs and pretenders could only have been sustained if there was a relatively low loss of life. Drought caused greater damage to economic life than war, and the wealth of India survived the effects of ceaseless conflict because there was a comparatively low level of destruction of life and property. Even so, the humble *ryot* (*raiyat*) prayed for the day when armies did not trample across his fields, requisition his provender and forcibly conscript his sons. The success of small units of professionally drilled sepoys with a stiffening of European gunners in conflict with the cumbersome armies of India had been first demonstrated when the French in 1676 intervened to help Sher Khan Lodi against the governor of Gingee. They were soon to be the hallmark of Company armies, both British and French. The sweepings of British gaols and poorhouses, which Company crimps sent to India, seldom survived two fevers or the country liquor, and were less valuable than sepoys whose resistance to disease and resilience in the face of fatigue or hunger were legendary. Moreover, bravely led, they could be as brave as lions, somewhat to the surprise of their European officers who observed the poor performance of enemy armies in the field.[7] Where the French had shown the way, the English company followed. To the military commanders of Europe, sepoy generals like Lawrence and Clive, and Clive's detested subordinate, Eyre Coote, and the great Wellington himself were to change the face of India more substantially in the course of a century than the commanders, who presided over the slaughters of Malplaquet, Passarowitz, Belgrade and Kunersdorf, changed that of Europe.

Events were now to give the British the chance to create an Indian client state, like Bussy's Hyderabad, in Bengal. In April 1756, just as Europe was on the brink of another conflagration, Alivardi Khan died. His only blood relative was his grandson, a youth of 20, Siraj-ud-daula, described even by his own Bengalis as 'cruel rapacious, vindictive, insolent and tyrannical. A coward, a profligate and a traitor'.[8] But whatever his true qualities, Siraj was determined to hang on to his inheritance, and the events in south India gave him good reason to be suspicious of both the British in Calcutta and the French in Chandernagore. Both settlements were strengthening their defences, ostensibly against each other, but they could just as easily have been preparing to support one of his rivals. When the English refused his demand that they dismantle such fortifications as had been erected contrary to the treaty, he overran both Kasimbazar and Calcutta in June. The British took to the ships in the river, leaving a miserable garrison to face the Bengali horde. Once it had surrendered, their captors, not knowing what to do with the prisoners, consigned them to one of the vaults of Fort William. The legend of the Black Hole is largely the work of one of its survivors, Surgeon John Zephaniah Holwell, member of the Calcutta council, who wished to prove that, unlike the governor, he had not only not deserted his post but been almost martyred, and should now be made governor. As a horror the 'Hole' was mild in the annals of man's inhumanity to man, but to obliterate the shameful ease with which Calcutta had been overrun, it was necessary to present Siraj-ud-daula as a monster, abusing his overwhelming power with an act of cruelty, of which he was certainly quite ignorant at the time. Unhappily he inspired enough terror in his servants to ensure that, once asleep, he could not be wakened to countermand an order to confine the prisoners to a small dungeon in the height of summer.

Despite the threats of another European war, the Company wanted no adventures in India such as had reduced profits during the last conflict, but Calcutta had to be recovered. Unknown to Leadenhall Street, Clive, that 'heaven-born general' (actual rank, lieutenant-colonel 'only in the East Indies') and now governor of Fort St David, was chosen to be avenging angel with all the troops that could be spared from Madras, 600 European and 900 native, on ships of the Royal Navy commanded by Admiral Watson. Calcutta was stormed on 2 January 1757. The factory, the elegant houses, and the church were in ruins. Siraj, realising he was up against something more powerful than a swarm of mosquitoes on the hides of his elephants, agreed to confirm the Company's privileges and compensate it for its losses. But Clive had another object, the removal of the French presence from Bengal. What doomed Siraj-ud-daula was, not the Black

Hole or the seizure of Calcutta, but the presence of a small French force in Chandernagore. Rebutting the nawab's ban on private war in his territory Admiral Watson threatened to 'kindle such a flame in your country as all the water in the Ganges will not be able to extinguish'.[9] The deputy *foujdar* of Hooghly, Nanda Kumar (Nundcomar), charged to keep the peace between the two sides, had put a price on his betrayal. The rich Panjabi banian, Amin Chand (Omichand), a merchant so rich that 'he could produce a third of the Company's Bengal goods, costing just under a million rupees, without needing to receive any payment in advance',[10] and the Seth bankers, who had been locked in their houses and threatened with circumcision, jointly urged the nawab to put his trust in British good faith (about as little to be relied upon as the nawab's own). Clive, without a by your leave, mopped up Chandernagore in March 1757 on his way to confront a possible assault on Bengal by Nadir Shah during one of his filibustering raids into India. He assured Siraj that, unlike the French, the British constituted no threat to his rule. See how they had sprung to his defence against the Afghans! But, knowing that the Hindu money-lords now believed that a nominally Christian Company might prove a useful ally against Muslim exploitation, he hastened on a conspiracy to replace him. Siraj was persuaded to scotch it by one more assault on the Company. On paper his army was a far more formidable one than Clive had ever faced before, 50,000 strong, and stiffened by a corps of Pathan cavalry, but he was surrounded by as many waverers and traitors as Richard Plantagenet at Bosworth Field. The Battle of Plassey was fought and won in palace corners, but it was the death in action of Siraj's only reliable commander on 23 June 1757 that led to the rout. His intended supplanter, Mir Jafar Khan played his treacherous part to the end and the nawab paid the price of all losers, being knifed to death by order of the Mir's bloodthirsty son.[11] Mir Jafar became nawab and sent a suitably humble letter to the emperor in Delhi to inform him that he had a new viceroy in Bengal. Meanwhile the vultures gathered. Clive claimed that, confronted with the nawab's treasury at Murshidabad, a city as large and as rich as London, he was amazed at his own moderation. But its contents were to be inadequate to meet all the demands that were now to be made on it, and the lazy and luxury-loving Mir, who had become its master, was to see it evaporate before his eyes. Clive himself received a modest gratuity worth £240,000 and William Watts, the agent at Kasimbazar, who had spent some time as an unwilling guest of Siraj, received £100,000. Other 'deserving' members of the Calcutta establishment were rewarded with purses of between £5,000 and £60,000. Clive increased the soldiers in Company pay and sent the bill to Mir Jafar, to meet which the Company was assigned zamindari rights over an area of 900 square miles, known as the Twenty Four Parganas – a *pargana* being like a county – which stretched from the south of Calcutta to the sea. Even these could not meet Mir Jafar's engagements to the Company which were re-scheduled for payment through the Seth banking house.

The most devastating effect on the nawab's income, however, came from the way Company servants, through their agents, pounced on the internal trade of Bengal, to which they had had only limited access. They stretched the Company's exemption from customs duty to cover their own private merchandise, by issuing to their *gomastahs*, or agents, free passes, or *dastaks*, which afforded the protection of the Company and of the British flag to goods described in them. So widespread did this practice become that Warren Hastings, travelling up the country in 1761 to his agency at the nawab's court, was 'surprised to meet with several English flags flying in places which I have passed; and on the river I do not believe that I passed a boat without one'.[12] Mir Jafar was powerless to prevent it, though he tried to hold on to his salt, tobacco and betel-nut monopolies (he lost that of opium) and the profitable farming of their custom duties. But even these had been invaded by Company servants claiming exemption, so much so that the new nawab could not sell the right to collect them. Crippled by obligations he could not meet to nurture a nest of vipers in Calcutta, Mir Jafar was beaten before he started and, as he lacked the energy to overcome his problems, it was not long before he too was replaced. Clive, feeling some responsibility for the man he had elevated to the principality in a privately managed palace revolution, refused to abandon him while he was president of the council. He was shocked by the speed with which the residents of Calcutta returned to their old ways, to the back-biting and venomous rivalry between senior merchants, claiming that 'the riches of Peru and Mexico should not induce me to dwell amongst them.'[13] When he left for England in February 1760 the affairs of Bengal began to slip into the morass.

Henry Vansittart's grandfather had been a director of the Company and when the 13-year-old Henry proved too much for Winchester College, he was shipped off to Fort St David as a writer. His rise through the ranks as factor (1750, aged 28), senior merchant (1756) and member of the council of Fort St George (1757) was pretty standard for survivors, and in 1759 he was summoned to preside over the council in Fort William. A frenzy of greed now possessed the merchants of Calcutta, always in a hurry to beat the apocalyptic horsemen who regularly traversed the province. Vansittart badgered Warren Hastings at Murshidabad to advise him how it might be done, but Hastings knew that the wealth of the province was exhausted, 'dissipated in idle schemes of luxury and ill-timed vanity, mis-spent on useless alliances, and so scantily and injudiciously employed in the expense of war, that the sepoys are starving... the country left a prey to every invader'.[14] Only years under a capable ruler could restore its fortunes and, when he recommended that Mir Jafar be replaced by his son-in-law, Mir Qasim, Vansittart agreed. Qasim was in the mould of the late Alivardi Khan and as soon as he became nawab he set energetically about the restoration of his state. The price of his elevation had been yet another cession of territory to the Company, the rich districts of Midnapur, Burdwan and Chittagong, and more gratuities (£50,000 to Vansittart and £37,000 to Holwell). He had given up most of west Bengal as lost and, as he refused to be a Company puppet like his father-in-law, Mir Qasim moved his capital from Murshidabad to Monghyr, and decided to develop Bihar and its Ganges trade to Delhi and beyond, from which Company merchants were to be excluded.

That was not what the merchants Holwell and his party wanted. Vansittart was only chairman of a council of 16, he had no casting vote, and the chiefs of Patna, Dacca and Kasimbazar were among the 16 and often absent. They had their own priorities and held that 'the dignity of our *dustucks* are the chief badges of honour'.[15] The Company protested, to which Mir Qasim replied very reasonably: 'The *gomastahs* of the English gentlemen purchase from the country people by force and extortion… and wrangling with my officers, so that the poor, the inhabitants, the merchants and manufacturers of my country are oppressed'.[16] He had an army to pay and a state to run, and the privilege of freedom from duty was confined to the imports and exports of the Company alone, not of its servants and certainly not of their servants. Vansittart, despite being himself involved on a huge scale in the internal trade, could not, in conscience, object, but the members of his council had left their consciences on the way to India at the Cape.[17] Hastings recognised that they were bent on 'absolving every person in our service from the jurisdiction of the government… [It] will prevent their suffering any oppression; but it gives them a full license of oppressing others, since, whatever crimes they may commit, the magistrates must patiently look on, nor dare even to defend the lives and properties of the subjects committed to his care without a violation of our rights and privileges'.[18]

Every reasonable accommodation with the nawab that Vansittart tried to negotiate was rejected out of hand by the hostile majority on the council, whose view was epitomised by one Company servant writing to the commander of the Company troops in Bengal: 'Let 'em grant the increase of duties, it won't hurt – but to oblige us to withdraw our protection from our gomastahs and sacrifice at once the privilege of our dusticks [sic] must ruin us all'.[19] The violent and arrogant chief at Patna, William Ellis, behaved as if the Company was above the law. He arrested the nawab's servants and broke into his go-downs to check that there were no confiscated goods covered by a Company dastak. Exasperated beyond patience, Mir Qasim, in January 1763, abolished at a stroke all internal duties on the movement of merchandise in his dominions for two years, thus removing all the benefits that false dastaks provided. The howl of rage in Calcutta was almost audible in Patna. The majority on the Council was determined on war if the nawab should persist in his impertinence. Ellis took it upon himself to deliver a reprimand and led an attack on Patna on 25 June 1763. The response was immediate and terrible.

Ellis and his marauders were rounded up, and eventually slaughtered at dinner after a gallant defence – chairs, knives and forks were no weapons against fully-armed men. The Hindu governor, suspected of being friendly to the British, was hurled into the Ganges and hundreds of his co-religionists were rounded up and killed. The Seth bankers who had followed Qasim's court were shot. The nawab invoked military support from his neighbour of Oudh and the pretender to the throne of the Great Mughal. Meanwhile the council in Calcutta had deposed him and restored the feeble and uxorious Mir Jafar. The army of Bengal chased the nawab into Oudh, where on 23 October Colonel Hector Munro demolished the combined army of Qasim, the nawab-wazir and the imperial pretender, at Buxar. It was a more fateful and bloody battle than Plassey. By the end of the day the triple alliance was destroyed and its treasure, valued at between two and three million rupees, was in Munro's hands. It was typical of the time that victory was measured in booty rather than loss of life, but the British lost 816 dead, the heaviest losses in battle so far in India.[20] The real booty was the undisputed control over the provinces of Bengal and Bihar, achieved, not by the diplomatic subtlety of a Bussy, but by force of arms.

Meanwhile the fortunes of the French had crashed. In 1758, Thomas Arthur O'Lally, Baron de Tollendal, landed in India with a French expeditionary force. He had commanded the Irish brigade at Fontenoy in 1745, and accompanied Bonnie Prince Charlie to Scotland. He suffered from excess of family pride and a short temper. As commander-in-chief and governor of Pondicherry he refused to take the advice of a mere sepoy general like Bussy, and treated his native troops little better than slaves, their caste traditions as mumbo-jumbo. With too little energy he finally invested Fort St George. But it was not to be a repeat of 1746. No fewer than 26,000 shot, 8,000 shells and 200,000 rounds of small arms fire assailed it in vain between December and February 1758–9. When a British squadron appeared, O'Lally withdrew.

He had summoned Bussy to join him in June 1758 and, obeying his superior officer, the marquis left his base perilously exposed to invasion from Bengal and the nizam to the intrigues of his younger brothers. O'Lally was decisively defeated at Wandewash in January 1760 by Eyre Coote, another Irishman, unlike O'Lally never to be worsted in battle, and Bussy was taken prisoner. O'Lally tried to redeem his poor performance by enduring eight months of siege in Pondicherry, but he finally capitulated in January 1761. He, too, was to pay the price of failure. Indian princes were usually stabbed or strangled. Count O'Lally was beheaded for treason, after trial in Paris, to which he had voluntarily returned from imprisonment in England. What was also beheaded was any hope of a resurgence of French power in India. British command of Bengal and the Bay meant that it could assume the provisioning and protection of Fort St George, and by putting Indian affairs into the hands of a deracinated Irishman with no experience of the east, France had destroyed her own power-base in the Deccan. Buxar changed the fortunes of India. British troops marched as far west as Allahabad, Mir Qasim had a price on his head, and the nawab-wazir of Oudh, Shuja-ud-daula, was mulcted of 50 lakhs of rupees and forced to grant the same exemption for Company goods from duty in Oudh as they enjoyed in Bengal. Had he reduced Oudh to the status of Bengal, Clive feared that 'the princes of Indostan' would conclude that the Company's ambitions were boundless. In fact, they seemed very little worried by what was happening in the east.[21] For the Matter of India that pre-occupied the 'princes of Indostan' was the imperial ambition of the Marathas. Their confederation had adapted the Mughal revenue and military systems they had found in the Deccan, and now constituted a successor state, ready to wrest control of the trade routes of the Ganges and the Cauvery from Oudh and Hyderabad. They would cleanse the holy places on the sacred rivers from Muslim defilement. But first they must control the emperor in Delhi, the legitimate authority for the chauth, off which they lived. By 1750 they had imposed tribute on most of south India, on Gujerat and much of the Deccan, on Bengal and on the Mesopotamian *doab* between the Ganges and the Jumna (Yamuna). They had watered their horses in all the rivers of India except the five rivers of the Panjab. On 11 April 1758 they occupied Lahore. They were at the zenith of their power.

They were, however, to prove no match for a new Afghan invader, Ahmed Shah Abdali, who had seized the kingdom from Nadir Shah. India was the granary of his otherwise poor mountain kingdom that stretched from the Oxus to the Gulf, from the foothills of the Tibetan plateau to the Indus and the Sutlej and Ahmed Shah was to be three times in India on missions of plunder. Though he repeatedly put Delhi to the sack it was to bribe his mountain-loving cavalrymen to stay in the plains. Preaching holy war against the 'Maratha kafirs', he met the Maratha army on the plain of Kurukshetra, the field of a legendary 18-day battle of all nations between the Kauravas and the Pandavas in the Máhabhárata, near Panipat, the site of two other great battles in historic time, at the first of which Babur had broken the Delhi sultanate. The plain ran red with blood, as at Kurukshetra of old, and chroniclers counted 28,000 dead on the field of battle and another 35,000 Maratha prisoners, hunted down and slaughtered. Ahmed Shah gave thanks at the Panipat mosque arrayed in his finest robes with the great Kohinor diamond, wrested by Nadir Shah from the regalia of Aurangzeb, in his turban.

Panipat broke the peshwa's heart; it even tempted Vansittart to invade the Maratha country to put an end to their menace once and for all.[22] But within a few years they had recovered their poise and imperial pretensions. What Ahmed Shah had achieved was the ruin of the Mughal empire. Unwilling to spend more time away from the mountains, he installed a client emperor and left, never again to appear near the city.

Panipat was fought on 14 January 1761. On 15 January, Company Major Carnac beat off Shah Alam who had invaded Mir Qasim's former nawabi in pursuit of booty, accompanied by French fugitives from Chandernagore. On 16 January Pondicherry fell to the investing armies of the Madras Presidency and the nawab Muhammad Ali of Arcot. These events were as remote from each other as would have been conflicts in Europe at Saragossa, Warsaw and Otranto. But each was prophetic.

The sensational campaigns in the Carnatic and in Bengal between 1751 and 1761 seemed to confirm the supremacy of European dash, vigour and discipline against oriental armies. In fact the Marathas had more dash, the Pathans and Afghans, who were the sinews of every Muslim army in India, had more vigour and French-trained gunners as much discipline. Where the Europeans had triumphed was in the regular payment of their troops, the steadfastness of their march and the speed of their small-arms fire. Against it Indian cavalry stumbled and fell, elephants were driven berserk and the ranks of peons were shot to pieces. The days were over when small European forces made little impression on the roving mass that was an Indian army, and the approach of a Company force was enough now to make even Afghan mercenaries on the loose and Maratha marauders in search of loot more circumspect. Panipat was, in fact, the last battle in India fought on traditional lines. Thereafter no army was without its European gunners and its European trained infantry, and defeated and turned-off French officers and men had little difficulty in finding an employer. The princes might be short of cash but the Company entered enthusiastically into trading weapons on credit to its clients, like Oudh and the Carnatic. Europeans could be bought in an open market as gunners, to destroy the cavalry, which had until recently determined victory in battle and which had given the Marathas their superiority, and to batter hitherto impregnable fortresses into rubble. Just as the peshwa and nizam had fenced for the services of Bussy, so Bussy's lieutenants and O'Lally's men were snapped up by the peshwa, the Bhosle rajah of Berar, the nizam and the new ruler in Mysore, Haidar Ali Khan. And not only Frenchmen. British deserters and Indian mercenaries were also available. After Panipat there were more non-Maratha mercenaries than Marathas in the armies of the peshwa and of the Maratha warlords like Tukoji Holkar and Mahadji Scindia who, like a Mughal himself, employed as many Muslims as Hindus in his forces. Money being short to pay mercenaries, ruthless looting became a feature of princely, particularly Maratha, armies moving like locusts across the country, which made them hated and feared everywhere, even within their own heartland.[23]

Dupleix had recognised that south Indian princes were little more than village chiefs, and Bussy had eliminated the smaller units of power to create one, French-dominated central power in the Deccan by reviving the Mughal authority of the nizam. The British, by taking over the defence of the nawab-wazir of Oudh in the north and the nawab of the Carnatic in the south, now also became part of the alliance system of India, a system shot through with intrigue and betrayal and fuelled by greed, a bewildering kaleidoscope of shifting combinations as the different parties, both European and Indian, pursued their ambitions. Indian princes were rich in land and they bought alliances and ruled over a people of clients and favourites whose loyalty was secured by gifts of rent from lands or jagirs. They were the basis of Bussy's wealth in the Northern Circars, they were the cause of the nawab of Arcot's famous debts and they were the subject of a motion of censure on Clive in the House of Commons.

From being the son of an undistinguished country lawyer, Clive had become richer than any European before him in India. Apart from his commission for provisioning the Company in Madras, his wealth consisted of Mir Jafar's stupendous gift of quarter of a million pounds on his accession, later supplemented by the grant of a jagir, worth another £27,000 a year. In fact he was not by the standards of the century enormously rich. He might have been worth £40,000 a year, but this fortune did not compare with the annual rent-rolls of over £100,000 enjoyed by the great landowners of England. His offence, if offence there were, was to have grown rich too quickly. Though he held, successfully and truthfully, that he had never acquired wealth by oppression, extortion or by any dishonest means, but only from the free generosity of a nawab whom he had helped to put on the throne, he was not to enjoy it without challenge. The directors were uncomfortably aware that events in India during the two recent wars had changed the political map, but they were not sure how. Shareholders were even more bemused: could that Sir Roger Dowlett, who had behaved so badly, really be a baronet?[24] They were mainly concerned about what effect the changes might have on the dividend. The future was clear. Now that the French establishments had been reduced to impotence, the merchants in India must return to the business of making money, balance the Company's books and pay a good dividend. If Clive had his way half their capital 'would be buried in stone walls'.[25] Furthermore, virtually supreme in a province so legendarily rich, the Company in Bengal should need no further remittances of bullion from London, except to finance the investment in Indian goods for export to Britain. And if, as Clive contended, Bengal was not so rich as imagined, then where had all the wealth gone if not into the pockets of its merchants, living extravagantly, accepting gifts which they then repatriated by drawing bills on London? What could be more visible evidence of this than Clive's jagir? If Clive felt he could not offend the nawab by refusing it, let him at least pay the rents to the treasury in Calcutta.

The usual financial adjustments following Mir Jafar's reinstatement after Buxar shocked the directors whose servants were adding so greatly to the miseries of a province 'involved for years past in continual war and drained of its riches and the blood of its inhabitants'.[26] As if this were not enough, when Mir Jafar died the next year, his son had to find another 12 lakhs for presents, so that 'the selection of the rulers of Bengal formed one of the most lucrative occupations of the Board at Fort William'.[27] Even the governor, Henry Verelst, felt impelled to write to his employers that the 'transactions of senior servants of the Company seem to demonstrate that every spring of this government was smeared with corruption, that principles or rapacity and oppression universally prevailed, and that every spark of sentiment and public spirit was lost and extinguished in the inordinate lust of unmerited wealth'.[28]

The Company's credit was at a low ebb, its stock valuation was depressed and its bonds discounted at a loss. What many had suspected was now plain for all to see. The Company had been systematically defrauded by its servants for years. Profits that should have accrued to the Company treasury had gone instead into the pockets of Company men who were also impoverishing the province from which the Company's wealth came. For those who were able to influence business, there was nothing so lucrative as a gift from Indians who required a favour, and a lakh of rupees (between £10,000 and £11,000) was the minimum gratuity a man of honour could be offered. Francis Sykes, the Company's resident at Murshidabad in 1773, milked the nawab of a princely fortune to represent his interests to the governor-general in Council. He argued that this was entirely proper, for not a rupee he ever received would have found its way to the Company. It was merely a matter of 'whether it should go into a black man's pocket or my own'.[29] The select committee of the House of Commons calculated that, from Plassey in 1757 to Clive's return to Bengal in 1765, £2,169,065 (almost certainly an under-estimate) had been received by Company servants in gifts, over £112,000 in 1765 alone, surpassing anything that disgraced the annals of Tacitus.[30] Even Clive was honest enough to admit that the minds of civil servants were possessed by 'corruption, licentiousness and a want of principle'.[31]

On Clive's return to London in 1760 he set about building up a party in the Commons. He was elected member for Shrewsbury, his father for Montgomery and his secretary for Worcester. The new King's government needed the Company's support in the city, and both ministerial and opposition supporters began to buy stock so that they could influence Company decisions by using their votes. Ministers even used funds from the paymaster-general's office. Having failed to prevent the election of his sternest critic as chairman of Directors, Clive was saved by Mir Qasim. The nawab's alliance with Oudh and the imperial pretender threw the Company into panic and Clive was sent back to India as governor and commander-in-chief of Bengal. He went on condition that his jagir was safe. Otherwise he was free to cleanse the Augean stable. His reports on reaching Calcutta on 3 May 1765 depressed the directors further, for the 'vast fortunes acquired in the inland trade have been obtained by a scene of the most tyrannic and oppressive conduct that ever was known in any age or country'.[32] He had already decided what must be done. 'We must... become the nabob ourselves in fact if not in name.'[33]

Shah Alam II was only too ready to oblige. On 12 August 1765, he received a pension of 26 lakhs of rupees a year to keep his eyes fixed on Delhi and 'the noblest of exalted nobles, the chief of illustrious warriors, our faithful servants and sincere well-wishers... the English company' was granted the right to collect the revenues of the province of Bengal, all 'in the time that it would have taken to sell a jackass'.[34] Clive genuinely believed that the grant would stop the regular pillaging of the nawab's ever depleting treasury, diminish the all-pervading stench of corruption and enable the Council to put the administration on a sure footing. It did the first, if not the others, for there was in fact very little left to pillage, and the demoralised nawab, Naim-ud-daula, was pathetically pleased to be guaranteed enough money to keep his dancing girls. But the diwani effectively elevated the Company into the constellation of Princes of Indostan and, in the words of Edmund Burke, constituted the 'great act of the constitutional entrance... into the body politic of India'.[35] Yet that event passed almost unnoticed outside Bengal, and Shah Alam thought virtually no more about it as long as his pension was paid.

Clive believed that the diwani had fallen into the Company's lap as if from heaven and that was enough. The Company should engage in no further military adventures. The revenues would enable it to support a purely defensive force, and he was careful to emphasise that the Company now only managed the money of the nawabi not the nawabi itself. Company servants were ill-equipped to collect taxes, being ignorant of the Mughal system and not having the language. Indians would still exercise judicial and administrative authority and collect the revenue. The diwani did not make the Company masters of Bengal but only of its revenue, estimated at £2 million a year, a fountain of rupees, half of which, in the short run, would revive the investment, threatened by the Company's poor trading performance in the face of war and competition from its own servants, *and* finance the trade with China and Japan.[36] The other half would pay for the civil and military establishment and enable Calcutta to provision Madras and keep Bombay solvent. From 1765 to 1770 not an ounce of bullion left England for India and this, to Clive, justified the whole transaction. Being diwan did not, however, reduce the costs of the nawab's administration, while the Company acquired new liabilities under the Treaty of Allahabad with Shah Alam, which gave it control of Bussy's old stamping ground, the Northern Circars, linking Bengal territorially with Madras, and which committed it to the defence, not only of Bengal, but also of Oudh. In 1765 the Bengal army numbered some 15,000 Indian and 3,000 European officers and men. By 1769 that number had risen to nearly 30,000 men in all. Two thirds of the costs of the Presidency went to the military.

Clive's despatch to the directors, over his sole signature on 30 September 1765, nearly five months after his return to Calcutta, was a mission statement for the government of Bengal which passed from chairman to chairman, until the end of the century, as received wisdom. He had always maintained that he had been well rewarded but not corrupt and so felt safe in stating at the outset that 'the sudden, and among many, the unwarrantable acquisition of riches has introduced luxury in every shape and its most pernicious excess… in a country where money is plenty, where fear is the principle of government and where your arms are ever victorious; in such a country it is no wonder that corruption should find its way to a spot so well prepared to receive it'.[37] Senior civil servants had set a bad example to junior and on his arrival he had seen nothing that bore the form or appearance of government. The army was no better a case as 'an independent fortune was no distant prospect even to a subaltern'.[38] But Clive knew he could not do as the directors wanted and arbitrarily stop all private trade, recalling all agents to Calcutta. Company servants could not be expected to relinquish the promise of affluence for the certainty of beggary. They must be rewarded in other ways. Fortunes should not be made too quickly and, by reducing the opportunities, the Company might persuade its senior servants to be content with salaries that would cover the true costs of living in India, not £300 a year but £3,000. For, 'if we see nothing but rapacity among councillors, in vain shall we look for moderation among writers'.[39] The diwani now made it less imperative for private bills to be drawn on London to raise ready money in Bengal, and this would remove one of the commonest ways of remitting fortunes back to England. He was quick to add that he hoped these measures would not be applied to the revenue from his own jagir.

By 1767 Clive had succeeded in covenanting civil servants, from the governor down, not to accept improper or excessive gifts in return for more adequate salaries, paid from diwani revenues. He had made a start on removing trading abuses by bringing private trade under regulation by a trading society, which paid a dividend to its members. He had faced down a mutiny of military officers who did not want field allowances instead of the right to trade on their own account. But he had only reduced the worst excesses of the more senior civil servants, who had made a tidy fortune already and whose successors wished not to be denied the chance to do the same. When he left India in 1767, the old evils returned. Civilian and military servants knew that time was short and 'a whole horde of *zamindars*, *amils*, *qanungos*, *mutasaddis* and other minor officials were let loose to raise what they pleased from the cultivators and merchants'.[40] Complaints to the nawab were a waste of time. He had no officers able to redress them, no soldiers to enforce the law, no courts that could afford to do justice. Even the Resident at his *dorbar* thought that the Bengalis had fared better under their former despotic and arbitrary government.[41] Clive had staved off the collapse of government but he had not cleansed the stable. Already one ministerialist was prophesying that 'the affairs of this Company seem to become much too big for the management of a body of merchants'. They would soon have to become the subject of parliamentary enquiry.[42]

4. 'THE MIND THAT GRASPS AT SUCH WEALTH MUST BE VICIOUS'

> The suspicions which I find generally attached to East Indian riches sit heavy on my mind... The mind that grasps at such inordinate wealth must be vicious.
>
> Letter from Caroline Ashburn to
> Sibella Valmont in *Secresy or
> The Ruin on the Rock*
> by Eliza Fenwick, 1795

> Cats and dogs and serpents could easier unite in society than so incongruous a composition as Clavering, Monson and Francis.
>
> Richard Barwell

> Bengal is stript of a considerable part of its defence, and the flower of our army sent to ramble through the heart of Indostan... to support a new competitor, hitherto unthought of, in his pretensions, if he has any, to the succession to the Ram and Son Raja.
>
> Philip Francis, 5 August 1778

THE AFFAIRS OF INDIA had hitherto figured little in Parliament. The Company traded its patronage for ministerial favours when it needed them, and ministers were not above squeezing the richest corporation in London when they needed money to buy support. Two things were to change this permissive indifference. First, the spring elections of 1768 returned no fewer than 17 'Indians' to seats in the Commons, bought with fortunes made in the east. Secondly, the Company, which had been considered beyond financial weakness, only four years later declared itself broke, unable to pay a dividend or to meet its creditors, ruined by the greed and insolence of those very fortune-hunters who now sat in the House. It was their creature, Muhammad Ali, the nawab of the Carnatic, whose financial affairs were, indirectly, to bring about a catastrophic fall in the value of Company stock and its virtual bankruptcy in 1772. The nawab was a familiar figure in the life of Fort St George. To Clive, he was 'the best Mussalman I ever knew'. To a bamboozled governor Dupré 'no devil had a blacker heart'. Warren Hastings probably summed him up accurately: 'a polite man, of a very agreeable address, and the worst man in the world to transact business with'.[1] He was a charming, shiftless and genial rogue, but no worse than the merchants to whom he owed money. Indeed his debts became, under the word-spell of Edmund Burke, not a princely malfeasance but one of the great wrongs to which an innocent and well-meaning prince had been subjected by a corrupt and ruthless Company. He owed his *masnad* to Clive and the peaceful occupation of it to the Company's army in Madras. He had assigned jagirs to the Company worth 400,000 pagodas (about 12 lakhs of rupees) a year to pay for ten of its 21 battalions. Jagirs worth rather more had been given to Company servants in return for cash advances to buy weapons, so that, as a result, some 40 per cent of the nawabi's income found its way to Madras. Without a formal treaty, the Company was hog-tied to the defence of a nominally independent prince, while it had no control of his foreign policy. That policy was to consolidate his nawabi and to rely on the Company to protect him from the nizam, the Marathas and the new ruler of Mysore, with all of whom he was bound sooner or later to come into conflict.

The last was an adventurer determined to carve out a kingdom for himself between the Indian ocean and the bay of Bengal at the expense of Maratha, nizam and nawab of Arcot alike. Haidar Ali was born in 1721/2, the son of a Muslim mercenary in the service of the Hindu rajah of Mysore. His childhood was passed in camp, so that he never learned to read or write, but in observing the British championship of Muhammad Ali he concluded that they were 'like the jackal who burned his skin to imitate the tiger'. He hired French deserters to train 500 peons and 200 cavalry, armed with European flintlocks, as a personal army.[2] From then on his career was marked by a ruthless vindictiveness, influenced neither by loyalty nor by gratitude, but accompanied by a shrewd sense of timing and unusual powers of organisation. Bribing the nizam for the title nawab of Sera, north of Bangalore, he assumed virtual independence and minted his own coins which, oddly for a Muslim, carried an image of Parvati seated on the knee of Shiva. He confined his royal Hindu master in gilded captivity at Seringapatam to provide symbolic legitimacy to his conquests. His success in holding off the universally feared Marathas prompted the governor of Madras to warn Calcutta that 'we must fix Hyder as a friend or overthrow him as an enemy'.[3] Fixing him as a friend proved too difficult, for his French sympathies were too powerful. When Eyre Coote reduced Pondicherry in 1761, Haidar took 300 of its French defenders into service. At this stage he had no quarrel with the Company and, indeed, while his principal enemies were the Marathas, he made overtures to both Bombay and Madras for a treaty of friendship and alliance. Bombay with its eye on concessions in Malabar was inclined to accept, but Madras could not overlook Haidar's French mercenaries and, besides, he was the implacable foe to Muhammad Ali. It had become painfully clear to the council of Fort St George that, if Haidar dispossessed Muhammad Ali, the nawab would never pay his debts and his creditors would be ruined. As they numbered nearly all the members of council, the Company must protect him. Haidar's overtures were rejected, the council hoping that either the nizam would hold him in check or the Marathas would crush him, and Haidar was convinced that the British were the principal obstacle to his ambitions. As the directors were to complain, with ample justice, had the presidency not tried 'to play the part of umpire in Indostan... [the country powers] would have formed a balance of power among themselves', and their quarrels would have left the British at peace.[4]

In 1767 Haidar settled his differences with the nizam and, to assert his claim on the nawabi, he led their joint forces into the Carnatic. In March 1768 his troops plundered the garden houses of San Thomé, wrenching out the doors and window frames for fires to boil their rice, while terrified refugees cowered under the walls of Fort St George. At this point the nizam, persuaded not to allow the Carnatic to slip from a feeble Muhammad Ali to a powerful Haidar, deserted the alliance, while Colonels Smith and Wood (the latter subsequently court-martialled for disobedience, incapacity, profiteering from the sale of arrack, illegal seizure of grain and fraudulent connivance in the sale of cattle to the army by his wife) plodded dourly after Haidar's standards, poking here and there, standing firm, retreating, weaving and reeling with the punch, but always holding him away from Madras. In April 1769 Haidar accepted a truce, for the Marathas had attacked him in the rear.

He had beaten the Company on points. The Madras army was crippled by a shortage of bullocks, due to control of the supply by middle-men like Mrs Wood, who fixed the price too high, and by the civilian deputies the select committee sent with the army to double-guess its field officers. Haidar's well-trained cavalry cut out convoys, outwitted British intelligence, retreated and reformed rapidly. 'I never saw black troops behave so bravely as Haidar's,' one British officer observed with surprise, 'all his foot were led on by Europeans.'[5] The Court of Directors was appalled by the terms of the peace agreed by the governor at the gates of Fort St George. The Presidency was ruined and the Company's interest and influence in India had been so gravely damaged that 'the most consummate abilities, persevering assiduity, unshaken fidelity and intrepid courage in our future servants, may perhaps be found insufficient in many years to restore' them.[6] More seriously the news from the Carnatic caused a catastrophic run on Company stock in London, knocking 60 per cent off its value. The 'Nabob' of Arcot's debts had brought the Company to the point of bankruptcy.

After the conquest of Bengal, Company stock had been the subject of massive speculative activity in London, Paris and Amsterdam and, in about 18 months from April 1776, its value had all but doubled. Clive ordered his agent to raise his holding from £30,000 to £73,000 and, in an unhappy moment for the Company, Edmund Burke's cousin William was to sink his all in Company stock. The directors knew that they could not afford to pay the sort of dividend speculators were expecting, but stayed silent. Vox populi, or rather the voice of Alderman William Beckford, the surprising father of the surprising author of *Vathek*, spoke louder: £2 million had been 'acquired, God knows how, by unjust wars with the natives, their servants come home with immense fortunes and proprietors receive no increase in dividend'.[7] To force the directors' hands, large holdings were bought and split to create 300 new voters and on 26 September 1766 they voted up the dividend from 6 per cent to 10 per cent. As there was no proportionate rise in the price of stock, there was not enough money to pay it yet, still deaf to all but the cry for gold, new voters, created by further splitting stock, urged the directors on 6 May 1767 to raise the dividend yet higher, to $12^1/_2$ per cent. The ministry, fearful that its share of Company profits would slip into the pockets of international financiers, rushed through a bill limiting the dividend to 10 per cent. When the crash came it was like the bursting of the South Sea Bubble. Among those ruined were many small-time stockholders who had plunged deep, like Edmund and William Burke, who now had a score to settle with the Company. Moreover, the gods, having driven men mad, now took a hand. Perpetual rains swept Bengal and destroyed the harvest. Famine carried off perhaps a quarter of the population. The revenue dropped alarmingly, while an ever increasing slice of it had to be spent on preparations for war, with Haidar, the Marathas, even the nizam, whose courts were filled with French and renegade English mercenaries. In London scribblers began to uncover the sins of the east. In 1772, William Bolts produced his *Consideration on Indian Affairs, particularly respecting the present state of Bengal and its dependencies*, while Alexander Dow, translating a history of Hindostan, decided to write volume three himself. Both attacked Clive so fiercely that Horace Walpole could believe him 'a monster in assassination, usurpation and extortion... monopolising in open defiance of the orders of the Company'. These monopolies were now held to be the cause of the famine and death of three million people.[8]

Everyone had thought the Company was safe, rich and powerful. It behaved as a private bank, second only to the Bank of England, taking up government loans and raising capital in the money market. It was also a source of powerful patronage. Writerships were sold like debenture shares for anything between £1500 and £2000, almost like permits to coin money. And yet Indian trade was not profitable to the Company. The investment, that annual outlay on Indian merchandise, most of which was sold in Britain, was always greater than the value of sales of British produce in India. Up to the grant of the diwani there had been a chronic net ouflow of specie from Britain to make the investment, and one of Clive's reasons for accepting it had been the hope that this would now stop. But rising costs soon meant that the diwani revenues were inadequate for that purpose, and the Company allowed its servants to fund the investment out of their gains, in exchange for bills payable in London. The fortunes thus repatriated had, many of them, been made from illegal trading, from lending money at high rates of interest (to people like Muhammad Ali), or from cornering essential supplies (like Mrs Colonel Wood's bullocks) and selling though an Indian agent at scarcity prices. Now the bills had mopped up the available cash. To add insult to injury, the 'nabobs' who had cashed them reflected little credit on the Company.

The habits of the east, the silks and perfumes, scented tobacco, spiced food, the trains of servants, palanquins, carriages and, above all, rank and title bought by money, were all culturally offensive in Britain to both rich and poor. Wherever they lived, 'nabobs' raised the price of everything 'from fresh eggs to rotten boroughs, their liveries outshone those of dukes... their coaches were finer than that of the Lord Mayor', and their 'ill-governed households corrupted half the servants of the country'.[9] Their style was disgusting, their habits ridiculous but their country and parliamentary seats meant that they had to be taken seriously. Their very existence proved that the government of Bengal was based on greed, that 'every village and district was ruined' by it and it was time that the Company started to govern its servants.[10] Clive's reforms had only touched the problem at its edges. Services were still provided, often by its own servants, through their wives or gomastahs, on a commission basis, and the abuse of dastaks was blatant. When the Earl of Chatham in 1770 inveighed against 'monopolies in the company's account... [which] operate to the unjust exclusion of an oppressed people, and the impoverishing of those extensive and populous provinces. The hearts and good affection of Bengal are more worth than all the profits of ruinous and odious monopolies', the directors could only agree.[11] Yet huge profits were still being made by private traders in salt and opium, two traditional Mughal monopolies now exercised by the Company. To make a fortune, however, was still what brought people to India, be they merchants, surgeons, apothecaries, lawyers, artists, soldiers or seamen.[12]

Chatham had been interested in India since the proceeds of Thomas Pitt's great diamond helped to buy him into Parliament, and in December 1756 the Secret Committee of the Company sent him an account of their expenses 'during the periods of the French embroils', in the course of which it asserted that the reduction of Mauritius, Pondicherry and Chandernagore (beyond the resources of the Company) would enable it to trade peacefully without the need to spend money on fortifications.[13] Seeing the sense of that he sent a squadron of ships and troops (*Primus in Indis*) to Madras, and the bill to the Company. He did not demand any return, for he distrusted the effects of any government's acquiring too much power or patronage in case it infringed civil liberties. But his mind was changed by the flow of 'nabob' money into Britain. 'When we see the opulent fortunes suddenly acquired by our servants... it gives but too much weight to the public opinion that this rage for negotiation, treaties and alliances has private advantage more for its object than public good.'[14] A Parliamentary select committee was set up to investigate the abuses and a Committee of Secrecy worked on the Company's accounts through the winter of 1772–3.

To his disgust Clive was cross-examined in the House as if he had been caught stealing sheep. The House must accept that it could understand no better than the Pope in Rome 'how a monopoly of salt, betel and tobacco in the years 1765 and 1766 could occasion want of rain and a scarcity of rice in the year 1769'.[15] On 10 May, after a debate in which Francis Sykes, now one of the 'Indian' MPs, suffered more than 'when I was a prisoner of Sir Serajah ul Dowlah',[16] the House decided that the member for Shrewsbury had rendered the country great and meritorious service. He could keep his jagir and, as Edmund Burke remarked caustically, came 'out of the fiery trial much brighter than he went into it. His gains are now recorded and not only not condemned, but actually approved by Parliament'.[17] All eyes were now on Lord North. He knew that the government would never be allowed to take over control of the Company and thus acquire its patronage, so it must be made better able to manage itself. On 17 June 1773, a Regulating Act had an easy passage through the Commons. A governor-general would be appointed, for five year periods, only removable before his time by the Crown on a petition from Parliament. He would preside over a council of four members, in the appointment of whom the government would have a say. The governor-general in Council would have superior, but not overriding, powers over the Presidencies of Bombay and Fort St George, and the mayor's court in Calcutta would be replaced by a Supreme Court, presided over by a chief justice and three puisne judges appointed by the Crown. In return the Company would be given a loan of £1,500,000 and the dividend be pegged at 6 per cent until it had been repaid.

The small print of the Regulating Act was not well drafted; the relationship of the 'governor-general in council' with his brother governors was ill-defined, and the jurisdiction of the Supreme Court was left vague. How it was to be made to work would depend very much on the personality of the new governor-general and, to the surprise of the proponents of a new-blood appointment, the choice was Warren Hastings, one of the old Bengal establishment, who had played his part in the deposition of Mir Jafar and the overthrow of Mir Qasim. But to those who knew him, there could be no better candidate. His forefathers had come to England with the Conqueror, so that the young Warren trailed clouds of patrician breeding, which stamped him as a born gentleman among many who had only achieved that dignity by making a fortune in India. He had been at Westminster with Edward Gibbon. Early death robbed him of his parents and of his guardian uncle who left him only £40 in his will. He had, therefore, to leave Westminster and enrol as a writer. He arrived in Bengal in October 1750, aged 18. Two years later he was ordered up the country to Kasimbazar to learn his trade.

His career path was in no way unusual. In three years, fluent in Bengali and Persian, he was secretary to the factory council. In 1755 he was a prisoner of Siraj-ud-daula, freed on bail paid by the Dutch agent in Kasimbazar, and in January 1757 he took part in the recapture of Calcutta. Then he was back at Kasimbazar, effectively chief of the factory, as his superior, William Watts, was almost permanently at the nawab's court, one of the spinners of the web that was fatally to snare Siraj. Hastings, in his turn, was to spring the gin on Siraj's successor, the extravagant and incompetent Mir Jafar. Vansittart recalled him to Calcutta where, in 1761, he took his seat on the Calcutta council. Mir Qasim used him as his intermediary, while a contract to supply the government with transport bullocks meant that he could afford a town house, and a garden home at Alipore.

In 1764, Hastings resigned over the second restoration of Mir Jafar and returned to England. Dr Johnson, whose circle he diffidently entered, was enthusiastic about establishing for him a chair of Persian at Oxford but as no one could be found to endow it the project languished. All the time he was in England, his mind turned over ideas for the reform of Bengal, high among which were the abolition of dastaks and the elevation of the magistracy, which should dispense the law for 'the ease and welfare' of the people which 'we are bound both by justice and policy to preserve; to make their laws sit as light on them as possible, and to share with them the privileges of our own constitution'.[18] In 1769 he rejoined the Company and was back in Madras as 'second' to the governor of Fort St George. It was not the centre of a great province of produce suppliers over whom the Company was diwan. It was a city-state, tucked behind its walls, trading with countries further east, dependent for necessaries on the 'nabob of Arcot' who, in turn, was dependent on a transport system based on bullocks, half-starved and slow, upon whose mangy backs was dependent in its turn the lavish rice economy of the Carnatic. In 1770 this had been so ravaged by Haidar's troops that rice and gunpowder had to be shipped from Bengal, which itself was suffering a shortage of food.

Madras was more like a Portuguese than a British settlement, moving to the rhythms of a society for whom time was an indefinite commodity. Hastings's reputation for integrity had preceded him into a government where corruption

51

was a way of life. If it did not stretch out, as in Bengal, to oppress a province, it could, as in Bengal, oppress a nawab. Hastings recognised how fatally linked the Madras Presidency was to a man of straw and how, as long as that link remained, it would always be under threat. But he was not destined to cross swords directly with Haidar Ali. In 1772 he was transferred to Calcutta to succeed Governor Cartier, than whom 'there never was a governor less capable, less active, less resolute'.[19] He accepted his 'crown of thorns' with alacrity, but was soon to find himself crucified between the directors who wanted a total overhaul of government, and the merchants who felt threatened. His temper was fermented to vinegar: he could not put his head out of the window without 'complainants from every quarter of the province hallooing me by hundreds for justice'.[20] He was assailed for the gifts of patronage. He worked through the day, through the night, through Sundays. His working documents were old charters for the chief of a merchant company, buying and selling silks and muslins, not for a governor-general arbitrating taxes, appointing to offices, restraining corruption and the lust for profit, surrounded by writers and merchants scarcely out of their teens, who broke every rule in the book, most of them ignorant of the local language and managed, like greedy puppets, by their banians.

Hastings had a grand design: to restore an effective, honest and Mughal administration. Such a challenge to the rapacious instinct of young men fearful of penury or an early death was like asking a Jew to turn Christian. For the 21-year-old son of the Archbishop of York, resident at the court of the Rajah of Benares, made £30,000 a year receiving bribes. To prevent the British in India from sinking beneath the burden of their own iniquity, he must dismantle the dyarchy, whereby the Company managed its commercial affairs for itself and the diwani, in theory at least, for the nawab. Civil administration and the collection of revenue should be firmly under Company control. Famine had so reduced the revenue that the Company could barely pay its troops, much less improve the condition of the people. Records were in chaos. No one knew what the peasants actually paid but, intercepted on its way by a chain of rogues and plunderers, native and European, it was certainly more than ever reached the treasury. He started by trimming the powers of the British supervisors. Collectors should not be allowed also to trade, lend money, or farm the revenues from monopolies. The actual collection would be done by Indian officials who understood these things. The Collector's duty was to protect the poor from fraud and oppression. Outside every office was to be a box for petitions. As for civil administration, there 'can be but one government and one power in this province'.[21] The dyarchy was replaced by a monarchy, and the monarch was the Company. The treasury moved from Murshidabad to Calcutta. Collectors and magistrates answered to the Company. The boy-nawab was relegated to a ceremonial function not unlike that to which Haidar Ali had reduced the rajah of Mysore and the peshwa the house of Shivaji. Collectors would preside over the diwani or civil court in each district and oversee the *foujdari*, or criminal court, with its Indian judges governed by Bengal's ancient laws, not laws made in Britain. It was 'a contradiction of the common notions of equity and policy that the English gentlemen of Cumberland and Argyleshire should regulate the policy of a nation which they only know by the lacs which it has sent to Great Britain'.[22] He set a team of Brahman pandits to codify Hindu legal principles in Sanskrit before being translated into Persian. Though he held that much Muslim law was barbarous, he was as absolutist as any tyrant in using it to suppress murder and brigandage.

In 1771, the directors put on Mir Qasim's shoes and prohibited the use of dastaks to cover private trade, and to enforce this ruling, Hastings did as Mir Qasim had done and reduced all duties to $2^1/_2$ per cent, prompting a future governor-general to complain that Warren Hastings was making a lucrative career for a Company servant impossible.[23] By acting as an archetypal eighteenth-century enlightened despot, 'the seat of government' being 'most effectually and visibly transferred... to Calcutta,' Hastings did not despair of seeing it 'the first city of India'.[24] But where Hastings differed from other despots was that he did not have undivided power and could expect only a limited time in office. London, moreover, had served him a vicious card in the nomination of his fellow councillors.

The government accepted the nomination of two 'Bengalis', Warren Hastings and Richard Barwell, to the five-man council under the Regulating Act. Richard Barwell was the son of a former governor, born and bred in Calcutta, a 'nabob'. His family had been trading in the East Indies since the 1660s and he had made a fortune from revenue farming and transporting salt. He spent it freely on a social life that included heavy gambling and convivial eating, in which his son, Daniel, excelled in the popular sport of shooting pellets of bread so dextrously that he could extinguish a candle. Barwell believed that the Company should use the diwani to enable the merchants to make fortunes and the directors to set a high dividend. It insisted on choosing the other three for their independence of the Company. General John Clavering had a modest reputation from the European wars and was to be commander-in-chief, with the right of succession to the post of governor-general. Colonel George Monson was a British army not Company officer though he had been present at the capture of Pondicherry and Manila. They were worthy but forgotten soldiers. The third was Philip Francis. No one could understand why he was appointed. If he were that incorrigible but anonymous royal scourge, Junius, then the King may have hoped to exile him to Calcutta to find another target for his pen. More probably he was a substitute for a late withdrawal, a placeman who could be expected to do the government's dirty work.

Francis was briefed by Clive and agreed to send a caucus of proprietors in London private despatches in cipher. His secretive, sceptical and clever brain was clouded by misanthropy, agnosticism and anti-clericalism, allied to a liking for drink, cards and fornication. At the same time it was fired by a Plutarchian sense of virtue.[25] Who else but the governor-general could be responsible for the misappropriated wealth of Bengal, the poverty of the Company, and the persistent reports of misgovernment and oppression? By the time the three councillors reached Calcutta he had converted Clavering and Monson to this view. From the start they were determined to be disaffected. They felt slighted by their welcome, four guns short of 21, and had to walk from the ship to government house, a hundred yards or so in the midday heat, both intended to 'lower them in the eyes of the natives'.[26] They set about picking over every aspect of policy, questioning all the governor-general's decisions and appointments, 'a very tribunal of inquisition'.[27] Hastings was astonished. If the directors saw fit to send three inquisitors to Calcutta, why did they appoint him governor-general? Even Barwell resented the ignorant and self-righteous judgements of the three strangers. He gambled and drank with Francis but never became an ally.

To the newcomers, Hastings and Barwell were only 'two abandoned villains', so that they were determined to undo everything they had done.[28] They did not understand that, though the Company appeared to control Bengal, its powers were very fragile and depended on the goodwill and competence of Indian executors. The intricacies of landholding on which revenue was based were understood by Muslim landowners, Hindu bankers and Armenian brokers, for whom successful collection spelt fortune, failure ruin. For Francis and his colleagues it was not difficult to find some irregularity, some abuse of management which they could immediately attribute to the corruption of Company servants, the most important of whom was the governor-general. They made no attempt to hide from European and Indian that they believed there 'was no species of peculation from which the Honourable Governor-General has thought it reasonable to abstain', so that he 'wholly and solely has sold and ruined Bengal'.[29]

They found a complicit ally. Nanda Kumar (Nundcomer) 'dark and deceitful... whose gratitude no kindness can bind', had been one of the influential Bengalis who had helped to plot the downfall of Siraj-ud-daula.[30] Hastings neither trusted nor liked him and refused to appoint him to any position of honour so that he agreed to accuse Hastings of having accepted bribes worth 350,000 rupees (about £35,000). His evidence was forged, but good enough for the Three, who used it to challenge the governor-general in Council. But Nanda had used forged documents once too often. Evidence that he had himself feloniously forged a bond was examined by Hastings' old schoolfellow, the chief justice Elijah Impey, and Hastings and Barwell decided to prosecute. The trial was the showpiece of that hot and devastating summer, the judges changing their linen three times a day. The forgery was proved and, as this was a criminal offence, Nanda Kumar had to hang. No one expected him to die but no one lifted a finger to help the 70-year-old Brahman, who was hanged on 5 August, 'a miserable fate', confessed the governor-general, 'which he has deserved ever since I knew him'.[31] The indecent haste of his end (he had only been arrested in May) seemed almost expedient, as if Hastings could not lose such an opportunity judicially to dispose of an enemy. Most Indians, who would have expected no differently from a nawab, believed this was so, but had no pity for the old sinner. Hastings was the best nawab Bengal had had since Alivardi Khan, and as such deserved a propitiatory sacrifice.

Hastings never shook off the suspicion that he had disposed of Nanda Kumar, whose fall completely discredited the Three. They had banked on their attack on the governor-general being popular and it was not. In the meantime the climate and social life wreaked their deadly effect on both military councillors. Hastings, who went to bed without supper, drank little and lived chastely, seemed indestructible. Colonel Monson's death in 1776 gave Hastings control of the council. The general was not long in following. Francis continued his battle to the end, enmeshed by high gambling debts and scandal as he seduced the delicious Mme le Grand, the future wife of Talleyrand. He was now little more than a standing nuisance to the governor-general yet, in their ideas, they were not poles apart. Both believed that merchants made bad governors and that foreigners were not the best people to govern the destinies of people, different in race, religion and custom. Francis, too, had made a serious study of the revenue prospects and, as he believed that Hastings's policy of farming revenues was impoverishing landlords and thus the land, he was one of the proponents of the permanent revenue settlement which was installed by Lord Cornwallis.[32] But in seeking to restore the dual system, he showed his inexperience both of administration and of India. Hastings knew what he was doing and he was in charge. He had seen the disasters wrought by Clive's attempt to separate administration (nizamat) and revenue collection (diwani), 'a screen to private rapine and embezzlement'.[33] Hastings wanted the administration of the province conducted by native administrators, with the tried and effective methods of their former Mughal rulers, but governed and protected by the larger horizons of Company power. Those horizons did not extend beyond the borders of Bengal and Bihar, except as a network of alliances with friendly country powers, to act as a conduit of influence and a glacis against attack. Francis would probably have signed up to that had not bile, rancour and thwarted pride rendered him incapable of understanding it. Hastings had no more desire than he to extend the limits of Company rule, but for that to continue profitable and successful in its present confines, he must contain the ambitions of the Marathas, the nizam and Haidar Ali.

Warren Hastings was a man of peace, yet his period as governor-general was marked by conflicts which the Company would have preferred to avoid, which it was hard put to fight, and which were to set it ineluctably on the road to territorial expansion. Panipat had reduced the Maratha threat to Bengal, but they still had a pliant instrument in the fainéant Mughal emperor, Shah Alam II. 'Relic of the most illustrious line of the eastern world', his sovereignty was universally acknowledged 'though the substance of it no longer existed', and from its ostensible bounty, as Hastings fairly admitted, 'the Company itself derives its constitutional dominions'.[34] No one was ready to strike it down, root and branch, not Afghan, Maratha, Jat nor Rajput, not nizam nor nawab. Once, the emperor whined, crores of rupees had been paid 'by the *subahs* of Bengal, Bahar and Aurissah,' but today he could not persuade the Company even to honour an order for fire arms![35]

In 1771, the emperor, to secure what was left of his hereditary throne, threw himself unequivocally on the mercy of the Marathas, forcing Hastings to reinforce the nawab–wazir of Oudh, with a garrison – for which he paid. He was also persuaded to allow the nawab to incorporate the territory of the Rohillas, originally Pathan mercenaries of the Great Mughal, settled in the fertile doab between the Ganges and Jumna rivers. Allowing Company troops to act as mercenaries for an Indian prince looked like doing its dirty work by proxy, and Edmund Burke was soon representing the Rohilla bandits as unhappy heroes of liberty, crushed under the heel of a megalomaniac. The bile of Francis and the greed of Company officers in Oudh, disappointed at being denied any share of the spoils, contributed between them to a dossier of atrocities and accusations that Hastings was more interested in furthering his own career and fortune than the good of the Company.

Hastings certainly wanted Oudh to be a reliable ally, and a safe buffer state and, with this at stake, the Rohillas barely counted. He also hoped to bind other country powers to Britain's interests by treaties with the British crown. 'Nothing,' he told Lord North in 1775 could 'so effectively contribute to perpetuate [British dominion in India]'.[36] A treaty between personages of royal rank would appeal to men of proud stomach if uncertain lineage, better than one with a company of merchants. He saw the extension of British influence, not by conquest, but by a series of pacts, which would enlarge 'the circle of its defence without involving the Company in hazardous or indefinite engagements'.[37] First the nawab of Bengal, then the nawab-wazir of Oudh and the nawab of the Carnatic, next the Maratha rajah of Berar, the peshwa in Poona, the nizam in Hyderabad and Haidar Ali in Mysore. Francis and his allies greeted the proposition with the gravest suspicion; if Hastings' relentless subjugation of Oudh was what was meant by a Treaty of Alliance, then this was hegemony masquerading as club membership. George III, however, would not treat as an equal with nawabs and rajahs, and the idea languished until reinvented as paramountcy fifty years later.

The peshwa, who was certain that 'once the English plant their feet in Delhi, no power will be left independent in India', relied on the Maratha viceroy, Mahadji Scindia, to keep the emperor in a gilded cage and the British out of Delhi.[38] The *padishah* lived out his days in twilit palaces among mullahs and concubines, an object of occasional interest to French adventurers who came to assess his talismanic value in any alliance against the British, but the puppet of a Maratha warlord.[39] If Calcutta were safe from Maratha threats, Bombay was not. Of the three presidencies, it had so far cut little figure in the sun. The volume of its trade was low. Cut off from the sea breezes by a permanent miasma of mist and midges, rising from the thick plantation of toddy palms, nurtured by liberal layers of rotting fish. fevers and fluxes still made Bombay 'the burying ground of the English'.[40] Whereas Surat may have numbered 500,000 inhabitants in 1773, more indeed than either Paris or London, Bombay mustered only 100,000, of whom barely 1,000 were Europeans. To a young writer, Bombay was a place of exile, its society only half awake. Men outnumbered women by three to one and even at the end of the century that much travelled naval wife, Maria Graham, found the ladies 'underbred and overdressed... very ignorant and grossière'.[41] There was plenty of business to be done, especially with the Marathas who were in the market for arms, but no great fortunes to be made, comparable to what the 'nabobs' were making in Bengal and the Carnatic. Indeed the presidency was only kept solvent by remittances from Bengal through Benares, arranged by Hindu merchants. The future of 'the narrow barren island' of Bombay lay in its superb harbour and dockyard, opened in 1736, to exploit the country trade, and with the Parsis from Surat who came to manage and develop it.[42] Neither Hindu nor Muslim, observing no purdah and no dietary exclusions, dressing, speaking and drinking like Europeans, their principal distinguishing feature was the Zoroastrian manner of disposing of the dead, recycled through the guts of birds of prey from the tops of their tall towers of silence. They had no one country of origin, they aspired to no tribal or political power and were content to make money and prosper in their endogamous community. Parsis were venture capitalists and noted philanthropists. They prospered, principally from shipping and ship-building, employing British sea captains and sailors in the merchant fleet and the country trade it carried. This partnership of British and native was unique in India.[43] Perhaps because they were carried on the back of Parsi capital, in palanquins and in carriages drawn by oxen rather than horses, the Bombay council seemed, to one visitor, to be selected from the most corpulent members of the community, to whom the Indian population paid special respect.[44]

In 1772 the Bombay council sent an agent to Poona to negotiate the purchase of the islands in the bay, Salsette, Bassein and the Maratha-held parganas round Surat. When he arrived, he found the peshwa, Madhavrao I, mortally ill. Hoping to gain from the inevitable dispute over the succession, he sat like a spider in his web, waiting for the Maratha princes to fly into it. The most prominent was Raghunathrao (known to the English at the time as Raghobar), the uncle of the dying peshwa. When in August 1773, Madhavrao's younger brother was killed and Raghunathrao seized power, he was widely believed to have been the Richard III behind the killing. Madhavrao I, however, was reincarnated in the posthumous son of the murdered peshwa, and Raghunathrao was deposed by a cabal of nobles, whereupon he approached the British chief in Surat for help. In March 1775, he agreed to cede the islands in perpetuity to the Company, in return for the loan of a force of 2,500 men, 700 of them Europeans, to restore him to Poona. Bombay had no authority to make such a promise and should, under the provisions of the 1783 Regulating Act, have consulted the governor-general. It was just the sort of adventurism that Clavering, Monson and Francis said they had come from London to prevent. Bombay had 'imposed on itself the charge of conquering the whole Maratha Empire for a man who appears incapable of affording you any effectual assistance in it'.[45] Negotiations with Poona should be left to Calcutta.

They were protracted and unfruitful. The Marathas would neither accept Raghunathrao in any position of authority in their affairs nor give up Bassein, a port fit to rival Bombay. They could not understand how the Company made 'such professions of honour. How disapprove the war... when [it was] so desirous of availing [itself] of the advantage of it?'[46] Into this impasse, in March 1777, marched a French agent, the Chevalier de St Lubin. He had served as a surgeon in French East Indiamen, and had talked himself into the confidence of the new navy minister in Paris with a plan to overturn the British in India. He had a draft treaty of friendship in his pocket and in April he was received in full dorbar, where he presented the infant peshwa with a large painting, done in France, of... Raghunathrao, his father's murderer. St Lubin, moreover, was authorised to convert any trade treaty into an offensive and defensive alliance, the principal terms of which were the attachment of 2,500 French troops, together with experts, to train a Maratha army of 10,000 men in European-style warfare. The shadow of Bussy began to lengthen across the land. 'This diabolical scheme,' his envoy informed Hastings, 'has opened a door the most destructive to our interests that could have been thought of.'[47]

News now reached India of France's alliance with the American colonies, and General Burgoyne's surrender at Saratoga. It aroused panic and dismay. Francis and his colleagues wanted Bengal put on alert against a French invasion, but Hastings was able to use his casting vote to confront the threat where it existed, if it existed at all. He instructed Bombay to occupy all neighbouring ports that might receive a French expeditionary force and to put Raghunathrao on his masnad at Poona by force of arms. The 4,000-strong force that set out from Bombay with Raghunathrao in its excessive baggage, maundered at two miles a day through the Ghats towards Poona, while the land was devastated in its path. As soon as it decided to turn about and retreat, it was trapped at Wadgaon. There was enacted an Indian Saratoga. In order to return to Bombay, the Bombay army had to surrender Raghunathrao and restore the Presidency's conquests in Gujerat. Only the prudence of the warlord, Mahadji Scindia ensured that the terms were not harsher still. He understood that the capitulation owed more to the incompetence of the British than to the discipline and cohesion of Maratha arms. Wadgaon moreover was not really a Saratoga. The Marathas were not disaffected colonists with a cause to fight for, but a divided people, used to battles that seldom settled anything, and more concerned to secure chauth and personal power than to defeat a possibly conquering power. Even now they were quarrelling about the future of Raghunathrao, while a Company army under Colonel Goddard marched from Allahabad across India to Surat.

Hastings feared that Wadgaon might encourage both the nizam and Haidar Ali to resume hostile action against Madras. The Marathas, moreover, had a secret weapon – the French. Here were a people who frightened the British, who could give any alliance of country powers the allure of possible success, either in reducing the Honourable Company to the status of mere traders again, confined to their factories, or wiping it out altogether. Hastings had recognised the danger as early as 26 January 1778:

> I lay it down as a point incontrovertible that if a detachment of much less than 1,000 Europeans, with arms for disciplining a body of native troops in the European manner, shall have once obtained a footing in the Mahratta country as allies of that government, all the native powers of Indostan united will lie at their mercy and even the Provinces of Bengal be exposed to their depredations.[48]

Bombay had not exactly covered itself with glory, and it was only the powerful presence of Colonel Goddard and the moderating influence of Scindia which preserved an uneasy peace. The escape of Raghunathrao and his flight to British territory did not help negotiations for a settlement. The Company's demand to be indemnified for a war for which it had been solely responsible (and which it had lost) was additionally offensive to a people who earned their indemnities by victories. By September, Goddard sniffed a confederacy in the making, the prime mover being the nizam. The catalyst of trouble was the governor of Madras.

5. 'A STORM OF UNIVERSAL FIRE'

> Then ensued a scene of woe, the like of which no eye
> had seen, no heart conceived, and which no tongue can
> adequately tell... A storm of universal fire blasted every
> field, consumed every house, destroyed every temple.

> Edmund Burke, 1785, from his speech on the
> Nabob of Arcot's debts

> No man ever served the Directors with a zeal superior
> to my own, nor perhaps equal to it.

> Warren Hastings at his impeachment

> The Company's Civil Service is the only certain track to
> a Fortune or Preferment, and more and more on the
> Bengal Establishment than any other.

> John Topham to Charles Burrington,
> 22 September 1765

THE GOVERNOR OF FORT St George in 1775 was Lord George Pigot. For successfully enduring the siege of Madras and accepting the surrender of O'Lally and Pondicherry in 1761 he had been created a baron in the peerage of Ireland. Twelve years after leaving Madras in 1763 he was back on his old stamping ground, impatient and choleric as ever, but also believed by many who knew him in his earlier incarnation to have been asleep or intoxicated ever since. The nawab's debts were now calculated at about £3 million, and the jagirs he had assigned his creditors only paid the interest.[1] Muhammad Ali was believed to have eight members of Parliament in his pocket and to be rich enough to bribe a whole government, but he was, in fact, too poor to pay his own agents in London.[2] When he suggested in 1773 that the possession of Tanjore, a Maratha principality since 1674, standing at the head of the Cauvery delta, and criss-crossed by dykes and canals which watered the rice basket of the south, would enable him to meet his obligations to creditors, the Madras presidency captured it for him. Pigot's orders were to hand it back to its legitimate ruler.

At once the governor was attacked by those merchants whose loans to the nawab were underwritten by rents from Tanjore. They demanded a guarantee that the Tanjore assignments, worth a quarter of a million rupees a year, would continue after the restoration. When Pigot refused, the nawab's creditors deposed him and, before he could be reinstated, he was dead, either from the spells Muhammad Ali had paid pandits to weave with the help of poisonous snakes, or from the effects of his choler. Hastings, in his short time in Madras, had concluded that every member of the select committee, except himself, was mired in the 'Nabob' of Arcot's financial slough.[3] From the governor down, including the military men, they had invested some 20–30 per cent of their capital in the nawab. Pigot's successor, Sir Thomas Rumbold, in trying to carry out his instructions from London, then managed to offend all the Company's most dangerous enemies at once.

Each had cause to resent the Company. First the nizam: war with France had broken out and as there were French mercenaries still in the Northern Circar of Guntur, the only one of Bussy's jagirs still to belong to the nizam, Rumbold handed it to Muhammad Ali, to be worked over by his efficient leeches. Such an offence to a powerful prince suggested that 'this government contains the seeds of death in it'.[4] Second, Haidar Ali: on the French declaration of war, the Madras army had immediately mopped up Pondicherry, but Mahé, the other French factory in the south, was under Haidar's protection. If the British 'created a disturbance' there, he would punish them by devastating the whole country from Madurai to Madras, and 'totally efface them from the earth'.[5] The ground had thus been carelessly prepared for the young peshwa's all powerful minister in Poona, Nana Phadnis (Farnavis), to erect an alliance against the Company. The Marathas, under their two warlords Mahadji Scindia and Tukhoji Holkar, would engage it on the Konkan coast, recovering the lost estates round Bombay and Surat. Mudhaji Bhosle of Berar would establish his right to chauth in Bengal. The nizam would recover the Northern Circars and Haidar would conquer the Carnatic. Hastings, barely allowing the crisis to alter his accustomed style and hours of work, decided that the first priority was to fracture the alliance. When Bhosle's army moved into Orissa, Hastings ordered it to be provisioned and paid 16 lakhs of rupees towards its expenses. Appeasement paid off. Mudhaji's army turned on a neighbouring rajah and expended its energies on conquering his lands. The nizam was disarmed by the return of Guntur. That left the Marathas. Rumour had it that Paris was preparing a mighty expeditionary force, led by the Marquis de Bussy, already gathering in Île de France, and it was vital to neutralise them before it arrived. Raghunathrao was to be abandoned, all territorial acquisitions were to be restored and Mahadji Scindia was encouraged to stake out his power in Delhi and the north. When the first overtures were rejected, Goddard in February 1780 captured the great fort of Ahmedabad for his Gujerati Maratha ally, the Gaekwad of Baroda, and on 4 August Captain Popham, with 2,400 sepoys, four field pieces and one howitzer from Oudh, pulled off a great coup, the capture of Gwalior fort, the heart of Scindia's power in Malwa. No one who has seen this fantastic fortress can dispute its distinction as the key to Indostan. Occupying the loop-shaped perimeter of a sandstone table-top, nearly two miles long and at its broadest half a mile wide, its sheer scarps rise 300 feet above the plain, surmounted by man-made walls another 30–35 feet high. Like the impregnable Achilles, it, too, had its heel, and Popham discovered it, a narrow scarp only 16 feet high, with a forty-yard ascent of scree to the foot of the wall. At dawn, it was scaled and, within minutes, 20 sepoy grenadiers were inside the fortress. It was not the campaigning season, the camp-fires were not alight, and on empty stomachs the exiguous garrison fled. There were no deaths apart from the Maratha governor. The effects of this action, 'were not to be described', Hastings wrote jubilantly. 'That the consequence may be peace is my firm opinion.'[6]

The victory was, however, swamped by dreadful news from the south. In July the great Mysorean army had erupted into action, and Haidar's fearful horsemen poured into the Carnatic for a second time, 'laying all waste with fire and sword'.[7] By 22 July, they had sacked Porto Novo, burned all the villages round Vellore and plundered Kanchipuram (Conjeeveram). Worse was to come. In September, Colonel Baillie was overrun at Palur (Pollilore). Ten miles north of Kanchipuram, and he and 80 other officers were led into captivity at Chidambran. The hero of Buxar had failed to come quickly enough to his rescue and was beaten off. 'There is not in India,' crowed one of Haidar's French officers, 'an example of a similar defeat.'[8] Hastings had only one choice: to strip the Bengal treasury of its reserves and send them down to Madras with as many men and as much military material as he could spare, led by Eyre Coote, 'to recover the Carnatic which is lost or to save Madras. He must be the distinguished favourite of heaven if he succeeds'.[9] Still in pursuit of the fortune he feared would elude him, negligent in dress, bizarre in manner, foul of tongue, a legend of greed, with his long nose and angular chin, close-cropped hair and stilt-like legs, Coote crossed the Indian scene like a warlock in uniform. The ladies of Madras were confident that 'his very name will strike [Haidar's] undisciplined hordes with terror'.[10] They were neither undisciplined nor in terror. Coote was to find that Haidar had 'taken every measure that would occur to the most experienced general to distress us and render himself formidable. His conduct... has been supported by a degree of political address unparalleled by any power that has yet appeared in Hindustan'.[11] His advantages over the Madras army were legion. He was moving like a liberator through a country disaffected by the nawab's tax collectors, his men and horses had been carefully selected and well-trained by French mercenaries, his field intelligence was better and his use of small groups of horsemen to act as spies was more efficient than anything the Marathas had managed and he had assembled herds of well-fed and sturdy draft cattle. The guns that reduced the walls of Arcot in November were expertly handed. Against him were sepoys ready to desert, draft cattle in short supply, and those available poor in size and strength, officers who blundered and a select committee divided against itself. Rumbold's temporary successor, John Whitehill, was rumoured to have a stake in a French privateer. Coote had orders to assume full executive powers (not to speak of a supplementary stipend worth £18,000 a year for all the time he served outside Bengal).

He was lucky to find Madras still intact. The closest the Mysoreans had come to the city was 'to plunder the washerwomen of their linen and cut off a small supply of fowles and vegetables'.[12] Coote wasted no time in taking the war back into the Carnatic, relieved Wandewash and set off down the coast to deny landing places to any French expeditionary force. At Cuddalore he found a French squadron off the coast and Haidar hastening to cut him off. But the French commander had strict orders not to risk his squadron before reinforcements reached Île de France and sailed off, the British squadron under Sir Edward Hughes arrived in his place and, with support from the sea, Coote delivered a smart rebuff to Haidar at Porto Novo on 1 July 1781.

61

It was not a decisive victory but Haidar, with all his advantages, could not seize the initiative or win a crushing victory in the east. The Mysoreans were resourceful, intrepid and better-fed, but were continually checked by Coote's greater tactical brilliance. The British also had control of the Bay of Bengal. Though Coote could never turn a victory into a rout, or match Haidar's greater mobility, he was not crippled by the desert that the Mysoreans created round him. 'The defeat of many Baillies... will not destroy the English,' Haidar lamented in *dorbar*. 'I can ruin their resources by land but I cannot dry up the sea'.[13] Rumours there were in plenty that Bussy was on his way back to India, and French agents were active at Poona, Seringapatam and Hyderabad, but the position on the ground was discouraging to the country powers.

The loss of Gwalior fort brought Scindia to the peace-table and, on 17 May 1781, the Marathas agreed to a treaty at Salbai, 20 miles south of Gwalior. Under its terms, Bombay kept Salsette but nothing else. Raghunathrao set off into exile, the Marathas agreed to allow no new European factories other than Portuguese or British (neatly excluding the French) to be established in Maratha lands, and the peshwa committed himself to bringing Haidar to terms. But Haidar had staked his hopes on Bussy. In the event the French intervention was only a fiery and dangerous squib. The French squadron returned to the Bay of Bengal in February 1782, commanded by the one indisputable hero of the *ancien régime*, the Knight of Malta, the Bailli de Suffren, consumed by a burning ardour for battle against the British. Finding himself with a tiny squadron in the backwater of the great dispute between France and Britain in the Americas, Suffren was determined to make it a glorious campaign, in which he would first destroy the East Indies squadron of the Royal Navy and then, with the magic of Bussy's name and presence, create such a coalition of force that John Company would be destroyed in India and replaced by the French. He fought five bitter battles against the unflappable Sir Edward Hughes in which, but for the mishandling of some of their ships by French captains, the result could have gone hard with the British; he captured Trincomali in Ceylon as a winter base and landed a French expeditionary force at Cuddalore. But there it ended. The force was only a meagre one, commanded by an indifferent officer who succeeded in antagonising Haidar Ali, on whom he relied for supplies. The legendary Bussy arrived in March 1783 but turned out to be the walking shadow of his glorious self, 'a painted caricature covered with decorations', wearing 'a mechanical contrivance which, drawing the skin to the back of his head, diminished the wrinkles in his forehead'.[14] His mighty expedition was decimated by scurvy, late in coming, and ineffective when it came. Only the peace in Europe (actually signed in January before Bussy ever reached India) prevented its destruction.

Haidar by this time was dead, killed by a gangrenous ulcer on his neck on which he would not allow the French surgeon to operate until the day was propitious, and his son, the ever more fearsome Tipu Sultan had to defend his possessions in Malabar, under threat from Bombay. It was not until March 1784 that the Company found itself again at peace. It had survived the worst test since 1756 and was not to be so tested again until 1857. It had survived because, however much the country powers feared and distrusted the Honourable Company, they feared and distrusted each other more. The ambitions of Scindia in Delhi and the Panjab prevented him from breaking all his contacts with Bengal. Haidar Ali was too successful to be an easy ally for either the nizam or the peshwa. British usefulness as allies in furthering the territorial ambitions of the country powers was greater than the fear of them as foes.

The French, moreover, were hardly to be preferred to the British as an intrusive mercantile company with a lust for power, and their performance in the event proved disappointing. By a practised combination of diplomatic subtlety and military success, Hastings had pulled off the peace. He had quarrelled with his governors and often frightened his friends and supporters. In June 1781, urgent letters from London, where panic had set in, urged him to 'give them one [peace] in India, Sir, for the love of God and your own good fame. Nothing ever hath done you more honour, than a general peace in India will do you almost on any terms'.[15] No other war-leader can have had so many shackles secured to him by the factions within his council, by the poison and subversion his opponents poured into the counsels of the Company and Parliament in London, by the short-sighted opportunism and greed of his instruments in all theatres of war and by funk in Britain. Philip Francis, resigning his seat on the Supreme Council in 1780, to Hastings's undisguised relief, had been confident of disaster. 'The British Empire in India is tottering to its foundation in spite of everything I could do to save it'.[16] These words were to be read by Edmund Burke. As Francis had resisted every step proposed by Hastings on the grounds that it was unsound, unsafe, corrupt, prepotent, provocative, a recipe for disaster proceeding from a mind crazed by self-interest, secret ambition and greed, Hastings could have hoped that his final success would stand him in good stead. Little did he expect that the peace which settled over India was only the lull before his own Calvary.

In 1781, the disasters of the Carnatic were added to the news from America, the setbacks at sea and unemployment and unrest at home. The loss of the investment was, to the directors, like the knell of doom, and the Marathas and Haidar Ali seemed to be trampling through their drawing rooms. Another select committee was formed to look into the causes of the war in the Carnatic, and its evidence became a torrent when Philip Francis returned in October from Bengal. Burke and Francis fed each other's paranoia, Francis providing the samples of Hastings's perfidy from a dossier laboriously collated in Calcutta, Burke embellishing them in prose, some of which would be recorded as among the greatest flights of forensic oratory heard at Westminster, a new Cicero come to accuse Verres. For there had been nothing like the trial of Warren Hastings since the great civil war trials of Strafford, Laud and the King himself. It was, indeed, as if a lord protector were in the dock. Behind the cynicism and mendacity of the accusation lurked both a belief that the accused had broken the trust of the nation, behaving arbitrarily towards those whom the nation was expected to protect, and a resolve that there should be no more almighty subjects, immune from the supervision of Parliament. What was surprising was that, given the corruption and incompetence that had just lost the American colonies, it should be Hastings who was in the dock, a peepshow for the fashionable world, as he stood in Westminster Hall over a weary period of seven years, while Britain's neighbours slithered into revolution and war, her own King went mad and constitutional crisis shook the land. Richard Sheridan claimed that there was 'nothing in the

63

nervous delineations and penetrating brevity of Tacitus; nothing in the luminous and luxuriant pages of Gibbon... which can equal, in the grossness of the guilt, or in the hardness of the heart... or in low grovelling motives, the acts of Warren Hastings'.[17]

As his defence was ultimately to prove, he had never acted beyond the provision of either the law or his constitutional authority. He had faithfully obeyed all the decisions of the directors in London, and accepted those of the majority on his Council in Calcutta, even when he knew they were dangerous and unsound. He never transgressed the bounds of his legitimate power, though he had often conspired to achieve the majority that gave it to him. He had not been corrupt, but he had not been particularly abstemious. Though, on leaving India, his fortune was modest (estimated at about £75,000); he had remitted home over the years something like £200,000, swallowed up in gifts and pensions to relatives and friends, and he had found it difficult to live within his salary of £25,000 a year. In comparison with what contemporaries took home with them, it did not amount to a fortune. He had, moreover, cleaned up the worst vices of the Company in Bengal, saved it from extinction at the hands of its enemies and salved the pride of Great Britain during a disastrous war. He expected at least a knighthood, if not a peerage. Instead he found himself accused on 22 counts, forced to kneel, like an already convicted criminal, at the bar of the House of Lords, to sit for 145 days to hear his accusers, almost rabid with hate and anger, rake over every action of his that might bear any construction which envy and malice could contrive and, in the end, to be acquitted on every count.

It was his misfortune to be one of the scapegoats for national shame in a political establishment reeling from defeat, searching for the causes that had reduced Great Britain within 20 years from world leader at the end of the Seven Years War to the pariah of Europe, the object of hostile combinations and the victim of armed revolt. The euphoria of 1763 had given way to anxiety, as the British became uncomfortably aware that their empire had expanded beyond mainly Protestant and anglophone colonies in America and the Caribbean. It now incorporated at least 70,000 Roman Catholic, French-speaking subjects in Canada, and countless millions of Indians of different races, religions and cultures acquired, not by commercial activity or settlement, but by force of arms. The subject peoples were not Britons and had only a feeble loyalty to their rulers. If rebels of British stock had thrown off rule from Britain, what could these aliens not do? And in 1764, the year after the Treaty of Paris, Hastings's old schoolfellow Gibbon began his chronicle of the greatest empire the world had yet seen, destroyed by its constituent peoples and an imported religion. The first volumes of *The Decline and Fall of the Roman Empire* appeared in 1766, the second batch in 1781, in the midst of a war that threatened to end in the loss of both the American colonies and the Company's possessions in India, and concluded in 1788 when the trial of Hastings for the suppression of these dangerous peoples had become one of the established public entertainments of London.

Edmund Burke had already asked how traditional British liberties were to be preserved in the face of the stern centralising power that such a diverse empire needed to rule it. Britons must beware of a despotic government on an Asian model.[18] The constipated Horace Walpole was quick to sneer that 'having starved millions by monopolies and plunder in India' the newly returned 'nabobs' now threatened to create 'a famine at home by the luxury occasioned by their opulence, raising the price of everything, till the poor could not purchase bread'.[19] The Earl of Chatham, conveniently forgetting that it was his grandfather's diamond which had bought his first seat, was heard to protest that 'without connections, without any natural interest in the soil, the importers of foreign gold have forced their way into Parliament by such a torrent of corruption as no private hereditary fortune can resist'.[20] As so often in his bursts of rhetoric, Chatham exaggerated. The fortunes were substantial (£200,000 to £300,000 was not an unusual sum with which to retire from India in the 1760s) but once invested in land and Company stock, it produced an annual income way below that available to most of the older families of England with Parliamentary interests.

The 1763 Regulating Act had not pleased the Rockingham Whigs, who feared that locking the government into the affairs of the Company risked extending its already dangerous powers of patronage. When Burke had gone for Clive, Clive had got away. He was determined that Hastings should not. His reasons, like everything to do with India, were a mixture of principle and pique. Had anything changed since Clive's governorship of 1765–67? According to Burke's chief informant, Philip Francis, they had not. Clive had spent 15 years in India, only two of them as governor of Bengal. Hastings had been governor-general for 13 years and, despite the known anxiety of Parliament, he had conducted himself throughout with absolute disregard for the interests of Britain and of the Company, solely with a view to making and consolidating his fortune and those of his cronies. Moreover, Hastings had ignored the best interests of the Indians themselves. India was a polity of village republics. 'God forbid that we should pass judgement upon a people who formed their laws and institutions prior to our own insect origins of yesterday'.[21] Hastings's crime was to have done just that.

These were the principles. But the Burke family had plunged deep in East India stock and lost it all in 1769, after which disaster Edmund's kinsman, William, had been appointed the agent of the Rajah of Tanjore in London, whose interests, he averred, Hastings had sacrificed for fear of losing Muhammad Ali's creditors the Tanjore rents. Hastings, moreover, had not favoured William with a post, yet he had granted so many 'contracts, allowances and agencies' to Scots, further proof of his attempt to create 'a prodigal and corrupt system of government in India'. For what, to Burke's slightly crazed mind, were Scots, if not 'tinctured with notions of despotism', hard men, ready to sacrifice native interests to ruthless centralisation and self-aggrandisement?[22] This was the pique. The principle was the corruption and greed, and his audience was ready to believe the worst of India. Had the 'nabobs' merely wished to become country gentlemen they might have passed into history without comment, but they also wished to enter politics. So powerful had the Company become as a dispenser of posts and patronage that, if it fell into the hands of a government party with the help of 'nabobs', it could be independent of parliament. The attack gathering on Hastings was to be, in Burke's mouth, as much a defence of constitutional freedom as the impeachment of a corrupt public servant. The dress rehearsal for impeachment was Burke's canonisation in February 1785 of Muhammad Ali, an elderly, decayed gentleman living in modest retirement in Madras, hounded by creditors who, for the most part were covenanted civil servants of the Company, had lent him money on terms he was too innocent to understand. By April 1786, Francis and Burke were ready with their 22 charges which the former governor-general should be compelled to answer. Battle was joined in June 1786 when the annexation of Rohilkund by the nawab-wazir of Oudh was presented as a wicked plot by Hastings to reduce Oudh to a client state which his cronies could then milk. The English in Oudh, as Hastings was the first to admit, behaved as if they were sovereigns, claiming 'the revenue of lacs as their right, though they could gamble away more than two lacs... at a sitting'. The House, however, agreed that they were not cronies of the governor-general, and that the annexation had kept the Marathas out of the province.[23] Hastings had been confirmed as governor-general three times since that unlucky war and members could hardly pursue the matter now.

The next charge concerned a bizarre and dangerous incident in Benares when Hastings was threatened by the sudden explosion of native anger, a long foreshadowing of the great surprise of 1857. But for Burke and Sheridan, Rajah Chait Singh and the Begums of Oudh would never have become household words, now lurking somewhere in the detritus of memory, for wronged humanity. Chait Singh was a petty rajah who had done well out of the pilgrimage business and was putting his considerable fortune into building a personal army. When Hastings asked him for a contribution of five lakhs of rupees to help with the Maratha war, he gave the governor-general two lakhs as a personal gift he would have done better to refuse. But so short was Hastings of money to pay the sepoys in Scindia's territory that he took it. Like Muhammad Ali, the rajah was now presented as a sunnily innocent prince, only too happy to play chess with British officers and have his portrait painted by a Company artist, oppressed by a rapacious governor-general. The news of Haidar's victories encouraged Chait Singh to talk freely of declaring his independence. Hastings decided on firm action. As both Oudh and Benares were late with their agreed contributions to the army that was to defend them, he decided personally to collect them. Chait Singh, openly obsequious and privately truculent, remained evasive before a demand to pay 50 lakhs, not five, as a fine for his waywardness. The troops sent to arrest him were attacked. Not armed, through a fatal oversight, with live ammunition, many, both sepoys and their officers, were killed. Soon, the entire city was in revolt. The governor-general did not lose his head, unlike many captive British officers whose bleeding visages, paraded through the fields on bayonets, startled the farmers. Knowing that a vengeful nawab-wazir would remove him if the British did not, Chait Singh decamped and was deposed. William Pitt, since 1784 effectively prime minister, instead of dismissing the incident as an episode of war, gave his opinion that the fine Hastings had imposed on the rajah had been too high. Immediately there was a case to answer, and at this point Hastings's seven-year torment began.

Richard Sheridan took up the next charge. The Begums of Oudh were the queen-mother and queen grandmother of the reigning nawab-wazir. They had modest needs in their *zenana*, and were happily ignorant of how extensively they were being robbed by their attendant eunuchs. Asaf-ud-daula, moreover, was an idle and dissolute prince, gambling heavily on his fighting cocks and maintaining a veritable army of concubines and catamites, sponged on and cheated by the British officers quartered on him at his expense. Unable to manage money, he found it impossible to meet his obligation and if he was to pay what he owed the Company – and Hastings was determined that he should – he could only do so if he clawed back some of the jagirs which his father had bestowed on the two Begums.

Hastings knew that the Company had guaranteed their settlement, but he was desperate for cash to meet the costs of the war. Asaf's men, accompanied by Company troops, moved into the Begums' palace and routed out the most corrupt and venal of the eunuchs. In the mouth of Sheridan, this assault on two harmless grannies was a gross breach of faith, a crime more horrible for being so coolly calculated, putting the impetuous passions of a Nero or a Caligula in the shade. At the height of Sheridan's peroration, ladies had to be removed from the hall, overcome with nervous exhaustion at this parade of offences against their sex. In truth neither Begum was so much as offended, nor did either know, so great was the fortune still left to them, what they had lost. But when Hastings went on to clean up the nawab-wazir's finances and to expel most of the Company servants and officers who had battened onto them, he provided a large army of ready witnesses to his perfidy.

The other items of the indictment, which took, with the accused's refutation, two days to read to an audience that included Sarah Siddons and Edward Gibbon – bribes taken, commercial monopolies granted, connivance at misdemeanours and conspiracy to defraud the Company – were hardly enough to make of him a Caligula, much less a Nero. 'I gave you all,' Hastings groaned bitterly, 'and you have rewarded me with confiscation, disgrace and a life of impeachment'.[24] He may have given all, but he was a reformer in the sense that the great European autocrats were reformers; they did not abolish the abuses of the time nor change the institutions of state, but they cleared the way for ability to replace mediocrity. Hastings boasted that he had never shown himself an enemy to the Company's servants.[25] He was guilty of allowing petulance to govern his treatment of Chait Singh and he did break the agreement to protect the settlement on the Begums. He failed to support Governor Pigot against his select committee, and he accepted money, not for himself, but for the Company to which it had not been given. He steered as close to the wind as he dared, when the government of British India lurched from military disaster to bankruptcy, but he did save it, to leave Great Britain at the end of his government-general with her power in India stronger than ever. This was more than could be said for those responsible for the 13 colonies in America.

It was not unreasonable for him to have looked to the government to vindicate him, but Pitt proposed to stay above the fray. Otherwise he would have found himself obliged to defend every past action in India. As it was, he soared free from any Indian shackles, and Burke it was who sank, as he began to bore the House with day-long speeches which increasingly abandoned truth for false witness and abuse. Finally, the whole apparatus of innuendo and lies collapsed, Hastings was virtually ruined, his £100,000 fortune had melted away, but he was declared an innocent man while Burke was spent and discredited. The desire for reform in India was now unanimous and it would be achieved, not by purges, leaving a free-standing and still independent Company, but by increased government control exercised through India House. Burke's warning of the danger that would come from government control of Indian patronage died on the weary air.

What had Warren Hastings achieved, unrecognised by Parliament and people? What he had not achieved was the India of friendly alliances with the country powers for which he had striven. The hostility of Francis, Clavering and Monson to all treaties, and the folly of the presidencies of Bombay and Madras had rendered this a pipe-dream. Instead the country powers were united in thinking, like the Maratha minister when he wrote to Haidar in 1780, that the Company's 'blind aggression has led them to violate solemn agreements and plighted words. They never observe written agreements and solemn promises, bent on the subjugation of Poona, Nagpur, Mysore and Hyderabad one by one, enlisting the sympathy of one to put down the other'.[26] By 1785, when Hastings left India, the capital of India had moved from Delhi to Calcutta. The emperor in Delhi might still be the arbiter of titles, under the Regent Plenipotentiary of the Empire, Mahadji Scindia, but the arbitrament of power had shifted unmistakably from the Jumna to the Hooghly. The East India Company was now a country power. It treated with the other country powers as an equal and had learned to play the power-game in the Indian way. By guaranteeing generous wages, it hired the cream of Indian warriors; by preserving order it exploited the credit network of Indian shroffs and commercial magnates; by keeping the legists of Cumbria and Lanark out of India, it had preserved the customary Mughal and Hindu codes, thus inspiring confidence in these men of wealth; and by using the Mughal revenue system it hired servants who understood the complexity of Indian land-holding and the rents that produced the revenue.

The directors in London did not understand what had happened, but those who wanted the Company to return to the relatively simple business of trading, were whistling in the wind. There was no retracing 'the perilous and wondrous paths' or redescending 'to the humble and undreaded character of trading adventurers'.[27] Company servants had become revenue-farmers, monopolists and money-lenders and, in order to control them, Hastings, against his better judgement for he would have preferred to keep the administration in Indian hands as the people who understood it best, was forced to increase the number of Britons in the administration of Bengal, a process which accelerated after his departure. The Company had irreversibly crossed the rubicon between being merchants and being rulers.[28] The Indians, for their part, could see that this process would provide only a humble and safe mediocrity for themselves. Sir Thomas Munro understood clearly in 1806 that 'it was a mistake to suppose that the higher orders have any respect for the Company's government, for they would prefer that of any native power, Mussalman or Hindu, because under such governments they can not only acquire wealth but also fill the highest civil and military offices of state'.[29] As Warren Hastings advised a future governor-general, his namesake Francis Rawdon, Marquess of Hastings, in 1812, 'among the natives of India there are men of as strong intellect, as sound integrity and as honourable feelings as any of this kingdom'.[30] The winning of hearts and minds was only just beginning to impinge on these merchants become rulers.

Hastings had wanted 'to eradicate every temptation for perquisites, embezzlements and corruption', but reform was one of the many tasks from which he was frequently distracted. He did succeed in banning all those involved in the collection of revenue and the administration of justice from private trading. He retained saltpetre, salt, grain and opium as Company monopolies, and left private traders, including Company servants, free to exploit the internal market in textiles, sugar and indigo as well as all other imported goods. Salt tax alone yielded annually half a million pounds sterling, though its expense to the consumer was to be a source of perennial grievance. The preparation of opium, which had in its time made immense profits for the Patna factors, was put out to contract, which was often sold on profitably as soon as it was granted. The opium monopoly became so valuable that it kept the Company in profit and the revenue from its export, mainly to China, was second only to that from the land tax.[31] The production of textiles, particularly of cotton piece goods and silk, was always profitable and the import of Bengali cottons into Britain had already begun to worry factory owners. Silk had no rival. From 1769 French and Italian artisans were imported to improve the quality of the thread.[32] The first industry to use local capital was indigo. When it was planted in Bengal and Bihar it benefited from more favourable market conditions, better transport and investment. One good crop in three could keep an indigo farmer going, a crop every second year could give him a surplus, three crops in three years could make him rich. The Baptist missionary, William Carey, who translated the scriptures into Sanskrit and Bengali, became a master of the process in order to earn enough to pay his *munshi* and buy a printing press.[33] The great indigo capitalist was John Prinsep, founder of a notable dynasty, who had come to India as a writer, turned military cadet and resigned his commission to make his fortune by supplying British textile manufacturers with the dye. He opened his first indigo factory in 1783 but the indigo boom was brief. Between 1827 and 1833 many over-capitalised ventures failed, leaving bad debts, and dragging some large agency houses down in their wake. It was a small comfort to their workers, whose wasted and purpled figures were a frequent scene of destitution in Bengal. The failures, moreover, dented confidence in European investment in India's industrialisation and exacerbated the general depression of the time.[34] The industry, however, picked up when it became an outlet for Eurasian enterprise and was concentrated in lower Bengal. It was never a popular crop with the farmer for it had no surplus, like rice, off which his family could live, and it could only be sold at a fixed low price to the factories. Conditions in these were among the worst examples of labour exploitation outside the slave-based economies in Brazil and the Caribbean. Until the synthesis of the aniline dye in 1856, it provided a living for planters whose hospitality was legendary and whose plantations resembled the *Casas Grandes* of Brazilian sugar and coffee barons. Prinsep, indeed, tried cultivating sugar, but though the Indians could actually undercut producers in the Caribbean with its slave labour, there was no profit in it. To placate British industrialists, the directors discouraged the exploitation of metals. Traders, whether Company servants or private, knew that it was not enough to exploit the raw materials of India, but that they must develop and improve them. By the 1790s the *Pax Britannica* in Bengal and its offshoot in Oudh and Benares began to show results.

Areas of stable farming expanded and immigrant labour moved in to open up new land, and the old Mughal system, of a successful agriculture with surpluses to trade and merchant communities with extra income to invest, had returned.[35] An increasing amount of that investment was now British. When the Company and the merchants, who lived under its protection began to invest in India, they had at last signified their intention to stay.

Clive had accepted the diwani of Bengal because the province, not London, would henceforward provide the bullion to fund the Company's 'investment' but, even before the famine, traders were complaining of a shortage of silver and, in 1768, Clive was warned of 'the almost universal bankruptcy of the shroffs' and that 'business and trade' were 'at a stand'.[36] A year later, the Bengal council was told that every merchant faced bankruptcy, and by 1775 one of Calcutta's commercial magnates believed that 'no advantages are to be derived... from the inland trade'.[37] Though allowance may be made for the habitual pessimism of traders facing a challenge, regulation and famine between them had made money harder to borrow and profit margins smaller. That, more than anything Hastings did, cut down individual fortunes and helped to put an end to 'nabobry'. The golden age for fortune-making had been in the 12 years after Plassey. Sudden death and disaster ensured rapid promotion for the survivors, who might find themselves on the Presidency Council within ten years and able to retire after another two or three. Though none quite amassed the £401,102 that Clive calculated he was worth in 1767, Zephaniah Holwell, survivor of the Black Hole, was thought to have retired worth £96,000, and William Ellis, slaughtered at Patna, died worth £100,000. The civil servant thought to have amassed an amount closest to Clive's was the Scot, John Johnstone, with a fortune, ruthlessly made, of £300,000, while Francis Sykes, Resident at the nawab's court at Murshidabad, Thomas Rumbold, the governor of Madras who mishandled Haidar Ali, and James Alexander, the only Ulsterman to do well out of India, were not far behind. Richard Smith, to whom the nawab of the Carnatic owed £60,000, retired as commander-in-chief of the Madras army with between £200,000 and £300,000, largely made from army contracts and prize money.[38] And, as in Clive's case, gifts. When the Company managed to control the giving and receipt of presents the big fortunes began to vanish. The early merchants had been slow to learn the language of gifts, so that their presents to local governors, even to the emperor, seemed woefully inadequate. It was when they began to receive gifts that they learned their value. Their extravagance turned all heads, for gratifications were more easily earned than profits. Once Indian princes knew that officials, from the governors-general and their ladies downwards, were obliged to buy any presents they were given from the Company chest to which they had been surrendered, and that presents from Company officials had all been bought by the Company according to a special scale, depending on who was gratifying whom, the practice became sordid. By the third decade of the nineteenth century, Ranjit Singh would not give the finest shawls to the governor-general's sister, Emily Eden, because he knew that she could never afford to buy them back, while Bishop Heber of Calcutta exchanged trumpery trinkets with the King of Kings in Delhi, when the whole exchange had become a routine to save face.

Fortunes being harder to earn, it became necessary to stay longer in India to earn what was in effect a comfortable retirement provision. A growing sense of permanency was reflected in the number of Company servants. Before Plassey, there had been only 80 or so civil servants, costing annually each about £150 in official pay and allowances. By 1774 salaries had risen to £455, and by the time Cornwallis arrived in 1786 these costs had reached an average of £2,261.[39] Warren Hastings was uncomfortable in 1781 with the thought that, of the 252 covenanted servants in Bengal, too many were 'the sons of the first families of the kingdom [of Britain] and everyone aspiring to the rapid acquisition of lacs and to return to pass the prime of their lives at home'.[40] The directors shared the discomfort. They were additionally worried that natives were being employed to do many of the tasks formerly consigned to writers. They feared that this would prove 'subversive of all order and introductory of every species of idleness and dissipation'.[41] Writers had started off by writing cargo manifests; now they were secretaries to the various boards which had been set up to manage the affairs of the Company: the Board of Council, the Military Board, the Board of Revenue and the Board of Trade. Since the Company required at least five copies of all papers, they had also become copywriters, which was too humdrum for young men who had come to make a fortune and enjoy themselves. So they sub-contracted scribes.

The civil service should have been kept to an economical size, since each civil servant was now costing a great deal more than before. It was actually increased by the steady pressure in Britain on proprietors and directors to provide jobs for clients and relations. Each director could nominate six persons to the Company's civil or military service and the President of the Court of Proprietors and Chairman of the Court of Directors each had the right to nominate 26. A governor-general could not refuse recommendations from his employers, so that by the time Warren Hastings left India there were more civil servants than there was work for them to do. A core of senior servants were overworked and underpaid, but an increasing number of others had to be given special sinecures to give them the illusion of being needed. In 1785 the directors froze the number of civil servants but did not abolish the privilege of nomination. Of covenanted servants appointed to Bengal in 1775, 20 were still soldiering on 30 years later, managing on their salaries and hoping to put by enough for old age.[42]

The Court of Directors, moreover, while repeatedly agreeing that the governor-general must exercise his initiative and judgement in any situation, in which it was at least six months and often longer out of date, remained throughout the century fussily preoccupied with detail, both to show that it was watchful and to ensure that the government Board of Control, set up under the 1784 act, could find no excuse to interfere. The Company, they declared sententiously, had always to remind itself that the object was profitable trade, not territorial expansion, that neutrality in the disputes of Indian princes must be the rule unless they impinged on obligations prescribed by treaty. 'The fundamental principle which we must rest upon is the preservation of treaties inviolate, and while we continue to act invariably upon that principle we shall be warranted to insist upon holding in our favour every right to which we are entitled by treaty.' To do otherwise, 'there would be no country in our possession which we could expect quietly to hold for a moment'.[43]

71

Even 225 civil servants were inadequate to keep a watchful eye on corrupt practice in *mofussil*, where collector would connive with zamindar, for a consideration, to take a lower rate of tax than was properly due, and where collectors, being also magistrates, could put the matter beyond redress. So bad had the practice become that Charles Cornwallis, who succeeded Hastings as governor-general, could not accept any statement by a Bengal civil servant at its face value. If the civil servants were hard to control, the military were, with their own traditions and command structure, harder. Each presidency had its own army and its own commander-in-chief (until 1895), obedient in theory to the overall command of the governor-general. The growth of the Bengal army after Plassey made it the largest in India; it also inflated the number of officers, since cadetships were items of patronage, so that in 1784, 70 per cent of them were subalterns with 20 years ahead of them before promotion to a captaincy. Their pay and field service allowance, or *batta* – which was paid whether they were in the field or in barracks, to discourage them from trading – was as low as their standard of living was high, and an attempt to remove batta when not in the field caused a mutiny in 1766. By the time a man had achieved his captaincy, he expected to take his retinue of servants with him wherever he went. Even at the height of the Carnatic campaign, when Haidar Ali appeared to be carrying all before him, a British officer went to war with his steward, cook, 'boy', groom, grass cutter, barber and washerman, the coolies who carried his palanquin and frequently that of his 'comfort girl' and her entourage, not to mention the wine, spirits, camp furniture, animals and tents. If not coolies, then bullocks had to be requisitioned and, as there were two to three camp followers to every soldier, a brigade might march with a train of 35,000 people. Thus, the perennial headache commanders in the field had with logistics and the supply of draught animals.[44]

By the end of the century, salaries of both civilians and soldiers had improved, but they were also living longer. The quick rewards had become slower, and something had to be done to sustain the attraction of Company service. It was no longer a guarantee, if you survived, of early retirement and a life of affluence in Britain. Behind each governor-general, as a result, was a growing and increasingly vocal lobby, urging him to provide more opportunities by conquest and expansion.

6. 'English Man, Very Good Man'

English man very good man, drinkee de punch, fire de
gun, beatee de French, very good fun.

Refrain of the bumboat men at Johanna,
Cape of Good Hope

He came; and, lisping our celestial tongue,
Though not from Brahma sprung,
Draws orient knowledge from its fountains pure,
Through caves obstructed long, and paths too long unsure.

Sir William Jones, *Hymn to Surya*, 1776

We sent you some time ago a box full of gods and
butterflies etc., and another box containing a hundred
copies of the New Testament in Bengali.

William Carey to Dr Ryland, 15 June 1801

THE FIRST EUROPEAN ARRIVALS followed Indian habits, wore light cotton clothes,
slept in cots under muslin, kept a concubine, ate moderately, smoked a hookah
and showed little interest in their Indian neighbours except by way of business
or as providing access to ready money. It was rare for them to learn the local
tongue. Clive, for all his mesmeric influence over sepoys, used a makeshift
Portuguese, picked up in Brazil, to talk to his *dubash*, 'his two-tongued man' or
interpreter. The average merchant mastered a vocabulary of sounds that evoked
a response from his servants. Zephaniah Holwell, who mastered colloquial Arabic
and Bengali and a written command of Persian, was an exception. Only towards
the end of the century was Persian an obligatory language for all Company
servants stationed up the country and attached to the courts of princes.

By 1760, merchants and writers had ceased to live in the factory. In Calcutta
the rich had dwellings on Chowringhee, bordering the maidan round the new
Fort William, with high Ionic colonnades and large rooms framed by venetian
windows open to whatever breeze that blew. This was the imperial style from
Virginia to Dublin, from St Petersburg to Calcutta, which Indian builders quickly
learned to imitate, though the pillars were plastered rubble and the floors made
of crushed limestone, *chunam*, which polished up to look like marble.[1] Their
country houses along the Hooghly, north of Fort William, presided over gardens,
with stepped ponds and secluded arbours and orchards, landscaped like those
on the Thames at Twickenham and Chiswick, which their owners would build in
Britain. Even the handsomest houses had rather a desolate air for, though the

furnishings were elegant, they were sparse, since clutter harboured vermin.[2] There were enough Europeans to create a lifestyle with European amusements.

Social drinking was high among them. Poorer Europeans drank country spirits, distilled from sugar or rice (toddy) or cut from the coconut palm (arrack). Both were cheap and mildly intoxicating, 'good for the gripes' and were safer to drink than water. By mid-century their consumption had been overtaken by the stronger spirits of Europe, and drunkenness was rife. The Dutch had introduced the drinking of tea, with sugar and lemon and spices, cried up as good for 'headache, gravel and griping of the guts', mainly because the water had been boiled.[3] Originally consumed as a way of taking sugar, by the time Belinda's lock was raped at Kensington Palace, tea had overtaken coffee as the popular beverage, the English drinking on average something like two pounds per person each year. Tea came from China and the Canton merchants insisted on being paid in silver. In 1757, there was a world shortage of silver which coincided with the Company's seizure of the Bengal opium monopoly so that opium was shipped instead as the return cargo for tea.[4] By the 1770s, the value of the Canton tea trade equalled that of all other trade goods from the Indian settlements put together.[5] In 1788 the directors commissioned Joseph Banks to report on its cultivation in Bengal. He chose Cooch Behar and Rangpur in north Bengal as the best sites for cultivation, both gateways to Assam which, in the middle of the nineteenth century, became the tea-garden of the world. By 1834, when opium ceased to be a Company monopoly, its sales accounted for 15 per cent of the Indian government's income and, until 1856, 30 per cent of the value of India's export trade.[6]

Food to excess certainly contributed to the mortality among young Europeans. Eliza Fay in 1780 'never saw such a quantity of victuals consumed': pilaus and curries were supplemented by 'soup, roast fowl, ... a mutton pie, a forequarter of lamb, a rice pudding, tarts, very good cheese, fresh-churned butter, fine bread and excellent madeira'.[7] The climate was considered too severe for much bodily exertion. Violent activity was for servants. Solitary riding, or duck-shooting on the salt lake was about the only exercise Europeans took. Europe and Asia met, above all, in a shared passion for gambling. Despite draconian regulations that empowered the chief agent to repatriate a merchant for gambling, the passion grew until they became unenforceable. A scene of that passion is brilliantly lit by Johannes Zoffany, when he painted the challenge of Colonel Mordaunt, commander of the nawab-wazir's bodyguard, master of ceremonies and the Earl of Peterborough's illegitimate son, to his master, Asaf-ud-daula. At stake is the prowess of teams of fighting cocks, British versus Indian. Mordaunt is wholly confident of the superiority of his cockerel, which has already started to bait its opponent. The nawab-wazir's servant, on the other hand, enumerates on his fingers the fighting qualities of the champion of Lucknow. The only person in the composition not interested in the contest is a uniformed officer under the *nim* tree to the left, whose hands are round his prize for the night, a nautch girl being made up for the dance. Even the effeminate catamite in the centre and the dancing girls to the right have eyes only for the birds.

By the middle of the century the principal exercise for both men and women was dancing. As more unattached women arrived, at the invitation of their sisters and their cousins and their aunts, dinners and balls began to follow the season, as in Europe. Concubines retreated to the servants' quarters and, though the frequently lubricious entertainment, known as the nautch, continued to be patronised by Europeans, it degenerated into a tourist attraction. The three women journalists who wrote their accounts in the early nineteenth century, Maria Graham (1809–10), Emma Roberts (1835) and Emily Eden (1838–9) found it a dull spectacle. 'These screaming girls' left Emily Eden cold and the seemingly automatic movements, gestures and songs went on, hour after hour, even if no one was listening.[8] Indians for their part could not understand why the British wanted to dance with their own women. 'The natives look on in surprise,' wrote Emma Roberts, 'wondering why the sahibs should take so much trouble, since professional persons are to be hired in every bazaar to perform for their own amusement.'[9] Emily Eden was diverted by the reactions of Indian visitors at the balls given by her brother, the governor-general. 'They think the ladies are utterly good for nothing, but seemed rather pleased to see so much vice.'[10] Eurasian and native girls, who had married Europeans, were careful not to be taken for nautch girls and dressed so sombrely as to be dowdy, a fashion that surprised the Indians even more. Emma Roberts felt sorry for 'the spinsterhood of India', the daughters of civil and military servants returning in their mid-teens from school in Britain, the sisters, like herself, who came out with betrothed brides to try their luck, and the orphan daughters educated in India at Company expense. The matrimonial market was not extensive and many of the couples who arrived at the altar were very young. Marriage was encouraged as an antidote to vice and extravagance; and life for the newly-wed was often hard and penurious. They were not always unhappy. Companionship up-country was better than loneliness.[11] The British did not imitate the apostasy of the Portuguese who Roman-Catholicised Hindu polytheism and created, in their polygamous zenanas, the topass, as in Brazil and Goa, a half-way class between the ruling caste and its helots. It was the fear that young writers in their celibate factories might end up marrying Roman Catholic topass brides or, worse, Indian women, that induced the Company to encourage European women to come to India.

With their arrival so the numbers of servants rose. Not that bachelors lived in slovenly isolation. William Hickey, whose household was free of a wife if not of women, employed 65, and many families had over 100, being hard put to it to remember who or how many there were. Honoria Lawrence, newly arrived in India, asked her hostess how many servants she employed. 'I am not sure,' was the reply, 'but we are very moderate people. I can soon reckon.' The number was nearly 30.[12] Wages being minimal, there was no reason why a merchant should not feed and fee a veritable army of retainers. On arrival he would have been recommended by his banian (Calcutta) or dubash (Madras) to take on a gomastah (Bengal) or agent and ubiquitous fixer, who would then organise a household, paying himself by commissions from those employed. Until 1764, African boys or India ocean islanders (*coffres*) could be imported as slaves to be pages and postillions.[13] European servants were generally considered to be unsatisfactory; they were fleeced in the market, were a constant source of complaint and often left without notice to open bars or businesses on their own account. European women servants were even more unreliable, leaving, usually soon after arrival, to get married.

'A set of thieves,' expostulated Eliza Fay, horrified at the household she and her husband were expected to maintain on their modest expectations. She scrutinised the cook-book, and challenged the prices so fiercely that her servants left her, complaining that there was no profit in her service. It shocked her that, being paid so little as wages, they expected to make a rupee a day from the housekeeping.[14] The shortcomings of servants afforded, perhaps, the most enthralling object of casual conversation, and in the domestic Plasseys and Buxars was born the legend of memsahibdom. *Khansama* and *kitmutgar* (head steward and head waiter, now known as bearers) were men of power in their own communities, despots in their own right, part of the hierarchy of Indian society that started with the nawab or subahdar, and cascaded down to the sweeper, whose status was so low that he could not be polluted only pollute, and who alone could perform most of the essential cleaning tasks, for which he was given the Persian title of *mehtar* or 'most important person'.[15] Between them servants made the climate supportable and social life possible and were the principal props of European life for the next 150 years. To many, Indians and Europeans alike, British women performing lowly domestic duties during the sieges of the Mutiny was the most shocking spectacle of that unhappy time.

Idleness for women was almost invariably the order of the day. When they travelled anything up to a hundred people would accompany them, for the domestic servants, the relays of palanquin porters, the tent pitchers, the sepoy guard were themselves accompanied by their female dependants. Progress was always slow, for women were usually condemned to travel over almost non-existent roads in a hackery, a light bullock-drawn carriage, or a palanquin from which they could be tipped if a porter stumbled and fell. The tents at camp were often large enough to allow for discrete sleeping quarters, sitting rooms, dining areas and washrooms but, in the rainy season, they became water-logged and leaked, while the ground became a sea of mud. 'What I hate about camp,' wrote Emily Eden, in a moment of concern for the patient army of attendants and animals, 'is the amount of human and brute suffering it induces.'[16] Such danger as there was came from the forces of nature rather than of man. Even in the great *melas*, or fairs, where 100,000 pilgrims might come together for a festival, a European could leave his wife and children quite safely in their tents, while he went for a day's shooting.[17]

The European community in city and cantonment enjoyed race meetings, in which the officers dressed as jockeys, bookies, trainers and owners, or theatricals with all parts played by men. Of intellectual activity up the country there was little; reading was never a great occupation, harassed as one was by the army of retainers omnipresent in house and garden. European women, who did not write or sketch, studied fashions, bullied *darzis* (tailors) and *malis* (gardeners) and tried to keep up the standards of a European household. They were probably more bored than the multiple wives in the zenana whom they were sometimes allowed to visit, and who had the companionship of their kind. Meals and dances were spun out for as long as possible to consume time. Emily Eden, who did not want for stimulation of the mind, was mightily relieved 'when dinner was over – and I have every reason to believe it did finish at last, though I cannot think I lived to see it'.[18] New arrivals, full of the wonders of a London they had left far behind, found Indian society uninterested. 'Persons who rave about Paganini, Sontag or Taglioni are much in the same predicament as narrators of tiger-hunts at home. They are voted bores.'[19] Few Europeans were exempt from the 'home-sickness of the heart'.[20] For a few moments, at their dances, at the race-course, during their promenades in fashionable rig, run up from magasines by the ever compliant darzi, while the regimental band played overtures by Handel, Mozart, Rossini and Weber, they might believe they were 'at home', but the relentless heat, the servants, the insects and the dust could not be shut out. Emily Eden counted the hours until her brother's governor-generalship ended and she and her sister returned to their little house at Kensington.

Despite contact since the end of the sixteenth century, Europeans knew very little about India. Philosophers and politicians were more interested in China, about which they knew even less. The image of the Celestial Empire as a nation ruled, without fear of God or gods, by an immemorial caste of scholar administrators, applying reason to human affairs, appealed to the eighteenth-century mind, escaping from dogmatism and credal tyranny. India was different, dedicated as she was to a pantheon of grotesque and often bloodthirsty deities, burdened with ritual known only to a hereditary caste, ruled by caprice and corrupted by sex. Early travellers could not tell Hindu from Muslim and Sir Thomas Roe's chaplain was sure that Brahmans shaved their heads, except for one notch of hair, so that Mohammed could snatch them up to Paradise. They jumped readily to conclusions they wanted to reach. The fastidious Jains, for example, who would not destroy life in any form, must be followers of Pythagoras, for only from him could they have learned about the transmigration of souls.[21] Some early visitors had detected echoes of a great literary and religious tradition, but eager Company chaplains were only too ready to believe that the intense religious sense of the Hindus was a Judaeo-Christian theophany, corrupted in the transfer, and spent much energy trying to reconcile the Hindu creation myths with the Book of Genesis. In Britain, the civilisation of India did not penetrate the universities. Oxford was the centre of oriental studies but the languages studied were Hebrew and Arabic, spiced with Turkish and Armenian.

When Edmund Burke warned the House of Lords of the fateful influence of Indian forms of despotism on people like Warren Hastings, he peddled one of the commonest beliefs about Asian monarchy. By the middle of the century, closer proximity to Asian rulers had showed that they might be despotic but they were not always powerful, and while some might trace their descent from Gods, Vedic heroes, planets, caliphs and sultans, they were often of pretty modest (even recent) origins who used adoption to renew the dynastic stock. With this realisation came a diminishment of esteem. Strong prejudice soon formed stereotypes. Robert Orme, the first chronicler of Clive's campaigns, accused Muslim princelings of a domineering insolence, ungovernable wilfulness, cruelty, insensibility to remorse, sensual excess, an unbounded sense of power and 'an expaciousness of wealth equal to the extravagance of his propensities and vices'. He even distrusted the Indian's innate courtesy and generous charm as 'the deepest disguise and dissimulation of the heart'.[22] Zephaniah Holwell, having survived the Black Hole, might perhaps be forgiven for believing that 'Gentoos' in general were 'as degenerate, crafty, superstitious and as wicked a people as any known race in the world'.[23] Other Europeans learned to repeat the litany. Mrs Kindersley, writing home to describe their gentle, temperate, regular, charitable and pious lives, felt obliged to add that the Indians were also 'superstitious, effeminate, avaricious and crafty, deceitful and dishonest in their dealings and void of every principle of honour, generosity and gratitude'.[24] Someone who benefited conspicuously from their generosity and loyalty, the mercenary, Benoît de Boigne, held that 'all Hindustanis, whether Hindus or Muslims, Brahmans or low castes, are vile and treacherous, entirely unreliable. While professing friendly sentiments, they will not scruple to cut your throat,' an opinion that he apparently shared, even acquired, from his master, Mahadji Scindia.[25] Haidar Ali was sure that 'no man of common sense will trust a Maratha, and they themselves do not expect to be trusted'.[26] By the time Arthur Wellesley wrote to his brother urging him to accept the government-general, it was as if he was copying straight from a manual. Among the 'mischievous and deceitful *dubashes*' he had not come across a Hindu with one good quality and 'the Mussulmans are worse'.[27] The contempt was mutual. Marathas never ceased to be amazed at how Company servants in Calcutta could repudiate agreement made by their colleagues in Bombay, so that no pact with them could be trusted to hold. For the Indian peasant, according to Luke Scrafton, Company agent at Murshidabad, it was 'a matter of the utmost indifference whether the tyrant is a Persian or a Tartar, for they feel all the curses of power without any of the benefit, but that of being exempt from anarchy, which is alone the only state worse than what they endure'.[28] Villagers in Bengal thought their new overlords worse than tigers.[29]

What really shocked Europeans was sex. A sense of sexual insecurity hovered over the European presence throughout their stay in India, which was entirely unjustified. Siraj-ud-daula's zenana was filled with women, seized, stolen, bought or donated, but none was a European. They were safe from oriental interest, being big, white, not generally attractive and impure, so that sex with a European meant loss of caste. Not being on offer as merchandise, loot or bribe, they were left alone. No white woman suffered outrage at the capture of Calcutta in 1756 and, if Mary Carver was in the Black Hole, she was only there because she would not leave her man. Even the ferocious Marathas or the frightening Mysoreans did not make war on women. At the battle of Kirkee in 1817, the palanquins of General Briggs's wife and children and two other ladies were surrounded by enemy horsemen, but once they were satisfied by their screams that they were women they were left unharmed.[30] It was part of the popular case against Tipu Sultan that he allowed the wives and daughters of his European prisoners to be enslaved to his henchmen, but it could not be proved that any of them had been violated.[31] None of the women who died in the Cawnpore Bibigarh massacre in 1857 was sexually assaulted. Eliza Fay, whose mental equipment, in Morgan Forster's view was 'that of an intelligent lady's maid... who has read Mrs Radcliffe, Pope and *Nubilia in Search of a Husband*, and can allude at a pinch to Queen Christina of Sweden' made the most of her frightening but actually uneventful experience as a woman 'in wretched confinement, totally in the power of barbarians'.[32]

She was impressed by the dancing snakes, sword-swallowers and prestidigitators, and vaguely curious about the books of palm leaves that she saw being composed so painstakingly by Hindu scribes, but she showed no interest in what was written in them.[33] It was hardly to be expected of a woman with the mind of a lady's maid. But others were beginning to find out. Holwell, whom Voltaire admired as 'un homme qui n'a voyagé que pour nous instruire', wrote the *Mythology of the Gentoos* and a study of metempsychosis authoritative enough to convince the Sage of Ferney that Greek philosophers, especially Pythagoras, had instructed Hindus in their sublime ideas, and that Brahmans preached a God desiring only charity and good works.[34] The excesses of their macabre rituals could be compared to the popular practices of Christianity.[35] Holwell had not mastered Sanskrit, so his claim to have read the *shastras* in their original form must be held in doubt.[36] But where he had pioneered, others were to follow. The Company now held the destinies of many millions of people in its hands so that it must 'conciliate a great people to a dominion which they see with envy and bear with reluctance,' and set up 'a system... for reconciling the people of England to the natives of Hindostan'.[37] Nathaniel Halhed, a young writer of 23, who had studied Persian at Oxford and come to India when the love of his life married Richard Brinsley Sheridan, was selected to preside over a team of Brahman pandits, charged in 1766 to produce the codex of 'Gentoo' laws, translated from the Sanskrit, first into Persian and then into English. Because the pandits and *maulvis* were reluctant to open their books of law too wide for translation, his *Gentoo Laws* was riddled with faults, but it was a start.

Warren Hastings had learned enough Persian and Bengali while in Kasimbazar to exchange abstract ideas. He would buy manuscripts in the bazaar which he later sold to the Company to help pay his debts when broken and ill, and which were to form the foundation collection of the India Office library. He instructed Halhed to set up a government press, supported virtually from his own pocket, to print works in Bengali and Persian. He sponsored a translation of the *Máhabhárata*, a work that could 'open a new and most extensive range for the human mind'.[38] In 1778 he gave the management of the press to Charles Wilkins who, while writer and superintendent of the factory at Malda, 300 miles north of Calcutta, had learned both Persian and Sanskrit. He made himself the master of oriental scripts and of all printing techniques, being at once metallurgist, engraver, foundry-manager, type-maker, setter and editor. In 1783 he was joined by the father of oriental studies in India, a linguist who had been appointed one of the three supreme court judges, a lawyer whose first love was antiquarianism, an acknowledged expert on India before he ever set foot on her shore. Sir William Jones collected his knighthood before he sailed, aged 37, but plain Jones had been a boyhood wonder. At Harrow he soon knew more Greek than his teachers and also learned to read Arabic. At Oxford he learned more from his Syrian amanuensis than from his professors, and while tutor to the Spencer family was commissioned to translate into French the history of the Afghan Nadir Shah, spoiler of Delhi. It made Jones's name as an orientalist. But not his fortune. Dedicating himself to a Ciceronian discipline of reading to prepare for the law, he discharged himself from noble patronage and in 1778 was offered a judgeship in India.

Gibbon saluted him as the only lawyer 'equally conversant with the year-book of Westminster, the Commentaries of Ulpia, the Attic pleadings of Isaeus and the sentences of Arabian and Persian cadhis'.[39] Warren Hastings, from a perusal of his grammar of the Persian language, a present from Dr Johnson, enthusiastically endorsed his appointment. Sir William was very clear about his objects. It was to make a modest fortune of £30,000 upon which to retire, to devote himself to study and to perfect his knowledge of oriental languages. Only by his own perfect understanding of Indian laws and customs could he provide the natives with 'an effective tribunal for their protection against the British', for he believed, with Hastings, that only by being governed fairly and justly by their own laws could the Company's subjects come to respect British justice. He was not encouraged by what he knew of the Honourable Company, a formidable engine for the corruption of Britons and the enslavement of Indians.[40] To avoid the first he imitated the simplicity of life he had detected among the Arabs of Yemen and the poets of Shiraz, living in a bungalow at Alipur, a close neighbour of the governor-general's in the jagir of Clive. There, in pastoral seclusion, accompanied by two large English sheep which had escaped the knife on board *The Crocodile* in which they had all travelled to India and, lulled to sleep by the bulbul, he followed the plan of work he had devised on the voyage out.[41]

In the six years he had proposed as sufficient for him to make his £30,000, he would study the laws of Hindus and Muslims, the history of the Indian ancient world, the proofs and illustrations of sacred scriptures to be found in India, particularly of the deluge, the modern politics and geography of the subcontinent, how best to govern Bengal, the mathematical, chemical, physical and medical sciences of India, her natural products, trade, manufactures, agriculture and commerce, the poetry, rhetoric, morality and music of Asia, and the Mughal and Maratha constitutions. The task was never completed. But his capacity for hard work was undimmed by the climate and ill-health, and he achieved what he did only by following the routine regularly advised to all newcomers and almost invariably rejected. He rose an hour before sunrise, walked the three miles to Fort William, whence he was carried to the court in a palanquin. There he bathed, dressed and breakfasted. From seven to eight he was closeted with his pandit, learning Sanskrit. From eight to nine he improved his Arabic and Persian. Attorneys started to brief him at nine, after which he spent five hours in court. At three he returned home, dined, relaxed in conversation until sunset and was then driven in the public gardens for an hour, after which he would read Ariosto or Tasso with his wife. Both were in bed by 10 o'clock.[42]

Jones spent ten years in India and died before he could return to England to enjoy his fortune. Much of the work he did on the juridical system was of little long-term value. He had aspired to be India's Justinian, 'to give the natives of these Indian provinces a permanent security for the due administration of justice among them'.[43] Pandits and maulvis should not be able to hide behind corrupt or partial texts, for to every judge would be available a sound translation from the Sanskrit or Arabic original. The vast ambition was never quite realised for, as Jeremy Bentham unkindly put it, he 'sent spinning cobwebs out of his own brain and winding them round the common law'.[44] His passion for authenticity was the enemy of practicality. It assumed that Indian justice had been engraved in tablets of stone, whereas it was constantly changing and adapting. Even his own pandits betrayed him by adapting rather than translating the classic works of jurisprudence. Sir William Jones did not become a lion under the governor-general's throne, his judgements passing down from precedent to precedent. His most distinguished niche in the pantheon of Anglo-India was as founder of the Asiatick Society.

He had arrived in 1783 to find a small group of Company servants, as part of their busy schedule, engaged on an investigation into the civilisation of Asia. Charles Wilkins has already set the first Bengali type-face, had published his book on the Monghyr inscriptions of Devapala and was translating the *Máhabhárata*. Halhed had followed his *Gentoo Laws* with a grammar of the Bengal language in 1778. Francis Gladwin had translated and abridged Abul Fazl's *Institute of the Emperor Akbar* (*Ain-i-Akbari*). Captain William Kirkpatrick was working on a grammar of Hindu dialects which the directors ordered to be published in 1785, and Joseph Champion was translating the first part of Firdousi's heroic poem, *Shahnama*, or the complete history of Persia in 60,000 verses (from which Matthew Arnold was to glean the story of Sohrab and Rustum). But for the great expense of printing there would have been more. Gladwin successfully asked the Company to purchase 150 copies to bring costs within his means. All these pioneers were generously supported by Warren Hastings, but they recognised in the Welsh judge that a greater than they had arrived. Because Jones could not find a Brahman willing to unlock the secrets of the *Ordinances of Manu*, which he proposed to translate into Persian, he set himself, single-handed, to learn Sanskrit.

The Asiatick Society (so called because it extended its interest to all lands east of Europe and was modelled on Boyle's Royal Society) provided Jones and his associates with a platform for research and a stimulus to intellectual exchange. It was never a popular part of the Calcutta scene and struggled against general indifference, but among those who did attend its meetings – it met on average ten times a year – were nearly always the governor-general and members of the Supreme Council and Supreme Court. Their deliberations were reproduced in *Asiatick Researches*, edited by Jones, who occasionally had to write most of the material himself. Indians were not admitted to the Society until 1829, but they were virtually corresponding members from the start, as Jones ransacked their brains for information and their *almirahs* for manuscripts. Brahman suspicion was exchanged for friendship and a shared dedication to learning, and his leisure hours were spent in the presence of pandits, discussing literature in the garden of his thatched cottage at Krishnagar, 60 miles up-country on the road to Plassey, whither he retired as often as he could to find perfect peace. 'I never was unhappy in England, but I was never happy till I was settled in India.' There he would rather be a valetudinarian all his life than leave unexplored the Sanskrit mine he had just opened.[45] From his nest of bulbuls he presented to English readers the work of Kalidasa, whose *Shakuntala* was written two thousand years earlier. 'Suppose Greece to have been conquered successively by Goths, Vandals, Tartars and lastly by the English; then suppose a court of judicature to be established by the British parliament in Athens and an inquisitive Englishman to be one of the judges; suppose him to learn Greek there, which none of the countrymen knew, and to read Homer, Pindar, Plato, which no other European had heard of!'[46]

Jones's life at Krishnagar, epitomised by the month-old tiger cub suckled by a goat, and by the Brahman pandits sitting cross-legged on the lawn, may have seemed to his colleagues like an affectation, but international recognition came when the president of Yale College wrote a huge letter of 148 pages to challenge his chronology of the Hindus. The first four volumes of *Asiatick Researches* were translated into German, two of them into French, while individual articles were reproduced in London and Dublin. 'Orientalism', which was to become part of the Romantic cult infecting Coleridge, Southey, Moore, Shelley and Byron, took its source from the quiet judge's garden in Bengal.[47] Both Byron and Shelley considered seeking either political or diplomatic careers in India. Shelley even wrote to his friend, Thomas Love Peacock, who worked in India House, for advice on how to set about it.[48] John Keats considered applying for a surgeon's post on an East Indiaman.

The Asiatick Society is credited with clothing with scientific evidence the Jesuit theory that there was a common origin to the Indo-European languages. Halhed had already noticed an affinity between Sanskrit, Arabic, Persian, Latin and Greek, as he struggled with his own unfinished translation of the *Máhabhárata*. When Jones acquired Sanskrit he was convinced of it. The Jesuits had taught that all languages derived from the common tongue at the tower of Babel; Jones believed that Sanskrit was that tongue. Unwilling to stray too far from sacred text, he thence tried to adduce the origin and families of nations by reference to the Book of Genesis, convinced that the sacred scriptures held the key to history. He worked out the mathematical probability of the human race deriving from the loins of Adam and Eve, and found both the flood and Mosaic law confirmed in the Puranas and Vedas, while the doctrines of the Vedic School were Platonic.[49] Contrary to the impression that Holwell, Halhed and Dow had managed to convey, that the Indians were the most ancient people on earth, Jones found that nothing in Hindu mythology disturbed the authenticity of the first books of the Bible.

He divided world history into historic periods, post-diluvian, patriarchal, Mosaic and prophetic, and found correspondences in Indian mythology that fitted the shared chronology of Christian and Muslim alike. The discovery, from this elaborate work of fiction, of one historical figure in Indian history, who answered to the Sandrocottas (Chandragupta) encountered by Alexander the Great, lent his construct a factitious authenticity and, more usefully, provided a date which linked Indian history to that of Europe. Jones and the Asiatick Society uncovered rather than discovered ancient India, and provided the foundation for the more scientific attempt to write its history that unfolded in the next century. Despite his enthusiasm for the treasures of Sanskrit literature he was unveiling, this saint of serendipity believed, throughout, in the superiority of Greece over the Asiatick handmaid, in the Hebrew Bible as the touchstone of all truth and in the British constitution as the summit of human wisdom.[50] 'Indians must and will be governed by absolute power' for, having no sense of freedom over many centuries of despotism, their natural and juridical sciences were inferior to those of Europe.[51] Liberty, if forced upon its millions, would make them as miserable as would the cruellest despot; absolute rule by the British would provide them with the peace, prosperity and wisdom which would allow them to substitute ritual and superstition by an understanding of the rational basis of all good law. If so sincere a devotee of Indian civilisation believed this, it was hardly surprising that it should also be the belief of the new rulers of Bengal for another century and a half.

Jones may have been a brilliant jurist but he is remembered as the first linguist to find the key to Indian philosophy and literature. He was also to unlock those treasures to Indian themselves, so long baffled by brahmanical secrecy and ignorant of the riches of a literature that could hold its own with any other in any age.[52] Like many other pioneers, he was too ready to find the relationship between languages that he sought, and was encouraged to find what he wanted by pandits who knew less than they pretended. Above all, Jones was too steeped in the Hellenic culture of his youth. Like Shelley, he would have confessed that 'We are all Greeks', from whom came 'all our laws, our literature, our religion, our arts'.[53] He might compare the best of Hindu writing with Homer, Pindar and Plato but they could never supersede them.

The real Sanskrit master was another Company servant, magistrate at the brass and carpet emporium of Mirzapur. Henry Colebrooke was the son of a Company director, pressed on Hastings by patronage in 1782. Disgusted by the gambling and drinking of his fellow writers, he threw himself into the study of Indian mathematics, astronomy and the art of prediction and, finding that his legal duties, first as assistant collector and then as magistrate, required him to learn Sanskrit, he did it thoroughly. He sat at the feet of Brahman pandits at Purnea, the greatest centre of Brahmanical learning after Benares. As a judge, Colebrooke reckoned to hear from 300 to 500 cases a month; even so, he produced in 1798 *A Digest of Hindu Law* (the project Jones had started and an Indian jurist had continued), and was appointed to the Court of Appeal in Calcutta in 1801. Here, with a little more leisure, he doubled as professor of Hindu Law and Sanskrit at Fort William College, edited a Sanskrit grammar and wrote extensively on Sanskrit and Prakrit poetry, on religious ceremonies of the Hindus, on the Jains and on the Vedas, the last providing the first access for western readers to Hindu scriptures.

Colebrooke benefited from Jones's mistakes. He refused to subscribe to the theory that Sanskrit had been invented by the Brahmans to conceal their secrets and confirm their power. Instead, he was to expose to a surprised Asiatick Society, of which he rose to be president, the mastery of the Indians in astronomy, contract law and prosody. His research into the Vedas revealed the subtlety and sophistication of Indian theology. Max Müller, in admiration, called him 'the legislator of India'. But Colebrooke was sufficiently a child of his time to admit that he had been resolved 'to conquer the admirable craft of the devil, which led the Brahman to form a language at once so rich and complicated.'[54] He thus spoke in the same tone as the self-taught Baptist cobbler and missionary, William Carey, who, in his enthusiasm to preach the good news in Bengali and to argue the scriptures with Brahmans in Sanskrit, made himself master of both. Carey became a colleague of Colebrooke's at Fort William College, but under his influence, the learning of Sanskrit was to be the key, not primarily to knowledge but to conversion. The twin trinities of Holwell, Halhed and Dow, and of Jones, Colebrooke and Carey were the fathers of the 'Orientalists', who believed that, behind the contemporary India of corruption and superstition, was a golden age of learning, when there were no gods but One God, no images, no objectionable practices, like suttee (sati) and infanticide, but a morality to which all men could subscribe, no priests, no temples, no idols, but only wholesome scripture. They believed that the way to return India to this blessed state was to investigate her history and civilisation, 'with the hope of facilitating the amelioration of which [it] may be found susceptible'.[55]

John Company may have started off as a godly association but most of its servants were in search of a fortune, not salvation. They had no interest in converting the Hindus or Muslims among whom they lived. Indeed the Company refused to license missionaries, and used its regulations against interlopers to keep them out. Its chaplains administered only to the spiritual needs of the Protestant merchant community. Their duties were not onerous. When in 1688 the directors decreed that any East Indiamen of 500 tons burthen or upwards must carry a chaplain, they were built not to exceed 499 tons. A godly man on his way to India had to endure 'a five months' imprisonment with carnal men on board the ship'.[56] For good religion was not a Company priority. Calcutta's first place of Protestant worship was only licensed in 1704 and as late as 1776, the directors ranked the building of a church after accommodation for its servants, barracks and go-downs.[57] The chaplains were 'useless freight', carrying with them a weight of learning, solemnity and piety which was not merchantable. It became progressively harder to find dedicated men to work in India *ad majorem dei gloriam*, so that by the end of the eighteenth century church-going had given place to dancing and race-meetings. The evangelical John Shore, when governor-general in 1795, blamed 'our clergy in Bengal [who] with some exceptions are not respectable characters'.[58] When, on 1 February 1800, Richard Wellesley ordered a Te Deum to celebrate the fall of Tipu Sultan, a jaundiced Baptist remarked that 'the inauguration of the Christian religion, as the religion of the rulers of British India, was announced by the booming of cannons and the parade of 2000 troops'.[59] The ban on missionaries was not due to crass mercantilism. The directors wanted no religious strife where they did their business. Besides, they believed missionary enterprise would be futile. The Hindus believed the English were a race without religion, the Muslims had their own book and stood apart. Most converts were made among the Roman Catholics of Portuguese descent.

Holwell, Halhed and Jones had tried to demonstrate that Hinduism was a monotheistic religion, sharing the worship of the Supreme Being and a moral code with Jews, Anglicans and deists everywhere. Not everyone was convinced. In 1792, an evangelical Scots senior merchant, Charles Grant, published his *Observations on the State of Society among the Asiatic Subjects of Great Britain*, a loud blast of the trumpet against a people 'unusually and wholly corrupt... as depraved as they are blind and as wretched as they are depraved'.[60] It was 'hardly possible to conceive any people more completely enchained... by their superstition'.[61] The Protestant conscience in India seemed undisturbed by this sad fact, but on 11 November 1793, this was destined to change. Among the non-merchantable freight of a Danish vessel anchoring at Calcutta were William Carey and his two sons, sponsored by the Baptist Society for Propagating the Gospel of Kettering in Northamptonshire. A self-taught cobbler, which trade supported him as an itinerant preacher, Carey had been fired by Wesley's mission to the West Indies, and by the discovery in the Pacific of lands wholly ignorant of the Good News. When the brethren of Kettering indicated 'a gold mine in India... as deep as the centre of the earth', and asked 'who will venture to explore it?' Carey ventured.[62] Within a year, he had shipped himself and his family to Calcutta. Like St Paul, to whom he often compared himself, he would work for his living while he learned the necessary languages and prepared the sacred text of Christianity for translation into Bengali.

At Carey's first sight of Calcutta, as at Paul's of Athens, the spirit stirred within him. He was not dismayed by the absence of the One True God, crowded out by the 300,000,000 pretences for Him, three for each head of population, who prostrated themselves before the 'monkey, the serpent... idols the very personification of sin... the lecher Krishna and his concubine Radha... No Bibles, no sabbath, no God but a log of wood, no saviour but the Ganges... no morality, for how should a people be moral whose gods are monsters of vice, whose priests are their ringleaders in crime... whose heaven is a brothel?'[63] Abominations surrounded him: girls allowed to die at birth, child brides, widows encouraged to mount their dead husbands' funeral pyres or submit to being buried alive with his corpse, unmarriageable women 'married' in scores to Brahman priests as licensed concubines – half the population condemned to ignorance and servitude by the accident of their sex. It was a challenge of Herculean proportions which the Moravian missionaries at the Danish enclave of Serampore had already abandoned. Not only were there the teeming masses lost in Hindu darkness, there were also those who had been seduced by the Jesuits who dragged down Christian doctrine and worship to the level of idolatrous heathenism. And thirdly, there were the other members of a missionary faith, the Muslims. Carey was undaunted. Given a hut by a Hindu money-lender, Carey roamed the streets like a mendicant, disputing the Koran with Muslims in the broken Bengali he had taught himself on board ship, while he struggled to translate the Book of Genesis with the aid of a munshi. When he was moved on by the authorities, he withdrew to a jungle clearing 40 miles east of Calcutta, built himself a bamboo house and preached to the bemused peasants who pitched their cabins near the man with a gun who would keep the tigers away from their animals. They may have learned little about the message of salvation but Carey learned demotic Bengali.

'Preachers are wanted 100 times more than people to preach to,' he wrote wearily to his sponsors in Kettering. 'There is not one soul that thinks of God aright.'[64] To remedy this he accepted the post of supervisor to an indigo planter of evangelical persuasion at Malda (later English Bazaar, some 300 miles north of Calcutta) for a salary of £150 a year. With these riches he bought a printing press on which, with the help of native compositors who thought it was his god, he produced by 1798 his first Bengali Bible, complete except for the books from Joshua to Job. Suspicious of the knowledge and reliability of munshis, he taught himself Sanskrit and, like Jones, practised on the classics. By 1807, he was the most active member of the Asiatick Society, and between 1806 and 1810 he worked on a version of the *Rámáyana*, with a prose translation and explanatory notes. The *Máhabhárata* he admired as heroic literature but abhorred as religious error. He found no words for divine love or repentance, no ideal of religion, the lack of which made it more difficult to preach to both great and humble on the evil and universality of sin, and the grace of conversion through the love of Jesus Christ.

It was only when Carey settled on Danish soil in Serampore that his mission took off. There, on 29 December 1800, he 'happened to desecrate the Gunga by baptising the first Hindoo', a caste Brahman, Krishna Pal, and his family. 'The chain of caste is broken,' he boasted. 'Who shall mend it?'[65] The labourer had worked long in the vineyard and the harvest was small, but Serampore was to become a centre for the desecration of the Ganges, operating subversively in the heart of Bengal. In the beginning was the Word, and Carey's labours with the word were as prodigious as those of Sir William Jones. Between 1801 and 1825, he oversaw the translation of the whole Bible into seven Indian languages and the new testament into 21, while editing a further eight translations by others. Between 1811 and 1818, against the Vedas and Upanishads, Brahmans and the Hindu epics, he set his Sanskrit Bible, and from his mastery of Sanskrit he learned the meaning of four out of five words in the languages of northern and central India. Every morning he read a chapter of the Bible, first in English and then in the language into which he was translating it. Charles Wilkins' own type-caster came to work with him, assisted by a blacksmith who could only work on this godly task under the gaze of his personal Hindu idol. Carey also learned the art of making paper until he could afford imported sheets, and later he built a steam-driven pulper, so that Serampore became the principal paper manufactory in Bengal until 1860. When, in 1812, the entire press and its store of material ready for printing were destroyed by fire, Carey remarked that God moved in mysterious ways to punish his servants, and started all over again, the Hindu blacksmith casting new type from the molten metal on the morning after.

In 1810 there were 32 Baptist missionaries operating out of Serampore, only a little yeast in a population of hundreds of millions, but Carey always hoped that the whole lump would by degrees be leavened. Despite the ban on missionary activity, they had made 300 converts in Company-ruled Bengal. When, for lack of anyone better qualified, Carey was appointed professor of oriental languages at Fort William College, the government in Calcutta effectively connived at his work. By day he taught Company servants Sanskrit, Bengali and Marathi. In the evening he preached in several tongues and at night he translated the *Rámáyana* and the *Veda*. Like St Paul, he wrote to like-minded company servants or private traders, who read the newly translated scriptures together. The communities of Corinth, Ephesus and Laodicea had started thus, and Carey had great faith.

The Danes had had missionaries in the Danish-held port of Tranquebar since Frederick IV established the Royal Danish Mission in 1706. There were never more than six at any one time but converts were more easily made in south India, among both Roman Catholics and low-caste Hindus. Being Lutherans, the Danes were acceptable as chaplains to British troops in the presidency of Madras. The Carey of the South was Frederick Christian Swartz. First in Trichinopoly, then in Tanjore, Swartz evangelised the Tamils and the soldiery. Visibly ascetic, tireless and disinterested, he was able to influence the brutal and licentious soldiery like none of their officers, and was considered good for discipline. Like Carey, he aimed his message primarily at the children he could persuade to come to his two schools, one for Tamil Hindus, one for Roman

Catholics. Even a Sivaite ascetic could not quarrel with his breakfast of hot water poured over tea into which he and his helpers dunked their mouldy bread. Against him was ranged the devil, not among the poor and lowly whom he served, but among the complacent merchants whose church-going was perfunctory and whose devotion to the word of God was slender. When Swartz reassured a young Hindu neophyte that no one wicked could reach the kingdom of heaven, she sighed, 'Then, alas, in that case hardly any Europeans will enter it.'[66]

Carey had declared war on Hinduism, as had St Paul on the pagan cults of Rome, and declared he would only be happy when the infamous 'swinging post' was no longer erected, when no widow burned on the funeral pile, when obscene dances were seen no more and when the gods were thrown down to the moles and bats.[67] Company government tolerated these practices, even undertaking responsibility for maintaining temples and holy places, collecting the pilgrim tax and appointing custodians of religious property. Its policy was not to disturb the religious practices of India and, as there was no evidence that the Indians themselves resented or feared them, the government merely assured itself of their voluntary nature. Now it was being challenged by a superior morality. The missionaries, being closer to the people, claimed that some of the practices were often far from freely chosen. A family's desire to satisfy an elder's wish to die by the banks of the Ganges often amounted to a form of euthanasia. The practice of casting oneself under the wheels of the tremendous vehicles that carried Juggernaut or Jaganath, an idol as detestable as Dagon or Baal, should make any Christian shudder. 'Idolatry destroys more than the sword,' Carey sighed as he considered the numbers carried off by disease and exhaustion while on pilgrimage, and the 10,000 victims of suttee.[68]

Nothing illustrates the Company's nervousness about interfering with religious custom better than its attitude to suttee. The practice appeared to be sanctioned by centuries of tradition. No European liked it, even if he could admire the fortitude of its voluntary victims. But therein lay the problem – who were real and who forced volunteers? In 1805 the civil court of *nizamat adalat* in Calcutta ruled that suttee was acceptable provided that it was voluntary, but added that a widow could achieve purification as well by a life of austere good works as by allowing herself to be immolated. No pregnant or nursing mother or girl under the age of puberty could commit suttee. Any form of encouragement, constraint or the use of stupefacients rendered suttee an illegal act and it was the job of the police to ensure that this judgement was observed. It was not until 1812, after vigorous prompting by Carey, that this judgement was made public, but the government was deaf to any call for abolition.[69] It was impossible to police all suttees. Some were stopped, but no one conniving at an illegal suttee was prosecuted, because it was so difficult to prove illegality. Worse, the agonised intention of the government to remain neutral but attempt to enforce correct religion appeared to revive a practice that had been slowly falling into disuse. Successive governors-general carefully avoided uttering any decisive opinion on abolition, fearful of unrest among sepoys or the rural masses, until the arrival of Lord William Bentinck in 1828.

Despite the protests of the missionary societies, the directors supported their government in India, and their stand against interference with religious practice was not without its supporters in the established church. In the *Edinburgh Review* of 1808, the Reverend Sydney Smith commented on the mutinous insurrection at Vellore on 10 July 1806. The commanding officer, seeking to introduce a form of Prussian efficiency into the Madras army, ordered the removal of moustaches and caste marks from all faces. Fearing that they were to be forcibly made to lose caste and christianised, in a sinister premonition of 1857 the sepoys torched their officers' houses, before running amok through the hospital, slaughtering any sick Europeans they found, until overwhelmed by the local garrison. The governor-general held missionaries responsible for fuelling fears of forcible conversion, and the Rector of Foston, indulging his dislike of Methodism and all forms of enthusiasm, and reinforced by his brother, Bobus Smith, advocate-general of Calcutta, accused the Anabaptist missionaries, as he persisted in calling them, of being 'quite insane and ungovernable; they would wish deliberately, piously, and conscientiously to expose our whole Eastern empire to destruction, for the sake of converting half a dozen Brahmans'. If a tinker were devout, he infallibly set off for the east.[70]

It was one thing to tilt at a proliferation of gods but quite another to preach the equality of man and universal brotherhood. What was to prove an insurmountable obstacle to conversion was caste, the most effective of 'Satan's arts to render men unhappy'.[71] To lose caste was to lose all the social supports that enabled life to be lived without breakdown in a society always on the verge of human or natural catastrophe. 'A change of faith might increase the immediate happiness of any other individual,' Smith argued sagely, but 'it annihilates for ever all the human comforts which a Hindoo enjoys. The eternal happiness which you proffer him is, therefore, less attractive to him... for the life of misery by which he purchases it.'[72] The ancient Christian churches in Malabar had accommodated to it and Christians attended churches which catered for their castes or which were divided in such a way that castes did not mingle. The Jesuits had even experimented with a priesthood of consecrated Brahmans. But in the end, Christianity was irreconcilable with Brahmanical Hinduism, for whom there was not the One Book but many, and the missionaries were to find that their uncasted converts became dependent on them.

Vellore reinforced the Company's resistance to interference with religious practice, but public opinion in Britain was beginning to think otherwise. In April 1809, Robert Southey came to the defence of the low-born and low-bred mechanics who had acquired the gift of tongues, and done more than any prince, potentate, or university to spread the scriptures among the heathen and overthrow the tyranny of superstition. In 1810, his best-selling but now forgotten epic *The Curse of Kehama*, a gigantic promethean epic, exalted the overthrow of a degenerate and evil despot by a simple Indian peasant, purged to heroic stature by the tyrant's curse which condemned him to eternal suffering, and who was now beyond the power of any god. In the poem, Southey denounced the now well-known litany of Hindu religious tortures: suttee, temple prostitution, female infanticide, and the immolations before Jaganath. And when Sydney Smith urged the Company to root out from Bengal 'the nest of consecrated cobblers', he roused the powerful voice of William Wilberforce. On 16 July 1813, during the debate on the renegotiation of the Company's charter, the great emancipator returned to a crusade he had started in 1793, to have the ban on missionaries in India overturned. The House should know that Milton's plan to write *Paradise Lost* in his old age and blindness was a lesser instance of the moral sublime 'than that a poor cobbler working in his stall should conceive of the idea of converting the Hindoos to Christianity'.[73] God's hand could be seen in the subjugation of so many Indians by a handful of Englishmen, but to what end, if not to persuade them to abandon the 'absolute monsters of lust, injustice, wickedness and cruelty' that were their gods.[74] For him the conversion of India had always been a greater object than the abolition of slavery.

Already there were cracks in the inner walls. Charles Grant had become Chairman of the Company, and strove to send as chaplains to Bengal men of the same strong evangelical views as he. One of these, Claudius Buchanan, vice-provost of Fort William College, toured the Hindu temples and historic Christian churches of the south between 1805 and 1807 to report on what passed therein for religion. Before an audience of bankers and merchants in London, Buchanan claimed that 'the message of kindness' would inspire the Indians 'to reach up and receive gospel and commerce together'.[75] God had saved Britain from the wreck of nations so that she could have the power and means to promote Christian knowledge.[76] With Grant and Buchanan behind Wilberforce, the Company was outvoted. The new charter was granted in 1813 on condition that the ban on missionaries was lifted. A bishopric was created in Calcutta, and archdeacons appointed in Madras and Bombay. The gates were open. The demand for the Bengali Bible could not now be satisfied from Serampore, so another press was set up in Calcutta. A Hindostani (Devanagri) version was expected, the demand reported to be insatiable. The Baptist brotherhood had stationed the gospel in 20 towns. Indians, Christian, Hindu and Muslim alike, had access to the Word in 126 schools, and native-born missioners were under training in Serampore. The net was now to be drawn to the shore, yet the catch, as Sydney Smith complained, was meagre. Of one clerical fisherman, Meadows Taylor felt moved to ask in 1852: 'Would it answer any good purpose, in Italy, where there is much image-worship very like idolatry, to call Saint This a rogue? Or Saint That a thief or Saint t'other an impostor?'[77]

William Sleeman was impressed by the tolerance of Christianity on the part of simple Indians. But, as the Jesuit Father Gregory at Agra explained, they were puzzled by how much less wonderful Christian miracles were than those of their own scriptures. If they were told that St Paul had seen the sun and moon collide with the earth and bounce off, they would relate an even more extraordinary wonder observed by Krishna.[78]

Christianity now began aggressively to challenge the traditional religion and customs of India, exposing their often corrupted scriptures to textual criticism, and in the struggle for their souls it persuaded its auditors to borrow some of its clothes, its assumptions and its dynamic. In due course Hinduism began to recover its confidence and to make converts among the converters. The catalytic factor was not Carey's stream of translations, but his other passion, education and science. The quest of Jones and Wilkins for Sanskrit's literary pleasures had been expected to create a bridge to the suspicious and solipsistic Brahman pandits who, persuaded by their enthusiastic interest, would yield up their medical knowledge, submit their systems of divination and prediction to mathematical scrutiny and discuss their philosophical achievements in logic. They did not. Brahmans bought up manuscripts in the bazaars to prevent them from falling into European hands. They resented the efforts of Jones to verify Biblical truths with the assistance of evidence from Hindu scriptures, and suspected Wilkins of using their mathematical constructs to help map the land for revenue. They were contemptuous of efforts to use Hindu astronomical calculations either to refute or to support the creation of the world in 4004 BC.[79] They were disturbed by the use to which Europeans put their sacred texts and suspected that all this interest was to be used to convert them to Christianity, which fear the enthusiasm of Carey and his colleagues and the withering contempt of Grant and Buchanan only seemed to support.

The Christian missionaries believed that the tyranny of crafty and imperious Brahmans could only be broken by the acquisition of useful knowledge, in which was included sound Christian doctrine, which would liberate the mind and effect a moral revolution. By 1818 there were 10,000 young Indians at Baptist schools in and near Serampore alone and Carey, always on the look-out for ways of spreading the word, was sure that commerce was creating a demand for English which, if met, would add a thousand more every night. But they did not convert. Ever optimistic, Carey accepted that they were at least rising from the servile and idolatrous posture of their parents. The completion in 1815 of his *Dictionary of Bengali and English*, in three quarto volumes, unique in its time in the world for the industry and erudition of its author and its philological completeness, was as important an event as the harnessing of electricity. If the gospel was to convert, its servants must preach in the language of the market place. The appearance, even intrusion, of Christian scriptures in the vernacular, moreover, advertised the need for authoritative versions of the Hindu and Islamic scriptures in the same tongues. Just as the recovery of Greek had in the fourteenth and fifteenth centuries forced scholars in Europe back to the originals of works they had accepted in corrupt texts, so the treasures of Sanskrit in good Bengali translations enabled educated Indians to re-examine their classics. As Bengali became the medium for a new generation of Indians to assert their culture and to become as well educated as, if not better educated than, their masters, the real achievement of Carey was not the conversion but the educating of Bengal.

7. 'We Must Go to the Orient'

> We must go to the Orient. All great glory has always been acquired there.
>
> Napoleon Bonaparte

> There never was in the world a more singular spectacle than to see a few thousand Europeans governing so despotically fifty or sixty millions of people, of different climate, religion and habits – forming them into large and well-disciplined armies and leading them out to the further subjugation of the native powers of India.
>
> The Rev Sydney Smith, *Edinburgh Review*, 1810

> We are necessarily very much confined to our houses by the heat: all our wants and business, which could create a greater intercourse with the natives, is done for us, and we are, in fact, strangers in the land.
>
> Lord William Bentinck in Madras to the Governor in Council, Calcutta, 26 September 1807

THE PRIME MINISTER, WILLIAM PITT, was bored by India, and left the choice of Hastings's successor to one of Burke's hated Scotsmen, Henry Dundas, president of the Board of Control. His choice of a defeated general may seem strange to a generation that only rewards success, but the career of Charles Cornwallis showed only proved capacity. His surrender at Yorktown was the result of irresolution and incompetence on the part of his colleagues. Above all, he had no past to expiate in India. 'Here there was no broken fortune to be mended! Here was no avarice to be gratified! Here was no beggarly, mushroom kindred to be provided for! No crew of hungry followers, gaping to be gorged.'[1] Cornwallis accepted the position on 23 February 1786. He had already shown his reforming mettle in America, where he fought corrupt practices in army supplies, and was resolved to eradicate corruption from Company service once and for all. He had been assured that he could overrule his council if necessary so that he need never suffer like Hastings and, at £25,000 a year, his emoluments compared to those of the Lord Lieutenant of Ireland, and put him above temptation.[2]

The Company's civil service was condemned in his eyes, less by the high rewards its members had secured for themselves, than by its dependence on Indian subordinates. In his patrician way he convinced himself that 'the principles and practices of native Asiatic governments' had contaminated the civil service, and had even corrupted Hastings himself.[3] They had to be removed. Hastings, moreover, had had to accept civil servants wished on him by directors whose protégés hoped to make a quick fortune. Cornwallis would not. Too much of the revenue found its way into private pockets by way of presents and perquisites, if not from straightforward bribery. This had to stop. To his prim and tidy mind, caprice in the collection of revenue and miscarriages of justice were as lamentable as the employment of agents to carry out corrupt practices, fornication with native women, excessive drinking and gambling. They must be rooted out of the administration of British India.

The genius of the Mughal system had been for rule not commerce and, having surrendered the rule of Bengal to the British, the Mughal aristocracy witnessed helplessly the rise of a new urban class of bankers, discount brokers and banians, mostly Hindus, whose fortunes were identified with their new rulers. The shortage of cash after the British stopped importing silver, exacerbated by the famine and floods of the 1770s, led to the increased use of bills of exchange, and the shroffs believed the Company was more likely to meet its obligations than local princes.[4] The days of nabobry were over. The economic crisis meant that the revenue was inadequate to support the expense of government so that there should be no more presents or perquisites. Cornwallis's first priority was to increase one and reduce the other. Bred among the rolling acres of England, he believed that a happy and prosperous people was one led by landed aristocrats. They would provide both efficient husbandry of their estates, which would ensure the revenue, and the political stability in which commerce flourished, while government merely looked after external security and internal order. The key to this was a permanent tax settlement in Bengal. Its principal architect was John Shore, son of a Company supercargo, who had been to Harrow with Nathaniel Halhed before coming to India as a writer in 1769. What Shore proposed was to convert the zamindars into titled landowners, in imitation of the landed gentry who were the backbone of Britain. Cornwallis, as part of that backbone, concurred. Shore thought that the revenue settlement should be for ten years in the first instance. As a third of the Company's territory in Hindostan was still jungle, inhabited only by wild beasts, ten years were not enough to encourage the new proprietors to clear the jungle and inculcate profitable apiculture among their ryots. Cornwallis made the settlement permanent.

The future backbone of Bengal, however, was composed of anything but gentry. The zamindars had acquired their lands in various way, none of them on terms of permanence but, 'under Indian governments, Moslem or Hindu, anything that was enjoyed, whether office or possession, had a tendency to become hereditary'.[5] No one really knew what their titles or their lands were worth for, under the Mughals, zamindars had been tax farmers, and the ryots, from whom they collected tax, were not their tenants, but enjoyed the possession of their land under the sovereign. Cornwallis expected the zamindars to become a benevolent aristocracy, and made them proprietors of the soil in return for the payment of tax. The ryots were handed over to make what deals they could with their new landlords. The expense of the war against Mysore, the threat of war with the French, the needs of civil government, meant that the assessment was fixed high, to yield 286 lakhs of Company rupees each year.

The zamindars, secure in their absolute right to their property, which the courts in Bengal would uphold against even the Company itself, very rarely performed as expected. They did not make new pacts with their ryots, but either sold up – one tenth of the land in Bengal, Bihar and Orissa had changed hands by 1796 – or sought, not to nurture, but to ruin their tenants, so that they could install new ones at higher rents. The settlement destroyed the old Mughal zamindars, both Muslim and Hindu, and created a new class of landed proprietors as new owners of capital, accumulated under Company rule, bought up their estates. It did, as Cornwallis expected, bring more land in north Bengal and the delta under cultivation, but it did not result in better, more scientific and therefore more productive farming. The Bengal zamindars proved to have too much in common with the absentee or rack-renting landlords of Ireland. And the revenue did not pay off the debt. Without such a settlement, however, he told Dundas on 7 April 1793, India would have become 'the resort of all the most unprincipled ruffians of the British dominions'.[6]

Cornwallis instinctively distrusted the mélange of Hindu and Muslim law dispensed by junior Indian judges, because he was convinced that it had been corrupted by the requirements of oriental despotism. Justice should be delivered under a western-style code by British circuit judges in local tribunals of civil and criminal justice, with provision for appeal to provincial courts. The collector of revenue should no longer sit in judgement on boundary disputes or revenue assessments, or have responsibility for the police, which was instead vested in the magistrate. This recipe for disinterested justice seemed unexceptionable but, though it promised a juster verdict in the end, it deferred that end by imposing a rigmarole of procedures on litigants which may have been customary in English tribunals but were incomprehensible to Indians. As a result, a log-jam of cases grew so overwhelming that, in one district, there were so many undecided cases no pretender to justice could be satisfied in his lifetime. Justice had once been capricious, but it had been swift and cheap. Now it became dilatory, distant and dear, and the government, unable to create enough courts and magistrates, proposed to charge fees as a way of thinning the back-log.

If Pitt and Dundas, persuaded by Burke's theory that the Company was in effect 'a delegation of the whole power of sovereignty of this kingdom sent into the east', intended in 1784 to transfer it from the Company to the Crown, by 1793, with a war on their hands, they were sufficiently reassured by the reforms to leave things as they were.[7] Cornwallis left Bengal in 1793 a better governed place than he had found it, but it was not governed better by Indians. He fed his prejudice by replacing as many as he could by Europeans; as a result, there were not enough of them to conclude the land settlements. Though Dundas had emphasised that Britain's priority in the east was to 'maintain and preserve the empire, which she has acquired, in comparison with which, even Trade is a subordinate or collateral consideration', the directors had also instructed the governor-general to engage in no more adventures in India, no more conflicts with country powers.[8] He was to regularise the Company's untidy and open-ended commitments to Oudh and the Carnatic, but no more.

Cornwallis dutifully assured all parties that the Company would not interfere in disputes between Indian princes unless another European nation chose to meddle in them for its own advantage. He feared that the French were doing just that for, in May 1785, the new governor of Pondicherry wrote offering a defensive alliance with any prince who sought one. In fact, Paris had neither the will nor the resources for any conflict with Britain, but no one knew that in India. When Tipu, fearing a hostile coalition of Poona, Hyderabad and Madras, sent a mission to Paris in 1787, it secured nothing beyond vague promises of friendship. Speaking Tipu's ambassadors fair and allowing Pondicherry's governor to croak like a bullfrog served France's purposes well enough, since it confused Britain about her intentions, which were actually to withdraw from India altogether. While Tipu's obsessive hatred of the British ruled out any accommodation with the Company, the fear he inspired in his neighbours rendered another coalition against it improbable, and there was little temptation for France to commit men and money to a campaign there. When in 1790 Tipu appealed for direct military help in the war he had provoked with his neighbours, he was refused. Cornwallis personally supervised the campaign against him but, in 1792, obedient to instructions, after his allies had helped themselves to territory they considered theirs, he left a truncated Mysorean state intact and, in the hands of a ruler as implacable as Tipu, capable of further trouble.

Cornwallis was a man of impeccable probity and sober habits. 'I do not think,' he wrote, 'the greatest sap at Eton could lead a duller life.'[9] He was succeeded by John Shore, whose devotion to duty and Christianity both inhibited any change of life-style at the top. He fretted at the way the climate seemed to sap the religious devotion of even committed Christians and feared that indifference was a worse foe to good religion than sin. He boasted of 'every native of India, whatever his situation might be, as having a claim upon me, and that I have not a right to dedicate an hour to amusement further than it is conducive to health'.[10] The permanence of British dominion in India would only be secure if its rulers persevered in true principles. Extraordinary ability was not necessary, only sound judgement and hard work. That may have been a specific for permanence of what Shore left in 1798 when he departed for a barony, a seat on the Board of Control and the presidency of the British and Foreign Bible Society. His successor wanted to replace permanence by paramountcy.

Richard Wellesley, second earl of Mornington in the peerage of Ireland, from 1793 to 1797 a member of the Board of Control, was 37, the eldest of three brothers, each of whom was resolved to shine. Arthur had preceded him to India, arriving in Calcutta as brevet-colonel of the 33rd regiment of foot in 1796. There he had abandoned cards for a careful study of the management, especially of supplies, of Indian armies. Richard had originally been designated for Madras, but Cornwallis was needed in Ireland and, with Arthur's warm commendation, he accepted the greater post. He burned to make his own mark and be rewarded by an English peerage.[11] Like Napoleon, he believed that 'all great glory has always been acquired' in the east.[12] He took his youngest brother, Henry, as secretary. The choice of a Pittite from the Anglo-Irish ascendancy, whose acquaintance with trade extended little beyond dealing with his tailor, was a bold step, and it was assumed that Mornington came with an agenda devised, in conclave with Dundas, to transform the trading company into a sovereign power and achieve what Pitt and Dundas had agreed was necessary in 1784. There is no evidence for this. The addition of 40 million people to British India and £10,000,000 to its revenue was not planned. The new governor-general was sent out to protect British interests from the Franco-Dutch, for which the directors in 1800 revived Sir John Child's title of Captain-General and Commander-in-chief of all forces in the East Indies.

Like Napoleon, Wellesley was short of stature, known to his acolytes as 'the glorious little man', but his stature was all that was small about him. He had energy and brilliance and the self-importance of Toad of Toad Hall. His despatches wearied all who read them, including Dundas. He was determined that India should be 'ruled from a palace not a counting house; with the ideas of a prince, not with those of a retail trader in muslins and indigo'.[13] The governor-general, William Hickey remarked sardonically, 'was in no way sparing of the Company's cash. His Lordship's own establishment of servants, equipages etc were extraordinary in the superlative degree, not only in point of numbers but splendour of dress, the whole being put to the account of the chaste managers of Leadenhall Street'.[14] He had the government house and 16 other recently constructed dwellings torn down to make room for a majestic Palladian palace set in a broad park, faced on the south by a colonnade and massive pediment and on the north by a false dome. It rose like an exhalation in three years, at a cost of 15 lakhs of rupees, not one of which was sanctioned by the directors. The public rooms were the finest the much travelled Maria Graham had ever seen. Great Doric columns of chunam lined the floor of dark grey marble, between which were placed the busts of 12 Roman Caesars. Upstairs Ionic pillars ran the length of the polished wooden dance-floor, lit by crystal lustres. For a few years, before being eaten by white ants, the ceiling was 'adorned with gods in many a string/in imitation of basso-relievo-ing', while at the south end on a raised dais was installed, in 1799, Tipu Sultan's throne of crimson and gold from Seringapatam.[15]

Wellesley would have built something as large at his river retreat at Barrackpore but he left before the second storey was started. Its extensive park housed a menagerie and aviary stocked with beasts and birds collected from all quarters of the globe, and the governor-general and his court would be rowed there, like a doge (which he may well have fancied he was), in a state barge painted green and gold, its watermen clad in scarlet. Chowringhee became a town of palaces, and he would have laid out the entire embankment from Fort William to Barrackpore had he been given time. To preserve its elegance, elephants were banned from the city because they frightened the horses.[16] Wellesley had only a limited understanding of economics, paying ritual tribute to free trade – which meant wresting it from rivals so that London 'was the throne of commerce in the world'.[17] The busts of the Caesars in his state-room reflected his collection of obedient allies, like the tributary princes to Rome. If their sovereign were to be a mercantile company so be it, but it should behave like a mercantile republic, like Venice or Genoa, and the governor-general should rule more like the Lord Lieutenant of Ireland than the president of a council. He did not think it important to square his concept of grandeur with that entertained in Leadenhall Street.

In that spirit he packed his private office with able civil servants, a nursery of talent to draft the interminable flow of despatches, letters and instructions.

Disgusted to find that young writers still arrived deficient in both education and languages, he founded his own 'university' college of Fort William where the cubs from Britain would be trained to become the lions who must rule India. It would inculcate 'habits of activity, regularity and decency... instead of those of sloth, indolence, low debauchery and vulgarity', which they would otherwise be tempted to acquire among the coarse indulgence of Calcutta society.[18] Britain in India needed a new class of administrators, aloof from the corruption of commerce, promoted on merit not on birth or influence, skilled, not only in tongues, but in diplomacy, a breed of superior mortals who must keep the Company's subsidiary allies in line, solvent, safe, harmless and obedient. Without them Cornwallis's reformed system would be undone, 'in the insufficiency of the instrument employed to administer its benefits to the native subjects of the British government in India'.[19]

Dundas viewed the venture with a jaundiced eye, fearing that the 'collection of literary and philosophic men... would resolve itself into a school of Jacobinism instead of a seminary of education'.[20] Wellesley, moreover, was beginning to show signs of insatiable ambition; the Company was assuming the character of a military despotism, wishing onto Indian princes alliances for which they paid, like a second Bussy or Clive. Oudh was crippled by the payment of troops it had agreed to support and the Carnatic was in hock to Company servants who milked their assignments to recover their loans. The extension of this benevolent arrangement was Wellesley's answer to the French threat. From 1789 to 1805, the British army in India became one of the largest standing armies in the world. In four years, according to Dundas, the number of European and native troops rose from 80,000 to 142,000, and the Europeans alone cost £500,000 a year.[21] The Bengal army was recruited from the traditional Mughal recruiting ground of eastern Oudh, mainly Brahmans and Rajputs. Regularly paid, well-disciplined and better trained than their enemies, in their red jackets behind their European officers, they were half way to victory before they fired a shot, 'like an immovable volcano spewing artillery and rifle fire like unrelenting hail on the enemy, and they are seldom defeated'.[22] European troops on the other hand were largely recruited by crimps in Britain at £5 a head, the 'refuse of our metropolis', a 'regiment of dwarfs' when compared to a battalion of sepoys.[23] Despite this, their presence as stiffening had always been considered essential. The sepoys being strict Hindus and Muslims, their caste and religious exclusions were carefully catered for, so that the expense of a native army was as much in its commissary as in its fighting men. To defeat the Marathas, the Company created a cavalry arm, supplying its troopers with superior steeds bred from European and South African mares. Arthur Wellesley had mastered the bullock supply system which had given the Mysoreans and the Marathas their fighting edge. The more country rulers improved their armies by recruiting European officers and gunners (usually French) and purchasing modern weapons, the more urgent it became to bind them into alliance before they could threaten British supremacy. Wellesley wished to fill the civil department with soldiers, owing to the 'scandalous ignorance and stupidity of the old civil servants... added to the scandalous corruption and idleness of the junior servants'.[24] He wanted to post them as residents and agents to Indian princes, to map the country as they travelled with the court and send back intelligence.

Wellesley landed in Calcutta, on 17 May 1798, two days before Napoleon left Toulon for an unknown destination. His briefing had told him Tipu Sultan still had the means to re-create an army even stronger than before, officered by French volunteers, that both the nizam and Scindia had large 'French armies' commanded by competent French generals, and that if none alone was a match for the Company, two with French support could be a threat and three, an unlikely combination, could be overwhelming. He decided, without communicating with his directors, that the elimination of these 'French armies' was his first priority. The nizam's French-led fighting force had distinguished itself against Tipu in 1790–2 and the Marathas in 1795. Its 'brave, magnificent, generous, affable and vigilant' General Raymond had been in correspondence with Pondicherry, and the lands he had been assigned on the Malabar coast happened to be the nearest landing point to the French base at Île de France.[25] He obligingly died in March, whereupon the nizam was persuaded, by a promise of protection, to disband his army on 22 October, without a shot being fired.

A French privateer captain, meanwhile, masquerading as a French envoy, had persuaded Tipu that a French expedition was already at Île de France. His supposed orders were to revolutionise the French troops in the Mysorean army and he soon had the French in Seringapatam dancing round trees of liberty in Phrygian caps. The arrival of a motley band of less than 200 scratch volunteers from Île de France, therefore, was for Wellesley 'a public, unqualified and unambiguous act of war'.[26] On 18 October he learned that Napoleon was in Egypt. Cairo to Delhi was no further than from Paris to Moscow and 60,000 men, on 50,000 camels and 10,000 horses, could, in theory, be at the Indus in four months, there to join Sikhs, Marathas, Tipu and the toothless Great Mughal, in a lethal coalition. He almost certainly did not believe it possible, but he acted as if he did.[27]

The governor-general knew that Tipu's removal would protect him from criticism at home. In 1794 John Murray had published the evidence of his atrocities: the 'Mahommedanisation' of young captives by compulsory circumcision, the poisoning of stubborn officers who would not turn renegade, the withholding of simple medical treatment from the wounded, forced labour and hideous beatings, the rumoured enslavement and prostitution of European women, the attempted subornment of honourable men by renegades who had accepted Islam and service with the enemy, put him beyond the pale.[28] A beleaguered Treasury released £500,000 and 5000 troops to destroy any possible French base in Mysore. When Tipu would not disband his 'French army', the governor-general launched the final war that left him hacked to death at the gates of Seringapatam. Tipu's end was immediately broadcast in the Red Sea and Gulf, so that the French would know that it was no longer feasible for even Bonaparte's 'innumerable and invincible army… to free [him] from the iron yoke of England'.[29]

On St Helena Napoleon convinced himself that he had a plan to invade India but, if he had, it was all in his head. The master of Egypt could, in time, have become master of India, but Napoleon had shorter-term objectives. What had begun as an adventure to secure control of the Levant was now an instrument to break the second coalition which had brought Turkey and Russia into the lists against France. For Napoleon never took his eyes off Europe. It is doubtful that he ever believed he had the resources to get as far, even, as Île de France, but Wellesley behaved as if he had and used this fear to subjugate all three major powers in India. Tipu's overthrow had happened more quickly than anyone had dared to expect. From the ruins of Seringapatam emerged, not only the 'man-tiger organ, prettiest of [Tipu's] toys', the ghastly model of a tiger in the act of mauling a European soldier which could be made to roar by the action of a handle, but also incriminating correspondence with almost every prince in India.[30] The nawab of the Carnatic paid for his part in it by the annexation of his prince-dom. Scindia with an impressive 'French army' still in existence became the next target. Scindia's general, Pierre Perron, had, under de Boigne, shown the sort of enterprise and dash that made marshals out of an innkeeper's son like Murat and a cooper's child like Ney. He gave teeth to the power and ambition of the only Maratha prince who could restore to the Maratha Confederacy some of its earlier *terribiltà*, and reassert the 'Brahman Raj'. Frightening but baseless rumours were rife that de Boigne was the 'close confidante of Bonaparte, ... constantly at St Cloud',[31] and that Perron himself had received a message to the emperor in Delhi that, the following year, Napoleon might be ready to march into India.[32]

Mahadji Scindia had died in 1794 and his adopted son, the 14-year-old Daulatrao, had only his horoscope to recommend him. Ten years later he had not yet become the 'disgraceful liar, living with buffoons and parasites, ... a babbling drunkard equally despised by his enemies or his pretended friends', but the seeds were already there.[33] In 1795, the young peshwa died in mysterious circumstances and was succeeded after a long gap by Raghunathrao's first-born son, the feckless, treacherous and ambitious Bajirao II, in whom none of the qualities of the first peshwa of that name could be found. To add to the disarray in the Confederacy, the head of the great house of Holkar died in August 1797, his inheritance passing to his youngest, and illegitimate, son, Jaswantrao, who burned to avenge the wrongs Scindia had done to his father's house. From 1799 to 1802 he led his tattered armies into Scindia territory and his military success made him the new paladin of the Brahman Raj.

Bajirao, confident of the support of Scindia and his 'French army', refused Wellesley's offer of a subsidiary alliance, until Jaswantrao drove him from Poona. On 16 December he signed the subsidiary treaty he had so far resisted, and protected by 6000 British troops, paid for by the cession of land worth 26 lakhs of rupees a year, he became a British dependent. Holkar was stunned. 'Bajirao has destroyed the Maratha state. The British will now deal the same blow to it that they did to Tipu Sultan.'[34] He was right. The Company had 60,000 men under arms, the largest force it had ever put into the field at once. Scindia could have saved himself if he had rid himself of Perron and resumed his office with the emperor in Delhi, but he knew that as soon as he did so he had lost all power in Poona, where his intrigues soon brought him again into conflict with the Company. He faced Arthur Wellesley on territory and at a season which favoured the British. In four months from August 1803 the future Duke of Wellington had cleared Maratha lands of Scindia's troops, assisted by Scindia's inability to pay his men. By 3 September, the French officers who commanded brigades, 45,000-strong, at Agra and Aligarh, had surrendered to General Lake, and Perron

98

was on his way to France with £280,000-worth of Company stock, countless diamonds and two copper-skinned children. On 14 September, the British flag flew from the Red Fort in Delhi and the blind, frightened Shah Alam II was once again a pensioner of the Company.

On 23 September Arthur Wellesley defeated Scindia's southern force at Assaye and again on 29 November at Argaon. Both were damned close-run things, for the Marathas, man for man, were as good as his own troops and their artillery better. He was saved by his resolve to attack and the inexplicable absence from the field of the Maratha command. On 1 November Lake surprised Scindia's camp at Laswari, 20 miles south of Bharatpur, and destroyed the last of his French-trained army. It was also a bloody encounter and, had the Marathas been commanded by their French officers, Lake might have recoiled with heavy loss. Though the defeat was heroic it was final. Scindia was broken, and his father's work in the north was dissolved. Daulatrao was a ward of the Company and the virtual sovereign at his court was the Company's resident, John Malcolm. Holkar, alone, was still untamed.

To his banner flocked the flotsam of Scindia's defeated army and the jetsam of deserters and freebooters turned off by other subdued princes. 'His empire... was the empire of the saddle, ... bold, lawless and unscrupulous.'[35] He commanded 60,000 horsemen and an impressive park of artillery serviced by what was left of Perron's veterans and defied the Company to restore the annexed lands that had once been Holkar's. Otherwise, he would 'overrun, plunder and burn countries of many hundred *koss*, and calamities will fall on lakhs of human beings... by the attacks of my army which will overwhelm like the waves of the sea.'[36] 'I was never so plagued as I am with this devil,' grumbled Lake. 'We are obliged to remain in the field at enormous cost.'[37] Holkar moved so fast that no one knew where he would strike next, but Lake was inexorable and, fly away as he might, Jaswantrao's plumage was increasingly tattered. No Maratha prince rose to help him and, in December 1805, he submitted to the British. He kept his hereditary principality, where he died in 1811, only 30 years old, driven insane by chagrin, drink and summer heat, through which he worked night and day making guns, the only weapon, he now realised too late, with which the British could be beaten.

In 1804, when Napoleon should have been setting off overland for India, he was considering the invasion of England, and in 1805, the Courts of Proprietors and Directors, satisfied that any French threat to India was over, recalled Wellesley with relief. He had infuriated them by his lordly disdain, excessive public expenditure and a reckless forward policy, financed by bullion that had been sent out to fund the investment. Brilliant gazettes from India could not justify any diversion from the deadly war with France in Europe. He may have reduced Hyderabad to vassalage and the Marathas to sullen neutrality, but as a result there were no profits to be expected from India. Castlereagh, president since 1802 of the Board of Control, had supported his policy but wished it could have been accompanied by less boastful and demanding despatches. Nothing, he told Pitt, 'can have been more unpleasant than the tone in which the despatches have been written on both sides'.[38] It was the annexation of large slices of Oudh and the Carnatic which stretched Castlereagh's tolerance too far. Oudh had been a loyal ally since the reign of Asaf-ud-daula and had paid its subsidies readily. They were high and much of the misgovernment, of which the governor-general complained, was due to the harshness with which the collectors were forced to raise it. A disputed succession, which gave Wellesley his excuse for annexing the best land of the nawabi, did not justify such arbitrary action. The Carnatic was a hopeless quagmire of debt for which the Company was now responsible. The governor-general may have been a man of destiny but his conquests had made the government of India so 'complicated and unwieldy' that it could be 'enfeebled and embarrassed in ordinary hands'.[39] Only the China trade paid the dividend. His peremptory recall was spiced with orders for the suppression of Fort William College. No more Wellesley nurseries, no more inflated despatches, no more adventures. Stout, tried and careful Cornwallis was to return to India, reverse the policy and restore the Company to profit. Immediately, he began 'a systematic demolition of all [Wellesley's] plans of policy', until his sudden death shortly after arrival.[40]

Arthur Wellesley also left India in 1805, a major-general and Companion of the Bath, with a fortune of £30,000. The battle of Waterloo may have been won on the playing fields of Eton, but the generalship was learned on the killing fields of Assaye and Argaon. Later, as a politician, he made India's defence a cardinal component of Britain's world strategy. Between them Richard and Arthur provided the ideological foundation for British paramountcy in India, erected on the tripod of British power, morality and the superiority of the British race. 'The bog-Irish Wellesleys used India to take a giant stride from the furthest fringe of the British oligarchy to the centre', and India went with them.[41]

Fear of the French had started the British on the path of conquest, which imposed on princes subsidiary alliances that bound them to the Company, and it postponed the final pacification of the Marathas until 1818. At the end of the Napoleonic war that fear was replaced by another: of an epidemic of banditry conducted by footloose soldiers no longer able to follow their princes into plunder. At their core were the Afghan and Pathan auxiliaries of Maratha armies who had customarily pillaged after battle, and the most formidable had served under Scindia and Holkar. Their bands observed no frontiers, raiding indiscriminately between the Narbada and Kistna rivers, and disposed of their booty at special fairs. In 1816 they wasted villages within 40 miles of Madras itself and carried their havoc into the lands round Hyderabad and Poona. Though they were feared and detested by landlord and peasant alike, some Maratha chiefs welcomed them as an instrument with which to flagellate their enemies and used them to raid their own subjects for money they could not raise by taxation.[42] The *pindari* menace was only over by March 1818, when the last leader was driven into the jungle where he was mauled to death by a tiger, and the peshwa, who had in desperation made common cause with them, was on his way to exile near Kanpur.

Lord Hastings (governor-general 1813–21) was now assailed by the directors for once again extending British territory in India. The conquered territories must be returned to a safe and obedient independence. In Maratha lands, the princes should not be pushed beyond the limits of their pride. One flame, warned John Malcolm, could light a forest fire 'and our whole empire tumble down like house of cards. It is a bad plan to swallow so many states, we have increased the sources of discord which it is our object to remove'.[43] Just as, once Tipu was dead, Mysore had been returned to its rightful Hindu rajah, so the house of Shivaji was brought out of its obscurity and restored to the titular sovereignty of the Marathas it had never legally lost. The Confederacy was divided into four divisions governed by commissioners. The princes kept their fiefdoms, armies and royal rank under the watchful eye of a resident or agent. Within 60 years of Plassey the Company had become the heir to Aurangzeb, having accomplished what he never accomplished – the subjugation of all India from the Himalayas to Cape Comorin.

'That a small western power should come to India from a distance of thousands of miles and subjugate this vast continent full of martial races and illimitable resources is an astounding phenomenon in human history.'[44] It was to be the stuff of the imperial legend, the British Alexandriad, and it does not diminish it to say that it was rendered possible by the endemic weakness of its opponents. They were, first, states only in name, not nations. Haidar Ali and Tipu Sultan were Muslim usurpers and the central state they forged depended on the naked use of power and on their survival. The Maratha state was at best a confederation of fiercely independent chieftains in loose allegiance to a dynastic head. They were the unrivalled masters of the art of mobile war and, though Scindia had a 'French army', it was always an implant not a feature of the 'empire of the saddle'. Since the death of Madhavrao I the dynasty of peshwas had produced only mediocrity and, as Arthur Wellesley remarked, 'there is not a Maharatta in the whole country, from the Peshwa down to the lowest horseman, who has a shilling'.[45] The richest and most powerful warlord, Mahadji Scindia, pursued his personal ambitions, with the Company's connivance, north of the Narbada. Bajirao II, Daulatrao Scindia and Jaswantrao Holkar were fated to challenge a unified power, directed by masterful men, who knew what it wanted. The object of Maratha policy was always shifting and 'the peshwa', Arthur told Richard Wellesley, 'is everything himself, and everything is little'.[46]

The defence of India had become a cornerstone of global British policy. India, after the loss of the North American colonies, gave her the extra-territorial weight in the power struggles at Vienna. Her national economy was roughly comparable to those of both France and Russia but with her Indian empire it was two and a half times larger than that of France and twice that of Russia.[47] Throughout the nineteenth century, particularly after 1840, that economy was set to grow in size, driven by the world-power imperatives of a small, rapidly industrialising nation, challenged by rivals in Europe. These developments were both to hasten India's unification and to retard her independence.

In 1783 'British India' comprised Bengal, Bihar, the Benares and Ghazipur districts of Oudh, part of Orissa and Chittagong, all ruled from Calcutta. Bombay controlled the island of Salsette and a 200-mile stretch of the Malabar coast north of Cochin. Madras governed strips of territory round Fort St George and the Northern Circars, north of Masulipatam, between the deltas of the Godavari and Mahanadi rivers, still technically on lease from the nizam. Hyderabad, Oudh and the Carnatic were tied to the apron strings of the Company by alliances. By 1818, despite the consistent assertion by the directors that the Company was a trading body only, with no territorial ambitions outside Bengal, it ruled all India along the great river systems from Chittagong to Delhi, which was now a protectorate, the emperor a helpless pensioner. It controlled the cotton manufactories of Gujerat and the pepper lands of Malabar. Madras had annexed the Carnatic, Tanjore and the Circars as far as Orissa, giving the Company control of the coastline of the Bay of Bengal. Mysore had been cut down to a petty principality, while the Maratha states in the Deccan were dependencies. The nawab-wazir, the nizam and the great princely houses of the Marathas, Satara, Scindia, Holkar, Baroda and Berar still preserved nominal independence over patrimonial lands, as did the Rajput princes, but all had surrendered territory to pay for the armies that now both protected and controlled them.

Successive governors-general had been admonished to limit expansion and reduce debt. Wellesley in return had asserted that if the directors could leave him 'unfettered by positive orders and undisturbed by ignorant, crude and hasty schemes of commerce and finance, formed without local knowledge on circumstantial detail, I entertain no doubt of bringing these revenues and expenses to a satisfactory proportion'.[48] Dundas, in despair, could only hope that 'nothing new is to be attempted without weighing well every rupee it will cost'.[49] It was a vain hope, and it was only in the government-generalcy of Lord William Bentinck (1828–35) that no territory was added to 'British India'. Between 1814 and 1823, the debt rose to £20 million, but it always seemed cheaper to occupy turbulent marcher country than to have unstable frontiers demanding constant surveillance. Even so, the Company never felt entirely secure, and over the next 30 years it continued to push its frontiers outwards, first into the foothills of the Himalayas, then into Burma, Sind and the Sikh lands of the Panjab, up to the mountain passes into Afghanistan and beyond. The driving motive was neither a lust for territorial expansion nor a passion for total security. The British government did not like spending money on India. The empire was expected to pay its way and make a surplus, and constant expansion brought new land into the revenue assessment. Wellesley spent the surplus raised by Cornwallis on his wars, and his successors fought a losing battle to keep expenditure below income. Revenue so often came in below estimate, and the battered state of so many of the new territories meant that revenue had to be set below valuation.

The system that the Wellesley brothers had imposed on India was intended to be the antithesis to that under which they had been brought up in Ireland, where an Anglo-Irish minority lived in quaking fear of its tenants. India was to be ruled by an exertion of physical power over a society whose religion, traditions, and customs the British had no intention of disturbing, in a land which it did not intend to colonise. As long as this power was never seen to retreat or condescend, it was safe. The Duke of Wellington, who had seen at first hand the power of nascent nationalism in Spain, feared only unrest in the Indian army. As a member of Liverpool's post-war government he favoured the creation of a buffer-zone of neutral Islamic states on the north-west frontier to limit the growing interest of Russia in the area. Turbulence there could only destabilise India's Muslim troops and lead to civil unrest, frontier wars, and attempts by subsidiary allies to recover their independence, all of which would put the power, not to speak of the income, of British India at risk. Indians were not invited to share that power, only feel it.

When, in 1812, the King of Sardinia claimed that the British considered him 'and all the rulers of Mediterranean islands as mere Indians and nabobs', he shrewdly understood that Britain had learned something from her conquest of India.[50] Subsidiary and unequal alliances, not dissimilar to those that bound Oudh and the Carnatic, were imposed on Portugal, secured by a British officered army paid for by her monarch, and on Brazil and The Two Sicilies, reinforced at Rio de Janeiro and at Palermo by squadrons of the Royal Navy. When Wellington thought that the Shah of Persia was behaving no better than the peshwa, the policy was exported to the Gulf. Yet, in India, there was no confidence that British rule was permanent. Twenty-two years after the Vellore mutiny, Charles Metcalf, resident in Delhi, warned the newly arrived governor-general that 'a very little mismanagement will cause our rapid expulsion', and in 1834 Macaulay nervously believed that 'a serious check in one part of India would raise half the country against us'.[51]

There were good reasons for this anxiety. The army that had reduced the principalities of the Deccan was a mercenary army, and mercenaries needed both booty and bounty. The European population in 1830 was estimated at 36,409 military officers and men, 3,550 Company servants and 2149 others, a drop in an ocean of potentially hostile people.[52] In the fear that familiarity would breed contempt, Company servants held themselves aloof, 'untouchables', in the fear that physical contact would only reduce the awe in which European demi-gods were held. The 'englishing' of government had been intended to reduce its size and expense but also to alienate it from the governed, while the zamindari class, between governors and taxpayers, distanced the conqueror from the soil. That the Cornwallis system did not spread throughout British India was largely due to those Company servants whose eyes were not fixed on the glebe lands and town houses of retirement. They spoke the local languages more often than they spoke English, and were as likely to read Hafiz and Saadi in camp as Horace and Anacreon.[53] They were as familiar with the saddle as any Maratha warrior, riding, hunting and fighting as fiercely, with the effortless superiority of those who had looked on nature and discerned themselves. For them, the challenge of conquest was slight in comparison with that of ruling the vanquished. They were the epigoni of Byron's tormented spirit, seeking fulfilment in action, privileged denizens of a society that was crumbling round them, and willing to shoulder the heroic futility of wrestling with uncompassionate nature and wilful man to improve it. Three of them were Scotsmen.

John Malcolm, born in 1769, was put up for a cadetship when he was 12 and, when asked what he would do if he met Haidar Ali, replied without hesitation: 'Why, cut off his head'. No one in India could resist 'Boy' Malcolm; always in scrapes, usually in debt, proud, penniless and always hungry. He was a fine horseman and a good shot, and so good-natured that he was never at a loss for a horse or a gun. He soon shook off a reputation as a careless, good-humoured, illiterate fellow and in 1801 joined Wellesley's cabinet as secretary and became 'the greatest man in Calcutta'. He then joined Arthur Wellesley's staff in Mysore and supervised the demilitarisation of the Maratha armies. As political agent in Malwa from 1817 to 1821 he was the most powerful man in central India, always accessible, conciliatory but firm. Bishop Heber, travelling through Rajput territory in 1825, heard nothing but praise of him. Whereas hardly a day passed in Rajputana without troops being called out to keep the peace, 'not a musket has since [Malcolm's time] been fired there except against professed and public robbers'. From a mere wilderness, 'it is now, I am told, a garden'.[54] His transparent good faith and honesty earned him the trust of Indians, friends and foes alike, so that his pacification of the central Maratha states was to endure. His natural conservatism prompted him to leave all social institutions undisturbed, with their own people in charge, so that his practice was in stark contrast to that of Cornwallis

A fellow Scot, Thomas Munro, the son of a Glaswegian merchant, two years older than Malcolm, had also preferred swimming, boxing and hunting to learning, and at the age of 19 joined the Company's marine. Once at Madras he transferred as a military cadet, fought in all Eyre Coote's major actions, and was on the personal staff of Cornwallis in the 1792 campaign against Tipu. Malcolm and he were both on the Mysore commission, after which Munro was sent to put down brigandage on the western coast. His enduring achievement, however, was to settle the land revenue system in the southern districts ceded by the nizam to pay for the Company troops that now protected him. He worked on it for eight years, perfecting a system that Haidar and Tipu had successfully operated, under which not a zamindar but a village headman was responsible for delivering the taxes levied on the landed peasants (ryots) of the village. A system very like it had regenerated the southern highlands of Scotland after the 1745 rebellion, and the Ceded Districts were larger than all Scotland, with a population of some two million souls.

Munro observed that the zamindari system, so beloved of Cornwallis, had reduced many ancient families 'from a state of influence and respectability to heavy distress, beggary and ruin',[55] principally because the assessment had been fixed too high. He believed that a thorough assessment of the value of land was the key to good government. Revenue would be regular, its levy would be fair, destitution could be avoided, crime would be reduced and prosperity shared. It could only be done by Indian civil servants, in which again he flew in the face of Cornwallis's policy. During the survey and the assessments, the village headman (*patel*), the village elders and the farmer would be present, disagreements would be settled on the spot and the final levy, based partly on past performance under native rulers and partly on the judgement of government assessors, would usually be set a few percentage points lower for realism. A key feature of the Munro system was that collector and magistrate were one, not two separate offices, as in Cornwallis's Bengal. His arbitration and judgement had the force of law, and disaffected farmers were not forced to have access to courts they could not afford and whose procedures they could not understand. Its success was demonstrated when, over his eight years in the Ceded Districts, Munro saw taxes reduced from a half to a third of the gross produce and revenue increased from ten to 18 lakhs of star pagodas. The Bengal system, on the other hand, was hurrying 'great Provinces off their hands as if they were private estates long before they can form any judgements of what they are worth'.[56] Better to preserve the village-based yeoman farmer, fix the rent of his fields and allow an annual agreement on how much land was to be cultivated each year. In this way the ryots were encouraged to practice good husbandry, while tenants on the zamindari estates tended to over-farm their fields to meet their landlord's demands. Under the Munro system collectors got to know the people, whose problems they had to understand when making the annual agreement. Better that land should 'be in the hands of forty or fifty thousand small proprietors than four or five hundred great ones'.[57] Munro and his colleagues believed that the governed had a right to be ruled by systems they understood and by people to whom they could appeal. By 1814, Munro's system prevailed as the general model for conquered districts. Though the demand for revenue continued to rise and assessments remained burdensome, Indian agriculture was able to bear both and still improve.

Mountstuart Elphinstone was the third in the trinity of Scots. Born in 1770 he was, unlike the others, an aristocrat, son of the governor of Edinburgh Castle. He was sent in a civilian capacity to Poona, served with Arthur Wellesley against Scindia, and went on a mission to the Amir of Afghanistan in 1809, his record of which was a generous and understanding account of the chieftains and people in a land popularly held to be a wilderness of savagery. Back at Poona as resident, during the last years of Bajirao's peshwaship, he was charged, after his deposition, with the political settlement. Impressed by Munro's settlement, he proceeded to introduce it into the new territories managed from Bombay.

Malcolm was a meteor, but Munro and Elphinstone were to fix British rule over most of the Indian cone outside Bengal. None of them was highly educated, but their delight in the memory of Scottish rural life predisposed them to find India as romantic and as beautiful, more colourful and diverse, but equally dependent on the labour and skill of the farmer and artisan. Indians might be inferior to Europeans in technical ability and political maturity, but they would have agreed with one of their disciples that 'if a good system of agriculture, if unrivalled manufactures, if the establishment of schools for reading and writing, if the general practice of kindness and hospitality, and if, above all, a scrupulous respect and delicacy towards the female sex are among the parts that denote a civilised people, then the Hindus are not inferior in civilisation than the people of Europe'.[58] If civilisation was to become an article of trade, Munro was 'convinced that this country [Britain] will gain by the import cargo'.[59] If the British could provide peace, protection of property, freedom from arbitrary arrest and an equitable revenue system, Indians could do the rest. If they were not yet fitted to manage their own affairs, it was because of recurrent defeats and conquests. It might take a century – 'I have no faith,' he wrote in 1821, 'in the modern doctrine of the rapid improvement of the Hindoos'[60] – but they should now be encouraged to take charge of their own affairs until, in the fullness of time, Britain could withdraw from an enlightened and independent India. Advancement in moral and intellectual stamina would certainly come from the adoption of ideas and practices of the west, but in their own time. 'I doubt if anyone can tell me what was good for the Mahrattas', Elphinstone might grumble, but the happiness of Indians was their immediate concern.[61] Liberty could come later. In due course the British would leave India. 'Better to have an early separation from a civilised people,' thought Elphinstone 'than a violent rupture with a barbarous nation.'[62] In that sense they were all paternalists. For all their sympathy with the Indian conquered and their hope that British rule would be accepted as preferable to what they had experienced before, both Malcolm and Munro knew that British power rested not on popularity but on power. The army tended to be cantoned where revenue collection was most likely to cause unrest.[63]

Munro died of cholera in 1827. Elphinstone retired from Bombay the same year, his hopes of being governor-general come to nothing. The post was too important to be denied to an aristocrat from the political establishment, for it was almost the greatest gift in the hands of government. As he was brutally informed: 'when the highways are broke up and the waters are out you may be sought for, but when all is smooth and clear any muffer who can collect the tolls will serve'.[64] Malcolm followed in 1830. Both wrote their India books, Malcolm *A Sketch of the Political History of India since 1784*, the second part of which appeared in 1826, and *A Memoir of Central India*, published in 1811, Elphinstone *A History of the Rise of British India*, in 1841, all recommended by Wellington to his sons to read. Both wished to give another view of India from that which had appeared in 1817, and which, in the words of Horace Hayman Wilson, then secretary of the Asiatick Society of Bengal, was little short of evil. The offending work was *The History of British India*, in seven volumes, written by yet another Scotsman, the father of John Stuart Mill, born the son of a shoemaker in 1773. James Mill, like so many Scots of his class, received a superior education and emerged from the university of Edinburgh a sound Greek scholar. He started his Indian history in 1806. In 1808 he met Jeremy Bentham and, from that moment, he was consumed by a second ambition – to promote the ideas of the great man. He only completed his history 11 years later.

He never set foot in India, nor learned a word of any Indian language. Had Tacitus visited Germania? Had his fellow countryman, William Robertson, any German before he wrote his *History of Charles V*? Mill used the best authorities, honed them on his knowledge of Greek civilisation and judged them against the template of Benthamite utilitarianism. 'Exactly in proportion as its ingenuity is wasted on contemptible or mischievous objects… the nation may safely be denominated barbarous.'[65] India did badly on every count. Her legends 'present a maze of unnatural fictions, in which a series of real events can by no artifice be traced'.[66] A single caste had, by imposing a set of meaningless rituals on the faithful, made themselves 'the uncontrollable masters of human life'.[67] 'An ignorant and fantastical age deems it a glory to render [its philosophy] in the highest degree perplexing and difficult.'[68] 'Volumes would hardly be sufficient to depict at large a ritual which is more tedious, minute and burdensome, … than any which has been found to fetter and oppress any other portion of the human race.'[69] The great mistake the British had made was to believe that the Hindus were a people of high civilisation, while in reality they had only completed a few steps along the road. Priestcraft and superstition, between them, had rendered them, in mind and body, the most enslaved portion of the human race.[70]

These nuggets of wisdom are only rare gleams in a relentless stream of prose, 'his Latinate sentences even clog[ging] the wheels of armies'.[71] His thesis, however, was clear. Only the provision of firm government could lead the natives out of a swamp of superstition into the modern age and only useful knowledge would civilise them. His villain was Sir William Jones, whose view of India as an ancient and worthy civilisation led to such frivolity as believing that the British were merely guests in a culture infinitely rich in things of the mind. Colebrook may have tried to prove that civilisation had its origin in Asia but, in truth, the institutions and achievements of the Hindu had been stationary for centuries and, 'in beholding the Hindu of the present day, we are beholding the Hindus of many ages past'.[72] The appearance of this opinionated work marked the appointment of its author to a key department of the Company and in 11 years he had risen to be its head. As Examiner of Indian Correspondence, Mill drafted the papers that the directors sent to the governor-general in council. He was thus in a prime position to influence policy for, though some of the directors knew India at first hand, they were seldom more than three or four out of 24 and few, if any, had the intellectual equipment to stand up to Mill. And here was a great continent, an open palimpsest upon which to write the doctrines of his master, Jeremy Bentham. The virus of utilitarianism entered the Indian body politic through the ink of Leadenhall Street. Horace Wilson may have feared for the minds of young men, sent to India inspired with 'an unfounded aversion towards those over whom they exercise their power',[73] but Mill was in tune with the movement of reform that was to change not only the constitutional, but social life of Britain. Bentham was the new stagirite and Mr Gradgrind his pupil. Mill's *History* encouraged the young men, for whom Wilson feared, with a similar desire to reform India, to bring her quickly into the modern age so that she could share the benefits of progress.[74]

8. 'OUR EMPIRE SEEMS DESTINED TO BE SHORT-LIVED'

> Our Empire can hardly be called old, but seems destined to be short-lived.
>
> Sir Charles Metcalfe, 11 October 1829

> The plains of India indeed present to mankind many a sad proof of the uncertainty of human glory.
>
> Thomas Daniell's commentary on his drawing of the ruins of Pilibhit near Rampur

> They all ascended the fatal drop together – refused the polluting touch of the hangman – adjusted the ropes round their own necks – and exclaiming 'Victory to Bhowanee!' seized each others hands, and leaped from the platform into eternity.
>
> Meadows Taylor, *Confessions of a Thug*, 1839

IN 1833 THE COMPANY'S charter was once more due for renewal. In 1813 it had lost its trading monopoly in India but retained the profitable trade with China, and was sole licensee for the export of opium and import of tea. Now it was to lose these too. 'A Company which carries a sword in one hand, and a ledger in the other, which maintains armies and retails tea, is a contradiction, and if it traded with success, it would be a prodigy.'[1] It should either govern a population greater than that which bowed the knee to Augustus Caesar and which increased every decade by conquests that exceeded those of Trajan, or it should trade profitably. It had shown that it could not do both. So parliament decided to free all commerce, buy up the Company's assets and liabilities, and receive an annual dividend of 10 per cent. The directors thus became trustees of a corporation whose sole function was to rule India. Gone with its monopolies was its power to decide who might reside in the lands under its control or to exclude any Indian from office and employment. To Thomas Babington Macaulay, rising on 10 July 1833 to support the motion in a thinly attended House, it was scarcely possible to calculate the benefits which must derive from the diffusion of European civilisation among the vast population of the east as a result. It was infinitely more profitable to trade with civilised men than to govern savages.[2]

Lord William Bentinck had been governor-general since 1828. In 1806, when governor of Madras, he had hoped to succeed Lord Wellesley but the Vellore mutiny put paid to that. Between 1811 and 1814 he was resident in Palermo at the Neapolitan court which had taken refuge in Sicily, where his role was not dissimilar to that of Company Residents at the courts of Hyderabad and Poona.

There he encouraged the house of Bourbon to introduce reforms that would make the inhabitants of that proverbially misgoverned island happy to expend their lives and fortunes in support of the dynasty and its allies. For liberals like Bentinck, the happiness of the governed should be the principal concern of their governors. The people of Sicily had not been happy. The people of India were not happy. Bentinck had no better opinion of Company rule in India than of Bourbon rule in Sicily. The peasants under both were wretchedly poor, their agriculture was built on beggarly stock, their lands were oppressed by extortionate landlords and plundered by brigands, their lives were burdened by revolting and brutalising practices. For all the British could show in India, the country might as well have been governed by 'police officers and tax-gatherers from the Sandwich Islands'.[3] Her economy was locked into a north-European cycle of trade, so that most Indians benefited little from it. The old Mughal centres of wealth sank into insignificance while Indian government loans, underwritten by banians, dubashes and Parsis who flocked to the Presidency cities, created a new class of rich British dependents. The Agency houses which invested heavily in the development of indigo, cotton, silk and opium, repatriated their profits. Bentinck concluded that British officials were ill-informed and heartily detested, their courts ineffective, their police oppressive and their Indian subordinates corrupt.[4] No wonder the Duke of Wellington, who had looked with a jaundiced eye at his behaviour in Sicily, expected 'some wild measure from Lord William'.[5]

Bentinck set a higher value on efficiency than on rank. He accepted the laws of political economy as Bentham had described them, and was sufficiently evangelised by the contemporary strain of Christianity to want to do good. In his eight years as governor-general, he had to make a set of uneasy compromises between reform and tradition. He had been brutally told to cut expenditure – the annual deficit was £3 million – and if he could not, someone else would be found who could.[6] He added no lands to Company rule and enforced economies that rendered him unpopular, even absurd. The ruler of India 'thinks and acts like a Pennsylvanian Quaker... riding on horseback, plainly dressed and without an escort or, on his way into the country, with his umbrella under his arm'.[7] He was the Clipping Dutchman. To meet a fellow sovereign, like Ranjit Singh, however, he would turn out 300 elephants, 1,300 camels and 800 bullock carts, together with the cavalry and infantry regiments, for his office was, after all, the highest situation in the world to which a subject could aspire.[8]

He accepted the Burkean thesis that the justification for British rule was the well-being of Indians, and the liberal belief that the separation of India from Britain would be the proudest day in British history.[9] A strong and united India could, with modern and enlightened administration, replace the former American colonies as a united, contented, even free, people under the crown. Symbolic of his commitment to modernity was a vision of steam navigation, shared by one Company official in Leadenhall Street, the sardonic novelist, Thomas Love Peacock. An up-river journey from Calcutta to Allahabad would be cut from three months to six weeks, passage time to Europe halved and Indians would visit Britain in increasing numbers, to return convinced of the superiority of western ways. Bengal coal would fire the boilers of paddle steamers, carrying merchandise up the waterways of Asia to its markets. Bentinck's arrival marked the end of an era dominated by Munro and Elphinstone. Theory rather than practice now dictated policy, as progressives of various kinds, utilitarian, evangelical, liberal or humanitarian, sometimes all four, urged government action. Their chosen arena was the abolition of suttee.

For 16 years the government had been sitting on the fence about suttee, and would have sat there for several decades more, had Bentinck not decided that suttee could be tolerated no longer. Though it was not widespread throughout India, in Bengal between 1814 and 1829, there had been on average about 800 known cases a year and Lord William feared for his happiness in this world and his admission to the next if he allowed the practice to continue for one minute longer than the happiness of the Indian population warranted.[10] The magistrates were united in favour; the army commanders thought that, as the greater number of sepoys came from provinces where suttee was not widely practised, there was little fear of unrest. On 4 December 1829, Bentinck disassociated religious belief and practice from blood and murder, and abolished it.[11] The offence to the Hindus was real.

The 1833 charter act opened all posts in the Company's service to Indians, regardless of race, creed or birth. Bentinck proposed to promote Indians on merit, over the heads of Europeans if appropriate. The governor-general considered it a sensible economy; his colleagues, even his directors, were annoyed by the lost opportunities for patronage. James Mill thought it dangerous Hindophilism.[12] Bentinck was undeterred. He also loosened censorship to allow criticism of the efficiency or honesty of administrators. He abolished flogging in the Indian army and tried to find savings from officers' field allowances and the promotion of Indian officers His countrymen were not so ready to believe that Indians were 'not sheep, good only for their fleeces'.[13]

For his two greatest reforms, however, he was indebted to the eloquence and energy of the new law member of Council. The failure of the house of Babington and Macaulay, and the precarious position in which that left the two daughters of Zachary Macaulay, persuaded their brother that he should seek a position more certain of rendering him a fortune than a seat in the House of Commons and fees from the *Edinburgh Review*. As a member of the Board of Control, Macaulay had helped the 1833 India bill through the Commons, and was well-placed to fill the one post it had created on the Supreme Council of India not to be held by a Company servant. With a salary of £10,000 a year, he hoped in five years to return with £30,000, which would take care of his father and sisters. Macaulay had supped on Mill, and he had been infected with utilitarianism. His work on the 1833 bill had been intense. 'I was,' he wrote to his nieces in 1832, 'already deep in Zamindars, Ryots, Polygars, Courts of Phoujdar and Courts of Nizamut Adawlat… Am I not in training to be as great a bore as if I had myself been in India?'[14] From February to June 1834, from Gravesend to Madras, he prepared himself by re-reading Mill, as well as 'the Iliad and the Odyssey, Virgil, Horace, Caesar's Commentaries, Bacon's *De Augmentis Scientiarum*, Dante, Petrarch, Ariosto, Tasso, *Don Quixote*, Gibbon's *Rome*… all the seventy volumes of Voltaire, Sismondi's *History of France*, and the seven thick folios of the *Biographia Britannica*'![15] But not a great deal about India, on which he felt he was sufficiently informed. Such spare time as he had in Calcutta he used to read and re-read the classics of Greek literature. The detachment these inspired in him helped him to shrug off the attacks on his penal code, in which, as law member, he advocated the equality of Europeans and Indians before the law. He had read in Mill that the only thing necessary for the happiness of the people of India was the sound administration of justice. Without a code there could be none.[16]

Between 1835 and 1838, his brisk mind produced codes of criminal and civil procedures that attempted to impose order on the mishmash of Muslim and Hindu law. He paid lip-service to the 'respect which must be paid to feelings generated by differences of religion, of nation and of caste'. His guiding principle was 'uniformity where you can have it, diversity when you must have it, but in all cases certainty'.[17] He illustrated punishable misdemeanours by references to Lady Macbeth, Wat Tyler, Robert Guiscard, the Sicilian Vespers and people who steal books from libraries.[18] It was an amazing intellectual feat which, though purporting to be that of a committee, carried Macaulay's trade mark on every page. It was government's duty to make lawsuits cheap and easy; 'why it has been so much the fashion... to darken by gibberish, by tautology, by circumlocution, that meaning which ought to be as transparent as words can make it' was a question he left to others to answer.[19] For all their simplicity, the codes were not immediately accepted. Would it not have been better to graft onto the Cornwallis system what was wanting to remedy its deficiencies than to level the whole fabric to the dust?[20] For 22 years, the draft lay under constant scrutiny, delayed by wars and the terrible events of 1857, before being finally introduced in 1860, to the eternal gratitude 'of Indian civilians, the younger of whom carry it about in their saddlebags, and the older in their heads'. Macaulay's successor on the council wondered 'whether, even in Scotland, you would find many people who know their Bibles as Indian civilians know their Codes'.[21] Grateful or not, Indian legists preferred secular to religious case-law, and administering it created the professional, English-speaking lawyers who were to become the nationalist politicians who saw the British out of India.

The Company had never expressed much interest in public education but, as a good Benthamite, Bentinck believed that only education would regenerate India. 'The ground must be prepared and the jungle cleared before the human mind can receive, with any prospect of real benefit, the seeds of improvement.'[22] There were only four lakhs of rupees a year to spend and the Committee of Public Instruction was split evenly between those who favoured instruction through the Indian languages and those who wanted to produce an English-speaking élite. They were also split on what should be taught. Revenue collectors wanted village schools to teach enough to extend the skills of farmers. The missionaries wanted useful knowledge bathed in the light of a correct and Protestant Christianity. Since the ban on missionary activity had been lifted in 1813, the churches had greatly extended schooling. The Baptists had learned that the scales were not going to fall from Hindu eyes at the first words of a bazaar preacher, and by 1815 they had 36 schools in Serampore and Chinsura (the Dutch enclave in Bengal), teaching by the Lancaster method and supported by the first general magazine in Bengali, which rolled off the Serampore press monthly with articles on general and useful knowledge, history, literature and science. In 1816 Hindu

111

College, Calcutta, was founded by Indian subscribers with a curriculum similar to that on offer at Fort William College and, later, at Serampore, without the Bible study, and by 1818 there were 166 schools in the city instructing geography and 'moral truths' in Bengali.[23]

On 2 February 1835, Macaulay, as president of a hung committee, cut the knot. The Company could not afford to educate its subjects through their mother tongue, so it should teach a significant number of them English, through which they would have access to the intellectual wealth all the wisest nations of the earth had amassed in the course of 90 generations. The four lakhs of public money should be used for teaching only what was worth knowing, not 'medical doctrines which would disgrace an English farrier – astronomy which would move laughter in girls at an English public school – history, abounding with kings thirty feet high, and reigns thirty thousand years long – and geography made up of seas of treacle and butter'. 'It is, I believe, no exaggeration to say that all the historical information that has been collected to form all the books written in the Sanskrit language is less valuable than what may be found in the most paltry abridgements used at preparatory schools in England.'[24] Never has an attack on a native culture been launched with such bitter eloquence and seldom has a good object been supported by unworthier arguments more brilliantly and devastatingly stated, but the notorious minute was enough for Bentinck, only too ready to be persuaded 'that the great object of the British government ought to be the promotion of European literature and science among the natives of India, and that all funds approved for the purposes of education would be best employed on English education alone'.[25]

The Orientalists rallied opposition. English could never be the lingua franca of India. Macaulayism would only 'widen the existing lamentable gap that divides us from the mass of the people'.[26] Macaulay's biting diminishment of oriental literature probably did as much as all the work of the Orientalists to convince Indians that it had to be cherished, but his minute also sounded the trumpet doom of Orientalism. Bentinck was ideologically unsympathetic to Fort William College, having supped on Mill's poisoned diet, believing that its alumni only helped 'to perpetuate the blight of oriental despotism by holding out the idea that there had been a golden age'.[27] To revive ancient learning was to revive a corpse, and he set about the College's demise from a thousand cuts. When in 1853 Dalhousie found 'no college, no buildings, no rooms, no professors, no lectures but only a few *moonshis* whom the government pays but who have no employment', he quietly dissolved it.[28] Sanskrit College, in Benares, almost predeceased it, but was saved by public subscription, an oasis of Orientalism. Bentinck even abolished the use of Persian in official correspondence, replacing it with English, the language of political and intellectual emancipation and of science, the key as he saw it to all improvement.

There were Indians who welcomed the light shed on their culture by the critical empiricism of the English language. At Hindu college, a young Indo-Portuguese teacher, barely older than the students he was instructing, mesmerised them with his presentation of English literature. His young Brahman auditors heard him use the drama of post-Elizabethan England like a sabre to cut into religious superstition and tradition. Henry de Rozio died only 21 years old, but in three

1. Pearl fishers, 'a cross between gods and satyrs, nereids and harlots',
by Alessandro Allori, *c.*1570, in the Studiolo di Francesco 1 dei Medici.

THE YOUNG CIVILIANS TOILET.

2. 'Young Civilian's Toilet', from *Manners and Customs of the Indians and Anglo-Indians*, 1842.
Young writers on arrival would borrow enough money to live surrounded by servants to
cut a dash.

3. 'Old Court House and Writers' Building, Calcutta', by Thomas Daniell, from *Views of Calcutta, 1786-1788*, showing the Imperial style.

4. 'Hog hunting in the Madras Presidency: The Early Repast', by Alexander William Phillips, *c.*1850. Much of an official's time was spent in camp, which often resembled a small canvas village.

5. 'Our Missionary', by George Franklin Atkinson, *c.*1856, from *Curry and Rice*, plate 12.
The picture shows a Lutheran missionary. George Cary started his mission as a street preacher.

6. 'South-East View of the New Government House, Calcutta', by James Moffat, 1805.
Wellesley's unauthorised building, showing a man in a palanquin.

7. 'Kandahar: A Lady of Rank engaged in smoking', by James Rattray, *c.*1840.
Could, painted earlier, have been a model for Moore's Lalla Rookh.

8. The Husainabad Imambara at Lucknow (1837), an example of the 'carbuncled palaces and perfumed gardens... that was to take physical shape in Britain's seaside piers and the pantomimes performed on them.' Photographed by the author in 1966.

9. Ranjit Singh, 'exactly like an old mouse', by Emily Eden.

10. Model of a Cutcherry, presided over by a Company magistrate, early 19th century, from the Victoria & Albert Museum.

11. The 1903 Delhi Durbar, by Roderick Mackenzie. The 'Curzonisation' of the 'magnificent state Barnum'.

12. A game of cricket in the dried moat of the Red Fort in Delhi,
seen through a lattice window. Photographed by the author in 1961.

years his extramural lectures on Locke, Hume, Rousseau and Tom Paine had made him a legend. Their attacks on the ramshackle conventions of western civilisation could be equally applied to traditions that kept India backward and subservient. If a new critique, based on English pragmatism, could purify Indian thought and remove the barnacles of centuries, a new and revivified Indian culture could stand up against the contemptuous missionaries and nostalgic linguists. The debate now shifted to the choice of texts for study in government schools. English literature could be subversive, as thoughts 'without religious principles' could 'produce an effect... of unmixed evil'.[29] If students were not to emerge from their exposure to the literature of Europe sceptical and unbelieving of all religions including their own, they should imbibe Christian virtues by the study of a literature drenched in Christian tradition. A committee of three, on which Charles Trevelyan, Macaulay's brother in law, sat with two missionaries, agreed that Shakespeare just about passed muster and that Addison's *Spectator*, Bacon and Locke, whose spirit of enquiry was grounded on sound Protestant principles, would do. The Bible, which was also literature, would have been ideal but adding it to the list would be too inflammatory. As an indispensable vade-mecum for the study of Shakespeare and Milton it could be put in the library. Students from Hindu College, as a result, knew more Bible than the average English public schoolboy.

Macaulay wished to give Indians the key to useful knowledge, with which they would drive the economy, operate the revenue collection and create a demand for British goods and services. The study of English was taken up most assiduously, not by poets and writers, but by lawyers, for there had always been a strong link between letters and the law in Indian society, and by helping to kill that interest in Indian literature, history and antiquity which the Orientalists had made their own, Macaulay's minute also contributed to the gap that yawned between two educated peoples. 'To the great unwashed today [1912],' cried one of them, Indians are 'simply niggers – without a past, perhaps without a future. They do not choose to know us.'[30]

Bentinck, by keeping out of frontier wars, transformed the annual deficit to a surplus of £500,000, all at a time when prices were falling and investment had dried up. But this 'busy, meddling governor of detail' was to break down before the end.[31] Dyspepsia, constipation, stone and poor circulation proved too much for one who was tied, like Curzon 70 years later, to the wheel of administration. Unlike Curzon, Bentinck had little aesthetic sense. The exquisite marble fretwork and mosaics of one of the Mughal bathrooms in the Red Fort at Agra, ripped out by the Marquess of Hastings as a present for the Prince Regent, had to be auctioned. Had they 'fetched the price expected, it is probable that the whole of the palace, even the Taj itself, would have been pulled down and sold in the same manner'.[32] In March 1835, at the age of 54, a very plain-looking, tired old man decided to retire, lamented 'by the sleek and timid inhabitants of Bengal, by the fat and greasy citizens of Calcutta'[33] and by Macaulay, but not by the majority of the European population. To them, he was 'the most infernal scoundrel' who united 'the treachery of an Italian to the caution of a Dutchman.'[34] To Macaulay he was the subject of an epitaph, which even the Marxist government of Calcutta did not wish, in the euphoria of independence, to efface from his statue – one 'whose constant study it was to elevate the intellectual and moral character of the nations committed to his charge'.[35] Though he encouraged Britons to come to India to settle, very few wanted to. Emily Eden probably summed it up when she remarked that 'the country was too HOT' – she could not write the letters large enough.[36] As Bentinck's reforms all had in mind a future India ruled by Indians, men and women continued to dream of retirement to Cheltenham, Buxton and Tunbridge Wells, and to spend as much time as they could in their Indian imitations at Simla, Ootacamund, Darjeeling and Pachmarhi.

Mill's *History* was intended to be a corrective to a Romantic view of India that was seducing the popular imagination in Britain. Aquatint sets of drawings made by artists for the Company in subscription editions, in which monkeys, tigers, elephants, sacred cows, fakirs and dervishes accompanied sketches of imposing forts and palaces and amazing temples, brought India live into the British drawing room. The first was the work of William Hodges. He had been assistant to the Romantic landscape painter, Richard Wilson, and had accompanied James Cook's second voyage to the South Seas as draughtsman and illustrator. From 1778 to 1784, he was engaged by Warren Hastings to record the countryside and its marvels during the governor-general's official perambulations. His first set of drawings appeared in 1786 and inspired Alexander Humboldt to become a traveller. His *Travels in India during the years 1780–83* was published in 1793 and brought him a celebrity his subsequent career did not support. In the three years of life left to him he abandoned painting to open a bank which failed.

He had, however, established a taste for and an image of India, disturbing to Mill, but which clamoured to be indulged. That clamour was met by Thomas Daniell and his nephew William. They came to India just as Hodges was leaving, and stayed ten years. Hodges had not travelled further than Warren Hastings and had kept, like his patron, to the river routes. The Daniells were to travel further, following Hodges, often view for view, up the Ganges to Benares and Allahabad, and then voyaging further, to the Garhwal Himalayas, escorted by two British officers and 50 sepoys to beat off brigands, and were the first Europeans to reach Srinagar in Kashmir. They crawled into ice-caves in search of rock temples, scrambled over scree to find the best viewpoint and descended into gorges, where the murmuring of a passing stream, the majestic grandeur of the mountains, the visionary effect of the twilight and the myriad swarms of fireflies 'diffused magical radiance equally beautiful and surprising; it seemed in truth to be a land of romance and the proper residence of those fanciful beings, the fairies and genii that appear so often in Asiatic tales'.[37] These sentiments informed the 144 aquatint engravings that appeared, loose-leaf, in pairs, between 1795 and 1808, comprising the six volumes of what came to be called *Oriental Scenery*, some of which reappeared in Humphrey Repton's original sketches for the Royal Pavilion in Brighton, and later, in the more modest plans of John Nash. When the retired Company official, Sir Charles Cockerell, commissioned his Indian villa at Sezincote in the Cotswolds, he instructed his architect to consult Thomas Daniell, to whom it owed its pavilions, fretted arches, Mughal gateways and onion domes. And, on the estate of Sir John Osborne at Melchet,

'An Ancient Hindoo Temple in the Fort of Rosas, Bahar' was surprisingly reconstructed as a memorial to Warren Hastings.[38]

If the Daniells affected a lament for former glory, epitomised in Shelley's *Ozymandias*, the more ebullient Romantic taste was indulged in a work of indisputable popular appeal which appeared in the same year as Mill's *History*. Thomas Moore had wanted to write an eastern tale, like his friend Byron. As the middle east had been poetically much travelled, he set his fancy of true love rewarded in the court of Aurangzeb, where the emperor's daughter, Lalla Rookh, is betrothed to the Prince of Bucharia, a land set somewhere to the north-west of Kashmir. To while away the long journey to meet her husband-to-be Lalla Rookh hires a poet to tell her stories. Hardly surprisingly, as the tales are all about the rough paths of true love, the princess falls in love with the poet who, predictably, on her wedding day, proves to be the prince she is to marry. Moore did enough background reading to satisfy John Malcolm that he had written an engagingly atmospheric poem, but its fantastical descriptions of carbuncled palaces and perfumed gardens created a crypto-Persian image of India that was to take physical shape in Britain's seaside piers and the pantomimes performed on them. No one much cared whether *Lalla Rookh* was authentic or not; it gave an occasional frisson of prohibited reading to its readers, who seemed to be every nubile lady in the land.

Another frisson was habitually provided by parents who chid refractory children with the threat that Haidar Ali or Tipu Sultan would come to carry them off, even from the safety of their British nurseries. Walter Scott, looking for a tale with which to launch his *Chronicles of the Canongate* in 1827, was intrigued enough by their oriental fearsomeness, reflected in the mechanical tiger mauling a European soldier which had so impressed John Keats, to locate one of his stories in India. *The Surgeon's Daughter* is, actually, a Presbyterian morality tale set, not among Scotland's self-justified sinners, but in Haidar's Mysore. Richard Middlemas is a native of Edinburgh who has gone to the bad. He kills his commanding officer in Madras, deserts to Haidar's service and trades his Scottish sweetheart to Haidar's harem. Lust and greed takes him to India in the first place, treachery keeps him there, but when he is discovered trying to sell Haidar's secrets to the British he is sentenced to be trampled to death by an elephant. In this nightmare of intriguing Brahmans, false Muslims and helpless victims, a Scottish surgeon redeems Scottish honour. Dr Hartley is the sort of man who should go to India, not Middlemas. His medical skill serves rich and poor, Indian and European alike. He is the angel of light on bloody battlefields. The tale is, however, not worthy of Scott's talent. His informant was an officer whose only service had been in the Muslim dominated north, and his *hajjis*, mullahs and fakirs were out of place in the south. Grave and inscrutable orientals, however, gave a specious verisimilitude to the melodramatic farrago, woven round European adventurers, ambitious villains and a Byronic orphan. Scott's India is as distant and unreal as Jonathan Swift's flying island of Laputa.[39]

Scott and Moore accepted the Hodges-Daniell image of the east, romantic, lubricious, beautiful but also sinister, more Arabian Nights than Indian Days. The ardent Mill belittled the efforts of Company servants who sat at the feet of pandits and wrestled with the anfractuosities of epitaphs and texts, and who took time off from surveying the source of rivers or garrison duty to dig in temple precincts. They wrote papers for the Asiatick Society, under canvas, by the light of rush lamps in a cloud of insects, and had them published, often at their own expense. They compiled dictionaries and lexicons of remote languages in the belief that they were releasing, from long darkness, a civilisation that would astonish the world. To Mill, the civilisation was a fraud, a long dark night. Their discoveries, like the rock carvings of Ellora, first reproduced by the portraitist, James Wales, for Sir Charles Malet in the early 1790s and engraved by Thomas Daniell, represented the dedication of wasted time to a gloomy and mendacious deity. The stranger might stand astonished 'whether he considers the labour which must have been bestowed on it in mere excavation, the rock being of red granite; or whether he considers the infinite pains which it must have taken to form the pillars and finish the numerous sculptural decorations: but when he is informed that the whole mountain is full of excavations and that many are larger and still more elaborate, he is quite at a loss how to credit what he hears'.[40] Indeed the monoliths of Mahabalipuram, and the mighty stupas of Sarnath and Sanchi were so colossal that many believed they could only be the works of great builders with whose works they were familiar, like the Babylonians, the Egyptians or the Greeks.[41] Mere Indians could not have created such wonders, despite the evidence all around them of towering and impregnable fortresses and massive, pillared temples. Mill's contempt did not deter enthusiasts, though it ensured there was no money to exploit their work. Slowly and painstakingly, the correspondents of the Assistant, later Assay Master of the Calcutta mint and secretary of the Asiatick Society of Bengal, James Prinsep, furnished him with the evidence that enabled him in 1838 to decipher the rock edicts of the Emperor Ashoka, and discover a golden age that had long forsaken India. Contemporaneously, Brian Hodgson, Company resident in Nepal, living the contemplative life of a llama, collected a vast library of Buddhist texts which suggested that, at one time, India had been the homeland not only of the Gautama but also of his doctrines. When in 1834 Lieutenant Alexander Cunningham, then 20 years old and professed as an engineer, began to explore a stupa near Benares he started on a pastime that was to become an obsession. Funded privately by Prinsep, he uncovered inscriptions that proved that the stupas were of Buddhist origin. The Ashoka edicts confirmed that the Gupta dynasty was Buddhist, while Chinese travel accounts of the fifth and seventh centuries after Christ, translated in 1834 by Horace Wilson, now incarnated as the first professor of Sanskrit at Oxford, and Prinsep's predecessor as Assay Master and as Secretary of the Asiatick Society, revealed that Buddhism was the dominant faith in India until well into the Christian era. That discovery was the last great achievement of the 'Orientalists'. Thereafter there was insufficient interest to do more. Their mantle fell on the Indians themselves.

Cunningham marched on, surveying and mapping, collecting and digging until 1861 when he retired with the rank of major-general, but the man, for whose first commission Sir Walter Scott had been a suppliant, was not going to rest on his laurels. He persuaded the governor-general to allow him to survey the monuments and sites of ancient India before they were completely destroyed in the search for rubble with which to build utilitarian roads and railways, or dismantled for building blocks. The Archaeological Survey of India was born. It could not dig and conserve – there was no money for that – but it did determine the historical sites worthy of protection. In 1861, Cunningham exposed the last great stupa of Boddh Gaya and the city of Taxila in the Panjab. His was a constant battle against vandalism and a race against developers. Like Wilson and Prinsep, he found that the British strangers in the land turned against him. James Mill's disciples held that the study of India's ancient inheritance was not worthwhile.

The dispute between 'Orientalists' and 'Anglicists' was essentially between the intellectuals on the Company establishment, and Macaulay's lapidary endorsement of 'Anglicism' seemed to many to finish the argument for good. The natural sympathies of the Bengali intelligentsia were with the 'Orientalists', and the man round whom the banner of Indian modernism was to wrap itself was the son of a zamindar who had made a fortune lending money to Company civilians. Rammohun Roy came to Calcutta in 1814, at the age of 44. For seven years he wandered round the north of India, as far as Tibet, in search of truth. He taught himself Sanskrit, Arabic, Hebrew and Greek and, in order to learn English he became a *sheristadar* (clerk to the court) at Rangpur, 230 miles north of Calcutta. There he immersed himself in the work of the Orientalists, discovering in the writing of Horace Wilson and Colebrooke proof of what he had long suspected, that there were serious discrepancies between the ancient scriptural texts and contemporary practice. In 1815 he produced his own translation of the Vedas into Bengali, and began a personal campaign to demonstrate how the Brahmans had hidden true religion in a Sanskrit fog, and how the ancient Hindu religion had been corrupted by idolatry. To awaken them from their dreams of error, he published his defence of the monotheist system of the Vedas, and a dissertation against suttee.

Rammohun Roy was no western clone. He upset the Serampore missionaries by applying to Christianity the same critical method he had used on Hinduism, holding that the divinity of Christ and his atonemental sacrifice on the cross were 'Brahmanical' corruptions of the master's teaching. He protested against the decree abolishing suttee, though he had argued that it had no scriptural warrant, because it was not for Europeans to interfere in Indian religious custom, however corrupted. In 1828, he founded the *Brahmo Samaj*, dedicated to the modernisation of Hinduism. Round him gathered some of de Rozio's students, and the staff at Hindu College. He corresponded with Bentham who congratulated him on casting off 35 million gods, while he attracted the venom of Sydney Smith, who derided him for losing his own religion but not finding another.[42]

The Brahmo Samaj, in addition to reforming Hinduism, had also to defend it against caricature and insult from Christians. Roy was an intellectual, a reformer, a gradualist, whose uncomfortable conclusion was that India would only be reformed under British rule because it was innovatory, rational and destructive. He recognised the truth of Macaulay's critique of Indian education and admired the way he supported his arguments with a passion for truth – as Macaulay saw it – and common sense. Roy wanted his people to show similar virtues. He endorsed the English language as a vehicle of new ideas from more dynamic societies, which were in turn to dynamise Hindu society. He ranged himself against the constraints imposed on women, and argued that caste, and the rituals and diet that went with it, were mere forms. His death in Bristol in 1833, away from his kind, was seen as a judgement for defying the prohibition against crossing the water. By not converting to Christianity he remained faithful to his roots, but by rejecting the cosy view of Hinduism held by some Orientalists, he upset some of them enough to keep him out of the Asiatick Society. By insisting on the pure religious philosophy of the Vedas he set himself apart from the radical secularism of Henry de Rozio. Coleridge in 1819 hailed him as the Luther of Brahmanism.[43]

Whether Rammohun Roy was an effective reformer or a visionary increasingly alienated from his people, he did begin to chart the direction of the Bengali mind. De Rozio used the examples of European political philosophy and literature to attack the sluggish Hindu mind; his loyalties were not to the deep culture that nourished it. He was after all, a very young man, burned up too soon by Romantic atheism, like Shelley. Had he lived he might have led a movement towards Anglicism, jettisoning traditional Hindu values for the European culture to which he half belonged. But Bentinck's frontal assault on suttee and Macaulay's sweeping advocacy of useful knowledge acquired through English, offended the subtle mind of Rammohun Roy. He set the Bengali intellectual against commitment to Europeanisation, in favour of Hindu cultural regeneration, which the English language was to assist. 'The better classes of the natives of India are placed under the sway of the Honourable East India Company,' he wrote in a petition to Parliament, 'in a state of political degradation which is absolutely without parallel in their former history.'[44] They must combine to pull themselves out of it, get government jobs and, with the English acquired, read the work of James Mill's greater son, John Stuart. English was to be the torch that welded the political liberalism of the left to a revived Hindu tradition, from which Indian nationalism took its origins.[45]

The end of the Maratha and pindari wars brought general peace but not pacification. Outside urban centres the former soldiers of native armies, unwilling to exchange the sword for the ploughshare, turned to brigandage. Some robbed with violence, some with stealth. Emily Eden had to admire the skilful robbers who could steal the bedclothes off a sleeping person, even in the well-guarded tents of regiments on the march. Travellers would disappear, leaving no trace or sign of violence, until a polluted well revealed its grisly store, or a jackal unearthed an inadequately buried corpse. Between 1809 and 1810, 60 bodies were fished out of wells round Etawah, a town in the Jumna basin between Agra and Kanpur, fuelling suspicion that it was the work of a brotherhood of murderers. In 1829 the suspicion became known fact. Because travellers felt safer travelling in company rather than alone, small caravans would assemble in the *serais* and bazaars, where they were joined by apparently bona fide travellers bent on their destruction. Part of the gang would go ahead to pick a spot for the murder and another would prepare the graves. The preferred method of despatch was a silk knotted handkerchief or *romal* with which the victims were bloodlessly strangled. If the victims were numerous, the knife would be used, the bodies dismembered to facilitate rapid burial, and the ground scorched by fire. Europeans were seldom victims, but sepoys travelling home on leave with their pay were favourite targets. The predators were both Muslim and Hindu, and known as thugs (*thags*).[46]

Emily Eden met one thug in 1837, who had confessed to killing 300 people. He professed pride in his skill with the noose and was only sorry that he would not be able to teach his son how to use it.[47] Thugs became one more legend about the mysterious, amoral east which it was Britain's destiny to civilise. Thuggee was not a new phenomenon. Murder by strangling was a time-honoured way of disposing of victims for pay or loot, and *phansigars* or noose-slayers were first recognised by Europeans as early as 1665.[48] If it started as a freemasonry of Muslims dedicated to secret murder, it was soon attributed to criminals of all creeds. Because thugs were supposed to be devotees of the goddess Kali, whose image was a corybantic hag with a chaplet of skulls and hands smeared with blood, or of Devi, the wife of Siva, or of Bhowani, whom Muslim thugs identified, however perversely, with Fatima, the prophet's daughter, thuggee came into the religious domain, which was off-bounds. Thugs were confident that their victims were 'saved' and destined for whatever paradise they believed in and, thus, felt no remorse. As with suttee, however deplorable the practice, while it was confined to native believers, thuggee could almost be tolerated as the latest manifestation of rural crime born of social dislocation.[49]

Its suppression is indissolubly linked to the name of William Sleeman. In 1820, like so many soldiers for whom there was no war to fight, Sleeman transferred from the Bengal army into the political department, and in 1819 was posted to Jubbulpore, a newly created military station in ceded Maratha lands, almost in the dead centre of India. Here he investigated an unsolved series of killings, which bore a marked similarity to each other. Thugs, being illiterate, committed nothing to paper and their gangs could only be penetrated by *pentiti*, known as 'approvers'. Sleeman was adept at turning 'approvers'. Having broken the thug code, *Ramasi*, which was little more than the Hindostani of thieve's kitchens, Sleeman's pursuit was systematic and unceasing. Records of rural crime were taken out of archives and studied. In 1835 he was appointed General Superintendent for the Suppression of Thuggee at Jubbulpore. Magistrates and police all over India were taught how to identify and crack thug operations in their districts. By 1840, 466 thugs had been hanged, 1,564 transported and 933 imprisoned for life. Fifty-six had turned 'approver', and with their help the remaining gangs were rounded up. For young thugs and children of convicted thugs, Sleeman created industrial schools at Jubbulpore and Saugor, from one of which Queen Victoria was to order a seamless carpet for Windsor Castle, measuring 80 by 40 feet and weighing two tons.[50] Small bands survived until the 1880s, many in the Panjab, where it was not a profession, handed down from father to son, but rather an avocation of the desperately poor. The Panjabi made a clumsy thug, often failing to despatch his victim who helped to put him behind bars. The government Thuggee and Dacoity Department stayed in existence until 1904, but its principal preoccupation was organised crime in native states, until the surveillance of political activists became part of its remit.

'Thuggee' Sleeman became a walking model for the ideal district officer. He would ride out into the countryside alone and stop to smoke and chat with peasants and travellers. It was while feigning sleep in one such encounter that he heard the *Ramasi* words that put him on the track of the Narsinghur murders. He knew his petty rajahs and nawabs and in 1844, during a Company dispute with the Scindia prince at Gwalior, he rode unarmed into the impregnable fortress to prevent a ruinous battle. Even though Company troops had crossed the frontier and were engaging the Maratha army, he was allowed to ride out unharmed. His advice to Richmond Shakspear, taking over as political agent in Gwalior, summed up his philosophy. 'As a general rule, do all the good you can in your present position,' as far as possible by stealth. He was worried about the apparently inexorable extension of Company frontiers. In 1836, during one of his rural rides near Meerut, he met an old Rajput, who complained that, while it was good that the British did not kill or suffer peasants to be killed in their dominions, they were taking kingdom after kingdom, yet there was not a rupee less to pay in taxes.[51] If the British ruled all India, they would be wholly at the mercy of the Indian army. Sleeman had absolute confidence in the ordinary people of India, who did not need to be watched by soldiers all the time. At the great mela at Allahabad, where the Jumna and Ganges met, a British magistrate could hold open court in the midst of at least 400,000 people, assisted by only two constables and two native writers. By and large British rule was accepted, but not with pleasure. Moderate revenue settlements, the abolition of the pilgrim tax, security on the highways, schools, the whole apparatus of Bentinckian benevolence would do more to pacify India than the demonstration of overwhelming military might.[52]

His last post in India was as resident at Lucknow. The nawabi of Oudh had become a byword for bad government, but all attempts to develop lucrative mono-polies and encourage surplus agriculture in the rich alluvial soil of the province had been thwarted by the predatory Company officers and merchants who battened on the court. Wellesley, fearing that the unpaid troop of the nawab-wazir's army would fraternise rather than repel invading Pathans, Afghans or Frenchmen, annexed half its territory to act as a buffer. The defence of Oudh became the responsibility of the Company. Without an army, the nawab-wazir was powerless to collect the taxes from the *taluqdars*, who enrolled their ryots as armed retainers and retired to fortified redoubts to defy the nawab's officers. Dacoits took service with taluqdars, sallying forth from their safe refuges to raid British territory.[53]

Such revenues as were surplus to the minimal obligations of state were applied to the beautification of the capital. This was no merit in the eyes of Company servants who were not disposed to admire a planned city of spacious roads, with a gateway superior to the Sublime Porte at Constantinople, and superb stuccoed palaces fit for prince and *peri*. The peri was often a petticoat wazir in the form of a possessive begum, and the Orchid House of Asaf-ud-daulah became notorious for voluptuous nautches, conspiratorial catamites, insinuating favourites, silken dalliance and sudden death. The cynosure of musicians and poets left the utilitarian British cold. The city was a pavilioned island cut off from its hinterland, where virtually independent landlords arrested anyone straying into their satrapies. This was the no-man's land into which Sleeman was posted.

In 1818, the Marquess of Hastings persuaded the nawab-wazir to become King of Oudh, in order to break the residual allegiance he owed to the emperor in Delhi, but also in the hope that royalty might encourage him to do something about the parlous condition of his kingdom. The principal products of this change were the portraits of the royal family by Tilly Kettle, who painted them all in coronation robes and coronets, like debauched Wittelbachs. Expenditure on ermine, gold chains and crown jewels soared, but the administration remained the despair of successive governors-general. The appointment of Sleeman seemed like a last throw. His opposition to the take-over of native states was well-known. 'Were we... to annex or confiscate Oudh, our good name in India would inevitably suffer and that good name is more valuable to us than a dozen of Oudhs.'[54] Princes might be served by incompetents and were often protectors of bandits and thugs, yet to absorb them all would remove the one visible standard of comparison between the oppression of natives and the benefits of Company rule.[55] The King of Oudh was, in 1849, a pathetic hypochondriac, terrified of being poisoned in his labyrinthine court. Sleeman took the administration into his hands and cleared out the lords of misrule. The work wore him out and he was to die at sea before he ever reached the shores of Cornwall where he hoped to retire.

Most of what the world knows about thugs comes, not from Sleeman's exhaustive reports but from a novel published in 1840, written by an officer in princely not in Company pay. Philip Meadows Taylor was 20 years younger than Sleeman and he had come to India at the age of 15 as clerk in a Bombay business agency. The agency being in financial difficulties, a friend arranged his entry into the military service of the nizam. *Confessions of a Thug* was his first, and only successful, novel, but a historical trilogy, *Tara, Ralph Darnell and Seeta*, tells us more about the India Taylor knew. They charted three climacteric periods of late Indian history, the origin of the power of the Marathas, the rise and fall of Siraj-ud-daula and the Mutiny of 1857. Of the three, *Seeta* is the most subtle, the most personal. In Cyril Brandon, deputy commissioner of Noorpoor, we see a portrait of Taylor himself, sent to a remote part of the nizam's territories without support, to hold a whole province loyal by sheer personality. 'It should be well for all,' he wrote as the story draws to an end, 'if... the English people cared to understand how, with a few assistants such as we know of, Cyril Brandon, like scores of others, governed hundreds of thousands, or perhaps even millions, with a province as large as Wales or Scotland.' The recipe was simple. 'Be just, be patient, be firm and true; be always accessible and courteous, never forgetting your position, and they will love you.'[56]

Brandon, however, was not as other commissioners, not in 1857, for he had married, according to Hindu rites, a young Sudra widow (the Sudra caste did not practise suttee), daughter-in-law to a rich goldsmith. Seeta is conventionally beautiful, almost fair enough to pass for a European, dauntless in courage and faithful to her love. Brandon cannot take her into European society, such as there was in Noorpoor, but he is never tempted to regret his action. Though it is his dearest hope that she will turn Christian he does nothing to bring it about, except to teach her enough English to read poetry, especially Shakespeare and the Bible. Seeta is befriended by Brandon's closest friends but the subject of malicious tittle-tattle from other wives. Her heroic act of self-sacrifice, saving Brandon's life when the mutiny reaches Noorpoor, reconciles all to her marriage, but only when she is safely dead. Taylor was not a covenanted Company servant and would always enjoy lower pay and lower rank than the twice-born. He was in sole charge of three very large districts on the Berar border, and never rose higher than deputy commissioner. But he was a freer agent and could push at the frontiers of prejudice. But even he could see no happy solution to Brandon's marriage but a beautiful and generous death, leaving Brandon to marry a pukka white girl and inherit his brother's title. When the call to mutiny comes, Seeta's father-in-law, two reformed dacoits, Seeta's husband's aunt, a pious old lady turned ascetic and a gentle Brahman priest all take the side of the British, of whom they see Brandon as the noblest representative, so careful is he of their caste rules.

Taylor's Noorpoor was partly based on the princely state of Shorapur to which, in 1841, at the ripe age of 33, he was sent to sort out a dispute that had baffled more seasoned officers. The widowed rani, a very Messalina, was withholding the succession fee due to the nizam from her late husband. She was encouraged by the palace soothsayers who, following British setbacks in Afghanistan, were prophesying their imminent departure from India. Clans of tribesmen, 'as wild looking as I ever saw', had gathered to die for their rani. Taylor's first encounter with their chiefs was only promising in that one of them saluted him with the parting words: 'You treat us with respect and we thank you for it.' What followed was the stuff of the Boy's Own Paper. The rani's little rajah ran at their first encounter into Taylor's arms and, while the rani was evasive about her intentions, she seemed ready to like the young Englishman. Her clansmen challenged Taylor about the succession.

> 'Your little Rajah is my son,' I told them, 'and I will put him on his throne with my own hands before I go.'
>
> 'And you give us your word about this?' they asked.
>
> 'Certainly I do,' I cried, 'and the word of the British government.'
>
> 'Enough!' was the general shout. 'And now, put your hands on our heads, and we will be your obedient children henceforth.'
>
> Then they crowded round me, and I placed my hands on a number of heads, many prostrating themselves before me, some weeping, and all much excited.[57]

Brandon/Taylor was as good as his word; the young rajah was enthroned on his *gadi*, his uncle was appointed regent, the rani paid her arrears and Taylor got them reassessed in her favour. 'My child is in truth yours,' concluded the rani, 'and you must guard him henceforth as a son.'[58] In pre-Mutiny, almost pre-lapsarian India, in a native state, a young official who steadfastly refused bribes and was unwavering, but just, in his demands, was as rare as in Britain. There, in the gothicising court of Victoria, the knightly cult of the Round Table was being paraded as an imperial paradigm. In India, a different prototype was being formed, and Taylor, as a colonial *chevalier sans peur et sans reproches*, was a walking model. His wife dead, his daughters at school in England, Taylor was able to dedicate himself, almost as a consecrated servant, to his people, even the rogues who made their living from dacoity. He found his next district, Nuldroog, 'a wild and barbarous district replete with disorder and irregularity of every conceivable kind' and he left it prosperous.[59] He was knighted but acknowledged no recognition higher than that he was 'father and mother to the *ryots*'. 'Never on any occasion,' they told him, 'have we seen that anyone was treated with indignity or affronted in your durbar.'[60] The 'sweet courtoisie' of the Round Table being resurrected at Windsor was Taylor's last advice to his public. All who went to India should 'use true courtesy to natives of all degrees. My experience has taught me that large masses of men are more easily led than driven, and that courtesy and kindness and firmness will gain many a point which, under a hard and haughty bearing, would prove unattainable'.[61] His novels are too long and too flabby. His ambition to be the Walter Scott of India was foiled by inability to transfer his genuine interest in people to the narrative, though it shines through every page of his autobiography. But he knew his India as well as Kipling and saw heroic qualities in the 'natives'. For Taylor, like Sleeman, believed Indians could be reconciled by kindness and fairness to British rule, and come to support it, so that there was no need for the largest standing army in the world, which swallowed up the money that could be spent on improvements.

Bishop Reginald Heber, crossing in 1824–5 from Calcutta to Bombay, thought that British rule, where he found it, was an improvement on what had gone before. Peace and security were great boons and, if the British could only unbend enough to take the same kindly interest in his Indian neighbour as the bishop did, it might even be popular.[62] Yet, not even Malcolm or Munro ever thought that the British could relax the role of occupying power for a long time to come. Confronted by the French revolution and the parvenu empire, the British had turned to their aristocratic and anglican traditions to protect themselves. Their naval and military heroes became part of a new meritocracy on a par with, if not so nakedly bourgeois as, Napoleon's marshals. The new British aristocrats had defeated Napoleon, conquered India, reduced South America to vassal status and, after 20 years of war, were looking for new opportunities to exercise the qualities those experiences had developed. They found them in India. There they could be free from the conservative traditions that dominated Europe, reinforced by fear of liberalism and revolution. In India the Company could cautiously consider promotion by merit rather than by seniority, but that was the limit of egalitarianism. Otherwise the rule of these new paragons would be paternalist, autocratic, military, anglican and superior.

Even Taylor saw being the father to his people as an indispensable part of control. The missionaries had accepted that, proselytisation being ineffectual, a bit of ecclesiastical grandeur, accompanied by a certain aloofness from religious enthusiasm, might help to convince the Hindu that the British also had fathers in God. The open and courteous Bishop Heber was gratified by the respect he received from mullahs, brahmans and *saddhus*. If Indians could learn to respect their rulers they might be less ready to rebel than had been the Americans.[63] It was an illusion. The British congratulated themselves on the benefits of peace but, had they been less anxious to keep the French away from a continent they could only reach by magic carpet, that peace would have been secured by the Indian princes themselves, if only to keep out the Company. They were pleased by the fairness of their revenue system, but it was based on Indian models that had worked, and would have been less onerous if the taxpayers had not had to meet the costs of their own conquest. They were boastful of British justice, forgetting that it was now so slow and expensive that victims of its delays would turn to dacoity.[64] They were proud of the suppression of suttee and female infanticide, their opposition to which had caused both to revive just as the practices were quietly dying out. They were flattered by the numbers who attended school to learn English, unaware that they were acquiring a weapon with which to match themselves against the British. William Sleeman believed that his countrymen had given 'what India never had before our rule and never could have without it, the assurance that there will always be at the head of government a sensible ruler trained up to office in the best school in the world and that the security of the rights and enforcement of duties... will not depend upon the will or caprice of individuals in power'.[65] It may have been true, but the British were still nervous that the Indians would seize the first opportunity to reject it.

9. 'WHY... DEPRIVE ME OF MY POOR AND BARREN COUNTRY?'

> I cannot understand why the rulers of so great an empire should have gone across the Indus to deprive me of my poor and barren country.
>
> Dost Muhammad, Amir of Afghanistan

> Unwarned by precedents, uninfluenced by example, the Sikh nation has called for war, and, on my word, they shall have it with a vengeance.
>
> Lord Dalhousie

> In India we must either keep all aloof or absorb. All our history shows that sooner or later connection with us is political death. The sunshine is not more fatal to a dew-drop than our friendship or alliance to an Asiatic kingdom.
>
> William Hodson, of Hodson's Horse, 16 November 1854

FOR ALL ITS FINE words, the Company had one overwhelming imperative in India, to pay for its mercenary army. The Marquess of Hastings may have hoped to see the ploughshare turning up soil that had never been stirred except by the hoofs of predatory cavalry, but 'the army in India must always be on a war establishment'.[1] By 1820, there were upwards of 200,000 men under arms in India, the largest volunteer force in the world, and the largest item of expenditure on the India budget. A sepoy's remittances to his home village fed and fee'd a whole domestic economy and the Bengal army sustained, in one way or another, between 15 and 20 per cent of the population. Regular pay encouraged long service. Fathers would dedicate all but one of their sons to the army so that they gave him status in the village. To bring that proud father's grey hairs to the grave by dereliction of duty was the most dreadful thing a sepoy could do. A flogging was an unnecessary sanction so Bentinck abolished it long before it was abolished in the king's service. William Sleeman was told, in 1841, by a senior native officer in his regiment, that abolition had improved not weakened discipline.[2]

Long service was also due to the slow crawl through the ranks, which affected both European and Indian troops. Promotion was strictly by seniority, so that it was not uncommon to find serving officers and men in their seventies. An ensign from England, joining the Bengal army in 1831, could wait 48 years to reach the rank of colonel and, in the Sikh wars, one commanding officer in battle needed two men to get him onto his horse, while on another occasion the brigadier was so short-sighted he could not tell, until his horse's mouth met the bayonets of the enemy, in which direction he was facing.[3] For the European officers of all its three armies in India, the Company now had its own training establishment at Addiscombe Place, near Croydon, where cadets, able to construe Caesar's *Commentaries* and write a decent hand, were admitted from between 14 and 18 to a two-year course which introduced them to sword exercises and regular drill, and instructed them in mathematics, fortifications, military drawing and surveying, civil drawing, Hindostani, French and Latin.[4] An engineer's mathematical training incorporated geometry, algebra, heights and fluxion (differential calculus) and rectifications and spherical trigonometry.[5] The head was a martinet in holy orders and the training was thorough for its time, certainly more professional than that given to civilians at Haileybury, enabling them to map and survey the new conquests. Despite the battle honours, experience of active service in battle was meagre. Most army time was spent in garrison duties, on internal security; bandit control and discouraging rural unrest could be left to Indian officers. Garrison drudgery prompted able British officers to leapfrog the promotion hurdles by volunteering for political service. They were often better skilled than civilians in the work of pacification, during which former bandits were transmogrified into policemen, and tribal and village elders elevated into rajahs. In the 1820s as many as a third and sometimes a half of the regimental officers were absent on non-military duties, furlough and sick leave at any one time.

By 1829 the Company's debt had risen to £50 million, largely the result of past conquests, and it seemed as if only new conquests could pay it off.[6] Part of this debt was incurred by the cost of nearly a quarter of the entire British army, a force of 20,000 regular British soldiers who, the British government believed, were necessary for the defence of India, and for whom the Company had to pay. They cost twice as much as sepoys and, despite being often incompetent, when not chronically sick, king's commissioned officers claimed precedence over Company officers of the same rank and filled the most senior posts. They had a poor opinion of sepoys and thought they were spoiled, 'belauded and bebuttered and bebattaed after a campaign'.[7] The sharp-nosed French naturalist, Victor Jacquemont, in 1829 tried to analyse the bond between sepoys and their officers and concluded that it could only be discipline.[8] It was more than that. A typical Awadhi sepoy like Sita Ram admired the reckless, sometimes irresponsible courage of European officers, whose success on the battlefield was often due to a combination of folly and good luck. In his opinion the English were invincible because they did not contemplate defeat.[9] There was, too, a degree of mutual tolerance and respect. A native regiment at the end of the Maratha wars, passing Dinapore where the King's 76th regiment of foot, alongside whom it had fought, was cantoned, invited them to an entertainment. The 76th accepted on condition that the sepoys should see them home to bed. After a glorious binge each man woke in his cot in barracks to which he had been carried by his hosts.[10] Only long years of familiarity could have allowed old men to make the crass decisions which were to spark off mutiny in 1857. The loyalty of native comrades in arms had become a property of easiness, but Bentinck could see 'no patriotism, no community feeling as to religion or birthplace, no influencing attachment from high considerations, or great honours and rewards. Our native army also is extremely ignorant, capable of the strongest religious excitement, and very sensitive to disrespect of their persons or infringement of their customs'.[11]

Anxiety about security, more than prospects of conquest, kept the enormous army in existence and, though Bentinck did his best to reduce its costs in order to reduce the national deficit, he met with obstruction at every turn. If Malcolm had stated that 'the only safe view that Britain can take of her empire is to consider it, as it really is, always in a state of danger,' it was the duty of the clipping Dutchman to set aside his reforms, not weaken the army.[12] Bentinck could not convince his countrymen that the native army was the principal danger to British rule, a fear shared by Macaulay and by a later governor-general, Lord Hardinge, who forecast that the Company's biggest fight would be with its own army.[13] There had been several garrison rebellions after Vellore, nearly all resulting from the sepoys' fear that their religious scruples were to be overridden in a drive to convert them to Christianity. In 1824 the garrison at Barrackpore resisted being shipped to Burma. They were ready to march hundreds of miles but not cross the water. In 1845 Hindu troops were also to resist crossing the Indus, the natural barrier to Hindostan, to fight in Sind. It was then that flogging was reintroduced into the Indian army. The envy and spite of British regulars were the real and not proximate causes of this reversal, but their reluctance should have reminded their commanders that Indian troops could be persuaded to do miracles, to fight against tremendous odds, to triumph over dangers that would have shocked Europeans, provided they could trust in the absolute respect of their officers for traditional customs and beliefs, no matter how irrational or inefficient. For a soldier who lost caste was a disgrace to his family and his village, as Sita Ram discovered when, grievously wounded and left for dead in Bundelkhand, he allowed himself to be succoured by an untouchable. For this defilement he had to undergo long and demeaning purification ceremonies that cost him five years' savings, a blow both to his pocket and his pride.[14] Units that demonstrated a personal and almost fanatical loyalty to their commanding officers were those almost private brigades raised by charismatic leaders, like Skinner's Yellow Boys, Hodson's Guides and Jacob's Scinde Horse, composed of soldiers of defeated armies, often adventurers of many faiths, former pindaris and bandits, for whom comradeship replaced caste. 'Well, Sahib,' the rissaldar of the Guides assured the commander-in-chief outside Delhi in 1857, 'wherever Hodson Sahib goes, we all go!'[15]

There were princely armies, too, for a prince in subsidiary alliance with the Company was allowed 'a court that preserved the forms of royalty, the right of keeping as many badly armed and worse paid ragamuffins as he could retain under his tawdry standard, and the privilege of occasionally sending letters of condolence or congratulation to the King of England, in which he calls himself His Majesty's good brother and ally'.[16] There were some 700 princely states, most of them small, ruling 604,717 square miles with a population of some 64 million.[17] Their very number prompted often intense discussion about the extension of British hegemony over the peripheral nations which might disturb the Pax Britannica – Nepalese Gurkhas, threatening to burst out of the valley of Kathmandu, predatory Burmese pushing into Manipur and Assam, trigger-happy Pathans, plunder-loving Afghans, wild Baluchi tribesmen from the Indus delta, and war-hungry Sikhs. The directors, the board of control and the civilians in Calcutta urged accommodation and patience. The soldiers in the marches wanted war.

The Company's expansion to the foothills of the Himalayan range brought it into conflict with a people on the move in the northern passages of India. The Nepalese were a mixed race of Indo-Tibetans, formerly Hindu Rajputs, seeking to ameliorate their hard mountain living by the sweeter enticements of life in the Kathmandu and Kashmir valleys. When they were blocked to the east by the Sikhs, also on the move from their mountain fastnesses, they were diverted to the valleys of Oudh. With great difficulty the tough highlanders were repelled and, when the British captured Kathmandu, a respectful peace confined the Gurkhas to their Nepalese homeland. Among the fruits of that peace was the acquisition of the small hill-state of Simla which the Gurkhas had recently overrun. Virtually no European had ever been there, but its sweet breezes and pine-scented air suggested an alternative to sweating out the long summers in Calcutta. Within 20 years there they were, 'with the band playing the *Puritani* and *Masaniello* and eating salmon from Scotland and sardines from the Mediterranean'.[18]

The Burmese, too, were lusting for the sweets of India, but the campaigns to repel them cost £5 million and 15,000 casualties, mainly from disease, and sparked rumours that the British had been beaten and would now leave India. Though the Burmese were eventually broken and surrendered their conquests, it had not been a glorious episode for British Indian arms. There was worse to come. By 1833, Russia's Asian intentions appeared seriously menacing to nervous watchers in Whitehall and Chowringhee. Since the Durrani kingdom in Afghanistan had split into warring factions, they might be tempted to adventure there, on their way to the clear waters of the Indian ocean. The most effective barrier would be a client amir on the gadi of Kabul. The opportunity came when the amir, refused a Company alliance to recover Peshawar from the Sikhs, approached the Russians. Even a perfunctory study of Afghan history, and Elphinstone's was readily available, would have revealed that, however much Afghans might fight among themselves, they fought more bitterly against any foreigner who interfered in their quarrels. The amir had no more intention of allowing the Russians into his kingdom than he did the British. But the forward party prevailed in Simla, a British client amir was put on the throne to cede the Indus delta lands to the Company, and allow it to exploit a river trade route to the khanates of central Asia. The sequel was to be the worst disaster to British arms since Wadgaon.

Between 2 and 9 November 1841, the entire British garrison in Kabul of 16,000 men was destroyed, and the civilians dragged off to captivity and domestic slavery. The causes of this débacle could have been foreseen. The troops were miserably unequipped for a winter of below-zero temperatures, they were accompanied by the usual shadow army of camp followers and garrisoned in an unprotected cantonment instead of in the citadel. The British commanders were in their 70s and the political chief had failed to notice that the English puppet was cordially detested by his subjects. When the blow fell, no one was ready for it. The re-treating troops 'fought like gods not men', but to no avail.[19] Extreme critics put the disaster down to the abolition of flogging in the Indian army. Kabul was recaptured in 1842, the prisoners liberated, and Afghanistan evacuated in an orderly retreat. The amir the British had deposed resumed his throne and reigned until his death in 1863. All this time the Russians had done absolutely nothing.

The new governor-general was greeted with the news of the massacre when he reached Madras. Lord Ellenborough had been president of the Board of Control since 1828, and shared Wellington's suspicions of Russian power in central Asia. He left London boasting that he would secure peace in Asia and arrived to face the shambles of Afghanistan. His first task being to restore the honour of British arms before disaffection spread, he greeted the withdrawal from Kabul as a victory. On 17 December 1842, he welcomed the troops who had sacked the city with a triumph at Ferozepore on the Sutlej, the border of British India. Their return was made glorious by the restoration to India of what the governor-general piously believed were the great sandalwood gates of the temple of Somnath, looted by Mahmud of Ghazni in 1025. Addressing the princes of India as brothers, he announced that the insult of 800 years had at last been avenged. Unfortunately, the gates, which had been looted from a mosque in Ghazni, did not date back to 1025 and were made of deal. Somnath, moreover, was a ruin and, in the face of so many more contemporary insults, the Hindus had forgotten that of Mahmud. The relics never got further than the lumber room of Agra fort. Ellenborough also marked his arrival with an assurance to those same princes that the British government had no territorial ambitions left in India and wished to live in peace and harmony with them all.

Yet, on 26 August 1843, with a stroke of the pen and without consulting his principals in London, he annexed the province of Sind. The flatlands of the lower Indus had never been an inviting prospect, regularly flooded, flagellated by dry winds from Baluchistan and bordered by a hard clay desert on the west and salt flatlands of the Rann of Cutch on the east. During the dry season the Rann was a dead arena of caked mud, in the rains a swamp, large enough to swallow an army without trace. Only the mighty delta sustained life and this had marked for centuries the furthest extremity of Hindostan. The Baluchi Talpurs, who ruled from Hyderabad, had little interest in commerce. In 1832 Bentinck, negotiated a treaty allowing steamboats to navigate the Indus with trade goods, but they were implacably opposed to the suggestion that it could provide an alternative route to Afghanistan for soldiers and military supplies. The British débacle in Afghanistan only made them more truculent.

On 12 December 1841, General Sir Charles Napier (aged 59) arrived in India. A veteran of Irish risings and the war in the Peninsula, he was not a man of peace. Contemptuous of comfort he believed that a man 'should have none but his pillow and his courage'.[20] Once his mind was made up there was no changing it, and here he was in Sind, 'with no orders! no instructions! no precise lines of policy given!'.[21] On his first visit to Hyderabad, he complained that only the Resident prevented him from thrashing those 'tyrannical, drunken, debauched, cheating, intriguing, contemptible Ameers'.[22] The mirs, feeling distinctly threatened by Napier's audible bluster, attacked the residency, Sind was conquered and Punch marked the event with the mock telegram *peccavi* ('I have Sinned'). The Indus was now a British river as far as the Sikh border at Multan, and Ellenborough justified his action by claiming that the mirs were interfering with the free movement of goods by surreptitiously levying tolls. The directors were not pleased by a conquest that could not pay for itself and where, despite Napier's economies, expenditure outran income by £500,000 a year. Wellington chid the governor-general for leaving decisions to the man on the spot. Mounstuart Elphinstone, opposing a Parliamentary vote of thanks, told the House that 'our conduct in Sind, immediately after the humiliations of Afghanistan, exactly resembled that of a bully who, having been knocked down in a street row, goes home and beats his wife'.[23] Ellenborough was impenitent. Fearing a return to the times of Richard Wellesley, the directors in 1844 exercised their constitutional right to recall the governor-general, even one who had been a member of cabinet, and in his place accepted a 50-year-old Peninsula and Waterloo veteran, Sir Henry Hardinge. Sir William Napier was furious at the recall of Lord Ellenborough. Was this 'the reward of zeal, ability, honesty and the saving of India? ... This mad step will do mischief... India is in great danger'.[24] Sind was uncomfortably close to Sikh territory and the view from the upper reaches of the Indus alarmed him.

The Sikhs were Jat yeomen who farmed the doab land of the five rivers, the Panjab, a light-skinned people in a well-watered province on the same latitude as the southern states of the USA. They had become a distinctive race as a result of the last great conversion in India. The first guru, the founder of a line of gurus who sprang from his loins, was born in 1469. Guru Nanak had read the Koran and the Puranas, but not found God in them. In the spirit of the author of Ecclesiastes, he could only urge men to worship the One, Invisible God, live virtuously and be tolerant of others. The tenth and last guru was assassinated in 1708. Their disciples practised a worship free of commands and prohibitions, free believers, not mosque or temple fodder. In the way of all religions, they acquired a holy book, a messianic mission and a physical distinction from a Hinduism that could so easily have re-absorbed them; if the worship of the one true God were to triumph over Hindu delusion and Islamic error, it must be at the point of the sword. Throughout the 18th century, the Sikhs had faced both ways, defending the land of the five rivers from Afghans, Mughals, and Marathas. The *akalis*, or saints, who ruled the Sikh confederacy, were seldom at rest from war, a condition they adopted as their way of renouncing the vanities of this world. The Sikh's dedication to war called for a single, secular ruler and, like King Saul, the Maharajah Ranjit Singh emerged at the end of the century to weld his people into a nation. Invested as a virtually independent monarch in Lahore, which he had seized in 1799, by the Afghan Zaman Shah, he proceeded to replace the *khalsa*, the armed farmers who responded to a call to arms from their religious leaders, with a disciplined army, trained by French and Italian veterans of Napoleon's wars. What he lacked in majesty – he was short, uncouth and blind in one eye, since childhood, 'exactly like an old mouse' – he made up in self-confidence. 'A very drunken old profligate, he has conquered a great many powerful enemies, he is remarkably just in his government... He has hardly ever taken away life, which is wonderful in a despot, and he is excessively loved by his people.'[25]

His kingdom was a Mughal successor state, which thrived on agriculture and the rich trade that crossed it, boosted by a monopoly of grain, salt and the sale of Kashmir shawls. The British were on his borders at Ludhiana but unlike Tipu, whom he resembled in many ways, he was careful not to fall out with John Company. He resisted the blandishments of Scindia and Holkar, and was neutral in the Anglo-Gurkha war of 1814–5. He was punctilious in paying his respects to the governors-general and in 1838, six months before his death, he invited a visit from Lord Auckland, made notorious by the pen of his sister, Emily Eden. To the British, he was an able savage, who retired into a corner of the magnificent tent in which he was receiving Lord William Bentinck to urinate, whose best dinner service was composed of palm leaves and who received Europeans barefooted.[26] He liked to be amused and he did not find the British amusing, but he knew better than to cross them. When urged to stand firm against them, he asked what happened to the 200,000 spears of the Marathas.[27] He kept his army down to 25,000 well-drilled men and a superb park of artillery, not enough to threaten the British, but enough to make other neighbours tremble. For Emily and George Eden they formed an aisle over two miles long at Amritsar, dressed all in yellow kincob, up which the governor-general's cavalcade swept to serried ranks stretching a further five miles before them. Nobody in the Eden party knew 'what to say about it, so they say nothing, except that they are sure the Sikhs would run away in a total fright!'.[28] Victor Jacquemont, the French naturalist, who did amuse Ranjit, was confident he would turn on the British if the Russians successfully invaded, for he was not above dreaming of a Sikh empire over India.[29]

By harnessing the messianic zeal of the khalsa, he had bound his Sikhs to a wheel which, in the absence of his controlling spirit, brought his people into conflict with the one power that could subdue them. Ranjit died in June 1839 and, the strong hand of the maharajah removed, the Sikh chieftains fell to quarrelling and the khalsa re-emerged to become the arbiters of peace or war. The British retreat from Kabul seemed to suggest that Ranjit had overestimated the strength of the Company and the chiefs remembered that it had denied them conquests in Sind, Afghanistan and Tibet. The number of men under arms rose to 60,000 and, to stop them tearing each other to pieces, the khalsa decided to turn them on the British. In December 1845 they crossed the Sutlej to liberate their co-religionists oppressed under British rule. The two Sikh wars between 1845 and 1849 had the result which Ranjit had always feared, of colouring the Panjab red, but the dye was blood. The British high command had not been ready for two savage and bitter wars and the expensive victories that broke the khalsa were massacres as costly as any battle in the Crimea.[30] The generalship on both sides was dire. Wave after wave of sepoys, stiffened by Europeans, were sent into the mouths of cannons which were more skilfully and lethally handled than ever they had experienced before. Lord Hardinge, unable to resist a fight, himself led an attack on the largest gun in the most effective battery, a sublime but pointless folly. The khalsa failed to destroy the British armies, which were left the almost defeated masters of the field, through divided counsels. After the first war, the British advanced their frontier to the Beas river, and as the Sikhs could not pay the war indemnity, the governor-general sold the province of Kashmir to a Dogra Rajput for cash down. Ranjit's reputed son was permitted to rule a truncated state round Lahore.

In 1847 Hardinge handed over to the youngest governor-general yet. James Andrew Ramsay, tenth Earl of Dalhousie, was a Scottish grandee with a longer pedigree than any of his predecessors. Ramsays had served Scotland and her kings since 1140 and it was the family's proud boast that none had crawled through seven centuries. Hardinge had made the peace, reduced expense, extended commerce and strengthened British rule by justice, kindness and wisdom.[31] 'It would not be necessary to fire a gun in India for several years to come.'[32] Within three months the Company was plunged into the second Sikh War. Resentment at defeat was compounded by the abolition of suttee (Ranjit Singh had been accompanied on his pyre by 11 women) and female infanticide, so that the Company had become a foreign tyrant interfering with the sacred rights of Sikh chieftains. They soon found common cause with paid-off soldiers who were still confident that they could lick the Company. The revolt started in the furthest south of the Sikh satrapies at Multan, and the Panjab was again in flames. Lord Gough, 69, had used his army in the earlier war like a battering ram in the face of artillery every bit as good as his own and he had won his battles with severe loss of life. The tactic being successful, he repeated it. At Chilianwala, in January 1849, he lost 2,336 British officers and men, an un-precedented slaughter for an Indian battle. He was suspended, to be replaced by Charles Napier, but before he learned of his supersession he had won, by the same tactic, the crushing victory of Gujrat, near the Chenab, with the loss of only 69 dead. The heroism on both sides became legendary, reconciling the Sikhs to the severity of their defeat, brought about by a leadership unable to profit from the stupidity of the British. The Sikhs surrendered their weapons and retired to their farms, their Afghan allies galloped home to boast of their glorious deeds of war, and the Company Bahadur moved up to their gates at Peshawar. Baron Gough got his viscountcy and the Panjab was formally annexed in March 1849.

The Sikhs had established that man for man, the Asian was as good as the European; only the endemic tendency of chiefs to seek their own ends before those of the khalsa led to defeat, just as it had the Marathas against Wellington. Sita Ram thought 'the Sikhs fought as no man had ever fought in India before, but it was clear that their commanders did not know how to command an army'.[33] Gough was no Wellington and was lucky to win. But there was an inevitability about the conquest of the Panjab which made it different from earlier conquests. It was an act of rehabilitation. The debacle at Kabul had to be set right, even at dreadful cost. George Meredith immortalised the pity of it:

> Chillianwallah, Chillianwallah!
> Where our brothers fought and bled!
> O thy name is natural music
> And a dirge above the dead!
> Though we have not been defeated
> Though we can't be overcome,
> Still, whene'er thou art repeated,
> I would fain that grief were dumb.[34]

Had the Panjab not been conquered, then the British fate in 1857 would have been catastrophically different, and the new governor-general believed that once and for all annexation was the right fate for states which had shown that they could not govern themselves.

Dalhousie annexed the Panjab, as Ellenborough had annexed Sind, without reference to London. For the people he was to govern, he professed the

Bentinckian view that their happiness was his first concern. The 20-year economic depression had lifted, partly due to the imperial telegraph service, the railways, the reliable survey maps, public works like the Ganges canal, the metalled roads and bridges, the imperial post offices, the new department of public instruction, the reform of the gaols and abolition of branding, the cultivation of tea, the protection of forests, the Archaeological Survey of India and the conservation of its ancient monuments, the systematic training of civil servants and improved conditions for the army. He was both despot and radical, to which contradictions he added conservative and Christian, and believed that God had given him a charge to complete the reforms that had faltered under Bentinck's successors. He listened to advice but once his mind was made up he was unmovable. He would not tolerate backsliding or equivocation, and his rebukes were couched in language honed to the cold precision of steel. He did not encourage familiarity. Not for him the modesty of Bentinck or the geniality of Emily Eden's brother, Lord Auckland. Short of stature, like Wellesley, he put on height with his uniform. Charles Trevelyan, testifying to Parliament before the renewal of the charter in 1853, had argued that British India should be ruled as one country not three; instead of three separate Presidency executive councils, there should be one supreme legislative council. Dalhousie proposed having Indians on it, but that proved too much even for the strong stomach of James Mill's liberal son, John Stuart. In the 1853 India Act, the governor-general was relieved of the government of Bengal but there was no legislative council. The other governors kept their virtually autonomous councils and, worse, their right to approach the Secretary of State direct. Like governors-general after him, particularly Lord Curzon, Dalhousie had cause to complain of this 'qualified privilege of insubordination'.[35]

Dalhousie did not suffer criticism easily. When Cunningham asserted in his *History of the Sikhs* that the bloody and costly battle of Sobraon (1846) had been fought unnecessarily, he was removed summarily from the political department and posted into the wilderness.[36] His assertion, however, was sound. The Sikhs were ready to treat but the British wanted a victory in the field. England, he wrote, must 'be certain that her sympathising labours in the cause of humanity are guided by intelligence towards a true and attainable end. She rules supreme as the welcome composer of political trouble; but the thin superficies of her dominion rests tremblingly upon the convulsed ocean of social change and mental revolution'. The subject princes were monarchs without power, the newly rich zamindars, bankers and merchants did not enjoy the respect accorded to Europeans, the peasants still laboured under taxation which may not have been ruinous but was still excessive. 'The husbandman is sullen and indifferent, the gentleman nurses his wrath in secrecy, kings idly chafe and intrigue, and all are ready to hope for everything from a change of masters.'[37]

That criticism continued to nag Dalhousie. The chaos of India was giving way to order. Why, then, did so many Indians pine for the days of their independence, when they were oppressed, tortured and plundered under their own princes? Sleeman might urge the retention of native states to demonstrate how much better things were under the British, but Dalhousie could see no point in preserving them. Dalhousies had been king-makers. The new governor-general was to be a king-breaker. The descent of Indian princes from their stellar ancestors was more than mythical, it was fraudulent, for in default of a natural heir, one could be adopted. If the prince had an overlord, his agreement was customarily secured. Between 1848 and 1854, Dalhousie exercised his overlord right to declare three inheritances null, annexing the disputed states to British India. None of them strained either practice or justice. The *chhatrapathi* of Satara, the descendant of Shivaji and prince of a state specially created for him in 1818, adopted an heir without approval and contrary to treaty. The state lapsed. The Bhosle rajah of the truncated state of Nagpur died without heir. As a tributary, not an independent state, it lapsed. The subahdar of Jhansi had never been an independent prince. His surviving rani proposed to adopt an heir post mortem. Permission was refused and the state lapsed. The decision earned the British the undying rancour of the rani who tried to get her own back in 1857. In all three cases Dalhousie was within his rights.

After Shah Alam's death in 1806, the Light of the World had progressively dimmed in the red fortress which was both his palace and his prison in Delhi. The padishah's 500 women and 70 sons, and the rest of his court lived in a cocoon of accumulated filth and bird-droppings that covered Shahjahan's once magic palace. Governors-general avoided visiting Delhi where they were technically vassals and it was not until 1827 that the emperor and Lord Amherst (governor-general 1823–8) managed an awkward meeting, at which the emperor received his visitor at the door and escorted him to a throne of equal height to his own. Thereafter, any pretence that the emperor was an overlord was quietly abandoned. Distinguished visitors to Delhi were encouraged to pay their respects, the cost of the shoddy gifts, accompanied by cushions bearing gold mohurs, being met by the Company. The squalor and desolation in which royalty lived saddened Bishop Heber, who hoped that 'no further degradation is reserved for the poor old man,' who reminded him of 'the druid's head on a Welsh halfpenny' 'whose idea was associated in my childhood with all imaginable wealth and splendour, under the name of the Great Mogul'.[38] He was now styled King of Delhi, no higher than his former wazir, the King of Oudh, and Emily Eden, in 1836, finding his guards asleep on charpoys in the splendid marble baths, mused on the power and wealth that had passed away.[39]

In 1835 the Company ceased minting the imperial rupee with the image of Shah Alam and replaced it with that of William IV. In 1841, however, the Jat Rajah of Dholpur, 'though indebted to [the Company] for all he had or ever will have, and though he has never had anything and never can have... anything from the poor pageant of the House of Timur... yet on his seal of office he declared himself to be the slave and creature of the imperial warrior for the faith of Islam'.[40] Lord Ellenborough in 1842 hoped that the *padishah* would surrender his title to the young queen of England, but the myth of Mughal majesty was still too strong in Leadenhall Street. Charles Metcalfe, the son of a Bengal army officer who later became a Company director, appointed Resident in Delhi in 1813, was the ruler of the Mughal state, the patron and the gaoler of the padishah, and as governor, chief justice, collector and commander-in-chief, he behaved much like a Mughal subahdar. Government, in his view, should be 'most simple, most free from artificial institutions'.[41] He preserved the old Mughal system of discretionary government, especially the network of village councils and headmen, responsible for raising the revenue, and combined the roles of judge, magistrate and collector in one person. Speed of justice was more important than justness, and commissioners were his agents, a permanent chief in each district, incorruptible, unsleeping, ruthless and fair. In reality, many commissioners were distanced by geography and language from their myrmidons, the district police, or *thanadars*, who were so poorly paid that they could be persuaded to turn a blind eye or to arrest the innocent. Plaintiffs feared to come to court if they could not purchase the support of the thanadars.[42] The Company paid its European servants adequately, its native officers badly. That was the basic inconsistency of its rule, which no amount of theorising about the happiness of the governed could disguise.

Only one member of the cabinet, the secretary of state for India, was in favour of the annexation of the Panjab; the others feared that Calcutta was bound to an Ixion wheel of conquest which they had been trying to arrest for two decades. Then, in 1852, following insult by the local governor to two British merchants, Dalhousie annexed Pegu and lower Burma, an area in which he had no political or economic interest. The emperor in Ava was warned that any further hostile action would be the end of Burma's independence and of his house. The governor-general had established the principle that an insult offered to the British flag at the mouth of the Ganges would be resented as fully as an insult offered at the mouth of the Thames.[43]

The dissolution of the kingdom of Oudh was something different. Dalhousie, observing the success of Thomason in the North-West Province, of Metcalfe in Delhi and of the Lawrence brothers in the Panjab, could only look with a jaundiced eye at the failure of the Company's oldest ally in India to bring order to his finances.[44] The Awadhi taluqdars were petty rajahs, Hindu and Muslim, with traditional powers of fief and fee, the equivalent of collector and magistrate. As long as they delivered the king's share of taxes, they could sustain their little courts and fortified ranches from the surplus. To the high-minded British administrators in the adjacent provinces, they were rapacious, dishonest and inefficient. What Oudh needed was fair administration and a sound system of revenue collection. On 7 February 1856, that was what it got. The graduates of the Thomason-Lawrence school were to start a three-year settlement of the land along the lines they had successfully established next door. The settlement was never completed. In its first year the taluqdars were required to deliver their share of revenue under the old royal contracts, without demur, on pain of penalty. Those who prevaricated had villages summarily removed from their control and those who were assessed saw their fiefdoms reduced by nearly a third.[45] Two years later, the secretary to the government of India concluded that it was a mistake. 'Because it reduced them to a level with the meanest before the law... because it compelled them to disband their arms, pay their revenue regularly and not oppress the *ryots*', the decree had been a decree too many. When Oudh went up in flames in May 1857, the traditionally conservative landlords proved only too ready to throw in their lot with rebellious sepoys and frightened peasantry.[46] Dalhousie could have made a similar mistake with the Panjab after the second Sikh war. The mantle of Malcolm, Munro, and Elphinstone had fallen on two disciples, in the biblical sense, for they were as often on their knees as on their feet, more deeply into the Bible than into Ariosto or Ovid. For Henry and John Lawrence the romantic challenge of ruling an alien people for their own good was spiced and sanctified by the Biblical precedent of the Book of Judges. The brothers Lawrence were inspired not by Bentham, Malthus or Mill, but by the word of God.[47] Alexander, George, Henry, John and Richard Lawrence were, through their mother, Letitia Knox, descendants of the grim apostle of Scottish Calvinism, which was bred into their bones and read into their brains. Their father was the only survivor of the four young officers who had volunteered to lead the storming of Seringapatam. Through a relation of their mother, they all secured Company appointments. Alexander, George, Henry and Richard joined the army and all became generals. John was the sole civilian and became Viceroy and Governor-general. Henry came to India, aged 17, in 1823, to join the Bengal Artillery. Despite an erratic temper and the habit of shouting at natives, for which his gentle wife, Honoria, constantly chid him, Henry inspired a passionate loyalty among his subordinates and a grudging admiration from the Indians in his charge. After marriage, he and his wife pitched their tent where duty took them like Old Testament patriarchs. It found him at the right hand of Lord Hardinge during the first Sikh war, resident at the court of Duleep Singh and in 1849 president of the board of administration for the conquered Panjab.

As the ceaselessly growing empire demanded an increasing flow of young cadets, John was hurried through Haileybury and, on arrival in 1829, attached to Fort William College to learn Persian, after which he was sent to assist the collector in Delhi, where, as assistant judge, magistrate and collector, he was required to pacify an area of 800 square miles with a population of half a million souls, and which included the ceded territories after the first Sikh war. Chasing marauders, giving judgements, mapping, assessing farms and encouraging agriculture, John had an infinite capacity for taking pains, driving himself with Puritan zeal. Nothing escaped him. 'Jan Larens,' whispered the peasants, 'sub janta.' ('John Lawrence knows all.')[48] Pestered night and day, travelling huge distances and living most of the year under canvas, he compiled for his superior officer, at the end of each day, a meticulous record of his activities omitting, more often than not, the details of 'hair-breadth escapes from assassination, from drowning, from wild beasts; of great criminals hunted down; of cattle lifting on a gigantic scale; of riots and raids; of robberies and murders; of thugs and dacoits'.[49]

John Lawrence accepted the Mughal model, championed by Metcalfe, of putting responsibility under one head and into one pair of hands. 'I give you these three (police districts),' he told Charles Raikes, assigned to him as assistant collector of Panipat in 1835, when Lawrence had only been six years in India. 'I put the police and revenue work under you. You are not to get in rows with the military... If you can keep crime down and collect your revenue... I will not interfere with you... Come and see me sometimes.'[50] His recipe for good government was 'Settle the country, make the people happy and take care there are no rows', and it worked in the Panjab.[51] After the second Sikh war he was made responsible for the finances of the Panjab. The Lawrence brothers should have been, but were not, a harmonious team. Henry in Lahore felt for the broken

Sikhs and wanted them to preserve their independence in a friendly state. John, the new model civil servant, wanted the Panjab to be a prosperous province of the British raj, with Sikh warriors converted to contented peasants, turning in a revenue surplus. Dalhousie eventually settled their quarrels by sending Henry to Rajputana, as agent, a post well below his seniority and capacity. Henry's passage from Lahore to Agra was like that of a much-loved king going into exile, but John was left to deliver his model Panjab, and this, because he was a Lawrence, was well done. The conquered province was divided into districts, each under a commissioner or deputy commissioner. Monopolies were abolished, land tax was swiftly assessed, the police were efficient, justice was speedy, simple and cheap, the power of recalcitrant chiefs was dissolved, fortresses were destroyed and private armies disarmed. A new force was created from the former khalsa to back the commissioner's will, public works were completed, a system of education imposed, and the conditions recreated in which agriculture and commerce could flourish. The pace was rapid and the effects heady, but they were solid and visible enough to make the Panjab loyal to its new masters. Put to the test in 1857, it held.

The lesser breeds might have their own ways of doing things, but if these were not the ways of the governors, that was too bad for them. Charles Napier, when told by the village elders that suttee was a religious issue, not affected by the 1829 regulation, concurred. 'The burning of widows is your custom. Repair to the funeral pile. But my nation also has a custom. When men burn women we hang them... My carpenters therefore shall erect gibbets on which to hang all concerned when the widow is consumed. Let us all act according to national custom.'[52] The epitome of the Dalhousie years was John Nicholson, another Bible-bred Irishman, who began swatting the devil with a knotted handkerchief at the age of three and continued swatting until shot down at the Kabul gate during the storming of Delhi in 1857. He fought the bullies and cheats at school and it was with some relief that his schoolfellows saw him leave at 16 for a cadetship in the Bengal infantry. In his first post at Ferozepore, on the Sikh frontier, he requisitioned supplies from reluctant village headmen by threatening them with a good flogging and showed that he meant it.

In 1847 Nicholson became Henry Lawrence's assistant in Lahore. They had Ireland and the Bible in common, but the special alchemy of Henry's character, so different from Nicholson's, gave him an understanding of what he had come to India to do. So far he had had little opportunity to put into practice the lessons of the Old Testament in ruling rough, independent peasants who respected firmness mixed with justice. Nicholson's theory was that rulers must stay on top. Any relaxation of watchfulness, any lowering of the guard, any misplaced kindness, any delay in taking action, any demonstration of weakness would be fatal among a people for whom lawlessness was a way of life. The second Sikh war gave him the action he excelled at: fast, decisive cavalry action, prodding, stabbing, keeping the enemy on the move, attacking unexpectedly and decisively in the tradition of James Skinner. His personal bravery and invulnerability gave him god-like attributes, so that he began to be embarrassed by adepts of a new cult who accepted 'Nikal Seyn' as their object of devotion. When he had them flogged in an attempt to disillusion them, it only made them more devout. Only after his death did the sect dissolve, some of its adepts accepting the worship of Nikal Seyn's own God.

In 1852 Henry Lawrence made him deputy commissioner for Bannu, a district of 6,500 square miles between the Afghan border and the river Indus. He dealt with refractory Bannuchis as he had dealt with the devil, cheats and bullies of his childhood. Desperadoes and tigers he hunted with a sabre with equal success. The desperadoes he often cut down in single combat, the tigers he confused by riding round them in reducing circles, too fast for the bewildered animal to spring and, when sufficiently close, delivering the coup de grace. He seemed moulded like a centaur to his horse, galloping immense distances to deal with disputes, and his court was open through the great heat of the day. He seemed to require no rest and, if he was impatient with evidence, the justice in shirtsleeves that he delivered was as close to fair as it seemed possible to get. He was an insatiable flogger, preferring peremptory justice to the injustice of prison. He despised the rule-book and was impatient of regulations. It was only his simple, biblical, imperative to fight evil and do good that prevented him from becoming a monster. He had the pride of the twice-born. When a tribesman spat on the ground in front of him, he forced him to lick it up. He had a mullah forcibly shaved for dumb insolence. There was not a man in the hills that did not shiver in his pyjamas when he heard the name of Nikal Seyn.

The 1857 Mutiny provided Nicholson with his apotheosis. John Lawrence had insisted that the disaffected sepoys in the Peshawar district should be disarmed. He had few Europeans to command, so he had to rely on officers like Nicholson, 'worth the wing of a regiment', to do the job with native troops.[53] At the head of a small troop of *sowars* (mounted camel corps), he chased a detachment of mutineers trying to escape into Swat. 'Seeming to multiply himself many times over he rode hither and thither, [he] laid low... dozens of men who, as he admitted afterwards with genuine admiration, fought desperately.' Only after 20 hours in the saddle, having ridden 70 miles without change of steed, did he give up the chase.[54] On another occasion, he pursued a batch of rebels through July's blazing midday sun and, when they took refuge on an island in the Jhelum river, he attacked them without boats and with only one gun, slaughtering them to a man. Slicing one wretched sepoy clean in two with his sabre, he commented laconically, 'Not a bad sliver that'.[55] Laid low by a bullet in the attack on Delhi, he survived long enough to threaten to shoot anyone who talked of retreat and died in great agony, only interested in one thing, the progress of the battle, before his soul crossed to Valhalla.[56] Not everyone was impressed. Victor Jacquemont observed with distaste the temptation of power that lurked in the path of deputy commissioners, often, like Nicholson, young soldiers. 'With an independence equal to that of the Great Turk, he acts as judge over his own subjects and, what is more, those of neighbouring rajahs, Hindu, Tartar or Tibetan, sending them to prison, fining them, even hanging them when he thinks fit.'[57] Nicholson was an alluring but bad example. Most of them were well-meaning and conscientious men, but afflicted by a corroding sense of racial superiority. Victory after 22 years of war against France had helped to imbue a sense of glacial arrogance into the British ruling class. The British had found themselves with strange, ungentlemanly allies: Spanish *guerillas*, Neapolitan *lazzaroni*, Sicilian peasants,

Brazilian planters and Spanish American *caudillos*, as well as the nizam of Hyderabad and the king of Oudh. Some of the rulers, too, with whom they had contrived to defeat Napoleon, seemed little better than the sort of monster to whom they had sold Kashmir after the second Sikh War. Rajah Gulab Singh treated as a calumny that he had flayed alive 12,000 men, insisting that he had only skinned three, but added on reflection, 'hundred'. His successor was credited with suspending a rebellious brother by his hair from a beam, lowering him a few inches a day into a cauldron of boiling oil until he was extinct. This, he warned his people, was a merciful death compared to what he would mete out to anyone rash enough to rebel.[58] Schoolboys reared on Livy and Cicero had been groomed to be representatives of a new Rome, ruling conquered nations. Brazilians, Spaniards, Portuguese, Sicilians, Neapolitans, even the civilised Florentines, learned what it was like to be treated like Indians.[59] Significantly, the word 'nigger' had entered the Anglo-Indian vocabulary.[60] Even Nicholson used it. Neither Haileybury nor Addiscombe flogged it out of new cadets who resented having to learn 'nigger language'. Indian vernaculars are rich in insults, but there is no insult like one applied to a race rather than an individual. The race must, sooner or later, hit back.

Flamboyant, inspired, sometimes brutal administrators there were, but by 1841 the reforms envisioned in the India bill of 1833 had come to a stop. Educators of an Indian middle class who were to be, in Macaulay's words, 'the interpreters between us and the millions whom we govern', were still locked in debate with the supporters of vernacular schools.[61] Would these 'interpreters' be faithful? Were they not more likely to learn and harbour treasonable thoughts? Charles Trevelyan, impatient for his brother-in-law's codes to be promulgated, urged Parliament to ensure that justice in India was cheap, swift and economical, whereas in most of British India, it was almost impossible to speed up the business of the courts.[62] Honoria Lawrence in 1852 observed the success of rough Panjab justice pronounced by village elders, whose principal weapon was to threaten a hardened malefactor 'with being handed over to the English courts of law, the delays and complications of which are looked upon with great terror'.[63] Macaulay's criminal code continued 'to repose in the Record Office as if in the Tower'.[64] The steam in the utilitarian kettle had boiled away. Other priorities had taken over.

10. 'EUROPEANS CANNOT RETREAT'

Europeans cannot retreat. Without rum, without beef, without success, they would soon be without hope, without organisation. Cabul would come again.

Herbert Edwardes to John Lawrence, 11 June 1857

The people of India have only seen England in its worst form in that country. They have seen it in its military power, its exclusive Civil Service, and in the supremacy of a handful of foreigners.

John Bright to the House of Commons,
24 June 1858

Be silent, O COOMPANEE BAHADUR! Cover up your brazen, seared, bloodstained old face, fold your sharp-clawed dirty old hands, and die... like an old Thug as you are.

Punch, February 1858

For a long time they accounted for the presence of the Queen's effigy on the rupee by setting her down as the wife of John Kumpani.

George Otto Trevelyan, *The Competition-wallah*

IN JUNE 1853 JOHN BRIGHT, in a speech of devastating criticism, opposed the motion to renew the Company's charter in the House of Commons. The directors may not have intended to misgovern India, but it was patent that they did, and the Board of Control, whose president changed every two years, was powerless to control them. The government of India had squandered its revenues on ruinous wars, bringing 100 million people living below subsistence under its rule, with no resources to improve their lot. Since 1784, when the Board of Control was set up, public debt had risen from £8,000,000, to over £50,000,000 in 1854, military spending had risen from £8,000,000 a year in 1833 to £12,000,000, accounting for 56% of all government expenditure and the Company had to borrow £16,000,000 to pay a dividend. All offices of government were open to Indians, yet not a single Indian had filled a higher post than he could have filled before 1833, and half-trained boys were still being sent out from Britain to enjoy all the privileges of a covenanted service. Why had so few Britons invested their property in India? Was it because Europeans 'had an absolute terror of coming under the Company's courts'? What had happened to Macaulay's promise that the Law Commission would change all that? Its report had been going to and fro like an unsettled spirit between Britain and India, as if the directors were intent on its extinction. And, out of an income of £29,000,000, why was only £66,000 spent on education? If the Company should goad the people of India into insurrection, the British government would have to 'reconquer the country or be ignominiously driven out of it'.[1] The government of India should be transferred to the crown.

The Sikh Wars, moreover, had called into question the value for that £12,000,000. Was it possible that Indian regiments, united and properly led, could beat Europeans? Lord Hardinge feared so. John Jacob, commanding his new-formed Scinde Horse, warned his superiors that they could, and General Napier, who had come late in his career to India, thought his colleagues were dangerously complacent about the loyalty of the Bengal regiments. They had proved staunch on so many fields of battle. They derived status and dignity from their service. How could they betray their salt? Yet they had mutinied, over field allowances, over serving outside Hindostan and, on occasions, they had answered invitations to cheer with 'yells and brutish scowls'.[2] Nor were sepoys a headless rabble without their European officers. Their own native officers often had more combat experience, especially as so many Europeans had opted for political service that the officer corps was never up to strength. When the revolt of the mercenaries came, it was very nearly successful. Had there been an Indian Lenin to take political control of the people's army, the mutiny would have been a war of independence.

Of political leadership, however, there was none. Disaffected princes merely tried to recover lost privileges and estates. When the Meerut garrison entered Delhi on 11 May 1857 it put itself under the green flag of Islam and the King of Delhi. Bahadur Shah had been twenty years on the throne, an accomplished if solipsistic poet, but otherwise almost an imbecile, believing he had the power to transform himself into other creatures.[3] Yet, for all his personal inadequacy, he was the *padishah* and *ghazi* (Sword of the Faith). His one wise action was to ban cow slaughter during the Id, so that Hindu and Muslim could be united against the British rather than each other.[4] The revolt was not a Muslim jihad and the rebels came from all communities except Christians. Muslims accepted the lead of Hindu rajahs and Hindus rallied to Muslim generals, as had been their custom through the ages. In Delhi the object of the revolt might have been the revival of the Mughal raj, elsewhere it was a return to the patchwork rule of former princes, to a less exacting financial regime for the ryot and the removal of meddlesome Christianity. As the war progressed it became a fight for personal survival.

The Mutiny was, moreover, confined to the Bengal army and not all regiments, even when exposed to the humiliation of being disarmed, mutinied. Of the 1700 men under siege in the Lucknow residency, 765 were native troops, 200 of whom were to be killed or wounded in its defence.[5] There was no rising in the south and only spasmodic unrest in the Bombay presidency. Even among the aggrieved aristocracy of Hindostan, support for mutiny was patchy and almost non-existent in Bengal itself. The Indian merchant community of Calcutta condemned it wholesale. Servants often remained faithful to their families and endured the horrors of siege with them in Kanpur and Lucknow. When the sepoys mutinied in Barrackpore, one family left the breakfast table to retreat to Fort William, leaving the house to their servants, with the china breakfast service, newly arrived from England, on the table, all their jewellery and a roll of 300 rupees in cupboards. When they returned it was all as they had left it.[6] Some mutineers saw their officers and their families to safety, some even hid refugees from their colleagues who would have killed them. Villagers and landlords risked their lives to save European fugitives from bands of sepoys seeking their death. Despite wild talk of flying chapatties, carrying the call from camp to camp, there was no single call to mutiny, indeed no single cause.[7] To some, the misplaced kindness of British officers was to blame. To others native education. The Scottish Presbyterian missionary, Alexander Duff, believed that schooling had concentrated too much on knowledge and too little on Christian precept. 'As Christianity has never taught rulers to oppress, so it will never teach subjects to rebel.'[8] If education was not set in a firm religious frame – in his view that of the Bible – education just put dangerous information into minds unable to use it properly.[9] To more secular minds, it was fear of Christianity. By their over-enthusiastic promotion of Bible study, proselytisers had encouraged the belief that schools were to produce a generation of government servants expected to turn Christian.[10] The new railways came in for their share of obloquy: they herded men and women of all castes and religions together and constituted a diabolic device for pollution. The telegraph, too, that relayed messages as fast as light, was being used for subliminal Christian persuasion. When governors-general, justices, commissioners and collectors went to church on Sunday, it was to receive their briefing on the next stage of christianisation. Brahman pandit, itinerant fakir and Muslim mullah had a religious duty to warn the faithful of the danger they were in.[11]

A prominent Muslim was probably nearer the truth than most. The British government had not cultivated the friendship of its subject people. It had kept itself apart, and 'at last came the day when all men looked upon the English government as slow poison, a rope of sand, a treacherous flame of fire.'[12] That no native could possibly be a gentleman was indicative of the contempt of the rulers for the ruled, and contempt was an ineradicable wrong.[13] Despite his noble sentiments, Dalhousie had shown that contempt when he bundled local princes off historic thrones. Sepoy and civilian could spend a lifetime in the army or administration and never earn the pay even of a British subaltern or rise higher than a deputy collector. Add the upward ratcheting of land-tax, the enforced selling-up of proprietors who fell behind with their payments or who could not pay their debts – land had traditionally been inalienable – and the corruption and venality of British courts that made justice too costly to obtain, the climate of fear was universal.[14]

Rumours about the greased cartridge for the newly introduced Lee Enfield rifle provided the trigger: that the use of pig and cow tallow was intended to make pollution doubly sure and so drive compromised and casteless sepoys into the arms of zealous Christian officers, excited chaplains and pious memsahibs, who insisted on preaching, passing on tracts and encouraging their men and servants to avoid eternal destruction by embracing Christ.[15] Suttee and female infanticide had gone down before government, so who could trust the word of the British? Certainly not that caste army of military priests, the Bengal army, 'almost wholly uneducated except in the ceremonies of Brahmanism'.[16] Muslims were reminded that they were once the proud rulers of Hindostan. A bogus fatwah, pronouncing a jihad against the infidel British, encouraged them to make common cause with infidel Hindus.[17]

Of the 120,000 troops in northern India, only 20,000 were European, and about 11,000 of these were in the Panjab, along with 36,000 sepoys and 14,000 irregular native troops. As soon as he heard the news from Delhi on 12 May, John Lawrence disarmed the Lahore sepoys, secured the Multan arsenal and the Sikh holy city of Amritsar, and then proceeded to strip the Panjab of men and weapons, sending as many as he dared to Delhi, relying on his Sikhs not to rise. 'If we are beaten at Delhi and have to retreat, our army will be destroyed.'[18] By 7 June, at the height of the blazing summer, 3,000 men, 20 field guns and a small siege train, had established themselves on the ridge to the southwest of Delhi, while mutineers with their weapons poured into the city from all over north India. The Ambala treasury, however, was safe, guarded by Sikh police, and the Sikh rajahs of Patiala, Jind and Nabha kept the supply routes open.

Numbers were to be the main headache of the British. At their greatest strength the fighting men outside Delhi amounted to 11,200 effectives, of whom 7,900 were Indians.[19] Nearly 4,000 either died of sunstroke, fatigue, sickness or in battle, or were wounded or unaccounted for, while the sepoy garrison within the walls was variously computed at between 40,000 and 70,000.[20] Of the four general officers commanding before the city, two died and one retired sick. Of the survivor, Nicholson wrote on 11 September, 'I have seen lots of useless generals in my day,' but 'such an ignorant croaking obstructive as he is, I have never, hitherto, met with.'[21] Only on 20 September did the British standard fly over the Red Fort. The rebels had contested every inch of the way and the city was like a charnel house. The liquor that the rebels had refused to touch was broached by the conquering soldiery who added a wild debauch to a combat in which no quarter was asked for or given. The reckoning was bitter. Any sepoy hiding or trying to escape was assumed to be a rebel and hanged on the spot. Even those who had supported the British were beaten up whatever their religion or loyalty, for being 'niggers', and 'niggers' had killed British women and children. The padishah was promised his life for abdication, but 21 members of his family were shot, in addition to his sons who had already been killed in a macabre action by their captor, Hodson of Hodson's Horse. Yet half of those who had recaptured Delhi were 'niggers', as were many who had risked their lives to harbour British fugitives and spies, even to act as spies themselves to bring information out of the city.[22]

The recapture of Delhi was to break the heart of the Mutiny, but for the British the living epic was the defence of Lucknow. Henry Lawrence had been appointed Chief Commissioner of Oudh in March 1857 and knew at once that the former kingdom was in a turbulent mood. He took such thorough precautions that the area of the Residency was able to receive, feed, water and defend most of the European community from the end of May to mid-November, together with Havelock's first relief force which fought its way into the area on 25 September, only to join the besieged. The mutineers had limited supplies of heavy ammunition but the damage from what they had was fearful. Lawrence was mortally wounded on the second day of the siege. Macabre stories of chapatti lunches, accompanied by a glass of sauterne, and preserved salmon dinners with sherry, champagne and claret – until the drink ran out – were overshadowed by the more macabre tally of death. It was not only the Europeans who died; there were 500 faithful sepoys in the Residency and a small army of servants, many of them Christian nannies. The rebels had all the best vantage points and the new Lee Enfield rifle, which they had no inhibitions about using.

The Residency endured four major assaults before its final relief. Sir Colin Campbell, aged 65, who had fought at Chilianwala and Gujrat, and retired from India after a tiff with Dalhousie, was back in India in August and, like Montgomery before El Alamein, he was determined to get the organisation right, before attempting a final relief, confident that Lucknow could hold out until the end of November. He only just made it, battering his way over four days into the Residency across a hecatomb of rebels on 16 November with a loss of 496 killed and wounded. All Mutiny battles were fought with brutal disregard of loss of life on both sides, on one side stoked by the spirit of revenge, on the other by despair. The sepoys, having failed in their prime purpose, knew only too well what to expect. Already by 1 June Herbert Edwardes in Peshawar was blowing mutinous sepoys from guns before the whole garrison. 'Five can be placed before each gun and two troops of artillery will throw sixty of them into the air at once. A second round will finish the matter.'[23] Even before the Lucknow mutiny, terrible tales had come up-river from Benares and Allahabad, where the dour Scots Calvinist, James Neill, and his Madras Fusiliers were hunting mutineers as if they were pariah dogs, and drum-head courts martial consigned 'niggers' to the gallows and villages to the torch.[24] John Nicholson, too, forgot the precepts of his Master and proposed, like a Turkish pasha or Japanese shogun, flaying alive, impaling or burning the slayers of women and children in Delhi. The Nawab of Farrukhabad, for his part in the Kanpur mutiny, was bound hand and foot to a charpoy, smeared with pig's fat, flogged by sweepers and then hanged.[25]

The Kanpur garrison exploded into mutiny four days after Lucknow's, on 4 June, after weeks of tension. Instead of joining their colleagues in Delhi, the sepoys declared as their leader the adopted son of the last Maratha peshwa, Dhondu Pant, known to history as Nana Saheb, whose proficiency at billiards and generous table had made him a favourite with the officers and ladies of the Kanpur garrison. The British had refused to recognise his adoption and he nursed that grievance with increasing bile. When the sepoys mutinied the Nana, 36 years old and growing stout from good living, seized his moment of destiny, which was to turn to ash in the butchery of the British garrison under guarantee of safety and the slaughter of the non-combatants in the notorious Bibigarh gardens. The horror of the mutiny was that it was not just a mutiny, it was genocide. Why did the garrison at Delhi put Englishmen, women and Christian servants to the sword? How did a Maratha prince come to connive at a general massacre of Englishwomen and children? By a strange miscalculation, the sepoy leaders believed that Britain's bolt was shot. The Crimean war had swallowed up the rest of her army, so that if all the British in India, men, women and children were eliminated, that would be the end of them. The Nana, too, had thrown in his lot with rebels, many of whom were unhappy about the betrayal of their duty, and their resolve had to be stiffened by being put beyond the prospect of pardon.

There was, too, a massive and spontaneous ebullition of religious and racial hate, a collective disgust with rulers to whom the sepoys had given the empire of India and whose reward was to be turned into Christians. Queen Victoria, so it was rumoured, had given the order, and those British women, who liked to think that they were her surrogates in India, were her agents.[26] Certainly the imperious memsahib was not an object of love and the massacre of women and children accounted for the ferocity, even madness of the retribution. Nothing did more to alienate Briton from Indian, and destroy such trust and affection as had been allowed to grow. A popular print showed half-naked European women chained to trees outside Kanpur, like so many Andromedas, waiting to be sabred. The most famous icon of the mutiny, Noel-Paton's *In Memoriam*, exhibited at the Royal Academy in 1858, was designed to commemorate 'the Christian Heroism of British Ladies and their Ultimate Deliverance'. It originally depicted, according to *The Times*, 'maddened sepoys hot after blood', but that proved too strong for most viewers. The purity of English womanhood being violated by black soldiers was a scene too horrible to contemplate, so Noel-Paton substituted the sepoys for Highlanders on the way to save them, but the expressions on the faces of the women and children still showed their expectation of rape, followed by martyrdom.[27] Yet, despite the horror stories, none of the victims of massacre was sexually assaulted. This would have added pollution to crime. Some women, mostly of mixed blood, preferred rather to disappear into the zenana than to be slaughtered, and stayed there when it was possible to emerge.[28]

Kanpur was recaptured before Lucknow was relieved and to disguise the paucity of his resources, Colin Campbell marched his English and Scots battalions twice through the city, hoping to frighten the Awadhis with reports of their numbers.[29] Fighting went on until the end of 1858. Tantia Tope, the rebel leader at Kanpur, took to the role of *pindari* and fought a brilliant guerrilla campaign, teaming up at one point with the 19-year-old Boadicea, Lakshmi Bai, Rani of Jhansi. The Rani died fighting, and Tantia was finally betrayed and executed. Oudh and Bundelkhand proved obstinate in resistance. 'Wherever our columns have marched they have literally walked over insurgent bodies, but directly they had passed, the rebels again formed in their rear, cut off their communications and intercepted their supplies.'[30] By January 1859, better weapons and a desperate fury, together with a general pardon for all rebels who had not committed murder and who turned themselves in, brought the long nightmare to a close.

The Raj survived because its neighbours were too preoccupied at home to attempt any distraction in support of the rebels. Had the Panjab fallen apart, or been forced to face an Afghan raid, Delhi would not have been invested as soon as it was. Fortuitously, the Crimean war had ended the year before so that reinforcements could be sent from Europe. A protracted civil war would have been a desperate blow to Britain's prestige and seriously have diminished her reputation in Europe. That would have been a bitter draught to swallow. As it was, on the level of myth, Britain had produced a new batch of heroes to encourage the young and she had retrieved some military laurels after a poor performance in the Crimea. Those who still nursed the ambition, that India would replace the United States as the pride of a great and beneficent British Empire, now realised that this would be more difficult than had been supposed by Bentinck and Macaulay, in the full flush of utilitarian optimism.

It had been a very frightening experience for the British. Even where there was no support for the rebels, there had been indifference to the result. There was no subscription drive among Indian capitalists to ensure the survival of the system that had made them rich, and whether ryots helped to round up and slaughter refugees or to hide and save them, seemed to depend on caprice. Most disturbing was the knowledge that the sepoys, with whom their children had played and who had shared the *servitude et grandeurs militaires* of the Sikh wars, had turned their guns on white comrades in arms. That comradeship could never be the same again. If they had risen once, they could rise again, specially if subverted by a foreign power. It was no longer possible to reconcile government with the limited vision of a trading Company. A wise and beneficent crown should now take over. The mystique of her office was so great that the band of the rebellious sepoys at Fatehgar concluded the day's fatigues by playing God Save the Queen throughout the mutiny.[31]

1857 was not the end of the British raj but it was the end of John Company. The insurrection had had to be put down by king's troops and now all the ravens, which had begun to croak before 1857, croaked in unison. Alexander Mackay, visiting Bombay in 1851 as a representative of Manchester's Chamber of Commerce, thought India was as backward as when Alexander of Macedon had crossed the Indus, hardly a rich market for British, especially Mancunian, goods. He was not impressed by all the Dalhousie improvements. Manchester wanted only a cheap supply of cotton and an inexhaustible demand for its finished goods. India was there to serve British commercial interests, and government action which did not serve this end was a waste of time and effort.[32] Free traders, like Richard Cobden, did not believe that honest trade required an empire. Britain had no mandate to continue ruling Indians, who should be equipped to look after themselves. 'Be it 50, or 100, or 500 years,' asked John Bright, 'does any man with the smallest glimmering of common sense believe that so great a country, with its 20 languages, can ever be bound up and consolidated into one compact and enduring empire?'[33] The evangelicals put their hope in Christian education, legislators in more delegation to Indian administrators, liberals in less government, covenanted servants in more. One soldier thought that India could be effectively policed by casteless sweepers, since no caste Hindu or Muslim would risk being killed by one![34]

Some voices defended the Company. John Stuart Mill believed that Committees and Boards on the banks of the Thames could never have the same feeling for the needs of India as a benign governor-general on the Hooghly. 'Few governments... have done so much for the good of their subjects' as the East India Company.[35] Whatever its defects, the Company had always had some servants with a larger vision than self-enrichment. Even Clive wanted to use the diwani revenues of Bengal to increase the prosperity of its people. Warren Hastings and Philip Francis, though locked in self-defeating hostility, were both committed to benevolent rule. Cornwallis hoped, by choosing a permanent land settlement, to create a wise and stable landed class, under whom agriculture and cottage industry would flourish. After the rapid conquest of Mysore and the Maratha lands, a new school of administrators tried to reconstruct the old native systems for the happiness of the people. But everyone knew that the Company's priority was to raise money. The utilitarians condemned the self-indulgence of the 'pseudo-Indians', who read the Indian classics with their Tasso and Ariosto, and were readier to chat with peasant and landlord in the field than to move paper in an office, but they were just as committed to improvement. Yet, even to so anglophile a Muslim as Sir Syed Ahmed Khan, 'the Hindustanees fell into the habit of thinking that all the laws were passed with a view to degrade and ruin them.'[36]

The Company had achieved a kind of internal peace from Peshawar to Cape Comorin, but the new landlords had not become an improving aristocracy and the peasants lacked capital and incentive, in the face of heavy tax targets, to improve their yield. Agriculture stagnated while administrative costs continued to rise. The occupation of Sind and Pegu, and the forced penetration of China markets, resulting in the occupation of Hong Kong, had provided new trade outlets, but they were dominated by British agency houses who used Indian revenues, not external capital, to finance them. Indian entrepreneurs, denied access to international market information and capital, could not compete. Even great Calcutta capitalists, like Dwarkanath Tagore, who had built up a prosperous business in shipping, ship-building and coal to bunker the new paddle steamers, could not command the same resources, and failed. So did many of the bigger agency houses whose early successes led them to expand too fast for the demand. The relentless call for revenue dampened when it did not destroy local endeavour. Few British had settled in India to develop plantations, the indigo market had collapsed and its replacement by tea and coffee was only just beginning. Only in Gujerat did the demand from Lancashire for cotton thread caused a transformation among farmers who began, however shakily, to be part of a prosperous agricultural economy, the 'yeomen farmers' of whom Munro had dreamed.

The Dalhousie years were overshadowed by the demands of financial and military security. The removal of 'sham kings' (and even real ones), and expansion to the natural frontiers of India had been intended to boost revenue, the first by adding some £10,000,000 to government income, the second by opening trade routes to central Asia. John Lawrence's heavy investment in irrigation in the Panjab helped to transform former warriors into successful farmers, and a wise tax assessment that fell on actual produce rather than, as before, on past harvests, allowed the Panjab to pay its way within a few years of occupation. Anxiety about the reliability, even before the Mutiny, of the Bengali sepoy was one of the driving forces behind the settlement of the Panjab and the recruitment of soldiers from more martial races than the pampered and caste-proud *purbiahs* of Bengal. If free traders and liberals, like Cobden and Bright, were dissatisfied with the Company's performance, how much more so were the displaced *taluqdars* of Oudh, the small chieftains of Bundelkhand, or the proud and defeated nobility of Rajputana and the Maratha lands. Trains, canals, the telegraph threatened all the ancestral certainties of a rural people. If agriculture, outside the Panjab, did not increase, population did. Industry was in decline. Once, India had produced the finest cottons in the world, effecting a revolution in the clothing of Europe.

Now the British had industrialised their finished textiles, silk apart, to as high a standard, and were replacing Indian with Egyptian raw cotton. Cottage industries faced ruin, for which the government seemed unable or unwilling to provide any protection. The English, too, seemed to have lost what affection they had for their faithful soldiers and servants, calling them niggers, and preferred the lighter-skinned denizens of the frontier lands, being more fun to fight and more entertaining to administer, and where additionally the sport was capital and the climate more like Scotland's. For the hard-pressed Awadhi farmers of 1857, the removal of the heavy hand of Company collectors and a return to the traditional practices of Mughal India, seemed a consummation worth fighting for.

The worm's eye view of the Company was a hostile one. Like a platonic philosopher king, it had taken Olympian decisions, often after detailed and painstaking correspondence with Leadenhall Street, without the participation of a single Indian. None had been admitted to Dalhousie's legislative council. Company servants had, with rare exceptions, convinced themselves that Indian society was beyond reform except from outside, and that it could only, over time, feel the benefits of European rule. On that issue there was unanimity. The religious and social structure of Hinduism, by which Islam had been corrupted, was inimical to the greatest good of the greatest number, since it was geared to the greater good of Brahmans. Herbert Edwardes, John Lawrence's fiery lieutenant, 'exactly,' thought Lord Canning, 'what Mahomet would have been if born at Clapham instead of Mecca', believed that lack of Christianity, not excess of it, was one of the causes of the Mutiny.[37] Had the sepoys been better instructed in its principles they would never have thought they were about to be forcibly converted. Study of the Bible in government schools should be compulsory, not voluntary; he objected to the endowment of temples and mosques from public funds, the celebration of non-Christian public holidays, the tolerance of caste and intermarriage and the government's stake in the opium trade. But as any pragmatist could see for himself, the harvest of Protestant Christians had been meagre. In 1852 there were 94,145 souls registered as converts with the Church Missionary Society. By 1862 that figure had risen to 138,543, but it is not known how many of these were converted Roman Catholics. It was certainly not missionaries who were going to drive 'brahmanism' out of India. George Otto Trevelyan believed that tolerance and secularism would do that. Most Brahmans, in his view, drew 'their creed not from the rolls of the Veda but from the pages of Locke, Adam Smith and Buckle... It is hard to conceive how one Calcutta Brahmin can look another in the face without a smile'.[38] The spirit of Bentinck lived on, but not in missionaries, either Christian or utilitarian, but in the philosophy of secularism.

John Stuart Mill knew that no one could force a people to become 'civilised', and as the civilisation of India, meaning its take-up of western techniques and its use of public instruction, proved disappointing, many of its providers had lost heart. The Mutiny had been a flight back into the past which, if successful, would have repudiated the civilisation that John Company had brought it. The challenge now was to find a way of involving Indians in the determination of their own future. The vision of an English-speaking, modernised successor state, which Macaulay had exposed to a rapt House of Commons in 1833, was still in

the shadows, to tantalise the new servants of the Crown. Queen Victoria's proclamation, transferring rule to her government, repeated the resolve of 1833,
that no office of service under the crown should be barred to Indians. In that
respect Her Majesty's government might do better.

The governor-general throughout the Mutiny was George Canning, third son
of the former foreign secretary. He was at school at Eton with both Gladstone and
Dalhousie, had taken a first class degree in classics and a second in mathematics at
Oxford, and acquired a reputation for thinking deeply before acting. He did not
speak unnecessarily and would often remain silent throughout a meal at which he
was host. 'A cultivated man of patient thought and perseverance, of most impartial
and yet inflexible mind, his great defect was want of decision in time of
emergency... the result of high conscientiousness, of almost morbid scruples.'[39]
Fortunately he was blessed in marriage to Charlotte Stuart, a London beauty of
such sweetness of temper that she enjoyed the undivided worship of her husband's
aides-de-camp. She also enjoyed the true affection of the queen, to whom she had
been a lady in waiting, and their correspondence was one of the principal agents
in engaging Victoria's interest in India. Indeed the queen thought that Charlotte's
letters were a far better source of information than her husband's despatches.

The Mutiny was an ordeal by fire for Canning, criticised for being too cautious,
for doing too little, then for doing too much. One young horse-coper, who had
volunteered for the militia to hunt out 'black devils', thought a good old washer-
woman would have done better.[40] At the Cambridge Union a speaker demanded
that there should be no talk of mercy until 'every bayonet is red with blood,
when every gibbet creaks beneath its ghastly burden, when the ground in front
of every cannon is strewn with rags and flesh and shattered bone.'[41] But 'Clemency'
Canning, so called first from disgust, later as a tribute, was determined not to
'govern in anger'.[42] The Bengal army was composed of simple villagers who were
strongly dedicated to their ancestral gods or to the Koran, and their grievances
had been sufficient to drive them to rebellion. Among them may have been a
few politicised rebels, many were *badmashes* or bad-hats, but the greater number
had been long-suffering and loyal over many years. Once the fury of retribution
had died down, the government and its servants knew that they must woo that
loyalty back. It was the passionate wish of the queen. 'I do feel so anxious that
kindness and a deep regard for their [native] feelings and susceptibilities' should
govern the policies of government and, after the death of the Prince Consort,
whose interest in India had been as lively as her own, it became a sacred mantra
of Her Majesty's and a repeated injunction to all viceroys, of whom, in 1859,
Canning became the first.[43] Those who were not government servants were not
so convinced. The Mutiny had driven a deep stake between native and European,
and friendship between Indian and Briton was accepted as impossible. Only a
respectful distance between the races would ensure that nothing like what
happened in Delhi, Lucknow, Kanpur and a host of smaller stations could happen
again. Natives were not to be trusted, the least trustworthy being those who had
a European education and the confidence to mix with Europeans. They were
still 'niggers', black of skin and at heart.

The son of Charles Trevelyan, George Otto, could not find in 1863 'a single
non-official person in India... who would not consider the sentiment that we

hold India for the benefit of the inhabitants of India a loathsome un-English piece of cant'.[44] But the queen, known only from her image on the rupee coin, was colour-blind; her viceroys, governors and lieutenants-governor must be gracious to all races, and her civil servants should know that all the inhabitants of British India were her subjects and must be treated with respect. She had accepted the transfer of India from the Company to the Crown with something like delight. She required the proclamation to be so drafted that everyone knew that it was 'a female sovereign who speaks to more than a hundred millions of Eastern people', and that it should 'breathe the feelings of generosity, benevolence, and religious toleration'.[45] No one was to be molested for his or her religious faith, and there should be no interference with the religious belief or worship of any of her subjects. She showed herself wiser than many of her subjects, for she had taken the lessons of the Mutiny more quickly to heart than they. She also accepted a sharp increase in work, and rode two private secretaries to death with the volume of despatches, drafts, appointments, and legislation that she demanded to see, and with her letters to the secretary of state for India.

Despite the sovereign's wish to speak to the hundred millions of her new subjects, her servants did not feel themselves obliged to do so outside the call of business. The viceroys and governors, being drawn from the ranks of either the British aristocracy or from the senior civil servants in India, were as twice-born as any Brahman. Grand galas at government house or dorbars for princes fulfilled the demands of exposure, and ensured that the Europeans were glued into a construct almost as socially rigid and snobbish as Saint-Simon's Versailles. Even without the Mutiny, such class and racial rigidity would have developed, for it was how Britain governed Ireland, her oldest colony, and the high sense of duty, now professed by the ruling class, meant that it was mostly too busy to behave in any other way.

The idea of equality before the law remained antipathetic to most Britons, official and non-official, and only while it remained a distant possibility could it safely stay on the agenda. When in 1876 a British barrister in Agra struck his groom so fiercely that he died of his injuries, he was fined only 30 rupees, a penalty upheld by a superior court. The viceroy, Lord Lytton, felt he could not overlook such a travesty of human justice and suspended the magistrate who had imposed the fine. He censured the barrister and the higher court and was exposed to bitter diatribes in the British-run press. Lord Mayo (viceroy from 1868 until murdered by a demented prisoner while on a visit to the Andaman Islands in 1872), believed that they were all British gentlemen who were engaged in the magnificent work of governing an inferior race.[46] The persistent British contempt for, even hatred of, Indians, ensured that that inferior race was always made to feel inferior.

Canning was more successful in solving the problem of the Bengal army for the Mutiny had virtually destroyed it, only five native regiments of infantry out of 74 remaining intact. He rejected proposals to replace Muslim and Brahman sepoys by Christians, Burmese, Gurkhas, Sikhs, even Africans.[47] The only practicable way to avoid another 1857 was to keep the artillery in European hands and to increase the ratio of European regulars to native troops. The European and native armies were amalgamated, all taking their oath to the queen, and the proportion of European to native troops was set at 1 to 2 in the Bengal army, 1 to 3 in Bombay and Madras. Economy dictated that in the event there were, in 1861, only 67 European regiments, both infantry and cavalry, but that was virtually double the strength in 1857. These dispositions were to survive, more or less intact, until the second world war.

Balancing the books was more difficult. The Mutiny had left India with a debt in both India and London of £98,000,000, which cost £2,000,000 a year to service. Even before the Mutiny a surplus of income over expenditure had been a rare occurrence. Yet the country was rich, individual fortunes were still being made by Europeans and Indians alike, and the export trade was worth £20,000,000 a year. In 1859–60, expenditure exceeded income by £11 million. By 1862 the arrears of debt had been cleared, achieved by a reduction in military expenditure, by administrative economy and by discreet taxation. For the first time expenditure was subjected to rigid scrutiny by Military and Civil Finance Commissioners, who carried out regular audits. For the first time, too, bankers and merchants also paid tax, which had hitherto fallen only on the workers of the land.

All this took its toll on a man who ignored leisure and exercise. On the sudden death in November 1861, of Charlotte Canning from jungle fever, her husband, like Dalhousie before him, seemed to lose heart. He died shortly after his return to England the following year at the age of 50, leaving the remains of his darling wife in the garden of her beloved retreat at Barrackpore. His successor was a schoolfellow at Eton and fellow collegian at Christchurch, James Bruce, 8th Earl of Elgin, in his prime, aged 51. Elgin was one of the newly emerging model colonial governors, and had, in both Jamaica and Canada, succeeded the old model colonial governor, Sir Charles Metcalfe, former resident at the court of the Great Mughal. He spent long enough as viceroy to be offended by the attitude of his fellow countrymen to their Indian fellow citizens before, like Charlotte Canning, falling victim to fever in November 1863, during a fatiguing journey through the Himalayan foothills on his way to Delhi.

Elgin's untimely death, and a renewal of trouble on the north-west frontier, led in 1864 to the appointment as viceroy of John Lawrence. He was the first Company servant to hold the exalted rank (of governor-general as well as) of viceroy, other than *pro tempore*, since Sir John Shore, and the first since Shore to speak any Indian language. The 'great pacificator' had lost none of his capacity for hard work during his nearly four years of retirement in England, but there were those who objected to his birth and lineage, being in the opinion of one of his juniors, 'a rough coarse man; in appearance more like a navvy than a gentleman'.[48] Many of his former colleagues, the stock of his 'nursery', were still in senior positions in India, but the sum of his virtues was the measure of his weakness. He had governed the Panjab by personal rule. He believed that a district officer should be always on the move, delivering judgements from the saddle. When one of them was accompanied to post by a piano, he had him moved so rapidly from post to post that the instrument was smashed. In Lawrence's Panjab, there was no room for a man who wanted time to play a musical instrument.[49] Now he tried to apply that experience to ruling all India. His very certainties ruled out new ideas, and new ideas were what were needed, if the widening breach between Indian and European were to be bridged.

The Mutiny had, for a time, interrupted the longer and more fundamental conflict at the heart of British India, between, on the one hand, expansion and security and, on the other, efficiency and economy. Within three months of taking office, Lawrence was presented with a budget that showed a surplus of £13,000,000, despite an increase in army pay and a reduction in duties, but he was not to find it easy to repeat such a record. He did not believe there were many opportunities to raise government income, whereas everyone was keen to spend it – on irrigation, higher salaries and the amalgamation of the armies, on new barracks and fortified centres at a cost of £10 million. 'Cantonments and arsenals, field batteries and breaching batteries seemed more essential to the government... than courts of law, normal schools and agricultural exhibitions.'[50]

In August 1858, India became the responsibility of the secretary of state, supported by a Council of India which met for the first time in Leadenhall Street on 3 September. (India House was to be pulled down in 1861 and the affairs of India were thereafter discharged in the sumptuous palace in Whitehall, designed by George Gilbert Scott, by a whim of Palmerston, in the style of the high Renaissance.) The new Council was not too unlike the old Board, being composed of 15 members, eight nominated by the Crown, seven by the outgoing Court, holding office for as long as they behaved themselves. Their functions were solely advisory. All Company servants became crown servants. The governor-general and governors of Madras and Bombay were appointed by the crown, their councils by the secretary of state. India had become a government department.

Messages from India to London could still, despite the telegraph, take a month to arrive, and for a complete turn-round of business, with explanations, qualifications, supporting papers, the period was seldom less than three. The relationship, moreover, between viceroy and secretary of state was uncharted, and the governor-general in India could sometimes feel that the real viceroy was in London. The Supreme Council in Calcutta was a seven-man executive council, almost a cabinet, made up of the commander-in-chief and the heads of the principal government departments: internal security, finance, defence, legislation and public works. The viceroy presided over its deliberations but he was not a prime minister with absolute power to dismiss colleagues and overrule their decisions. Every member had the right to express his opinions at length and, if that were not enough, he could approach Whitehall over the viceroy's head. The governors-general, from the time of Cornwallis, had had more power than any post-mutiny viceroy but the most resolute and determined. Lawrence complained that the influence of the governor-general 'is nowadays weaker than ever it was'. On taxation 'I have not the authority to resist. At every turn one is met by opposition'.[51]

When it met with a number of nominated members, the Executive Council became the Legislative Council, the organ by which non-officials, Indian as well as Europeans, could be represented. The Council could only propose legislation, not enact it – that was the job of the viceroy in (executive) council – but it was a very slight step forward towards involving Indians in government. The viceroy was his own foreign secretary, responsible for relations with sovereign states within the penumbra of the Company – Afghanistan, Burma, Muscat and Zanzibar – and with those princely states which had not been absorbed or annexed. The

Council was far from being its master's voice. In 1876 Lord Lytton found it in 'a very cantankerous and hostile disposition towards any advice or instruction from home'.[52]

Lawrence also initiated the transfer of government for a sizeable part of the year from Calcutta to Simla. By April, 'the amenities of life are over for the year. The last waltz has been danced in the Assembly Rooms, the last wicket has been pitched on the cricket ground, the last tiffin eaten in the botanical gardens, the last couple married in the cathedral'. From then on it was 'clammy, gloomy and hepatic for six grilling months', as Calcutta became 'a vast vapour bath in which those Europeans who had the will to work, must needs do so at half power'.[53] Calcutta, even in the smart areas, 'the filthiest city in India', which consigned 5,000 corpses a year to the principal sources of its water, the river, was also the worst place, geographically, from which to run an empire almost the size of Europe, being some 1200 miles from Lahore, 1000 from Bombay and 900 from Madras, distances equivalent to those of Bucharest, Naples and Madrid from London.[54] His doctors had insisted that he should only return as viceroy if he spent part of the year in the hills. If he, why not the rest of government? The cost of annual transfer would be covered by increased efficiency. 'We (the Council) will do more work in one day here (Simla) than in five days down in Calcutta.'[55] So the village, where Emily Eden had eaten sardines and listened to the band playing Bellini, became for half the year an oligopoly and a pleasure dome, where the spirit of Mrs Hauksbee presided over society and the viceroy dwelt in the comfort of a Scottish laird's castle, in what Lord Lytton described 'as a despotism of office-boxes tempered by the occasional loss of keys'.[56]

Back in London it was difficult to excite either House over the business of India, even if one were a Macaulay. Gladstone was surprised by the warmth with which his maiden speech on Ireland was greeted in the Commons, and put it down to the fact that it had just been bored by the debate on the India bill of 1833.[57] Parliament could be roused from 'its normal state of forgetting the existence of India', by issues of patronage, religion and the rights of the landlord and peasant.[58] Mutiny, moreover, had slowed down the momentum for economic and social change. The British were pre-occupied by the collection of revenue and by law and order. Conservation rather than change was the order of the day. The customary rights of landlord and tenant had, from the time of Cornwallis and John Shore, been high among the shibboleths of British rule. The Secretary of State in 1866 feared that Britain's 'permanent hold on India would be fearfully loosened if our cultivating population felt that their customary rights were in danger'.[59] In 1857–8, that cultivating population, in Oudh particularly, had not demonstrated its satisfaction with British interest in its welfare, and had sided with its former oppressors. It was now vital to win back the loyalty of that cultivating population, or rather of its landlords, to ensure that rural unrest on this scale was not repeated.

11. 'THE GREAT CHIEFS AND LANDOWNERS OF INDIA'

> You have seen that it is the desire and purpose of [the] government to seek out and encourage you, the great Chiefs and Landowners of India, those in whom it may safely repose its confidence and, having found them, to place power and confidence freely in their hands, and to uphold them in respect of their fellow subjects in every class.
>
> Lord Canning, 1861

> Don't forget that you're superior to everyone in India except one or two of the Ranis, and they're on an equality.
>
> Mrs Turton to Mrs Moore, *A Passage to India*

> Any foreign power, possessing a dominant influence over Afghanistan... would command all the passes into India in time of war, together with the support of a very warlike turbulent population, easily excited to plunder.
>
> Robert Lytton, 6 August, 1876

> They have looked each other between the eyes, and there they found no fault.
> They have taken the Oath of the Brother-in-Blood on leavened bread and salt:
> They have taken the Oath of the Brother-in-Blood on fire and fresh cut sod,
> On the hilt and haft of the Khyber knife, and the Wondrous Names of God.
>
> Rudyard Kipling

IN MARCH 1858, CANNING confiscated all the land of the former kingdom of Oudh, except for the estates of the half dozen taluqdars who had sided with the British. The ryots had been faithful to their old landlords; and those landlords should henceforward be loyal to the crown. Out of 23,843 villages, 22,659 were returned to their former lords. The surprised taluqdars had come to Canning's dorbar expecting to be shot and went home loyal tributaries of the Raj.[1] Any taluqdar who failed to promote agricultural improvements on his estate could expect, in theory, to lose it but, in the event, that happened rarely.[2] Canning's use of the local aristocracy as the native allies of British administration helped to identify an Indian class with the status quo so that, in any other challenge to their power from rural India, the British could count on influential support. It did not, however, make the Oudh taluqdar 'into a public-spirited country magistrate on the model of the English JP'.[3] By and large they proved to be indifferent to their new role as the agents of British rule in Oudh, but by the end of the century, they were the governing layer between the British and the governed, and their loyalty was 'the only breakwater between Bengal and the Punjab'.[4] They might abuse their power but it was 'far more important to retain (their) general goodwill than to start an enquiry which may have the effect of putting the whole of Oudh into a blaze'.[5] Knowing that the British would put up with much before taking action against them, they were often minor despots. Fifty years after independence, the malign effect of Canning's policy can still be seen among the 'goonda landlords' in the politics of Uttar Pradesh.[6] John Lawrence did not like it. He would have preferred to concentrate on improving the yield of the land, which had reconciled the Sikh to British rule. In the North-West Province and the Panjab, British rule was felt more directly in the villages where government appointed the revenue accountant (*patwari*) and Dogberry (*chowkidar*). As viceroy Lawrence, however, undid nothing, insisting, in his broad Ulster brogue, that the immemorial rights of the cultivators should be respected. It was not always easy to establish what these were.

In 1857–58, the majority of the great chiefs and landlords threw in their lot with the British. The Rajput princes stayed out of the conflict, the Maratha chiefs stood firm, and the Sikh lords were positively helpful. The Maharajah of Nepal was an active ally. They had their reward. Canning convincingly demonstrated that the Dalhousie policy of lapse was over. Adoption by childless chiefs was now accepted as both legal and desirable. He issued titles to enlarged fiefdoms to those princes who had remained demonstrably loyal and, as more than half the population of India was still ruled by princes, he provided them with privileges and ranked them for access to and affability from the representatives of the paramount power. In great darbars, at Agra and Lahore, like a latter-day Mughal, he rewarded loyalty and chastised backsliding. The Most Excellent Order of the Star of India, a double star with rays of gold and diamonds, set round an onyx cameo of the queen's head, with its suitable oriental motto, 'Heaven's Light be Our Guide', hung by a pale blue riband from the necks of 25 selected Knights Grand Cross, both British and Indian. Among the first to be dubbed were the nizam of Hyderabad, the maharajahs of Gwalior, Kashmir, Indore, and Patiala, the Gaekwar of Baroda and Duleep Singh, the grandson of Ranjit, out of honour to the Sikh nation that had rallied to the cause.

Successive viceroys, even the plain-speaking John Lawrence, understood that pomp spelled power. Lawrence held dorbars at Lahore, Agra and Lucknow, the seats of government of the faithful, the wavering and the disaffected provinces. None refused to attend. In Lahore, the great princes emptied the jewellers of Delhi's Chandni Chauk. Patiala 'blazed with diamonds'.[7] A huge assemblage of something like 80,000 armed men gathered outside the city, a motley of uniforms and regalia, a babel of languages, among whom there were the envoy from Kabul, and ambassadors from beyond the Oxus, seeking assistance to stave off the relentless advance of Russia. There were loyal Sikhs, Gurkhas, Rajputs and hill tribesmen, all of whom had helped to reduce Delhi and relieve Lucknow, for whom this was a feast of gratitude and encouragement. The viceroy informed them in Hindostani of the queen's devotion to the peoples of the Northwest Province, greeting them as faithful friends, with an exchange of gifts, as if he were the padishah himself. Some he decorated with the order of the Star of India, to others he presented silver vases, inlaid rifles, silk dresses, strings of pearls, ranged like the contents of Aladdin's cave from the *masnad* to the mouth of the tent. It all out-Mughaled the Great Mughal. Behind it all was the hope that if ordinary Europeans saw the viceroy honour and respect natives, they might be encouraged to do the same. Most of those the viceroy honoured and respected were the survivors of an old ruling class, not the new entrepreneurial, educated middle classes, and it was on these survivors of past glory that the British came increasingly to rely for 'popular' support. In November, the viceroy was at Agra, to impress upon the Rajput chiefs, of whom 94 attended, that Britain was now *sirdar*. The province had held, but only just, in 1857. At Lucknow, triumphalism was the order, for the viceroy entered the city, where his brother had died, with a train of 700 elephants. Nothing like it had been seen even in the days of the extravagant nawabs. A symbolic visit to the ruins of the Residency impressed on Lawrence's colleagues the need to enshrine Lucknow in living memory, so that it would happen Never Again.

The great princes of Rajputana subsisted in their palaces, some of them like small cities in themselves. The nizam kept state in Hyderabad like an independent sovereign. The descendants of the vanquished, the erstwhile emperor, the peshwa, the nawab of Bengal, Tipu Sultan, had virtually vanished, the descendants of the King of Oudh eked out a penurious life in Calcutta. Those who kept their thrones survived with only ceremonial powers, allowed to retain small armies. Each had to harbour a resident or commissioner, whose task it was to oversee his external relations and to ensure that he ruled with due regard to the rules of law and good administration. To him they surrendered their princely prerogative of life and death; capital crimes were reserved for his judgement and only with his agreement could a felon be hanged. Deprived of real power many of the princes spent their still lavish incomes building palaces – and sometimes public amenities for their subjects, like roads, railways and canals – and projecting their personalities in elaborate courts, ceremonial and collections of artefacts, mainly European – cars, china, glass, furniture and art – often in deadly bad taste. Apart from wooing the devotion of their subjects, they tried to ingratiate themselves with their European neighbours by lavish hospitality and quaint, almost touristic, shows of their native costume and custom.

Europeans responded to such approaches with flattered but cynical condescension. The very exoticism mystified and amused guests, mainly women, and among the most successful hosts had been Nana Saheb, the 'villain' of Lucknow. Indeed 'rajahmania' – the collection of titled exotics, the memory of whom would bring reflected light from the cascade of pearls and diamonds to Wimbledon and Surbiton – started in Lucknow with the visit by George Annesley, Viscount Valentia, to the nawab-wazir of Oudh in 1803. He was not a member of the Company, he was not even 'Lord Wellesley's sister's son, the grandson of Mrs Company', but he was a member of the House of Lords and Wellesley used him as a kind of roving ambassador from the king of England to the Company's allies.[8]

His visit to Lucknow set the style. Invited to breakfast, Valentia and the Resident arrived on their elephants, welcomed by the nawab's own caparisoned pachyderm, uniformed soldiers and a 17-gun salute. The meal was served on an English china breakfast set on an English table, under English chandeliers, though it rather resembled a dinner and was prepared by a French chef. There was the statutory offer of a *nuzzer*, consisting of gold coins, trays of shawls and food. The conversation consisted mainly of elaborate enquiries about Valentia's health and that of his family. This hospitality had to be returned, usually by the Resident. These encounters over, the tiger shoot was arranged. For all the pleasantness, Valentia was convinced that there 'was not in India a Mussalman prince who would not rejoice to throw off our yoke and expel us altogether'.[9] The Hindu rajah of Tanjore was more comfortable. His band had been trained to play the national anthem and *Marbrouk s'en va-t-en guerre*.[10] Always there were dancing girls, providing a continuous and mostly unpleasing background din to the occasion. As late as 1937, Betsy Macdonald, an indigo planter's wife, attended the *dassehra* festival of the local maharajah on elephants along with the diwan, the collector and his wife, to be entertained by an interminable nautch, during which the principal vocalist sang, over and over again, 'My lo-ove is like a leetle birrd, my lo-ove is like a leetle birrd, he flits from tree to tree, hee, hee, hee'.[11]

Every Indian prince was interested in his honour, the survival of his house and his reputation for splendour. His honour could no longer be demonstrated on the battle-fields of India, only his titles, salutes, precedence and decorations showed that he was still an important person. Oriental languages are peculiarly suited to the creation of pompous titles, which often only the princely herald can memorise and recite. His Highness Saranmad-i-Rajah-i-Hindustan Raj Rajendra Maharajadhirai, Lieutenant General Sir Sawai Man Singhji Bahadur the Second, GCSI, GCIE, known for short as the Maharajah of Jaipur, could not abandon a single syllable. Princely pride was a constant anxiety to the viceroy. Having decided to add the Maharajah of Patiala and the diwan of the Maharajah of Gwalior to his Legislative Council, Canning found that Patiala would not sit down with the servant of another prince. Only the firm reproof that he would sit with whomever the viceroy chose, or go home, brought him to heel.[12] The greatest and prickliest of the 'twice-born', the Maharana of Udaipur, whose father thought that the Star of India was beneath the dignity of a descendant of the Sun, travelled to the coronation dorbar of 1903, accompanied by a thousand retainers in two trains. On learning that Lord Curzon had put the ceremonial processions of Hyderabad, Mysore, Kashmir and Baroda before his, he did not even leave his train but turned it back to Udaipur with everyone on board.[13] To bring these descendants of heavenly bodies into a close and family relationship with the paramount ruler, Disraeli decided to proclaim Victoria, Queen-Empress. The queen had been enchanted by Charlotte Canning's letters from India and, were it not for the heat and the insects, she would have visited 'that luxuriant country full of such wealth and, I am sure, intended some day to become civilised'.[14] In 1876, Disraeli persuaded her to open the parliament that was to make her Empress of India, one of only three times between 1874 and 1880 that she agreed to do so.

To become the empress of a huge sub-continent was a distinction the proud matriarch of Europe could not resist. Emperors surrounded her from Napoleon III of France and Pedro II of Brazil, whose empires were to crumble in her lifetime, to her daughter's father in law, the recently proclaimed emperor William I of Germany. Then there was the emperor of All the Russias whose daughter had married the Duke of Edinburgh. When emperors' children married her children, there were awkward considerations of precedence. Emperors and empresses from medieval times had outranked kings and queens; more modern empires, like France, Brazil and Germany carried the suggestion that their sovereigns had been elected not only by God but also by the people, so that emperors were the chosen as well as hereditary instruments of the national will. To become Empress of India would remove, at one blow, any doubt about the primacy of the Queen-Empress in the constellation of monarchs, and imply that she had listened to the unspoken wishes of a subject people to give them wise and benign rule.

The bill did not pass through parliament without a struggle. Gladstone was against it. Empires were associated in history with tyrants, whereas the British mission in India was to do as much good as possible. Disraeli wanted it to give clout to his government in international affairs. When the imperial title was proclaimed in Delhi on 1 January 1877, Queen Victoria arrived at her celebratory banquet at Windsor festooned in Indian jewels like a *diwali* lamp. It did not stop there. Indian servants appeared in the palace, first as silent and attentive domestics, then as privileged attendants. The queen claimed to nourish an unfulfilled wish to visit India, but considering the anxiety with which she had the 30-year old Prince of Wales pursued by special messengers carrying coded instructions to stick to bottled water and to be in bed by ten, it was improbable that she would ever have exposed herself to the perils of Bombay duck.

Disraeli confided the proclamation to a man, himself part peacock, part coxcomb: the second Earl of Lytton. The son of the author of *Rienzi* and *The Last Days of Pompeii* threw himself into the arrangements with gusto. Russia was active in Asia, Afghanistan was querulous. Something was needed to secure the absolute loyalty of the princes, whose armies could police India if it came to war again in the north-west. He summoned them all to Delhi for an imperial assemblage in May 1877 – he preferred that description to dorbar. To his surprise, virtually none refused the invitation, and a limit had to be put of 500 armed retainers each, over and above household servants. To record the event he commissioned Val Prinsep, an artist of impeccable 'Anglo-Indian' credentials – his father was a former master of the Calcutta mint, his mother's father a Company man, and he himself had forsaken an Indian career for art. Lytton, who stood throughout the ceremony while his audience sat, for which he was criticised for sacrificing his dignity to a lot of nigger princes, felt that it would be prudent to be portrayed seated, in which posture his magnificent robes looked like a bundle of clothes. Prinsep had to reduce the whole canvas, so that an event, which had occupied 226 feet of space, was shown as occupying 30. In the event it was difficult for Her Imperial Majesty to identify her subjects.[15] Lytton staged the whole thing with great efficiency and panache. He designed the banners, with coats of arms, to present to each prince present. The pavilion might have been decorated for a Shakespeare history play, 'ornament on ornament, colour on colour... pieces of needlework (stuck) into stone panels, and tin shields and battle-axes all over the place, ... like a gigantic circus'.[16] The viceroy entered to the march from Tannhauser played by mediaeval trumpets. The 662 princes of India, however, were not barons of the realm. Some were subordinate to other princes, others had only their titles to support them, but they all became Highnesses, and their high-ness was measured by their salutes.[17] Only 118 had states big or old or rich enough to qualify for a gun-salute. The empress, if she ever appeared, would be greeted by 101 guns. The five leading princes, the nizam, the Maharajah of Mysore, the Gaekwad of Baroda, the Maharajahs of Gwalior and of Jammu and Kashmir, received 21 guns equally. They were overjoyed to find that they enjoyed the same number of guns as the viceroy, but were trumped when the viceroy entitled himself to 31.

The event did not impress the British. Lord Salisbury warned Lytton that his own countrymen would not accept a privy council, on which the leading princes would sit. They had been shocked to see the viceroy's wife introduced to dark gentlemen as an equal; they had complained that there were no balls for the European ladies to show off the dresses they had so laboriously acquired or made, and there were no receptions without dark gentlemen present. The whole lamentable business, following so closely after the visit of the Prince of Wales, who appeared to have come to India with secret instructions to snub whites, smacked of a 'Black Raj'.

Though the princes were rulers of states nominally independent, the viceroy could remove anyone who was deemed unfit to rule, but it was a delicate matter for, no matter how badly a prince ruled, he seldom lost the respect or devotion of his subjects. There was a divinity that hedged him around like a king, whose fellow princes were reluctant to be party to a fate which might be served on themselves. The removal of the plainly deranged *gaekwad* of Baroda in 1875, of a Holkar for complicity in murder in 1926, and of Dewas Senior (EM Forster's employer) in 1933, for bankrupting his state, demonstrated this only too clearly. Princes were left in perilous isolation to do pretty well what they wanted, so long as it was not positively harmful to their subjects or subversive of the Raj. They could, like some of the old taluqdar families of Oudh, create cultivated courts, dedicated to ancient culture and learning; they could, like Gwalior and Jaipur, spend and build or, like Patiala, play at being a councillor of state or, like Mysore and Hyderabad, improve the infrastructure of their kingdoms. Some were ready to work closely with the paramount power, others kept a polite distance. The Maharajah of Bikaner personally took his camel corps to China at the time of the Boxer Rebellion in 1900 and to Somaliland in 1903 when the British were attacked by the 'mad mullah'. Bikaners were prominent leaders in the Chamber of Princes and a Bikaner was a member of the Imperial War Cabinet in 1918. At the age of 70 the Maharajah of Jodhpur accompanied the Jodhpur Lancers to the western front in 1914. None wished to offend the government which preserved him in the simulacrum of power, though it was little more than that enjoyed by the king of Montenegro. The Maharana of Udaipur in 1911 travelled to Delhi to congratulate the King-Emperor George V on his accession, was met by the monarch at the station and, honour satisfied, went straight home. The Maharajah of Jaipur, on the other hand, went to enormous trouble to overcome religious obstacles to attend the golden jubilee of Queen Victoria. He commissioned Thomas Cook to equip the *SS Olympia* as a shrine for his ancestral deity, carried enough Jaipur soil for Him to feel that He had never embarked on water, and six months' supply of Ganges water to ensure that his lustrations were pukka. Bombay harbour witnessed the cautious propitiation of Varuna, god of the sea and winds, with gold and silver vessels, strings of pearls and precious silks. To accommodate the Ganges water, a special well was dug in the grounds of the maharajah's residence on Camden Hill.[18] He never learned any English and refused to ride in a motor car to the end of his life.

Once the princes were installed as semi-independent rulers, as local magistrates, as landlords, as emblems of British authority, the education of their sons became a live issue for British administrators. Private tutors ensured that a young prince would learn some English and, at the same time remain steeped in his own religion and culture but, as resistance to school came mainly from the zenana, this usually meant that he learned very little. The prospect of a half-educated chief finding himself in negotiations with a *babu* from an Indian university persuaded the aristocracy to patronise the newly founded chiefs' schools. Curzon on speech-day at Rajkumar College, Rajkot, in 1900, declared that 'we want the young Chiefs who are educated here to learn the English language, and to become sufficiently familiar with English customs, literature, science, modes of thought, standards of truth and honour, and... with manly English sports and games, to be able to hold their own in the world in which their lot will be cast, without appearing to be dullards or clowns, and to give to their people... the benefit of enlightened and pure administration'.[19] Edith Lytton in 1875 thought it 'so nice to see Captain Loch [the principal of Mayo College] with all the little native gentlemen round him, so happy and running and playing games like English boys almost'.[20]

Despite the retention of national dress, elaborate religious observances, trains of personal servants and respect according to rank not achievement, some western values rubbed off. But for the most part the knowledge imbibed was superficial. English teachers and Indian munshis competed for the souls of the young men who, apart from acquiring some good conversational English, emerged 'fashionable gentlemen only, playing hockey, smoking cigars, riding bikes, and aping European customs and manners'.[21] The princes propitiated the Raj to keep their ancestral gods, palaces and retainers, and they got little recognition for it. They were kept waiting by British officials, snubbed socially, lectured on the iniquities of their religion and subjected to insolent inquisitions into their domestic affairs. Viceroys were too distant to be models for Collector Turton and his wife. When Mrs Turton told Mrs Moore and Miss Quested that they were superior to everyone except a few Ranis, she believed it.[22] As one sympathetic official attached to a series of princely states observed, 'the *pax britannica*, a blessing as it has been to British India, has somewhat enervated the Indian states, ... [and] the life of a Chief was often one of dull boredom, tempered by intrigues and occasional assassinations'.[23]

The princes were the gelded eunuchs of British power. It was too committed to their survival to press them too hard to engage in better farming or in social change, for both of which most of them had little stomach. In 1926 the ruler of Limdi spent 150,000 rupees on education in his state, for which he was congratulated, until it was discovered he had spent the lot on the education of his heir. They wanted to live as royally as they felt was appropriate to their destiny. As late as the 1930s one of the Sindhi mirs would shop in Delhi or Karachi, though wholly indigent, ordering tens of thousands of pounds worth of jewellery for his Begums, only for his British finance minister, following in a car, to cancel the transactions.[24] Edwin Montagu, trying to sell constitutional reform in India in the winter of 1917–8, met many princes, and liked most of them, but 'progress with these chiefs is a very thin veneer, and usually comes from a trusted Diwan'.[25] The princes became distant, even alienated from the emerging nationalism of the towns, whose leaders were beginning to organise their tenants against them. To loyal Highnesses, like EM Forster's HH of Dewas, British India had become the home not of tyranny but of sedition.[26] It was not until the 1930s that the princely caste realised that British India could soon be ruled by their own countrymen, and that it might be in their interest to become involved in the Hindu Mahasabha or the Muslim League, or to stake their places in the provincial legislatures. As allies of the British in the struggle against nationalism they were broken reeds. As instruments in the achievement of independence they were, as a class, anachronistic and impotent.

The first rajah to visit England was Kolhapur and appeared at the Queen's Ball like a fairy prince, all cloth of gold tissue, necklaces and strings of pearls. By the new century, they were as indispensable to Edwardian society as orchids and champagne.[27] 'Every man with a turban,' Curzon sniffed in 1902, 'a sufficient number of jewels and a black skin, is mistaken for a miniature Akbar, and becomes the darling of the drawing rooms.'[28] He was so worried about the 'multiplication of the category of half-Anglicised, half denationalised, European women-hunting, pseudo sporting and, very often, in the end, spirit drinking young native chiefs,' that he did what he could to prevent them leaving their states.[29] He was also afraid that their heads would be turned in Europe by too much respect. Yet the allure lingered on, even in India. In 1930 Aldous Huxley wrote of New Delhi:

> And then there were the Maharajas... For a week Rolls Royces were far more plentiful in the streets than Fords. The hotels pullulated with despots and their viziers. At the Viceroy's evening parties the diamonds were so large that they looked like stage gems; it was impossible to believe that the pearls in the million pound necklaces were the genuine excrement of oysters. How hugely Proust would have enjoyed the Maharajas! ... It would have charmed him to watch some Rajput descendant of the Sun going out of his way to be agreeable to the official, who, though poor, insignificant, of no breeding, is in reality his master; and the spectacle of a virtuous English matron, doing her duty by making polite conversation to some dark and jewelled Heliogabalus, notorious for the number of his concubines and catamites, would have delighted him no less.

That they had become subjects for anthropological studies in *une recherche de temps perdus* was sad, but true.[30]

Their end bordered on farce. From the days of Lord Lytton onwards, the government of India had guaranteed their nominal independence and territorial protection, if not their immunity from change. They had opted for but failed to join a federated India so that, in 1947, they had no guarantees for their future. To both Congress and the Muslim League the future of the princes was a peripheral issue, to be settled at independence, when they expected to inherit all the powers and prerogatives of the crown which included relations with the princes. The princes resolutely held that their treaties were with the British crown, not with the governments of India or Pakistan. But, in practical terms, paramountcy could not be transferred, it could only lapse. All powers surrendered in treaties with the crown reverted to the 565 or so independent states who had, therefore, to negotiate a new relationship with the successor states of British India. With Britain's departure there was no way she could protect any princely state from one of the two new dominions except by an infringement of its sovereignty. Lord Louis Mountbatten, a prince himself, and a cousin of the ruling monarch, by bluff, rank and the embezzling power of personality, persuaded most of them to sign away their powers, salutes and prerogatives for the right to maintain their titles, palaces and a privy purse in either independent India or Pakistan. In India, by 1971, they had lost even these. Democratic processes were not invoked in any of their principalities to decide their future.[31]

With the gelding of the Indian princes, viceroys turned to the turbid states of the Hindu Kush and Transoxiana. The urge to intervene in Kabul would not lie quiet. It was not just the factitious threat from Russia for, if the menace were real, the Afghans could deal with it as they had dealt with the British. It was the lure of the mountains, of a type of warfare that most resembled hunting, the attraction that existed between men of infinite resource and sagacity, a mutual admiration for courage and endurance, a kind of *simpatia* that grew up between fundamental Muslims and equally fundamental Christians pitched against each other on different sides, all of which made up the Great Game. The amir in Kabul had warned Lawrence: 'Leave us and our country alone. We are poor in everything except stones and men'.[32] Both were soon in motion. With the Dost's death in 1862, sixteen sons had inheritances to secure, and Lawrence refused to entertain any thought of intervention in favour of one or another. In 1869, Mayo secured from the Czar a promise that Russia had no intention of expanding her empire in the direction of India's north-west frontier. If she did, war would spread like a forest fire from the Caspian Sea to the borders of China and Mayo would make 'of Central Asia a hot plate for our friend the Bear to dance on'.[33]

The Disraeli government which came into office in 1874, with Salisbury as secretary of state for India, was not disposed to rely on an independent Afghanistan as the best defence against a threat to India from the northwest. How long would it be before she became so independent that she could be tempted, by the loot of Hindostan and Russian support, to cross the passes? Disraeli wanted the world to know that the paramount power in Asia was British India, not the expanding Russian empire and there should be a strong British presence, preferably in Kabul, but if not there, at Herat and Kandahar. Afghanistan could not long remain outside either the British or the Russian sphere of influence. In vain did Lawrence warn the secretary of state that British agents would be murdered, there would be war and another disastrous attempt at military occupation, all of which would so inflame the Afghans that an invitation to the Russians would be inevitable. It should, surely, be enough for Russia to be told that Britain would defend her Indian possessions by all the means in her power, and St Petersburg would back away.

In 1875 Lord Lytton became viceroy. Inheriting the literary ambitions of his father, the romantic novelist, he wished to be remembered as a poet. Books of verse never ceased to roll from his pen, none of it good enough to make him immortal, but most of it lively and clever in the style of Browning and Tennyson. His crowning oeuvre, a six-volume novel in verse, *Glenaveril*, is now totally forgotten. Disraeli did not believe that literary ambitions interfered with professional competence, and Lytton's scant respect for the conventions of social life, his rings, jewellery, curls and dandified dress were further recommendations. The prime minister guessed that the romantic streak in his nature would tempt him to take more positive action over Afghanistan.

Lytton, though he neither 'courted or willingly accepted the crushing gift of such a white elephant' as the vice-royalty, was ready to oblige.[34] The amir's refusal to accept a British agent in Kabul without a Russian counterpart sounded like a threat; unless he changed his tune, Lytton must regard him as an enemy. 'A tool in the hands of Russia I will never allow him to become.' The amir's envoy explained that 'it is firmly fixed in [Afghan] minds and deeply rooted in their hearts that if Englishmen or other Europeans once set foot in their country, it will sooner or later pass out of their hands'.[35] Lytton was sure that there was an agreement with St Petersburg. London's wish to avoid war and rely on diplomacy was 'dictated by the heart of a hen to the head of a pin'.[36] The Russian governor in Turkestan had more power than the viceroy of India, the greatest man in the greatest empire in Asia. *He* was not opposed by a weak and divided cabinet, public opinion, parliament; *he* could rely on his government to back him to the hilt. At this rate, he would be in Herat before the British and then they would have to invade Afghanistan to get him out. The amir might hate the Russians but he hated the British more. The Mutiny had been one great Muslim rising and Russia was bent on fomenting another.

Part of the problem was that London was only marginally more distant from Calcutta than St Petersburg from Tashkent, so that both Lytton and General Kauffman were isolated from the high diplomacy that determined peace or war between the two countries. In addition, since travel in the vexed frontier lands had been discouraged, there were few men who really knew them, and no maps. In the winter of 1877–78 jingoism was at its peak in Britain, when Russia had broken through the Turkish defence at Plevna, and threatened Constantinople. The British fleet was ordered to the Dardanelles and Lytton was ordered to send 7000 native, non Muslim troops to Malta, through the newly opened Suez Canal. The Begum of Bhopal put her militia at the disposal of the viceroy, the Maharajah of Kashmir undertook to help defend the frontier and Scindia offered to raise and lead a regiment. Then, in July 1878, war was averted by an agreement at Berlin. As far as Disraeli was concerned it removed any Russian threat to Afghanistan but, in India, things looked rather different. A Russian military mission had arrived in Kabul in July, received reluctantly but honourably by the amir. Not even the Russian foreign minister knew that its leader had encouraged the amir not to receive a British mission, promising to return with 30,000 troops if the British objected. It was hardly surprising, therefore, that a last minute ultimatum to receive the mission from India went unanswered whereupon, on 21 November, it set off. The amir called in vain on the Russian garrison at Tashkent, now informed of Russian policy towards Afghanistan.

A British Residence was 'permanently' established at Kabul while Lord Lawrence's phillipics were mocked; but his was the last word before he died. 'They will be murdered every one of them.' And they were. On 3 September 1879 the Residency was under attack and the garrison of 25 was all dead by evening. The new amir, who was not directly responsible for the attack, knew that his throne was doomed. Within days General Roberts was on the march and by 10 October all resistance in Kabul had been crushed and the British instituted a search for the bodies of their compatriots. Without success, but what they found were guns, uniforms and 13,000 Russian gold pieces in the Treasury together with evidence that the amir had entered into treaty with the Russian general in Tashkent, even after the Congress of Berlin had settled all British disputes with the Czar's government. Disraeli and Salisbury knew that St Petersburg had as much trouble controlling the freebooting Russian soldiery in Turkestan as Whitehall had had with the East India Company, for whom war never waited on British policy in London. Disraeli had allowed Lytton his head because, having brought the Indian empire into existence, he accepted the Lytton logic that, to keep India's Muslims quiet, the amir could not be allowed to defy the might and prestige of the Raj. It was an attitude the opposition did not share. Gladstone in his fervid Midlothian speeches, called upon the Scots to remember that the sanctity of life in the hill villages of Afghanistan was as inviolable in the eye of Almighty God as was that of their own Highlanders. The money voted for the relief of famine had been used to drive Afghan mothers and children from their homes to perish in the snow.[37]

By 1880 Gladstone was back in power, Lytton had resigned and the prime minister's choice for viceroy, Lord Ripon, was instructed to disengage wholly from Afghanistan, put a reliable ruler on the throne, keep him there, and leave Russia to London's diplomacy. By 1884 this had been achieved and the Russians had agreed to a joint demarcation of the frontier. It was not accompanied by sweetness and light. Bismarck was solicited to use his influence on the Russian government to get it to withdraw from disputed territories, when the absurdity was exposed of 'all England and India... thrown into a flurry of excitement and a deluge of expense every time that a wretched Cossack chooses to shake his spear in the top of a sand hill'.[38] In 1889, Lord Lansdowne, exasperated by 'the cantankerous and suspicious old savage', advised the ruling amir that it was 'absolutely necessary that he should stop gouging out his prisoners' eyes, boiling them in hot oil, or tying them up to posts and leaving them to die of cold and hunger'. But there was nothing the Indian government could do about it, except atone for the amir's brutality by treating the refugees from his excesses kindly.[39]

Gladstonian rhetoric thundered equally over Muslim *bashi-bazouks* and British oppressors of the Muslim poor in Afghanistan. But the frontier continued to have a dangerous fascination for the British. For a century they had fought across the massive plains of India burdened by kit, heat, flies, and thirst, cantoned in huts or tents that by mid-morning were as hot as a furnace, their companions in war vegetarians with strange beliefs and a multitude of perplexing gods. Now they were faced by a new foe, one who could, in stature, meet them eyeball to eyeball, men of a terrible and burning faith, worthy of a Caledonian Calvinist. It was one man's cunning matched to another man's skill. In the clean sharp air of the mountains, bullets cracked like whips, and dislodging a sniper from his lair was as much a game of skill as war, especially a war against peoples whose religion made warriors of them. From Siraj-ud-daula to Tipu Sultan, Muslims had been among the most dangerous enemies of Britain. From that, it was a short step to attributing the Mutiny to ingrained Muslim hostility to the infidel British, a hatred not, it was thought, felt anything like so strongly by Hindus. In 1871, W. W. Hunter published his book on *The Indian Mussalmans*, a thoroughly alarmist tract on what was hatching beyond the mountains beyond the five rivers, where a fundamentalist Wahabi movement among the Pathan tribesmen of the northwest frontier threatened a Crescentade against the Europeans.[40] Men of the book, they were not like the slippery and treacherous Hindu, who fawned while he hated and whose personality was infinitely adaptable. The British might find the frontier tribesman 'cruel and treacherous, shockingly addicted to unnatural vice and habitually given to stealing each other's wives', his only occupation 'considered worthy of manhood... the promiscuous shooting at each other, taken unawares, which they call war', but the annals of the border lands of Britain were stained with the same accusations and had been immortalised by Sir Walter Scott. The Pathan 'are fine manly fellows, "good sportsmen"'.[41] The Victorian Briton, schooled in single-sex establishments and tested by feats of endurance on the field of sport, failed to recognise the whiff of buggery. The Pathan might not have gone to your school but he 'could take a beating in the boxing ring or rugger without complaining, who could give as good as he got'.[42] The Pathan who appeared outside a mountain dwelling appropriated by the occupying British as an officer's mess, and whose entire flock of chickens had disappeared into the stewpot the night before, was still able to assure General Dunsterville, in truly hospitable fashion, that it was his house and that he should make use of anything he wanted.[43] How different from the imaginative and cultivated Bengali, like Kipling's Grish Chunder De. 'More English than the English', talking of 'Oxford and "Home"', with much curious book knowledge of bump-suppers, cricket matches, hunting runs and other unholy sports of the alien' he was no match for them. To the Pathan as to the Briton, he was 'a black man – unfit to run at the tail of a potter's donkey. All the peoples of the earth have harried Bengal. It is written. Thou knowest when we of the North wanted women or plunder, whither went we? To Bengal – where else?'[44]

Islam confronted Christianity like a reproach. The millions of Muslims in India, compared to the handful of Christians, testified to a faith simple and sublime in its certainties, not yet adulterated by doubt or riddled with scientific rationalism. It was a system of belief, false yet admirable, and the Muslim of the frontier, measured in steel, became a worthy, if still treacherous, foe. 'Border warfare, as we knew it best, had absolutely no ill-feeling in it. It was a war of hard-trained bodies, each against the other; a war of keen eyesight and straight shooting, a war of vigilance and of quick wits.'[45] India with its temple prostitution, lascivious statuary and subtle echoes of the Kama Sutra was like a huge, scented brothel. The Frontier on the other hand was womanless, a male paradise, seeded with new towns: Campbellpur, where Colin Campbell, of Mutiny fame, had between 1850 and 1852 cleared the Kohat pass of hostile tribesmen, thrashed the Mohmands and 'biffed' the rebellious tribesman of the Swat valley; Edwardesabad, for some time the popular name for Bannu where, in 1847, Sir Herbert Edwardes had cut his teeth as a district officer, pacifying the Afghans in the Tochi valley; Jacobabad, the frontier post of the Upper Sind, where John Jacob had subdued the Bugti, Dombki, Burdi and Marri clans, only abandoned in 1914; Fort Sandeman, 80 miles northeast of Quetta, where in the 1880s Sir George Sandeman tamed the Pathans of the passes into South Afghanistan and the main trade route to Kandahar along the valley of the Zhob; and Lawrencepur, near Peshawar called after George, the elder brother of Henry and John Lawrence. The Afghan invasions had both been disasters but the police actions on the Frontier were like training exercises. As late as 1944, an officer of the 7th Rajput Regiment told Cecil Beaton, that 'they provide us with a lot of fun. It's a great life – hard, but it's masculine: not a woman in sight'.[46] The respect that began to grow between the child of the Bible and the child of the Koran, two very different people, but sharing a common devotion to a Book, was reflected in political terms by what was perceived by Hindus as a sentimental preference for the minority religion. Islam produced soldiers for the faith as well as the queen.

Kipling's Stalky had his military baptism on the frontier and returned as General Dunsterville in 1915 to keep the Mohmand tribesmen of the Tangi pass from raiding the territories of the British raj. For him 'a tribesman with a rifle in his hand is very like a sportsman in the jungle. He wants to kill something, if he can... The sportsman is not actuated by any hatred of the animal he aims at – he merely wants the trophy with which to decorate his ancestral halls... So the Mohmands, in directing their fire on me, were not actuated by any particular dislike, but merely wanted to bag a General. One can sympathise with that feeling'.[47] Westward Hovians were taught to make light of danger and privation and Stalky, all of whose Indian experience was on the Frontier, did not share Beetle's wider sympathy with Indians of the Plains. The war-games he played, which included receiving a request for a blanket from a Pathan who was cold spending the nights on the hillside potting at British troops, made him easy in the company of 'natives'. He could sympathise with but not support their political ambitions. To the Pathan, freedom could only mean a return to the golden age when he 'will be free to ravage, loot and destroy without let or hindrance'. White officials would be replaced by brown ones, but such was 'the fierce, undying antagonism between Mahomedan and Hindu, no system of government for India that does not provide officials, and especially magistrates, from a race that stands aloof from both can ever give peace and security to the people'.[48] This sort of justification for British rule helped to encourage the accusation that their specific for ruling India was to divide the communities, and rule.

12. 'WORTH THREE HUNDRED A YEAR, DEAD OR ALIVE'

> The Civil Service was in those days an aristocracy in India, and we were the *jeunesse dorée* thereof... Mamas angled for us for their daughters for, as the phrase then went, we were 'worth three hundred a year, dead or alive.'
>
> John Beames in 1858

> There are no such things as office hours – an officer's services are at the disposal of the government at all hours of the day and night.
>
> Sir George Campbell,
> Lieutenant-Governor of Bengal

> Ruling India was a splendid, happy slavery... Looking back it seems a divine drudgery and we all felt that the world was good. We were proud of it; we were knights errant.
>
> Sir Walter Lawrence, 1928

> I suppose there never was an administration of equal importance which received so much information and which was so ill-informed.
>
> George Aberigh-Mackay, 1880

> The princes of India... both on easy and difficult wickets... have tried their best to play with a straight bat for the Empire.
>
> KS Ranjitsinhji at the Scarborough Festival, 1930

BY 1862, THE OFFICIAL object of British rule in India was 'to improve the native, reconcile him, if we can, to our rule and fit him for ruling himself'.[1] The sum of knowledge at Haileybury, 'rather a farce as far as learning was concerned', being 'beastly hot with niggers'[2] it was decided that from 1855, the covenanted service would be filled by 'competition-wallahs', 'bookish hobbledehoys who fell off their horses, misunderstood Hindustani and made silly mistakes about the ways of the country'.[3] Indian graduates of British universities could take the examination in London, but it was a rare Indian who could 'write succinctly and in Latin biographical notices of Theramenes, Polybius, Poseidonius, Arcesilaus, Pamenides, and Eratosthenes'.[4] It was not until 1969 that three Indians were able to pass into the covenanted service, but they filled an increasing number of uncovenanted posts.[5] Lord Salisbury, secretary of state, could 'imagine no more terrible picture for India that that of being governed by competition baboos.'[6]

That Indians should be able to take the exam in India was an annual demand of the Indian National Congress from its inaugural session in 1885. London agreed in 1893, and raised the examination age to 22, so that the covenanted service should be a career for graduates. Even so, by 1909, the number of covenanted Indians was only about 60 out of 1,142.[7] It was received opinion in India that Britain's continued rule relied on a constant entry of Britons, not Indians, and non-graduates continued to be recruited. In 1922 Eric Blair (George Orwell), not having distinguished himself academically at Eton, sat compulsory papers in English, English History, Mathematics and French, to which he added Latin, Greek and Drawing. His views on the greatest prime minister since Pitt, or the consequences of Nelson's defeat at Trafalgar, were less important than the riding test, since 'getting round their districts... weighted more heavily than knowledge'.[8] 'The Covenanted Ones' were recognised from their train of red-coated chuprassies, 'the Judges of the High Court and all those who dispense the Law of the Raj, the Scions of the Secretariat and other Departments... Commissioners and Collectors who are in authority throughout the land, the Army! Bow down.' 'Three hundred a year, dead or alive', and the prospect of a pension made them almost god-like.[9] If they lasted 20 years, they might earn £1800 a year and be pensioned with £1000 a year. John Bright thought that 'except for some high-salaried bishops... no men are so grossly overpaid'. Expenditure on the civil service should be cut by half.[10]

The beginner usually understudied a magistrate, and was then attached to a settlement review, when parcels of land were measured, checked against the *patwari*'s records, and the assessment adjusted. 'There is no work in the world like that of a settlement in India. He is always fighting for the people against the Government, who want more revenue: against the Forest Officer who wants more forest and cares little for cultivation: against the money-lenders who want more land: and against the privileged classes, who want something for nothing'.[11] After passing an exam in law to be gazetted second class magistrate, he would then be put in charge of a district. Leonard Woolf, having taken a rather lower degree at Cambridge than he had hoped, found himself governing an area one thousand miles square in the Tamil-speaking northern tip of Ceylon, where he 'was responsible for everything connected with the well-being of the people and the maintenance of law and order'. Though Sri Lanka (Ceylon) was never part of the government of India, Woolf served in a Tamil-speaking area and his experience was no different from that of an Indian civil servant. A major headache was the policing of a pilgrimage, but 'if one white civil servant was there, nothing could possibly go wrong'.[12]

Recently an Apostle at Cambridge, Woolf could not have found fifteen more unapostolic people than his colleagues who comprised white society in Jaffna and who all suffered from black melancholia.[13] They spent much energy complaining to each other, in writing, of slights and peccadilloes, yet met in all apparent amity on the tennis court in the cooler part of the day.[14] The women were all 'whores or hags or missionaries or all three', and all were bored.[15] The men took an interest only in their work and after dinner went to sleep in their chairs.[16] Even accounting for the tone he felt the need to adopt when writing to shock and intrigue the fastidious Lytton Strachey, whose 'Indian' ancestry was numerous, his comments were unusually bitter. Even so, he threw himself into the daily routine: 'pundit from 7.30 to 9.0 am, the loathsome breakfast at 10, the pure futility of the work here until 4.30, the inevitable tennis at 5.15, the foul and melancholy dinner at 8, the dreary grind at Tamil and half an hour's read before I go to bed'.[17] The office day started when it was really too hot to be out of doors, 'signing letters, issuing licenses, counting and receiving rupees, inspecting carriages, trying and fining miserable wretches, answering petitions, checking accounts, deciding questions about salt, and coolies and family quarrels and irrigation and injustices'. Add to this list, verifying causes of death and out-breaks of disease, attending hangings, checking weights and measures, 'counting out fish-knives, pillows and pos' for visiting dignitaries and their ladies, deciding exemptions from tax and writing the interminable and mandatory reports. It was small wonder that an average working day was of twelve hours, and that the work was ever done at all was due to his Indian assistants. 'Once you establish a *dastur*, a custom of fixed routine, they are all right. There is nothing they love so much as a *dastur*, they make themselves into machines and work admirably'.[18] There were few respites; convalescence after the usual bouts of dysentery, typhoid and other fevers, riding in the early morning when the horse, 'scenting the chance of a good gallop, stretches out his tail and tears away as hard as he can go – it is then that it is heavenly, ... better, I think, than copulation'.[19] Or a spot of leave in the district capital, a change of society, catching up with the latest gossip and books and magazines from 'home'. Back to the daily grind until after six or so years, a year's furlough had been earned and you boarded the P&O liner for Tilbury. In every respect his life was typical of all officers up country. He developed an affection for the people, who never ceased to amaze him, especially by their whole-hearted addiction to lying, even when telling the truth would have done as well, their fatalistic acceptance of whatever blows life might give them, their lack of triviality in face of the seriousness of life. Yet, like nearly all other civil servants, he did not want to mix socially even with educated Tamils, and did not feel properly dressed without a stiff collar and displayed god-like indifference to heat and discomfort like the most double-dyed devotee of the imperial mission, in which he never believed.

The other great disaffected, Eric Blair (George Orwell), was born in Bengal and chose to be assigned to the Burma Police, because his father had worked and his mother still lived there. Unlike the well-dressed Woolf, he was a tall, gangling youth, whose clothes did not seem quite to fit. He had to work out of his system the caste inheritance of Eton and the violence endemic to Europeans in the east. He remembered with a bad conscience the servants and coolies he had hit with his fist in moments of rage, and was once seen to lash out with a heavy stick at a student who bumped into him while larking about.[20] He worked for five years in Burma and never learned to like the Burmese but his mastery of spoken and written Burmese meant that, like Leonard Woolf, he was an efficient and effective officer.[21] Either of them, had he persisted, could have acquired a knighthood and even risen to be provincial governor. To his superiors, Blair did not appear to harbour any radical views and behaved like the usual remote and superior British officer. 'A sahib has got to act like a sahib, he has got to appear resolute, to know his own mind and do definite things.' White men have to hang together. To safe friends he might reveal that he was appalled that his grand-mother, born in Burma and still living there, had not learned a word of Burmese, and 'damn the British Empire'.[22] His anti-Imperial views were only made public ten years after leaving Burma. While, he wrote in 1936, he would have experienced 'the greatest joy in the world... to drive a bayonet into a Burmese priest's guts', he thought the British raj was 'an unbreakable tyranny'.[23] The dilemma, as he saw it two years later, was that in theory, the British civil servant was 'administer-ing an impartial system of justice, in practice he is part of a huge machine that exists to protect British interests'.[24] He resigned in 1927, adding some years later, 'because I could not go on any longer serving an imperialism which I had come to regard as very largely a racket'.[25]

Neither Leonard Woolf nor George Orwell served in traditional India, which may have helped to account for their special disgusts. In traditional India it was still held in 1870 to be 'fifty-fold more important that candidates for the ICS should be public school men than that they should be university men', products of an education which developed 'their capacity to govern others and control themselves, their aptitude for combining freedom with order, their public spirit, their vigour and manliness of character... their love of healthy sports and exercise, the self-subjugation which renders corporate action a possibility, the sentiments of affectionate reverence for ancient national institutions, and of just pride in national achievements.'[26] Public-spirited and admirable they may have been but being the Platonic guardians of society meant that they kept themselves remote from the people they were administering. And were they always efficient? Lord Lytton complained that he was required to do first rate work with fourth-rate tools. Did Leonard Woolf ever read the comments of Virginia's uncle, Fitzjames Stephen, to the viceroy? 'You must not forget that nineteen civilians in twenty are the most commonplace and the least dignified of Englishmen. They are in India ten times more fidgety and peppery about their dignity and independence than they are in England.'[27]

Paper was the great product of Indian administration. In six years of office, Canning may have written as many as 10,000 letters. In a single year in the 1860s, the finance Department received and answered 18,000 communications, the military department 25,000 and the home department 15,000. The Bengal office dealt with something like 40,000.[28] This avalanche kept the governor-general and senior departmental heads working into the early hours, sometimes until dawn. Everything had its own urgency. No wonder Lord Northbrook (1872–6) was warned that 'the Natives look on themselves as being hustled... into a state of premature civilisation and wish to be allowed to settle down'.[29] But India no longer lived in the silence of ignorance. By 1878 there were something like 200 publications that could pass as newspapers, in many languages. Since Macaulay had lifted the restrictions on it in 1835, the Indian vernacular press was free to say pretty well what it liked, and what it liked to say was how unequal was the treatment of Indians and Europeans before the law, and how arrogant were the British of all classes. In March 1878 Lytton decided to gag it.[30] 'Her Majesty's gracious opposition' to the 'despotism' of the government of India was muzzled because, Lytton reported, the bazaar rumours of a Turko-Russian alliance were being used by the Indian press to suggest that British rule in India was doomed to early extinction. It was ungagged in 1882 after Gladstone advised that a free press was of greater service to a government than one under constraint. Fortunately, for the spirit of censorship was omnipresent, Lord Dufferin (1884–8) convinced himself and the queen that 'the most extravagant Bengali Baboo that ever "slung ink"... cherishes at heart a deep devotion to your Majesty's person and a firm conviction that it would be destruction to him and his if ever English rule in India was replaced by that of any other power'.[31]

Since the object was to civilise India, and since Indians were not Europeans and carried, still, such a load of cultural baggage from their past, Indians could only participate in this process as junior partners. Darwinian theories suggested that there were superior and inferior races, rulers and ruled, survivors and losers. Even Kipling had little faith in Indian administration. Calcutta stank, yet 'in spite of that stink, they allow, even encourage, natives to look after the place! The damp, drainage-soaked soil is sick with the teeming life of a hundred years and the Municipal Board list is choked with the names of natives – men of the breed born in and raised off this surfeited muckheap!'[32] John Strachey in 1888 averred that the prolonged rule, benevolent but strong, of Englishmen was the only hope for the country. She had never been a nation, never 'possessed any sort of unity, physical, political, social or religious'.[33] The Olympian distance between rulers and ruled was virtually unbridgeable. In January 1884, Wilfred Scawen Blunt was being seen off by his Muslim friends on the platform of Patna station. 'Suddenly a furious white man leaned out of the next compartment window brandishing a cane and shouting: "Clear off. I shall strike you if you come in reach of me."' He was the Chief Medical Officer of the Panjab. On being challenged by Blunt on his authority to give orders, he shouted: 'What the devil is that to you? These people must move off – they're in my way.' Blunt was not to be cowed. Even though he was interfering with the white man's 'time-honoured privilege of ill-treating men of an inferior race to his own', he secured an apology, which came months later.[34] Only too credible was the remark of EM Forster's fictional Surgeon-Major's wife that the kindest thing a medical officer could do to a native was to let him die. '"How if he went to heaven?" asked the ingenuous Mrs Moore. "He can go where he likes as long as he doesn't come near me. They give me the creeps."'[35]

All Europeans found the Bengali babu a most irritating gentleman, but the emergence of an educated Indian class, for which Macaulay had planned, was inexorable, though there were not enough of them – and many hoped there would never be enough of them – to rule 180 million people. In 1888 there were fewer than 800 Indians with a university education and only 500,000 who had a reasonable command of English. By the end of the century there were nearly 2000 graduates a year from Indian university colleges, but a quarter of them were destined for the law. At this rate of production, there was nothing for it but to go on shouldering the burden. The secretary of state comforted himself that the masses did not want to be ruled by 'Baboos', so that 'it is our duty, as well as our interest, and still more the interest of the people, that there is English rule

171

and English justice and English consideration for the wants, the prejudices and the habits, religious as well as social, of all classes'.[36]

The involvement of 'baboos' in local government had been general since an elective municipality was created in Calcutta in 1876 and replicated in the other large cities of India. In Calcutta 75 commissioners constituted the municipal body, 50 elected by rate payers (perhaps 2% of the population), fifteen nominated by government and ten by the chamber of commerce. At the turn of the century, 23 of the elected commissioners were lawyers, and 39 of all commissioners were Hindu, 13 Muslim, the rest either European or Eurasian. 'The official sahibs' were obliged to 'keep up the farce of constitutional discussion and voting, though they well know that it is only a more cumbrous way of doing work that they would have to do in any case'.[37] Despite European scepticism of representational government, they could not manage large Indian centres of population without it. By 1915 everybody knew that British rule in India might not see out the century, but as Ruby Elliot, Viscountess Errington, from her place of honour at the viceroy's table, surveyed the senior civil servants and princes who assembled there, she worried about the concessions that would have to follow the war, an anxiety shared by most of the guests.[38] For they still had challenging jobs to do. The Orientalist tradition had never completely succumbed to dry utilitarianism or the disillusioning pressures of ruling a resentful people. There were constant surprises. One young ICS officer wrote a report in Virgilian hexameters, to be reprimanded by the Chief Secretary for a false quantity.[39] The professionals, engineers, surveyors, medical men, found much job satisfaction in the problems they had to solve and wrote monographs and papers which the ever hungry Journal of the Asiatick Society published and which gave them often a far from modest reputation in the intellectual world.

The part-author of that indispensable glossary of Anglo–Indian words and phrases, Hobson-Jobson, was an army engineer who made his reputation by developing the old Mughal canal system that fed water into Delhi. Henry Yule (1820–1889) worked on the most ambitious feat of engineering to date in India, the construction of the Ganges Canal, responsible for the mighty headworks at the pilgrimage centre of Hardwar, whence the canal started forth along 648 miles to water the doab. Among his contributions to the Journal of the Asiatick Society of Bengal was a paper on the Canal Act of the Emperor Akbar. The Sikh wars were fought among a network of rivers that armies had to cross and recross, and demanded constant bridge-building and improvisation, which led to the collapse of his health. He was attached to the mission Dalhousie sent to Ava after the annexation of Pegu and wrote an account describing its adventures, with verbatim reports of conversations with courtiers, chapters on Burmese Buddhism, on the administration of the country, and a contribution towards a definitive map, the first authoritative account of the country that was, piece by piece, being absorbed into the Indian empire. Until his departure from India in 1862, Yule worked in the Public Works department in Calcutta, on the design and building of barracks for the greatly increased number of European troops following the Mutiny and on the extension of the railway system, over 20,000 miles of new track being constructed during his five years there.

'Weariness of India' persuaded him to retire after only 22 years in service to embark on nearly thirty years of scholarship. His greatest achievement was the miraculous *Hobson-Jobson*, for most of which he was responsible, and which remains a treasure trove of Indiana never likely to be superseded. In 1875, he joined the Council of India and opposed Lytton's Vernacular Press Act in phrases of lapidary and crushing condemnation. His knighthood in the year before his death was of less interest to him than the presidency of the Hakluyt Society, the crowning recognition of his intellectual life.[40]

A very different introduction to India was the work of another Bengal soldier. Richard Burton came to Bombay in 1842 with the 18th Regiment of Foot, and immediately hired the foremost Parsi oriental linguist to teach him Persian, Hindostani and Gujerati, largely through the discipline of learning 300 words a day. He passed out first in the Hindostani examination and was appointed regimental interpreter. He kept a monkey in his bungalow to see if he could classify its speech patterns, and thought he identified at least 60 separate utterances. Dressed in native garb, like Kim, he went into the bazaars and brothels to pick up demotic speech, and kept an Indian girl for pillow talk. In his working time, he surveyed and mapped. Burton's linguistic skill may have attracted the quirky admiration of General Napier, who was not an old India hand and could therefore be indulgent about these things, and for whom the tidbits from the bazaar were as important as they were to Lurgan Sahib, but to his fellow officers Burton was a 'white nigger'. He produced a detailed report on the male brothels in Karachi, frequented by European soldiery which had therefore to be closed. It led to suspicions of paedophiliac sodomy and Burton came close to being cashiered. In 1849 Burton returned home with rheumatic ophthalmia, for which his remedy was to throw his notes together into three books, on *Scinde or the Unhappy Valley*, on *Goa and the Blue Mountains* and on *Sindh and the Races that Inhabit the Valley of the Indus*, only the last of which had pretensions to being a serious study, in which 'the incredible variety, the vast canvas of curious and bewildering data from gypsies to incest, from bayonet drill to Islam, in half a dozen languages, made it plain that the man was a protean Gibbon of analytic ethnology'.[41] His *Kamasutra* was the reworking of the two Indian love manuals, the *Ananga Ranga, or the Pleasures of Women*, and the *Kamasutra of Vatsyayana*. By the 1870s his mission was to free western women from self-imposed frigidity. To publish the explicit details of how to avoid the horror of the 'first night' and how to replace a spouse incapable of arousal, he established in 1882, with another scion of the covenanted service, Foster Fitzgerald Arbuthnott, a *Kama Shastra Society* of London and Benares and pretended that the text was entirely the work of two pandits and printed in the holy city. By the use of Hindu words for the most intimate parts of the body and perfumed euphemisms for conjugation, he avoided the charges of obscenity.[42] Though the *Kamasutra* was reprinted twice within two years, it was through pirated editions that it reached its readers. Its economy of style compares startlingly with 'the whole forests [that] have been felled to publicise a modern discovery of the female orgasm'.[43]

Henry Yule and Richard Burton represent the contrasted poles of Victorian orientalism, no longer trying to represent an idealised India to the west in order to correct European ignorance and contempt, but writing up discovery based on experience and observation. They had both come to India as soldiers but found something far more rewarding than the art of war. Frontier work apart, British army officers were not overworked in India and, for those for whom hunting, shooting and billiards were empty recreations, there was much original work they could do. Trained in the arts of precision – the Addiscombe graduates were engineers and surveyors – they eschewed the abstruse realms of Indian metaphysics for the observational sciences, and Burton's work pioneered that of anthropologists of the 20th century like Malinowski, Geoffrey Gorer and Verrier Elwin.

To a later soldier, Winston Churchill, the prospect of going to India with the 4th Hussars in 1896, when he might have gone to South Africa, was 'an useless and unprofitable exile'. Unimpressed by his fellow countrywomen in India, 'nasty vulgar creatures all looking as it they thought themselves great beauties', he threw himself into collecting butterflies and playing polo, at both of which he showed himself an adept. The civilians in Bangalore could tell him nothing about the country so that 'if I stay here twenty years as a soldier I see no prospect of my acquiring any knowledge worth knowing of Indian affairs'. So he settled down to prepare for his career in politics by reading Macaulay and Gibbon, Adam Smith's *Wealth of Nations* and 27 volumes of the Annual Register, all of which he devoured in cantonment at Bangalore. From the great Whig he formed a simple political theory for Britain: that the franchise should be extended to every British male East of Suez, but he agreed with Lord Curzon that 'India must be governed on old principles.' The master of the Ootacamund Hounds was surprised by his confident assertion that he would be going into Parliament and one day be prime minister. In 1898 he wangled an attachment to headquarters of the Tirah campaign at Peshawar, saw action in two exhilarating engagements, and was mentioned in despatches. But he upset the military establishment in Simla by the irregular way he had carried on, so that when he was later considered as a possible viceroy in 1910 and 1915, there was considerable trepidation in the war department. His memorial of the campaign, *The Story of the Malakand Field Force*, 'in style a volume by Disraeli revised by a mad printer's reader', was to start him off on his literary life.[44]

Churchill made the best of India as a place to mark time, but he remained curiously uninterested in her as a country. He barely noticed the existence of Congress, or the growth of civic unrest, and that lack of interest lasted through his life, constituting a toxic ingredient of his belief that India in 1930 was the country he had known in 1899, God-given to the British to rule. Empire was necessary to absorb the energies of the British people whom Tory democracy was going to produce. As he told the Southsea Conservative Association in 1898: 'To keep our Empire we must have a free people, an educated and well-fed people... You have two duties to perform – the support of the empire abroad and the support of liberty at home.' He never spelled out the duties of Empire, but it was there to be ruled by free Britons, voting Tory. To vote any other way was to vote for no Empire at all.[45] A spell as viceroy would probably not have caused him to modify this historic view shared by a fellow cinema-buff, Adolf Hitler, whose favourite film was *The Lives of the Bengal Lancers*, from the novel by Yeats-Brown, which proved to him conclusively that the British destiny was to rule black men, the German, white.[46]

Meanwhile the civil servants, whom Churchill despised, had to do their best to cope with Indian dissent, and still fulfil the mission that had taken them to

India. Curzon's secretary, Walter Lawrence, who served for 16 years in Indian states, believed that three things in particular – more office work than touring, the motor car which could not go off the beaten track and the decreasing use of the languages of the people – were 'destructive of that touch of nature which leavened and lightened the heavy regularity' of British rule.[47] There were still those who had not fallen for these snares. Frank Brayne (1882–1952), was an ICS officer who believed that physical uplift led to moral regeneration, and that this would neutralise nationalist aspirations in which he had no faith. Indian politicians were no more likely to improve their people's lot than British. That must be the work of the people themselves. He despised the desk-wallah, surrounded by files and rulebooks. The role of people like Brayne was to defend them from all that might otherwise exploit them, 'landlords, officials, moneylenders, traders, lawyers'.[48] His mission, which amounted to mania, was rural self-help and his promotion of well-digging, importing a superior breed of bulls, digging communal latrines, constructing *bhoosa-boxes* for slow cooking and saving cow dung for fertiliser were all intended to elevate subsistence farming. His one integrated experiment in uplift among the impoverished Meos at Gurgaon, just south-east of Delhi, from 1920 to 1927, had a factitious success, talked up as it was by Brayne himself, whose restless energy kept the lift up. What peasants needed was massive investment in the supply of water and power, in insecticides and pills to eliminate malaria, and relief from debt, but to Brayne these were dangerous specifics. By self-help the peasants would stay industrious and frugal (and probably poor). If they once became rich, no one knew what vices they would adopt. Yet further up the Panjab, the success of water schemes was making the Panjabi farmer rich, and his surplus was to feed the less fortunate.[49] For Brayne, uplift was a coherent philosophy of development, of which he became a remorseless missionary. It was the only effective way of ensuring that peasants did not fall for the wiles of politicians who would promise them the earth. If they seized the earth for themselves they would not need politicians to seize it for them, and support for the Indian National Congress would fall away. Gandhi recognised him for the enemy he was.

The sickness from which British rule would die was immediately clear to the two Cambridge 'apostles', Goldsworthy Lowes Dickinson and Morgan Forster, who visited India in 1912. For Forster, the muddied oafs and flanelled fools of Tonbridge School, with their physical arrogance and suppressed sexuality, were prototypes of the governing class in India. Dickinson blamed European women. 'There they are, without their children, with no duties, no charities, with empty minds and hearts, trying to fill them by playing tennis and despising the natives.' Why could not the races meet? 'Simply because the Indians *bore* the English. That is the simple adamantine fact.'[50] It was largely true. The British in India were prepared to work hard for Indians, to control and improve them, but not to love them. Their warmest sentiments were not for friends but servants. To the idealist don, India was 'supernatural, uncanny, terrifying, sublime, horrible, monotonous, full of mountains and abysses, all heights and depths, and for ever incomprehensible' and ungovernable. Though the British presence was a curse, their absence would be worse. That Cambridge shrug summed up the liberal view of the Indian empire. Forster was depressed by the racial pride that set up barriers between officials and the educated native. Yet when officials tried to be polite they were often snubbed; Syed Ahmad Khan's grandson met the offer of a berth in a railway carriage from a young British officer with the ungracious words: 'Don't do this sort of thing, please. We don't appreciate it any more than the old sort. We know you have been told you must do it.'[51] The bitterness of past rudeness had bitten too deep for cure.

Malcolm Darling, Eton and King's College, Cambridge, had been one of the Dickinson set, a fellow student with Forster, and he came to India drenched in the urbane culture of the *fin de siècle*. He kept Homer in his pocket, read Pater and Keats and did not mind who knew it. His wife, Josie, shared his tastes and his prejudices, or rather anti-prejudices, and they filled their house, at whatever station they were, with elegance and taste, and Indians. 'If our power here is the illumination of a great people,' he wrote to one of his university friends, 'and not a mere commercial exploitation, we must build on love rather than force'.[52] In making friends with Indians, there were difficulties that the Darlings had not expected. To the British, friendship is often cerebral, disinterested, a mutual juncture of opinions and tastes. To an Indian friendship is visceral, full of expectations and demands, incurring obligations, even duties, which often proved too difficult to meet. 'The view commonly held in India [is] that those who occupy positions of authority are under a moral obligation to help, and to go on helping their friends to secure appointments, promotion, increases of salary, and so on'.[53]

The arrogance with which British administrators were accused stemmed partly from their inability to enter into the sort of friendship an Indian might demand. Even so sympathetic an officer as Walter Lawrence, who tried very hard, had to admit that 'no one can ever boast that he really knows and understands the Indians'.[54] One critic of Forster's *Passage to India* claimed that his portraits of Anglo-Indian civilians were caricatures and that 'if a Collector behaved as Turton did he would be written off as a madman'. Forster was not impressed. He had only been to India twice but he had seen certain truths that had been hidden from his critic, despite his thirty long years service in the country and his highly specialised training. High-minded civil servants could often not see the boorishness of their countrymen towards Indians, to whom they might be invariably polite, if distant, themselves.[55] 'You do not treat us as equals and you do not trust us,' was the lapidary reply of a Madrassi pleader when Darling asked him what fault he found with the English.[56] As Britons had been brought up to believe in their own moral superiority, they would only break through the barrier if they lost it. When Forster confessed his buggery and had to depend on what his employer, the maharaja, would tolerate, he entered the circle of his friends. Such unbending was rare.

The transfer of the capital of British India to Delhi had first been proposed by Charles Trevelyan at the time of the Mutiny.[57] By the end of the century, Bengali nationalism having taken to terror, the government wanted a capital that could be more easily policed. Unlike Calcutta, Delhi was stitched to many regimental battle honours, and the heroic exploits on the Ridge in 1857 had been etched onto every British schoolboy's memory. With the example of Haussman's Paris before them, with its broad avenues and landscaped esplanades, which made crowd control easier, the capital would move to a new city built alongside Shahjahanabad. Delhi was where Lytton had proclaimed Victoria Empress of India in 1878, and it was at a Delhi dorbar that George V himself announced the transfer in 1911.

Despite all the pomp and circumstance it was to serve, the new city was to be built within a budget of half a million pounds, of which £200,000 would be for the viceregal palace. The Delhi public works department thought the project well within its competence, but the viceroy, Lord Hardinge, had no wish to be a cut-price Great Mughal. A capital to last 300 years should be 'as interesting... as the older buildings in the neighbourhood area'. If the Delhi town-planners had their way 'they will make our city look ridiculous'.[58] Edwin Lutyens had a powerful connection with India through his wife, Emily, daughter of Lord Lytton. Despite this possibly awkward relationship, Lutyens was recommended to the secretary of state, the Marquess of Crewe, by the president of the Royal Institute of British Architects, for his work on country houses in England and on the British pavilion at the Rome international exhibition. This make-shift edifice, reproducing the first order of St Paul's cathedral, gave the right indication that he could think imperially. He now joined the three-man commission for the new capital, along with Liverpool's city architect and the former chairman of the London County Council.

Lutyens galumphed over all the possible sites in high summer temperatures on the back of an elephant. He was baffled by the beauty and misery of its teeming life, the absence of drains, the ubiquity of flies and 'the extraordinarily unintelligent' housing of British and Indians alike.[59] George V had, during an exhortatory interview, revealed a strong personal interest in the project, and believed that the Mughal style would be most suitable, 'like', expostulated Lutyens, 'Queen Elizabeth instructing Shakespeare to write an ode in Chaucerian metre'.[60] Hardinge was obsessed by pointed windows (an abomination to Lutyens) and he was shocked when Lutyens told him the palace he envisaged would cost nearer £1,000,000 than £200,000 (an estimate that proved to be correct). As for Indian architecture, there was, in Lutyens's view, lots of 'veneered joinery in stone, concrete and marble on a gigantic scale... but no real architecture, and nothing built to last, not even the Taj'.[61] If *he* was to build something to last, it would have to be his own original, not an imitation, not a classical English building with captured Indian features, hung like pictures on a wall, but something which gave India a new sense of architecture, adapted to her craft tradition.

Lutyens did not like architects or Indians, and architects trying to be Indians least of all. The six volume work of Swinton Jacob, which contained 375 drawings in loving detail of the fretted carvings, capitals, brackets, kiosks, and cupolas of buildings, from Hindu temples to the sumptuous mausolea of emperors and saints, which were presented to clients as being in the 'Indo–Saracenic' style, aroused in him only contempt. There was no such thing as an Indo–Saracenic style; indeed there was no great tradition of Indian architecture, 'just spurts by various mushroom dynasties with as much intellect in them as any other art nouveau'.[62] Lutyens was impatient with his colleagues and took advice badly, though he was free with it himself. But the Hardinges, man and wife, warmed to him, and he was assured of the commission for the palace and forecourt. Like all great building complexes, the capital project was beset by compromises, and his two colleagues got on too badly with each other to overrule Lutyens. There were disputes over the site, the style, the size, the cost, the name. The last was, at one point, reduced to either Georgebad or Marypore. Lutyens, watching the committee sweat over the matter, suggested Ooziepore. His own name for it was Bedlampore. Unable to agree, they fell back on New Delhi.[63]

Hardinge was seriously wounded in a terrorist bomb attack on 23 December 1912, while making a state entry into Delhi, and during his long convalescence his mind kept changing. Lady Hardinge died and Lutyens seemed to slip out of favour. She had enjoyed his mischievous wit that did not go down well elsewhere in government house. His relationship with the vicereine was almost flirtatious and she enjoyed his form of cheek. He once apologised to her with the quip that 'I will wash your feet with my tears and dry them with my hair. True I have very little hair but you have very little feet.'[64] After her death, Hardinge reverted to his original wish that the palace should be built in the Indian style. Lutyens still wanted the classical, the only Imperial style, but he began to see the possibilities of the viceroy's choice. Lutyens was no democrat and Hardinge's idea of working in harmony with the old Indian élites appealed to him. 'To express modern India in stone, to represent her amazing sense of the supernatural, with its complement of profound fatalism and enduring patience is no easy task.'[65] All this against a declining budget and the jealous rivalry of his former associate in South Africa, Herbert Baker, whom he had invited to join the project and who had been commissioned to design the secretariat buildings. Baker believed, and made no secret of his belief, that he was the viceroy's real choice for the palace design, and disputed Lutyens's judgement about the lay-out of the 'acropolis', their name for the slightly concave plateau on the Ridge that had eventually been chosen as the site and which was being levelled.

Lutyens did not realise until too late that a sketch, drawn as it were from thirty feet in the air, in order to remove the effect of the concavity, actually consigned his palace to a dip in the plateau that rendered it invisible from the royal processional way, so that the first buildings to be seen by visiting potentates and ambassadors were those of Baker's Secretariat. Lutyens moved heaven and earth, and lobbied Their Imperial Majesties themselves, to have the plan changed, but he was defeated both on grounds of sightliness and cost. In fact, the gradual appearance of the stately pleasure dome, like the Buddhist *stupa* at Sanchi, which Lutyens intended to overawe its visitors, the tall thin row of classical columns and the huge bronze gates, rising like an exhalation in the Indian haze, is more impressive. Despite its size and grandeur, the close marriage of Imperial classical and Imperial mughal, the whole space has an air of intimacy and gentleness, of a prince lying among his *houris* in the surrounding gardens and lily ponds, of a residence more suitable for a cultivated gentleman than a mighty monarch. That is probably why it has been such a suitable residence for a constitutional, often humble, president. But it was not until December 1930 that the viceroy, then Lord Irwin, was able to move in. Until then he had to make do with a house in civil lines, now the vice-chancellor's residence of Delhi University.

The oriental traveller, Robert Byron, was ecstatic about it:

> Like all humanists, Sir Edwin Lutyens had drunk of the European past,
> and he now drank of the Indian... He has accomplished... a fusion of
> tastes, comforts and conceptions of beauty in different climates. The
> Mogul emperors, behind their gorgeous façades, lived in rooms like
> housemaids' closets... Lutyens has combined the gorgeous façade,
> coloured and dramatic, of Asia, with the solid habits, cubic and
> intellectual, of European building... Sometimes he has shouted for joy in
> his earth, conjuring rays from a dome, fountains from a roof and a glass
> star from a column, and smoke from an arch.[66]

Mughal colouring, bands of sandstone 'rich rhubarb red and ivory cream',
the deep cornice and the great copper dome, 'a shout of imperial suggestion, an
offence against democracy, a slap in the face of the average modern man' were
the supreme amalgam of east and west which he had put on the drawing board
in 1912. Despite the changes in plan, the quarrels over cost, and the vacillating
resolution of the viceroy (now he wanted the dome higher, now he wanted it
lower), the viceregal palace, Rashtrapati Bhavan, is one of the great buildings of
the 20th century.[67]

Lutyens's impish sense of fun is to be seen in the details, the stone birdcages
on the balustrades, the images that appear and disappear like mediaeval gargoyles,
the sudden visions of domesticity, corridors that open into bedrooms, the
incorporation of what was then modern technology (to keep the food warm) into
grandiose space. Its clean lines, its contrasts of shades and shadows, its use of
Indian motives sparingly preserved it from the bulbous pomposity and fretful
fussiness of the Madras Law Courts (1889–92), or Swinton Jacob's palace at
Gwalior, 'a white sugarcake looking building, with an inside of a third rate
Boarding House'.[68] Lord Hardinge had decided that, with the transfer of the
capital to New Delhi, the partition of Bengal could be reversed, thus converting
Bengal once again into a predominantly Muslim province. Hindus were not
impressed. Calcutta was a Hindu city, built by Hindu capital. Delhi had only
been capital of a declining Mughal empire. The plain around it was littered with
dead cities. The Maharajah of Burdwan was particularly scathing: 'One might as
well try pumping oxygen into a dead man as to pump life into Delhi!'[69]

Where Briton met Indian on equal terms was in the sports field. Understanding
race horses 'goes pretty far towards pleasing the British residents,' remarked
one jaundiced observer in 1864 of the Aga Khan.[70] But the man who pleased the
English more than anyone was Kumar Shri Ranjitsinhji (1872–1933) who, from
1893 to 1920 was every schoolboy's hero. Coupled with WG Grace for
performance, for style and grace he had no peer. Ranji was part of the anglicised,
dandified Indian nobility, educated at a prince's school, and was destined to be
Jam Saheb of Nawanagar and pillar of the Chamber of Princes. He was sent to
Cambridge in 1890 as part of an India Office quota of young 'leaders' and earned
his laurels with the bat, winning his blue in 1893. By 1895 he was playing for
Sussex and in 1896 for England. In 1899, 'Ranji saved England', in a match
against Australia, in which his team-mates did not shine. "E never made a
Christian stroke in his life' but sport proved to be a religion more easy to export

than Protestant Christianity and, today, budding Ranjis are to be seen on every open space in the great cities of India, on the maidans of Calcutta, Madras and Bombay, in the ditches of the Red Fort in Delhi, worshipping at the shrine of the MCC.[71] Ranji seldom disappointed his admirers, surpassing himself against Yorkshire at Brighton in 1896 as the only batsman ever to score two centuries on a single day, against Surrey at Hastings by scoring the highest number of runs in a pre-lunch session, the only player besides WG Grace to score a century in his test début against Australia in 1896, and the first to score 3000 runs in a season. As a batsman he was second only to Bradman for the highest career average in first class cricket.[72]

'The Indian has the eye of the hawk and wrists like Toledo steel, and the finest of the batsman's art is his, the art of timing the ball... [It] leaves his blade with the swiftness of thought.'[73] As a fielder he was like a panther, a deadly slip catch. He made scoring off the back foot an aggressive stroke and his cricket was the stuff of poetry. At one time he was held to be the most popular man in England, and the India Office must have been pleased by their selection when, in 1896, at a dinner in his honour at Cambridge, he hoped that 'the wrongs done in the past to Her Majesty's Indian subjects, and the injustice, if any, which they had suffered in days gone by, would be forgotten, and that England and India might form one united country, ready to show an united front to a common enemy, and be the admiration and envy of all other nations'.[74] They were sentiments his fellow Kathiawari and contemporary, Mohandas Gandhi, might at that time have seconded.

In Ranji's nephew, Prince Duleepsinhji, the great cricketer seemed almost to be reincarnated. Duleep also played for Cambridge and, like his uncle, captained Sussex and played against Bradman in test matches, but he had to retire early from the game with a weak chest, from catching pleurisy in the damp English May. He made more runs for Cambridge than his uncle, with 254 against Middlesex in 1927 scoring what was then the highest score of any Cambridge player. In 1929 he notched up 2,500 runs for Sussex, never took more than three hours to make a century, and in 1930 beat his uncle's 1901 record innings of 285 not out with 333 against Northamptonshire. His drives were so powerful that, in the Lords test in 1930, Bradman, fielding at mid-off and cover, had to bandage his bruised hands at the tea interval.

The first Indian team to play in England were The Parsees in 1886 but it was not until 1932 that an Indian test team came to England to play at Lords. Dismissing Sutcliffe, Hobbes and Woolley for a total of 28 runs between them, they made England sweat for her victory. Ranji had insisted that Duleep, having learned his cricket in England, should play for England not India, but that year saw Duleep's last innings. The side that sailed for Australia, however, included another Indian prince, the Nawab of Pataudi, who like his two illustrious countrymen, made a century in his first match against the Australians in the notorious body-line tour. Henceforward the Indian princes would play their straight bats for India.

The Indian chief schools took to 'manly sports' with greater enthusiasm than to learning. Rajkumar College produced Ranji, Mayo College produced the Maharajahs who captained the Patiala and Kotah polo teams. Polo, had come into India from Persia and was enthusiastically, if roughly, played by hill men in Manipur in the east and in the high valley of the Indus, in Ladakh, in Kashmir, at Balti and Gilgit where anyone with a horse would play. The sport was taken up by the Lancers and the Hussars, who developed the Indian rules in the 1850s while on cantonment duty in the hills. They brought the game down to the Panjab in 1864 and to England in 1869. Exercises on horse-back were all seen to be grand training for war. Winston Churchill became an enthusiastic player while based at Bangalore, where the 4th Hussars determined that they would win the inter-regimental cup. They did not, but they did win the tournament cup at Secunderabad within a month of their arrival in India, which no team had ever done before. Tent-pegging, hunting, especially wild boar, on horseback, additionally added the spice of danger, of measuring man against odds. The British never achieved the same speed and dexterity of their Indian opponents at 'polo on foot', as hockey came to be called, when the qualities of wrist and eye, that had made Ranji a prince among batsmen, had to be linked to speed and stamina. In 1899 the finest shot in the world was deemed to be the Nizam of Hyderabad. Sport had become the substitute for war and a good sportsman was considered less likely to be a vicious ruler, devoting his life to champagne, European women, bookmakers and trousers.[75] Indians could play cricket, tennis and polo for English clubs in England, but in India, civil servants might be willing to work with Indians but not to play with them, while boxwallahs preferred to do neither. The Yacht and Byculla Clubs in Bombay were exclusively for Europeans so that the Indians, lavishly supported by their princes, had to build a sports club of their own in a poorer location, with facilities just as grand for cricket, polo, tennis and football.[76]

The passion for slaughter of wild life was almost pathological with both races and united Briton and Indian, military and civilian, liberal and conservative. In the hands of a European the gun might have been the symbol of racial mastery, in the hands of an Indian it confirmed equality, even allowed him to show his superiority. The Maharajah of Alwar despised the viceroy, Lord Reading, for missing 'three tigers running'.[77] Tiger hunting was the necessary entertainment of India. Next to battle, it was the most exciting thing there was, a sport laced with the danger of death. 'What are the poor triumphs of the first of September compared to the noble warfare which we carry on against the masters of the wood, where the sharp roar of the tiger is followed by its deadly spring?'[78] Travellers could not return home without having run the slender dangers of a tiger-shoot, dignitaries had to be rewarded with a head or a pelt as trophies, proof that they had endured the ritual. Hunting provided its own special ceremonial of power, causing almost a levée en masse of local people, enrolled as trackers and beaters; to give the secretary of state a day's shooting, the maharajah of Patiala laid on '3,500 beaters, horsemen etc to kill 100 farmyard chickens'.[79] One of the attraction of Simla was the opportunity to kill a cold-weather tiger, more difficult to hunt than a hot weather tiger whose pads found the ground too hot to wander far and was easier to find.[80]

'An Englishman's life in India... is that of a man who works hard to maintain a wife and children whom he never sees.'[81] Wives were trapped in an environment as small as Cranford in a continent of darkness, saddened by absentee husbands, and lost children sent early from home to school, dominated by social tyranny, oppressive servants, fear of illness or sexual molestation. 'Two inquisitive black crows perched in the open window and surveyed the ceremony, flying off with coarse caws at the point of the blessing; from the world outside came the hot, bright glare of the afternoon sun upon the Maidan, and the creaking of the ox-gharries, and the chattering of the mynas in the casuarina tree, and the scent of some heavy-smelling thing of the country – how like it was to every other Indian wedding where a maid come trippingly from overseas to live in a long chair under a punkah, and be a law unto kitmutgars!'[82] The new bride of a civilian or a commercial would live in a rented house, her society would be other wives, who observed the intricate niceties of rank. Unconventionality and social mixing with the natives were not encouraged. No need to know the name of any educated Indian she met. 'Call him baboo; he will answer to plain "baboo"'.[83] Conversation with 'Baboo' was about necessities or business. Young Browne, clerking in tea and indigo on 500 rupees a month, nearly tipped a visiting MP out of his pony trap because he 'had been talking to a beastly baboo about the white women of Calcutta'.[84] From the highest to the lowest, everyone experienced loneliness in the midst of crowds. 'Words cannot describe the hugeness of this place [Government House, Calcutta] or the utter absence of anything like homely comfort,' moaned Lord Lansdowne '[the] colossal bed large enough for half a dozen couples, ... the vast tent of mosquito netting running all the way up to the ceiling so far up that one can hardly see it'. But what oppressed him most was the cloud of servants always at his door.[85] The grandson of Sir Richard Strachey found it 'hard to believe that, amidst the publicity and distraction to which my parents [in India] were subjected, they could have found the few moments in which to fuck'.[86]

The offspring of European fathers and native women could never be accepted as the equal of pure Europeans. Missionaries were interested in them as neophytes and Bishop Heber, during his pastoral visits, found them the most usual recipients of his spiritual attentions. None had been so marked a victim of this prejudice than Colonel James Skinner (1787–1841), famous for the irregular cavalry he commanded, known as the Yellow Boys from the canary-coloured uniforms and turbans which made it so distinctive a force. Skinner's parents were a Scottish army officer and a Rajput woman. As a commander of irregular cavalry, Skinner knew his business better than anyone, but it took the personal intervention of the sovereign to secure him the Order of the Bath and the rank of Lieutenant-Colonel. All the powers of a governor-general were insufficient to confer rank on one as black as he was.

The government persistently held that it could not afford to maintain a married European soldiery; there were no marriage allowances or special quarters so that, as enlisted men could not be expected to remain chaste, concubinage with, even marriage to, Indian women was tolerated as being preferable to frequenting brothels and being clapped. Hindu caste rules and Muslim endogamy meant that the women available were often of doubtful virtue. Sexual liaisons with topass girls, sometimes blessed by a local ceremony of marriage, were preferable, for they were, even if Roman Catholics, Christians and the descendants of Europeans, but these arrangements were usually made for the duration of the man's stay in India, and upon his leaving, the unhappy woman often found she was not married at all and she and her children not eligible for repatriation.[87] As the years rolled by and the Latin American empires and republics were forged by creoles, the growing number of Eurasians was thought to compose some sort of threat to British rule.[88] Though the disqualification of people of mixed blood from government and military service was repealed in 1853, their status did not improve markedly, despite their sterling service during the Mutiny in dangerous roles as spies and couriers. One of them throughout that turbid period had been the intrepid police chief in Bombay.

The morals of British soldiers in India remained a constant source of applied Pecksniffism. The army maintained mobile brothels in the cantonments, the whores were routinely checked and, if infected, sent to a lock or special hospital to be cured. This element of control meant that the women were often the least commercially desirable, and their allure could not compete with the girls outside the camp. Attempts to find younger and more attractive 'comfort-women' to keep the men from going into town, drinking bad liquor and contracting the pox, aroused missionary anger that the army was conniving at, even encouraging sin. The lock hospitals came under bitter nonconformist attack both in Britain and in India. Liberals and the chastisers of sin joined together, one to prevent an infringement of the liberty of women from forcible examination, the second to prevent encouragement of fornication, so that in 1881 the provision of hospital treatment and accommodation for licensed whores was banned in Calcutta and gradually ceased elsewhere. 'This official virtue cost our army,' wrote Kipling disdainfully, 'nine thousand expensive white men a year always laid up from venereal disease.'[89] The official statistics, however, showed that VD among the men rose in proportion to the number of them in the country, whether there were lock hospitals and regimental brothels or not, though probably less fast where they remained open. Sermons on purity at church parade were ineffective against the long hours of idleness and boredom, exacerbated by heat, which demanded diversion in the traditional way that the brutal and licentious soldiery knew best.

The prudish attitude to their behaviour was not wholly a matter of morals. Soldiers in congress with local prostitutes reduced the gap that should exist between the occupying force and the native population. Even missionaries who tried to span the social gap separating them from their Christian flock were viewed askance, since it reduced the gap between white women and black. Social, rather than sexual, particularism, was the canker at the heart of British rule. Curzon worried himself about European barmaids in India, not only because they might end up themselves in concubinage or encourage young men in drinking and frivolity, but because 'the spectacle of service is open to the eyes of natives... and occasionally... incidents occur which are profoundly degrading to the prestige of the ruling race'.[90] Princes were not considered appropriate spouses for European women. It might encourage them to take social liberties with their rulers.

If India was a hell for many women, it was heaven for children, the 'land of spoildom'[91] from birth. As there was no one to instruct them before they were sent to school there were no lessons. They had their own *pootly nautch*, or wooden puppet shows and, as they spoke the language of the servants better than that of their parents, they could tap into the endless delights of Indian story telling. For six or seven years they knew virtually no restraint, the *baba sahib* being a Lilliputian tyrant, a little prince or princess whose every whim was satisfied. Some parents, like Henry and Honoria Lawrence, tried to rein in their children, but for the most part their mothers, who knew only too well that they would lose them at seven, sometimes for ever, conspired with their households to spoil them. For Dickie-baba sahib Strachey 'the greatest gift that India gave me' was Love; the devotion of his ayah and personal bearer provided the parenting, the women of the compound fed him with cakes, honey, sugared almonds, dates and other fruits, with half a dozen flies for good measure, until he was sick.[92] Ayahs were 'singularly kind, injudicious, patient and thoughtless,' but 'to expect any-thing like common-sense from them is to lay yourself open to certain dis-appointment'.[93]

Writing was a suspect activity for wives, in case it encouraged levity or despair. When her dashing colonel husband died, Adela Cory, having produced, as Laurence Hope, a book of poems of exotic and banal sensuality, killed herself from excessive sensibility. Flora Annie Steel, wife of a Panjab civil servant between 1867 and 1889, in default of any other social life, decided that she would get to know more about India than was ever considered necessary for a woman. She entertained natives, interfered in her husband's work and wrote disrespectful articles for a Lahore newspaper on outrageous matters, like the sale of degrees of the Punjab University. She wrote a novel about the mutiny, in which the rebels were not mindless and depraved villains, and another about the court of Jahangir, as well as a History of India for bored memsahibs. Perhaps her most important work was *The Complete Indian Housekeeper and Cook*, exhorting women to stop whingeing about their lot and to master, if not the language and culture of India, at least its cuisine. She was, however, the exception rather than the rule. Most memsahibs found their only creative activity in the garden.

Some wives were able to travel with their husbands and do missionary-type work in their station, teaching, zenana visiting, butterfly hunting. Violet Jacob, another minor novelist, was tireless in her pursuit of flowers to paint, braving all the imagined dangers of riding out alone to find her specimens. An army wife, she was happy to be posted to a native state, 'twice and three times as interesting as British India', and was able to avoid the 'official, deadly social hills.[94] Often the wives of senior officials became adept at game shooting. One governor's lady was such a good shot she would cut canna lilies for her guests by shooting at them with her rifle.[95] In the hill-stations and larger cantonments, there being always more men than unmarried women, dances and dinners could sustain a social life almost as febrile as that depicted in the novels of Jane Austen, where boredom was always stalking at the end of the garden, rank and precedence were the constant preoccupation of social life and failure to marry a fate almost worse than lingering death.

For all their sacrifices, the women of the Raj were often stigmatised as being the sap that undermined British resolution in India. Life-time dedication to India was weakened as mothers went home to see their children through school. Wives, sweethearts and paramours sucked civilians into a life of dinners, tennis parties, picnics, dances, amateur theatricals and dalliance at the Club, from all of which

Indians were excluded.[96] The nostalgia for 'home' became unbearable, holly berries sent out to deck the table at Christmas helping to nourish this sense of estrangement.[97] Retirement in Britain became not a destiny to be dreaded but a consummation devoutly to be wished. If long-term residents found it hard to come to terms with India, it was harder for the occasional visitors, even the magnificently intellectual Sidney and Beatrice Webb. For them the great difficulty was that 'a stupid people find themselves governing an intellectual aristocracy'.[98] As children of the western myth that only liberty provided for the fullest development of the human personality, they feared that 'the ideal is wholly antagonistic to the Eastern ideal of restricting activity and assiduously cultivating a state of mind which seems to us to resemble blankness.'[99] Webb could sympathise with the Unitarian trend in Hinduism professed by the Arya and Brahmo Samaj, and could approve of all educational institutions run by them, because they conformed to his own secular and scientific attitudes. Both Beatrice and Sidney were in no doubt that India could be managed perfectly competently by the right people, but how to ensure that it was? Gandhi, in his own way, thought the same, but in his case *all* the people were to be the right people, by following his own prescription for *swaraj*.

Not all European women in India came as wives. Apart from the barmaids of whom Lord Curzon disapproved, there were some like Annette Ackroyd who came out to improve the education of Indian women. With no Christian belief, she answered a personal appeal in 1870 from the leader of the Progressive Brahmo Samaj, for British women to extend to India their campaign for women's rights in Britain. In Calcutta Annette was appalled at the attitude of her countrywomen. 'How these sweet and feminine souls,' she wrote to her sister, superintendent of the Working Women's College in London, 'whose sympathy is so tender and sensibilities so acute, can be so destitute not only of humanity but of simple courtesy and consideration for the feelings of others is a problem I cannot pretend to solve.'[100] Her idealism could not prevent her school for 14 young ladies becoming 'a drab affair of spoons and forks and filters, and drunken landlords and absconding servants'.[101] In 1875, she married the district magistrate, Henry Beveridge, and found more satisfaction in being wife and mother than the vain task of trying to improve the lot of Indian women. If she considered India an uncivilised country, it was not because she was British, but because she was a woman.[102]

The condition of women was increasingly used as a yardstick to measure readiness for self-government. The appearance of Katherine Mayo's *Mother India* in 1927 caused a *succès de scandale*. Winston Churchill found plenty of matter with which to feed his prejudices and 'would have no mercy with the Hindus who marry little girls aged ten'. Even the viceroy, who feared that she would make the Hindus see red, thought it might 'yet give a shock to the unsatisfactory conditions of Hindu thought on many of these subjects'.[103] *Mother India* was a sustained and detailed attack on Indian habits and customs. It was 'all true' in the sense that, to a superficial observer, what was described there did happen, but Mayo saw things only with the eyes of a fastidious Pennsylvanian who felt much as did Annette Beveridge. She made no attempt to analyse or understand what she was writing about and her book paraded many of the prejudices of

James Mill over a hundred years earlier. At this rate, it seemed to say, Indians will never be fit to run their own affairs. The book ran to many editions and probably did more than any other to perpetuate the myth that Indian society was unreformable.[104] Many of the customs and habits, which scandalised Katherine Mayo, also scandalised Gandhi who battled against untouchability, child marriage, illiteracy and dirt from within the system. It needed not a prophet come from deepest Pennsylvania to pass judgement on the customs of a continent almost as old as time. Her criticisms were levelled primarily at Hindus, suggesting an atavistic dislike of that system of faith among those who ought to understand it better, and the Hindus did, indeed, see red.

13. 'WE ARE PLEDGED TO INDIA'

We are pledged to India, I may say to mankind, for its
performance; and we have no choice but to apply
ourselves to the accomplishment of the work, the
redemption of the pledge, with every faculty we possess.

> William Ewart Gladstone to Lord Ripon,
> 24 November 1881

Can any Bengali honestly say that the [Congress]
resolutions passed... will be beneficial to any class of
natives except Bengalis and Maratha Brahmans?

> Syed Ahmad Khan, 1887

Let India be my Judge.

> Lord Curzon to the Bombay Byculla Club,
> November 1905

Try and suffer fools more gladly; they constitute the
majority of mankind.

> Lord George Hamilton to Lord Curzon, 1903

Is this Congress a nursery for sedition and rebellion
against the British government (*cries of no, no*); or is it
another stone in the foundation of the stability of that
government (*cries of yes, yes*)?

> From Dadabhai Naoroji's presidential speech to
> Congress, 27 December 1886

GLADSTONE DUBBED LYTTON THE Great Ornamental, 'floating loosely about in
wide pantaloons and flying skirts, diffusing as he passes the fragrance of smile
and pleasantry and cigarette'.[1] When he chose Lord Ripon to succeed him in
1880 he wanted someone to fulfil his pledge 'to India, I may say to mankind'.[2]
The test came when, in February 1883, Sir Courtenay Ilbert, the new law member, removed the immunity of Europeans from appearing before native judges.
Ripon's fellow countrymen, supported by the majority of British civil servants,
the chief justice, ten British judges of the Calcutta High Court and the
Lieutenant-Governor of Bengal, then showed that there were two kinds of justice,
one for Indians, another for Europeans. Even Annette Beveridge, née Ackroyd,

187

who was usually highly critical of British attitudes to India, was outraged by 'Mr Ilbert's proposal to subject civilized women to the jurisdiction of men who have done little or nothing to redeem the women of their own races'. Any attempt to use native police to enforce native judgements against Europeans would cause a white revolt. Such a threat of mutiny seemed to justify Lord Salisbury' s prophetic comment that 'the only enemies, I believe, who will ever seriously threaten England's power in India are her own sons'.[4] Because the *Pioneer* ratted over the Bill, Rudyard Kipling was hissed in the Punjab Club.[5] In the end it was decided that Europeans might be tried by a mixed jury of which half could be Indians.

In 1861 (the year that the Emperor of Russia abolished serfdom and licensed election to local councils), the Indian Council's Act of 1861 had sanctioned the appointment of Indians to the viceroy's and governors' legislative councils and election to municipal councils. Ripon was unhappy that in the intervening 18 years 'attempts at local self-government have been too often overridden and practically crushed by direct... official interference'. Officers of government should 'foster sedulously the small beginnings of independent political life', by encouraging the election rather than nomination of local people.[6] A judge of the Calcutta High Court spoke for most of his compatriots when he wrote to *The Times* that the government of India was 'essentially an absolute Government, founded, not on consent, but on conquest'. It could not 'represent the native principles of life or of government, and it can never do so until it represents heathenism and barbarism'.[7] Ripon was talking to the deaf.

In 1886, the Indian National Congress, born out of the experience of limited local government and an Indian National Conference in 1883, met in Bombay with the aim of devising an agenda for bringing Indians into partnership with the government. Ripon suggested that the governor of Bombay should preside over its meetings and his successor, the conservative Lord Dufferin (1884–8), agreed that it would be wrong not to 'give full play to the legitimate and praiseworthy ambition of the loyal, patriotic and educated classes in India' to play their part in framing the general policy of government.[8] Loyal and patriotic the first Congresses certainly were, in their aim to fuse the population of India into a nation and to consolidate the union between England and India by removing the causes of division or injury. It seemed about as dangerous as a college debating society, dissolving grievances into huff and puff. 'Self-government is very good,' Sir Charles Wood wrote in August 1861, 'if the people, who are to be so governed, are the people who govern; but self government is a mockery, if 9/10ths of the people to be governed have not & cannot have anything *really* to do with the government.'[9] The interests of the ryot were safer in the hands of British civil servants than those of their own countrymen.

Congress sought a partnership in government and hoped that, by making common cause, over social ills, like the legal age of marriage, it might convince the ruling power of its maturity and the responsibility of its members. But regulation of child marriage divided liberal Indians from orthodox and stirred both the Hindu and Muslim faithful to resist. The spectre of sectarianism was nourished by the appearance of a sect of self-deluded charlatans, many of them from Europe, who limpeted themselves upon the leadership. Madame Blavatsky, née Helena Petrovna Hahn, was a child of the German diaspora in the Ukraine, and exposed to the fantasies of Russian mysticism in early life, was convinced that she had passed seven years in Tibet in spiritual communion with two Himalayan *mahatmas*, who had alone revealed themselves to her and could send her telepathic messages faster than light. She set up as a highly accomplished medium in the United States, and in 1875 launched the Theosophical Society, with the modest aim of forming a universal brotherhood, inspired by the lore of ancient religions, and releasing the divine powers latent in man. Her study, in translation, of Brahman and Buddhist literature inspired a mixture of cabalistic, Egyptian, occult, and spiritual gobbledegook. Theosophy, according to Kipling, 'approved of and stole from freemasonry, looted the Latter-day Rosicrucians of half their pet words, took any fragments of Egyptian philosophy that it found in the *Encyclopaedia Britannica*, annexed as many of the Vedas as had been translated into French or English and talked of all the rest, [and]... would have adopted Voodoo and Obeah had it known anything about them'.[10] It was not long before this new priestess of Isis was attracted to India where, between 1879 and 1884, she absorbed the wide eclecticism of the Hindus into an even larger and more comprehensive cosmos. The Indians rumbled her at once, but one of her adepts, Annie Besant, who arrived in India in 1891, determined to build Indian nationalism on its Hindu past. Annie Besant was one of those Shavian women who consistently acted out of character, but that character had been moulded by the influences, hidden and experienced, of her childhood. Her aunt was Kitty O'Shea, the unwitting cause of Parnell's political demise, she was taught by Captain Marryat's sister, and she married the brother of the novelist Water Besant, an ordained priest of the Church of England, from whom she was legally separated when she lost her faith. In 1874 she joined the National Secular Society and, four years later, wrote her neo-Malthusian tract *The Gospel of Atheism*, as a result of which she lost the custody of her daughter. Under the spell of Madame Blavatsky, she, too, found that she had endured several incarnations in Tibet and had her own *mahatma*, who communicated with her 'phenomenally'. India was, clearly, her natural home where she enthusiastically proclaimed the identification of theosophy with Hindu values, superior to those of the West. With the conversion to theosophy of its founder, the disaffected civil servant, Alan Hume, she encouraged Hindus to rally behind the Indian National Congress which, she hoped, would become the inclusive ideological bed in which all religions could cohabit peacefully.

In 1898 Mrs Besant founded in her home in Benares the Central Hindu College, an experimental school to teach a new Hinduism, characterised by Beatrice Webb, who met her in 1912, as 'the attempt to appeal to the religious patriotism of the Hindu in favour of combining a maintenance of religious patriotism and mysticism, with the power of Conduct and a Power of Knowledge of Western Civilisation'.[11] It soon attracted support from rich and princely Hindus and had over a thousand students. Many of its staff were volunteers attracted by the 'new Hinduism' and, in 1916, the university college, became Benares Hindu University, her most enduring monument. Besant was not, like Blavatsky, a fraud. Apart from her Tibetan pre-life experiences, she never claimed mediumistic powers and her single-minded campaign for Indian self-rule, throughout the first world war, led to her election as the president of Congress. But the theosophical bed was not inviting to Muslims and the skewed direction in which Congress seemed to be heading, turned Muslims to look for an alternative party.

Many Britons believed that, as 'babus' did not have the stuff of empire within them, if they left India, it would be to the Muslims. One journalist in 1899 reported meeting a young Parsi 'shocked at our denial of representational institutions to India, conceiving that if they were granted, he would be a representative, and forgetting that, we once gone, the Mussulmans would straightway push him into the sea and take his rupees unto themselves'.[12] But the putative Muslim successors were not there to take over. The imposition of English as the medium of secondary education, rather than providing the catalyst for a great renascence of talent across all religions and castes, had entrenched the power of the old scribal castes, especially the Brahman.[13] Rich landlords had not been under any pressure to learn it, and Muslim élites were members of families wedded to the languages of the Mughal empire. One father told his son that he would rather see him dead than learn English.[14] An educated Muslim, moreover, wished to be literate in Persian, Arabic and Urdu, rather than in English and Bengali (a language he despised). As a result, an educated Muslim was lucky to obtain 'any post above the rank of porter, filler of inkpots and mender of pens'.[15] The effect could be seen in 1906 when there was no Muslim High Court Judge in Calcutta, where there were formerly three, and none in the Panjab, in both of which the Muslim population was numerically strong.[16] As late as 1911, only three out of ten literate inhabitants of Bengal were Muslims, and they were only four per cent of the total Muslim community. For the most part the demand for sons to work on the soil, the obligations of Koranic learning, the poor status of Muslims at large inhibited an adequate supply of teachers, so that the Muslim community would always fall behind.[17] In 1912 Sidney and Beatrice were depressed to see so many Muslim children droning out the sacred words, 'not learning anything that could be useful to them as independent members of a self-governing state'. Indeed they thought the British record of education provision since 1857 had been pretty abysmal, as 'only a tiny proportion of boys and a handful of girls were getting any decent education in the primary grade let alone in the higher'.[18]

The foundation in 1875 at Aligarh of the Muslim Anglo-Oriental College did something to redress the balance. By 1912, Sidney Webb believed that without it 'scarcely any Mussulman would have risen above the rank of artisan or subordinate of police'. The Muslim judges, barristers and civil servants he met seemed all to be Aligarh alumni.[19] In 1906 to advance the rights and interests of Muslims in India the All India Muslim League was founded. Meanwhile, in the alleys that surrounded the great mosques and in the world of the bazaar, Hindu-Muslim rivalry revolved round purity rituals and religious processions. Riots in Calcutta in 1891 brought the issue of cow slaughter to the fore as a threat to public peace. Cow protection societies sprang up to protect the life and honour of the sacred symbol of Hinduism, and parades of naked *saddhus*, leading crowds of inflamed faithful, aroused all the distaste of the Protestant European for religious fanaticism in a cause so patently, in their view, unworthy. By doing nothing they allowed the expression of Hindu solidarity to grow so that, by 1893, it outdid the National Congress, and by substituting the Cow-Empress for the legitimate sovereign, inspired one mordant observer to see a Hindu government in the making.[20] Hindu–Muslim tensions were never far from the surface. Curzon's secretary was told in all seriousness by his Rajput friend, Sir Pertab Singh, Maharajah of Jodhpur, that he would like to annihilate the 60 million Muslims of India. Even their mutual friends? 'Yes. I liking them too, but very much liking them dead'.[21] To a generalised dislike of British rule throughout the educated classes was now added a growing belief that it favoured one community over another, just as the boasted benefits of British rule to India grew less obvious than the benefits to Britain. Factory legislation, however humane in limiting the hours women and children were permitted to work, struck at India's principal advantage in the cheapness and availability of labour. By the 1890s 19 per cent of all British exports and 40 per cent of the total export of British cotton goods went to India, 20 per cent of British investment abroad was in India (about £365,000,000), and the balance of trade was in Britain's advantage annually to the tune of £51,000,000. India, too, bore all the expenses of her own administration, including the pensions of all former civil servants and the costs of British troops in the country, and some £10,000,000 of debt repayment and £17,000,000 'home payments' were transferred each year to London. India's exports to other countries, too, contributed a surplus that enabled Britain to balance her international trade, whereas in reality her own performance, vis à vis America and Europe, was declining.[22] For the economists of the day, this was a triumph of economic rationalism. India was not just an empire, she was a successful self-financing enterprise.[23] If that was so, why were there not more Indians in the boardroom?

From 1898 to 1905, the chairman of that board was a reincarnated Great Mughal. Lord Curzon was better informed, better educated, more extensively travelled, more industrious and more often right than his colleagues. At Balliol he had decided that 'there has never been anything so great in the world's history as the British Empire, so great as an instrument for the good of humanity'.[24] It followed that its servants must be 'as able and enlightened body of men as ever carried or sustained a conquering flag in foreign lands'.[25] In office, he was constantly to be disappointed by the unfired clay of so many of those who formed that body. He shared the queen's dislike of their 'snobbish, vulgar, overbearing and offensive behaviour', and her chagrin at the 'red-tapist, narrow-minded Council and entourage'. Authority should not 'make [Indians] feel they are a conquered people', but should be exercised 'kindly and not offensively'.[26] Curzon did not believe in representational government for subject peoples. He had a poor view of the competence of his own countrymen, and could not believe that the natives would do any better. Like Warren Hastings he was content to be a benevolent despot, finding opposition irksome when it failed to match arguments against his own. 'All these gentlemen state their worthless views at equal length,' he remarked of his departmental chiefs, 'and the result is a sort of literary bedlam'.[27] Of only one of his provincial governors could he say that 'it is such a Godsend in this pigmy-ridden country to find a man who at least has mental stature'.[28] Otherwise 'the government of India is a mighty and miraculous machine for doing nothing'.[29]

He lamented that the comparative closeness to 'home', brought about by the steamship companies and the rapid post, rendered its recruits less committed to the people they were sent to govern and more interested in home-leave and eventual retirement to Surbiton or Cheltenham. 'If I felt that we were not working here,' he told the Bengal Chamber of Commerce in 1903, 'for the good of India in obedience to a higher law and a nobler aim, then I would see the link that holds England and India together severed without a sigh. But it is because I believe in the future of this country and in the capacity of our own race to guide it to goals that it has never hitherto attained, that I keep courage and press forward'.[30] The standard he set himself was one, he was convinced, no Indian could ever reach. Bengalis rolled 'out yards and yards of frothy declamation about subjects which he has imperfectly considered or which he does not fully understand'.[31] He had a poor view of native rulers his sovereign so much admired who, when not absentees, led a life of pomp and frivolity, their minds 'about equally compounded of childishness and vainglory'.[32] He was infuriated that 'a third rate chief, of fifth rate morals', after being feted by the French president at Longchamps, went on to appear at a state ball in London. Not everyone 'who wears a turban with bad pearls in it' was to be regarded 'as a lineal descendant of Nebuchadnezzar or Tamberlaine'.[33] The temptations of a fast life, drink, white women, buggery and ostentatious expenditure set a disastrous example to the governed. 'For what are they in most part but a set of unruly and ignorant and rather undisciplined schoolboys,' needing 'a firm but not unkindly hand' and 'the sort of discipline that a boy goes through at a public school in England'.[34]

Curzon felt that he had been predestined for India. It was not just that, since 1888, the viceroy had been a Balliol man or that, between 1878 and 1914, 200 Balliol men were to enter the Indian service, but he had been taught at Eton that the British held 'an empire more populous, more amazing and more beneficent than that of Rome'.[35] As long as Britain ruled India, she was the greatest power in the world. Whoever was master of India was lord of half the world. 'If we lose it, we shall drop straightaway to a third-rate Power.'[36] Ever since then he had succumbed to the 'fascination and, if I may say so, the sacredness of India'.[37] He persisted in treating the Indian National Congress as a self-interested middle class movement and not as a potential partner. 'Efficiency,' lamented one of its future leaders bitterly, 'was his watchword… popular sentiment counted for nothing and in his worship of this fetish Lord Curzon set popular opinion at open defiance'.[38]

His capacity for work was legendary. 'Grind, grind, grind with never a word of encouragement, on, on, on till the collar breaks and the poor beast stumbles'.[39] His first 18 months were visited by drought, famine and plague. He toured all the worst affected areas and claimed to have inspected every plague hospital and seen nearly every sufferer. He tackled the required public works and, by the end of his viceroyalty, more miles of rail track had been laid than under any other viceroy. He confounded his advisers by knowing more than they about the border threats to India. He was the first viceroy ever to visit the stupendous caves at Ajanta and he personally adopted the Taj Mahal and Fatehpur Sikri as exercises in conservation, and ensured that, by his policy towards historical monuments, India had something enduring to thank him for.[40] By 1903 he was satisfied that no viceroy since Dalhousie had achieved as much as he.

His 'Curzonisation' was the great dorbar of 1903. Never was his fussy preoccupation with detail given such a public display. It was to outshine Lytton's mediaeval extravaganza of 1876, and be the consummation of India's loyalty to the new King-Emperor, of whom Curzon was the incarnation since, not Edward VII, but his uncle, the Duke of Connaught, represented the king and was content to play second fiddle. Curzon was the 'magnificent state Barnum, an imperial Buffalo Bill',[41] though what those attending remembered, those who saw her, was the vision of Mary Curzon in a dress, woven of silk thread and peacock's feathers, with a garnet for the eye of each feather, spreading out behind her like the tail of Juno's sacred bird, a silken paean to the American Madonna, an icon of majesty.[42]

Curzon's apotheosis had a sad and heavy sequel. In 1900 he had suspected that an Indian famine excited 'no more attention [in London] than a squall on the Serpentine'.[43] In 1904, during his long leave in England, he sensed that the great British public was almost wholly indifferent to India. It did not see the message, 'hewed out of the rock of doom – that our work is righteous and it shall endure'.[44] Though he quailed before the storms of criticism and personal vilification that met him on issues like the partitioning of Bengal and the staffing of Indian universities, he did not stop to question his own judgement. His dedication to an ideal of India prompted one Indian nationalist in 1902 to admit 'that God himself has led the British to this country, to help it in working out its salvation and realise its heaven-appointed destiny among the nations of the world'.[45] Curzon, alas, had a very limited vision of what that destiny might be. He judged himself and his acolytes as a headmaster might upon his retirement. He had loved righteousness and hated iniquity. 'No man has, I believe, ever served India faithfully of whom that could not be said, ... [who could not] feel that somewhere, among these millions, you have left a little justice or happiness, or prosperity, a sense of manliness or moral dignity, a spring of patriotism, a dawn of intellectual enlightenment, or a stirring of duty where it did not before exist.'[46]

Curzon's youthful travels in Asiatic Asia and Persia had convinced him that Russia's national ambition was dominance in Asia, and ultimately conquest of India. His colleagues considered him a 'regular jingo', 'with Russia on the brain'.[47] He did not believe that her ambitions were limited to the colonisation of the thinly populated steppes of central Asia, and insisted that the British government should remind her that south-east Persia and Afghanistan were within the British sphere of influence. It was only his persistence that persuaded his predecessor, Lord Lansdowne, now foreign secretary, to declare a kind of Monroe policy for the Gulf in 1903. It was more difficult to do the same for Afghanistan. The nightmare was to find Russians in Kabul before British troops had even reached the Khyber pass in sufficient numbers to repel them. Curzon also feared for that weak theocracy, Tibet, and believed that the Russians had made a deal with the Chinese to extend their influence there. Unless the Tibetans were impressed by British might, they might easily fall victim to Russian designs. His paranoia was fed by Colonel Francis Younghusband, who had been engaged in the Great Game for a quarter of a century, and relished the maleness of it, the adventure, the absence of humbug, the tang of danger and the pleasure of self-reliance. The viceroy trusted the adventurer as a fellow traveller in parts where few men had been and considered him sound. His expeditionary force, however, found only one Russian rifle on the way to Lhasa. London accepted Russian disclaimers of any interest in the country. But in India, the Russian threat was not so easily disclaimed and embroiled the viceroy in a losing battle with his commander-in-chief on how best to counter it. The row with Kitchener was not about anything that reasonable men could not have solved. It was a clash of titans, one high-minded, eloquent, rational and right, the other jealous, querulous, mendacious and wrong. The mendacious and wrong knew how to use friends and journalists, and the one who was high-minded and right believed that a just cause needed no pleading. Moreover Curzon had lost the friends he needed in high places by his well-known opinions on their limited competence.

The actual argument was about the role of the military member of the viceroy's Council, which was to tender technical information in support of policies the viceroy was determined to follow. The measure of the disagreement grew out of Kitchener's gloomy prophecy that Britain would soon be fighting for her very existence in Asia and his estimate of what would be needed to defend it. To fight Russia in Afghanistan, which had become his fixed expectation, would require an investment of between £20 million and £30 million. While he was commander-in-chief, military expenditure rose by nearly 40 per cent to £20,757,032 in 1905–6, in a vain attempt to comply with his requirements.[48] Soon the figures entered the realm of fantasy. Barely 20 years before, Roberts and his 13,000 men had consumed all available food near Kabul. Now Kitchener reckoned that Russia could put 150,000 men into Afghanistan which would need to be countered by a force of similar size. Given that there was no railway service from the Indian frontier to Kabul, this would require over three million pounds of food a day and three million camels to carry it. For such a contingency, he would also need an additional 150,000 men from Britain, which would leave barely 27,000 for home defence and 30,000 for the defence of the rest of the empire. Curzon thought it was absurd and, having delivered his opinion, which he had thoroughly researched, he left its sheer intellectual breadth and reasoning to prevail. Kitchener stirred up his friends at home, lobbied the king and prime minister and poisoned the ear of the secretary of state, only too ready to be poisoned. Curzon ignored those who opposed him, Kitchener conspired against them. 'He is Ignatius Loyola and Juggernaut.'[49] The cabinet was convinced that if it came to resignations, Curzon's would be more welcome than Kitchener's, though it would mean removal of an already arrogant and expensive military machine from civilian control.

Curzon's plans for the improvement of British rule in India were also contentious. The creation in 1901 of the North-West Frontier Province, resented at the time, made it easier to pacify the warring tribesmen and secure the peace south of the Afghan border. He accepted that Hindi, as the language of the majority, should be officially recognised. Muslim objections he trampled down as the 'spleen of a minority from whose hands are slipping away the reins of power'.[50] He insisted that British soldiers guilty of violence against natives should be punished: until one was actually hanged for the murder of an Indian, British justice would not have been vindicated.[51] Yet despite his resolve to improve the lot of Indians, nationalism became increasingly bitter and frustrated during his term of office.

The catalyst for discontent was the partition of Bengal. Just as Curzon had tidied up the North-West Frontier Province, so he had a solution for the over-sized, over-populated province of Bengal that sprawled over what is now both Bangladesh and the Indian state of West Bengal. Administratively there were good arguments for creating two provincial capitals, one in Calcutta (West Bengal), the other in Dacca (East Bengal and Assam), but arguments of good administration did not placate the mainly Hindu protesters, who would lose jobs in the east to Muslims. Curzon saw no reason to defer the decision because 'babu agitators' in Congress condemned it as a 'preposterous scheme'. 'The stale rehash of belated cries and obsolete platitudes' struck him as being devoid of intellectual argument.[52] Indeed he thought the people welcomed it. It would restore some of the identity of the Mughal state that had been ruled from Dacca, and bring the principal producers of tea and jute under a single administration. The partition finally came into force on 16 October 1905, not before there had been massive protests in Calcutta, and a boycott of British goods, particularly textiles. The actual promulgation of the decree was a day of mourning. Even the future Nobel laureate, Rabindranath Tagore, left his philosophic retreat at Santiniketan to protest in verse, prompting Ezra Pound to claim that he had sung Bengal into a nation.[53] Curzon sustained his lordly indifference to the protest, unable to see that had furnished an emotional cause to the 'frothy' Bengali mind, concentrating it on an affront to Bengali and thus a nascent, Indian, consciousness.

Curzon's was a personal tragedy of almost Shakespearean proportions. At times the viceroy seemed to turn into the 'roy' himself. The secretary of state felt that he was merely Curzon's representative at the Court of St James, and Balfour thought he gave a fair imitation of the head of an independent and not always friendly power.[54] He had come closest to being a legendary despot, and ruefully admitted that 'a sparrow can hardly twitter its tail in India without the action being attributed to direct orders issued by the... viceroy'.[55] But he could not forgive the Indians for counting 'justice, equity, sympathy, the even hand, as of little account' and continuing to want constitutional reform and more control of the executive 'for which they are as yet profoundly unfitted'.[56] When his secretary suggested the self-rule was bound to come, he was positive that 'it will not come in my time and I cannot say what may happen in the future'.[57] By his very refusal to contemplate such a possibility he had contrived to hasten forward the day when it would.

Curzon's frustration partly derived from the ramshackle way in which the government in London was constructed. Two great departments of state, the Colonial Office and the India Office, were a charge to the peoples over whose destinies they presided. If the secretary of state for India and Council were in agreement, no one, prime minister, foreign secretary, the House of Commons, had the power to move them. Within the India Office were discharged for India the functions of Treasury, Foreign Office, Home Office and Board of Trade.[58] The secretary of state was the viceroy's intermediary with government and, pro-vided they were in agreement, the powers of the viceroy were virtually unfettered. When Curzon encountered resistance from the India office, he attributed it to men, 'who, having trembled at the nod of the Viceroy for the greater part of

195

their lives are eventually in a position where they can with impunity dance a hornpipe on his prostrate form'.[59] In his 1903 dorbar speech, Curzon foresaw an India of expanding industry, increasing prosperity and more widely distributed comfort and wealth – but only through 'the unchallenged supremacy of the paramount power and under no other controlling authority... than that of the British Crown'.[60] For its part, the British crown gave little sustained thought to India whose budget was seldom debated before a house of more than six members. Governing India was seen by most MPs as an administrative matter. Indeed the one occasion on which Gladstone gave thought to India was when he invited Stafford Northcote and Charles Trevelyan to advise him on a competitive-entry home civil service on the Company model.[61]

If most members of Parliament knew that Indians now constituted one fifth of the human race they probably did not know that one tenth of the entire trade of the British empire passed through Indian ports, that India was the largest producer of food and raw materials in the empire, that she was the largest buyer of British goods, and that Britain had invested there between a sixth and a seventh part of her total overseas investment. During Curzon's viceroyalty the capital invested in Indian railways rose by 56 per cent, company investment in industrial development by 23 per cent, savings bank deposits grew by 43 per cent, India's imports rose by 35 per cent, her exports by 48 per cent. Net imports of bullion rose from £25 million to £46 million.[62] It was not surprising that the viceroy was impatient with this lack of interest and no less surprising that, despite Curzon's airy dismissal of their claims, Indians wanted a greater say in the managing of the enterprise. But in Curzon's estimate even the most intelligent Indians were 'still in the nursery, and no worse fate could befall them than to be mistaken for grown men'.[63]

By 1900 the government of India employed about 500,000 people, of whom only some 3,500 were Europeans, a quarter of these being civil servants. Most of them constituted the clerks or 'babus' who propelled the work forward or, as the case might be, round. As one chief accounts clerk in Calcutta was, perhaps apocryphally, recorded as having written to a colleague in a provincial government: 'Your accounts have come up quite correct. Do not let this occur again.'[64] Indian graduates virtually staffed the service of the princely states, were increasingly numerous in provincial service, and were beginning to make inroads into the covenanted civil service itself. Minimal government, the collection of revenue and the preservation of law and order, was increasingly inadequate to manage India's human problems. Famine and disease in 1900 forced the government to extend relief to some six million ruined farmers and other afflicted people, at the stupendous cost – unprecedented for any contemporary government – of £10 million. The flagellation of drought had, over six years, caused government in the Central Province alone to lose the equivalent of land revenue for 50 years. Even so, total revenue in India rose, over the same period, from £68.5 million to £83 million.

Curzon had always been able to count on the support of the queen-empress while she was alive. In Victoria he had a sympathetic ear to his complaints about officialdom. 'Red-tapeism', she once wrote, using a neologism that has since acquired enormous resonance in contemporary India, 'is, alas! our great misfortune, and exists very strongly in the India Office'.[65] After her golden jubilee, the queen increased her Indian establishment and was soon 'as excited about them as a child would be with a new toy'.[66] One of them resented waiting at table and, making himself out to be the son of an army surgeon-general and qualified as a munshi, the name given to letter-writers in Indian languages, he offered to teach her Hindostani. Hafiz Abdul Karim became her official instructor in 1888 and the queen learned enough words to greet visiting Maharanis. By 1892 he was Her Majesty's Indian Secretary, looked after her despatch boxes, assisted her in her Indian correspondence and constantly briefed her on Indian matters. Munshi informed her, and she informed Lord Salisbury, her prime minister, that she had more Muslim subjects than the Sultan. 'He is so useful to me,' she wrote to her daughter, the empress Frederick, on 26 February 1890, 'that I was quite lost without him. Poor things, one must feel so much for them, away from all their belongings and dearest and nearest.'[67]

Abdul Karim, now a Companion of the Order of the Indian Empire, was as close to the queen as John Brown before him. Not husband, not son, not companion, but an indispensable dependent (whose merits no one else could see), he was handsomely housed, warmly clad and provided, when he needed it, with a covered carriage. He was driving in it when it was not available to meet the commander-in-chief at Ballater station. 'One must have been in India,' Lord Wolseley noted grimly, 'to realise the position of a man who is thus provided with a carriage while the Field-Marshall, at the Head of the Queen's Army, drives in a fly.'[68]

One may admire his enterprise but Munshi did not deserve the queen's esteem. As he rose in rank, so he grew progressively more overbearing to his inferiors. He was too idle to keep house and too lascivious to make do with a single 'wife'. Visitors to Couper Cottage met a different woman each time, though the queen thought he was lodging his wife and mother-in-law, 'the first Mohammedan purdah ladies who ever came over and kept their custom of complete seclusion'.[69] When she learned that he was only the son of an apothecary's assistant working in a gaol, the queen did not hold it against him. She had known two archbishops whose fathers were, respectively, a butcher and a grocer![70] She refuted all criticisms of the man as inspired by racial dislike. Even when it was suspected that he was leaking state secrets back to India, she defended him, not because she was still deluded by him, but on principle. Munshi was the representative of an oppressed race, and she used all her majesty to ensure that he was protected.[71] Even her children, who detested him, would not challenge her. He was created additionally a Companion of the Victorian Order and given a prominent place in her jubilee procession.[72] Edward VII generously allowed him a last look at his mistress before her coffin was sealed. He then disappeared into obscurity. Munshi represented, for the queen, the innocent victim of racial superiority that unrivalled success induced in the British people in the second half of the nineteenth century. That superiority, Kipling warned, would soon be one with Nineveh and Tyre, and the curious tale of the queen and her munshi was worthy of the pen that wrote *Without Benefit of Clergy* and *Kim*.

The queen, having observed the treatment of Munshi, knew that over her long reign and despite her encouragement to successive viceroys, there had been little change in the 'snobbish and vulgar overbearing and offensive behaviour' of her British subjects in India. Time and again she warned Curzon not to be influenced by it. Not content with raising the matter at his last meeting with her before proceeding to post, she sent him no less than 30 letters in his last two years of office to keep him up to the mark. They steeled him to annoy the India Office by refusing to send Indian 'coolies' to the Transvaal after the end of the Boer War, at a time when the growing quarrel with Kitchener meant that he needed all the friends he had there, but he was resolved not to add to human misery.[73]

The queen-empress was genuinely mourned in India and, in Calcutta, the roadside vendors closed their booths on the day of her funeral, and a great crowd sat fasting and grieving on the maidan. She had expressed a genuine if naive interest in her Indian empire from the day of her proclamation, and had begged her viceroys (and their wives) to write often and at length, delighting in the letters she received from Charlotte Canning and Robert Lytton. Edward VII found the stream of information, which Victoria had always relished, boring. In this respect Edward 'the Caresser' was not a worthy son of his mother. His visit as Prince of Wales had been remarkable for its lack of impact, either his on India or India's on him, and now he was king, he let it be known he only wanted to hear from the viceroy when he had something really important to say. To Curzon this loss of interest resounded like a criticism.

If so fine a mind as Curzon's could not see that efficient administration was not an acceptable alternative to self-government and that this inexorable result of British education and economic progress could not be long delayed, politicians in Britain, who opposed self-rule in Ireland, were even less likely to see it. In 1905, the Indian National Congress sounded like a 'collection of half-Europeanised lawyers, belonging to a dozen different breeds and representing none'.[74] With Curzon's successor and the election of a Liberal government in 1906, however, the iceberg began to move. Both recognised some truth in the claim of the Congress President, the moderate GK Gokhale, that 'fully fifty millions of the population, a number yearly increasing, are dragging out a miserable existence on the verge of starvation', a condition largely due to 'the exclusion of the people of India from a due participation in the administration, and all control over the finances of their country'.[75] On 17 November 1905, Gilbert John Murray Elliot, fourth earl of Minto, arrived at Bombay with his three lively daughters. The 18-year old Ruby Elliot thought that Curzon looked 'more like a butler than ever' and was worried for her father.[76] Curzon's reputation as an administrator, orator and presence was almost too awesome for a man who, if his great grandfather had not been viceroy and he himself a fourth earl, would never have got the job. His career so far had hardly qualified him for it. On coming down from Cambridge he was commissioned in the Scots Guards, rode jockey in the Grand National, acted as war correspondent for the Morning Post in Spain and Turkey, and did service with Lord Roberts in India and South Africa. From 1878 to 1904, he served as governor-general of Canada where he performed well enough to succeed Curzon.

Canada was hardly preparation for India, as Ruby was quick to note. On being informed that on arrival they would sit down with the outgoing Curzons, 'quite alone', they were surprised to find the company numbered 44 at table.[77] The cloud of servants, the protocol, the load of paper, the travel, public speeches, handshakes, even a hereditary peer of Minto's sweetness of temperament found wearisome. For his five years as viceroy, however, he was to have a remarkable man as secretary of state for India. John Morley, born in 1838, was in 1905 at the height of his powers as a man of letters. Unlike Macaulay who became a great historian after a short parliamentary career, Morley entered the House as Liberal member for Newcastle-on-Tyne in 1883, after a long and distinguished literary career. Editor of the *Fortnightly Review* for 16 years, he had become one of the great pundits of the liberal, reformist, agnostic left, a radical in politics and Darwinian in science. He was appointed secretary of state for India, two years after he had completed his great life of Gladstone, and for the first time, liberal opinion about the future of India had an ear in government.

Morley was alien to the culture of a fourth earl but their two names were linked to reform. Morley was almost certainly the moving spirit, but he let Minto take the credit for the election to provincial legislatures, at long last, of a majority of 'natives'. They were chosen by local groups, like universities, trade unions, and religious associations, themselves chosen by electors from among rich Hindus and Muslims. Though officials still retained the majority, Indians were also elected to the viceroy's legislative council, thus effectively frightening 'that nervous animal (naturally nervous), the European-Indian'.[78] Minto, unlike Morley, who saw the reforms as a step to more representative institutions, hoped that he was disarming criticism of the government and keeping the educated class out of the arms of Congress.[79] Morley and he were agreed that reform must come bottom-up. Congress, however, 'wanted ready-made power', and Minto shared Curzon's belief that it was led by a very small class of men whom the people of India themselves would not want to lead them.[80] 'Representative government in its Western sense,' he told the first session of the enlarged meeting of the Imperial Legislative Council on 25 January 1910, 'is totally inapplicable to the Indian Empire... The safety and welfare of this country must depend on the supremacy of British administration – and that supremacy can, in no circumstances, be delegated to any kind of representative assembly.'[81] Nationalist criticism drove him to cultivate the support of the princes who were beginning to fear the politics of Congress more than the continuation of British rule. It became policy to co-opt or elect as many landlords as possible onto the legislative councils, despite the fact that many of them were known oppressors of the ryot, to protect whom the British government had eschewed democracy. The alliance between the princes and the Raj, which proved to be built on sand, was a substitute for any political initiative to secure the support of Indian popular opinion.

This had made formidable advances throughout the century as Indians came together in local associations and clubs of educated or like-minded Indians, who rapidly acquired the forms and disciplines of public debate in local government. Real change was brought about rather by those Indian members of the legislative councils and their political supporters than by the social *mela* of the annual Congress meeting, which was still rather an occasion for Indians of all persuasions to discuss a political agenda of a strictly limited kind, hoping 'to invoke the sense of justice which must surely lie in the heart of so great and free a people as the English'.[82] Students, mainly from higher caste families, found an icon in Kali, the goddess of destruction, to externalise their impatience with progress, and their sense that time was short if they were to change the economic and social world with the revolver and the bomb, hazarded an attempt on Minto's life in November 1909. Congress might repudiate them, but the Indian people could not rely on electoral swings in London, to return, from time to time, a liberal government, prepared to make a few cautious concessions in India. The 1907 Congress meeting at Surat broke up in confusion as delegates argued about a more effective way, short of terror, of reminding the British people of their aspirations and grievances. The form it took was a boycott of British imported goods in favour of *swadeshi* (home-produced), the adoption of which modest measure allowed moderate sentiment to establish its control over Congress. This now firmly proposed self-government on the Canadian, Australian and South African model as its aim.

14. 'MARCHING UP TO AN IMPOSSIBLE SOLUTION'

> In order to ensure the proper progress and development
> in this country, there can be no question as to the
> permanence of British rule in India. Colonial swaraj...
> must be absolutely ruled out.
>
> Lord Hardinge, viceroy, 1912

> There was no definite plan or purpose about the
> Government of India. Were we really trying to enable
> the Indian people to dispense with our guidance or did
> we intend to remain for ever in command?
>
> Sidney & Beatrice Webb, 28 January 1912

> I am strongly suspicious that our old friend, firm
> government, the idol of the Club Smoking Room, has
> produced its invariable and inevitable harvest.
>
> Edwin Montagu, on the events at Amritsar, 1919

> You've got to go to a place, see it and smell it before you
> can say what's got to be done about it.
>
> Clement Attlee, 1927

> I am now receiving... streams of letters from our people
> in India and the feeling that... we are throwing away our
> position with both our hands, that we are marching up
> to an impossible solution is enjoined by all.
>
> Winston Churchill to Stanley Baldwin,
> 24 September 1930

THE FIRST WORLD WAR did more than destroy the old certainties of Europe. It also marked the end of a century during which British power in India was seen to be invincible and her rule permanent. India's response to the war was magnificent. By November 1918, 1,302,394 armed volunteers had left India on active service, together with many thousands of non-combatant support personnel. Ranjitsinhji, who had stood shoulder to shoulder with his fellow cricketers to save an English innings, proclaimed that it was 'a high honour and privilege to fight shoulder to shoulder with the British army in maintaining intact this great Empire and its glorious and untarnished name'.[1] An Indian Corps of 24,000 men was in France by October 1914, and inspired a healthy terror in the enemy. 'Thousands of these brown rascals,' wrote one German soldier, 'rushed upon us as suddenly as if they were shot out of a fog.' In spite of destructive fire 'the others advanced, springing forward like cats and surmounting obstacles with unexampled agility... Truly these brown enemies were not be despised.'[2] Their casualties were appalling, 10,000 men being lost in the first year, but the cold, mud and filth of trench warfare were to demoralise them more than death or disablement. By the end of 1915 most had been withdrawn to Smyrna, whence, the English prime minister hoped, they might 'make their way sooner or later to Constantinople'.[3]

Questions were soon being asked about the invulnerability of the British army and the superior qualities of the British race. The Germans were more efficient and their weapons better, and the French were less hidebound about black troops among the civilian population. In England, fraternisation between the troops of different races was carefully avoided, hospital compounds with Indian wounded were surrounded by barbed wire and sentries, and British women were discouraged from visiting wounded Indian soldiers, in case the patients conceived from the freedom between the sexes in England 'a wrong idea of the "izzat" of English women'.[4] Twelve Victoria Crosses later, there was scarcely a village in the Panjab and Gurkhali without its dead and permanently disabled. And none in defence of any Indian interest.

In 1916, there had been a new viceroy. Of the possible candidates to succeed Hardinge, Winston Churchill would not 'be done out of this glorious delicious war for anything the world could give'[5] and, though Asquith would have been ready to off-load him on India, Kitchener was still considered too important for victory over Germany.[6] Lord Chelmsford had been governor of two Australian states, before joining up on the outbreak of the war, and was actually serving on the viceroy's military establishment and immediately available. In 1917, the Congress president, Annie Besant, reminded the world that, when the war began, 'India believed whole-heartedly that Great Britain was fighting for the freedom of all nationalities.' The silence that had greeted the demand, a year earlier, for the immediate introduction of self-rule was proof 'that the hatred of autocracy was confined to autocracy in the West; ... that freedom was lavishly promised to all except India'.[7] Now, in June 1917, there was a new secretary of state to hear Mrs Besant. As parliamentary under-secretary, Edwin Montagu had visited India in 1912 and, being 'somewhat oriental' himself, had felt quite at home. Within two months of his appointment, he proposed that Parliament should introduce 'the progressive realisation of responsible government' by 'increasing the association of Indians in every branch of the administration and the gradual development of self-governing institutions'.[8] The mountain was beginning to move.

Montagu spent that winter in India, sounding every significant person and association. 'The officials administrate and do not govern,' he concluded. 'They refuse to explain themselves, ... they misuse powers.' 'Grudging giving has always been the bane of Indian administration,'[9] which could not believe that 'full self-government under the Crown' could be on offer 'for decades to come'.[10] In England, the *Manchester Guardian* told its readers that Indians 'were sick and tired of being a subject race' to 'white men animated by a keen sense of duty but growingly inferior in their manners and consideration for them'. The end of the war made conciliation a top priority.[11] The dismemberment of the Ottoman empire at the peace table was unsettling traditional Islamic communities to which disillusioned soldiers were returning. The price of food grains had doubled, imported goods cost nearly four times more than in 1914, taxes were higher, shortages led to violent riots and looting, and inflation and recession were the background to an epidemic of Asian flu which carried off as many as six million people.[12] In 1919, a Sedition Committee reported the use of textbooks in Bengal which cited the Bhagavid Gita as a revolutionary manifesto and exalted the examples of Mazzini and Garibaldi![13] It frightened the European members of the legislative council enough for it to revive the repressive face of British India. The spine-chilling Anarchical and Revolutionary Crimes Act, known as the Rowlatt Act to his countrymen after the committee chairman, Sir Sydney Rowlatt, a former schoolmaster at Eton, now a judge of the King's Bench Division, but as the Black Act to Indians, allowed trial without jury of anyone accused of sedition, even if merely found in possession of seditious literature.[14]

The Panjab was to provide the flash-point for trouble. As the granary of the north, so much of its produce had been exported to Europe that prices had rocketed, leaving many on the verge of starvation. The 'Black Act', moreover, had given rise to rumours about police powers, even that an awkward husband could be disposed of by a policeman enamoured of his wife.[15] Unrest, too, was stimulated by public debate on what ought to be in Montagu's bill at the end of the year. Sir Michael O'Dwyer, who had impressed the secretary of state as the idol of the reactionary forces, determined to use the iron hand.[16] As an Irishman he thought he had a nose for subversion; as Lieutenant Governor, he believed in the thrifty, hardworking Panjabi ryot, who had fathered so many loyal troops, and not in the slippery, foreign-educated intellectuals who were only intent on making trouble. On 30 March a national strike (*hartal*) closed down Amritsar, while a huge meeting called for the repeal of the Rowlatt Act. On 10 April the crowd got out of hand, looted two banks, killed three European staff, and beat up a missionary lady. The Europeans fled to the Gobindgarh fort, fearful of another 1857. The following day, Brigadier-General Dyer and 1,100 soldiers arrived, ordered up from Jullundur to help keep the peace.

General Dyer, apart from a few years at school in Cork and at the Royal Military College, Sandhurst, had lived all his life in India, his father being the first to brew beer commercially there. He had fought in Burma in 1886–7, relieved Chitral in 1895, and blockaded Waziristan from 1901 to 1902. 'Biffing' frontier savages was Dyer's chief qualification for command. On the 13th, he 'biffed' once too often. His order to fire without warning on an unauthorised meeting in the Jallianwalabagh, a nondescript park almost wholly walled in and approached only by a narrow lane, left 379 dead. Many more were wounded. For Dyer, it was well done, for the peace of the dead fell on the city. But this rigidly self-disciplined man could not leave it there. On the 19th he ordered that any Indian passing by the spot where the missionary had been attacked should do so on all fours, interpreted by the soldiers enforcing the order, as on his belly. When six persons were arrested for the assault, he had them flogged on the spot before they had actually been convicted of the offence. It seemed like delayed revenge for the dead women of 1857.

Under martial law savage sentences of death and deportation were handed out freely and public floggings were almost a ritual in the surrounding countryside. Everything was done to prove that the dissidents had plotted to wage war on the Raj. Chelmsford, though appalled by the events, did not feel strong enough to condemn them in the face of O'Dwyer's reports that the situation had been touch and go. He could only murmur that the days when India could be ruled by displays of force were over. Rabindranath Tagore resigned the knighthood he had received in 1915, two years after the Nobel prize for literature; Gandhi surrendered the Kaiser-i-Hind medal for his work in South Africa. Edwin Montagu in London was sure that the judgements of the martial law courts were doubtfully lawful; an eminent British lawyer, Sir John Simon, was retained by the condemned for an appeal to the Privy Council, and one by one the sentences were overturned. In December, to much local fury among the British in the Panjab, George V exercised his royal clemency to quash those cases in which no threat to public safety had been conclusively proved. A Scottish judge, commissioned to chair an enquiry into what had occurred in Amritsar, produced a report which, though its Indian members thought it did not go far enough, was surprisingly forthright. Whatever Dyer's merits as a brave and resourceful soldier, he had made an appalling error of judgement. The commander-in-chief cancelled his promotion to divisional command and demanded his resignation from service in India within a few months of normal retirement age. To many Britons, this was an unconscionably severe punishment for a man who was only doing his duty, indeed who had 'saved India'. Dyer's public impenitence compounded the injury and, though he claimed he had prevented worse things by his prompt action, and his defenders moved a motion of censure against government for conniving at subversion in India, he was not vindicated. But a public subscription raised a £26,000 benefit which Dyer accepted and O'Dwyer led a long campaign to exonerate the general long after he was dead, before himself being 'executed' at a public meeting in London by a Sikh assassin.

The almost paranoid reaction of the British authorities in the Panjab was the worst possible prelude to Montagu's bill, but the disillusionment of Gandhi was to prove Britain's greatest contribution to Indian independence. He had returned to India from South Africa in 1915, to the great relief of Jan Smuts: 'The saint is gone from our shores. I sincerely hope for ever.'[17] Gandhi had supported the British position in the Boer Wars, believed that the allied cause in 1914 was just and hoped that the British sense of fair play would eventually accept the logic of self-rule. The 1919 Government of India Act did not impress him. Imitating Western practice in representative assemblies was not how Indians should prepare themselves for self-rule. The liberty rhetoric of Burke, JS Mill and Gladstone did not apply to a country so divided by race and caste and language, that four fifths of the population had never experienced it. The intelligentsia might demand, in the language of Westminster, a freedom that Westminster itself had not yet wholly devolved to its own people, but it meant little to the ryot in the field, the indigo worker in the pits, the weaver in the mills, or the tribal helot impressed to build roads and railways, upon whose support the Raj relied. Freedom from any raj, whether it was Mughal, British or even Hindu, was the only real freedom for all Indians. Gandhi, having championed the rights of people denied them on the basis of race in South Africa, recognised that untouchability was a form of discrimination as indefensible as that based on skin pigmentation. To render India free, she must be freed from herself.

His methods were often baffling, even to his own supporters. *Satyagraha*, defined by Gandhi himself as Truth-force, Love-force or Soul-force, would be vindicated 'not by the infliction of suffering on the opponent, but on one's self', and by inviting the penalty for the breach of an unjust law, one would shame the lawgiver into repealing it.[18] To Gandhi, Truth and God were synonymous, and it was neither Hindu, Muslim nor Christian. To be one or the other implied the overlordship of one set of beliefs over another and, thus, strife. Strife invariably led to the triumph of the physically strong, so that against a resolute repudiation of violence in the face of oppression there could be neither a physical nor a moral victory to the oppressor. This doctrine of *ahimsa* had its tap-roots deep in the heart of Hinduism, and reflected both the Jesus message, and the submission that was Islam, but it baffled the British. To them, Gandhi was either a mendicant saint, or an astute politician, who took refuge behind religion, the one thing with which the British rulers had tried not to tangle throughout their contact with India.

His ideals and life-style were equally revolutionary. Western society was based on violence, the fruit of an unsatisfied desire for material goods. India must repudiate its values, and return to the simplicity of the Indian village, where the seasons provided the cycle of work and the necessities of life, and prayer was the link with God. Gandhi had never been exposed to the grinding and malevolent poverty of such a life, so that there was a certain arcadianism about his ideas, but in his ashrams he exposed middle class acolytes to the realities of how four fifths of the population lived. There was no discrimination of caste, sex or religion, and both manual and menial labour was the task of all. This was a revolution for Indians. What was revolution for the British was a movement that embraced reconciliation between Hindus and Muslims, and the elimination of untouchability. If it succeeded, there would be union where there had always been division, and *swadeshi*, which could destroy the whole apparatus of production that made India a profitable enterprise.

Satyagraha, to the British, meant sedition and, in the Panjab, from the chief secretary down, they held Gandhi responsible for the disturbances there.[19] 'The present representatives of the empire have become dishonest and unscrupulous,' Gandhi thundered in *Young India*, (28 July 1920) as he justified satyagraha against an illegitimate government.[20] In the Ahmedabad Fort Prison Camp, Nehru invited a future historian to consider how far imperialism and racialism were responsible for 'England's decline from her proud eminence'.[21] While occupying a top bunk in the night train from Lahore to Delhi, he had overheard Dyer boast to his fellow passengers of what he had done in Amritsar. Only his sense of pity, the general claimed, had dissuaded him from reducing the city to ashes.

For Gandhi, revenge was no answer. Indians had now to demonstrate that they were morally superior to their masters and thus could use liberty. British rule might be evil, but taking up arms against it would only mean replacing it by something as evil. Peaceful, non-violent protest alone was to be the weapon. If it got out of hand, then it would have to be discontinued. Gandhi had no timetable; moral regeneration was not a matter for overnight adjustments. Montagu might believe that it was necessary to grow 'those conventions and customs and habits of representative government, without the acquisition of which democracy cannot stand', but Gandhi held little store by them.[22] 'Grudging giving', meanwhile, continued to be the British reaction to the 1919 bill. The Indianisation of services was spun out for as long as possible.[23] In 1924 the published aim was to replace half the Civil Service with Indians by 1939 – by which time there were 715 Europeans and 643 Indians – and half the police force by 1949, while the officer caste in the army should be wholly filled by Indians (who were only allowed to hold the King's commissions from 1918) by 1955. This was too fast for the commander-in-chief, who could not believe suitable officers could be found. Indeed by 1928 there were only 77. Resistance was partly owing to ideological prejudice – that Indians were just not up to taking decisions for firm administrative or military action – but more to fear that the 'three hundred a year men' were losing a career into which many, sometimes more than one generation of the same family, had put all they had, now to be turned off to satisfy the shibboleths of politicians at home. The snail-like progress only served to fuel suspicions that the British had no intention of ever handing over real power.

General puzzlement at the complexity of Gandhi's thought, inability to understand his moral position, fear at his growing popularity and charisma, all contributed to a palpable failure of imagination on the part of the British. Lord Chelmsford echoed Smuts: 'What a damned nuisance these saintly fanatics are!'[24] His successor, the former Lord Chief Justice, Rufus Isaacs, first Marquess of Reading, could not understand how he applied his high ideals to practical politics.[25] Gandhi had urged a nationwide satyagraha, to make British rule irrelevant by ignoring it. Non-cooperation broke no laws and, to his own surprise, in December 1920, Congress adopted it as the next stage in the struggle for freedom. It had not experienced a blinding conversion. Gandhi's thought processes puzzled Congress politicians too, and some, like Jawaharlal Nehru, found them antipathetic to his vision of independence won by democratic action and socialism, but they did persuade the viceroy in 1921 to have six private conversations with the Mahatma, conducted on both sides with exquisite courtesy. At one encounter Gandhi explained that as 'every action by the Government which appeared to be good, and indeed was good, was actuated by the sinister motive of trying to fasten British dominion on India', India had no cause to be grateful.[26] Clean water, public health and education might produce healthier people but, unless they produced better people, the gain was illusory. British rule was not going to do that.

Though non-cooperation was honoured as much in the breach as in the observance – only 24 out of 5,186 Indians with British titles surrendered them, few lawyers interrupted their careers and few parents withdrew their children from government schools for long – Indian opinion had not been bought by the 1919 reforms. Reading 'never quite know how strong the movement is among the ignorant masses', that reservoir of British support,[27] but he knew the fate of empires 'when they begin to withdraw their legions'.[28] To George Lloyd, arriving in December 1918 as governor of Bombay, treating with sedition was a form of retreat, and the government must stop retreating. He was appalled at the old fashioned apparatus of government house, with not a working typewriter to be seen, where 'five incompetent, inefficient, ill-paid people [did] the work that one good, well-paid worker could do better in less time'.[29] The strikes in the mills and on the railways, which poured unemployed men onto the streets ready for trouble, were caused by agitators against inefficient government. Remedy that, and unrest would go away. He raised police pay and a loan on the Indian money market, guaranteed by the Government of Bombay, to fund a housing project to change a system that amounted to 'a conspiracy of landowners'. He removed, from the dust of 60 years, a scheme to use the Indus to irrigate six million acres of rich alluvial land.[30] Projects of this size were beyond the powers of Gandhi's self-help programmes.

The Gandhian magic, moreover, did not work on the majority of the Muslims. The failure of his joint Muslim-Hindu satyagraha over the future of the Caliphate (Khalifat) in 1921 to prevent the arrest of its Muslim leaders for trying to provoke mutiny in the army, provoked a suspicion among their fellow Muslims that Gandhi enjoyed a special immunity from arrest. George Lloyd, wrestling with disobedience, thought the same, but Reading was not convinced that Gandhi was preaching non-violence and planning violent revolution.[31] The man who solemnly averred that, if the Afghans invaded India, he would go to conquer them by love was hardly likely to encourage a bloodbath of the British.[32] He offered a Round-Table conference and the release of all those arrested. The peppery Lloyd thought this was a sure way of losing the Empire. What actually happened was that Reading lost the secretary of state. Edwin Montagu, disenchanted by Lloyd George's cynical dismemberment of the former Turkish empire, foolishly allowed the publication of confidential telegrams urging the British government to avoid losing the support of moderate Islam in India. Montagu's eventual successor was FE Smith, now Lord Birkenhead, who had always distrusted his reforms and doubted that India would ever be ready for self-government. Lloyd George had put up with Reading's appeasement to secure a successful visit by the Prince of Wales and did not want now to be bothered by India.

In 1917 Montagu attributed the strained relations between government and governed 'to the government always talking to the people with reservations, which show they are founded on distrust than anything else'.[33] One day Britain would tire of trying to run India in the teeth of Indian protest but now, in 1922, with Gandhi urging the boycott and destruction of foreign cloth, and waning patience in London, even Montagu recognised that he would have to be removed from the public scene.[34] Almost as a symbol of the change about to overtake Whitehall, Gandhi was arrested on the day (10 March 1922) that Montagu resigned from office. Non-cooperation had foundered for a whole raft of reasons: the deep-rooted antipathies of Hindu and Muslim, non-cooperation in non-cooperation, and the wish among self-rule supporters to accept election to the new councils and so make constitutional progress by cooperation. The arrest was greeted with deep satisfaction by most of the British in India, and very little protest from Indians. Indeed imprisonment may have protected Gandhi from popular disappointment that so little had been achieved. His closest associates were already behind bars, and the cause seemed to have suffered a massive defeat.

The collapse of non-cooperation gave a chance for the Montagu reforms to breathe. Decisions were transferred from paternal, if disinterested, administrators to elected politicians who began to enjoy the sweets of office, the publicity, the patronage, the respect. With most local councils introducing universal primary education, on paper at least, there would soon be more educated people than could be found the sort of jobs they expected. The interests of India, even of an India ruled by Britons, began to diverge from those of Britain, her priorities were not those of a European off-shore island, gravely damaged by four years of war. Though the rate of Indianisation was slow, it was inexorable. India was close to becoming rather a liability than an asset. The reforms improved the lot of Indians generally, but they did not install a cheap form of government, and global depression, trade stagnation and the declining value of the rupee proved a greater limitation on power than any dispute with Delhi about where devolved power ended. Taxing income was bedevilled by the difficulty of calculating incomes, death duties thwarted by the complexities of the joint family, tobacco and alcohol were but little used. Land taxes had to correspond with productivity and the newly elected councils resolutely opposed new local taxes. The duty on the one profitable government monopoly, salt, was a tax on the poor. The British, in bowing to national shibboleths, and deferring to home producers, had produced a revenue system that was inelastic.[35] Indian export surpluses had to fund her own national debt. To generate more income to meet its liabilities and to sustain the elected assemblies, the government of India had to act against hitherto unquestionable Imperial assumptions, and raise tariffs on Imperial commodities to protect India's own products. In 1932, duties were imposed even on British produced cottons. India was still a major trading partner, taking ten per cent of British exports, but in certain sectors she had become a rival. Meanwhile the rupee debt rose as most of the investment into burgeoning industry came from within the country. Instead of being a major servicer of British capital, India was increasingly behaving like an independent country, solving its fiscal problems in its own way.

In 1926 a Yorkshire grandee took over from the barrow boy's son. Lord Irwin, though a Tory, recognised from the start what Lord Reading, for all his forensic brilliance, had been reluctant to admit, that India was set irreversibly on the road to self-rule, not immediately, as the more extreme nationalists were demanding, but over a suitably protracted period, while Indian politicians learned their trade. Those politicians differed not only over the rate of change but over its substance. Was it to be dominion status, which still implied some authority invested in Parliament in London – the Statute of Westminster was still five years away – or total independence? Irwin's brief from Lord Birkenhead repeated the line that the rich landlords and lawyers who appeared to constitute the Congress party could not possibly represent the toiling masses of farmers, whose taxes sustained the state, and the millions of the poor and illiterate whose interests it was Britain's duty to defend. Communal riots in Calcutta in April had caused immense damage and the loss of 110 lives, while copycat clashes, at least 40 in number, marked Irwin's first 12 months, and appeared to confirm Birkenhead's view that India was not ready for dominion status. The provisions of the 1919 bill being due for review by a statutory commission in 1929, Birkenhead decided to bring it forward by two years in order to secure its report before any Labour government was elected. Sir John Simon, after his defence of Indians accused at

Jallianwalabagh, was appointed to head three conservative, one unionist and two labour MPs, one of whom was Clement Attlee. But Simon, though a Liberal of impeccable pedigree, professed increasingly retrogressive views and Ramsay Macdonald did not want to send a Labour stalwart as part of a team expected to produce a report that would disappoint the party. Attlee's 'gas and water' socialism seemed safe enough. The experience convinced Attlee that the ills from which India suffered 'will require a giant's hand to remove [them], and I am certain that that hand cannot be an alien hand. It can only be done by the people of India themselves'.[36]

The Commission did not bring an offer of immediate dominion status, so both Hindu and Muslim political caucuses boycotted it. It took evidence as parties wrangled about whether to accept dominion status or stand out for independence, about safeguards for Muslims and other minority communities. 'What they are bound by past professions to demand,' Irwin wrote wryly to his father, 'is very much in advance of what I can imagine any British opinion at present willing to give'.[37] Before the Commission reported, a Labour government was elected in May 1929, whose leader had already committed himself in principle to dominion status. On 31 October 1929 the viceroy announced a round-table conference to discuss how to bring it about.

Reaction from the empire wing of the Tories was loud and brutal. Its leader, Winston Churchill, chose to express it, not in the House of Commons, but in the *Daily Mail*. Out came the old Imperial prejudices in the language of Macaulay. 'The rescue of India from ages of barbarism, tyranny and internecine war,' Churchill thundered, 'and its slow but ceaseless forward march to civilisation, constitute upon the whole the finest achievement of our history.' Dominion status 'can certainly not be attained by a community which brands and treats sixty millions of its members, fellow human beings, toiling at their side, as "Untouchables", whose approach is an affront and whose very presence is pollution... while India is a prey to fierce racial and religious dissensions and when the withdrawal of British protection would mean the immediate resumption of mediaeval wars... while the political classes in India represent only an insignificant fraction of the three hundred and fifty millions for whose welfare we are responsible'.[38] One Conservative member of the Simon team thought that Churchill was deliberately antagonising Indian politicians, to whom he believed India was being sold, in order to scupper the talks.[39] As Baldwin noted sadly when the Round Table opened in November 1930, Winston had become once more the subaltern of hussars of 1896.

To the disappointment of those who hoped that Congress might accept the outstretched hand of the viceroy and call peace while dominion status was discussed, Gandhi, while congratulating Irwin on his escape from an attempt on his life on 23 December 1929, claimed that only the people of India, not Round Tables, not Parliament in London were entitled to make decisions for their future. Congress, at its Lucknow meeting in 1928, had promised a campaign of civil disobedience if dominion status were not granted by 1 January 1930, and at the end of 1929 it called for the resignation of all Congress members from the central and provincial legislatures. Gandhi inaugurated the campaign in March 1930 when, after civilly informing Irwin of his intention, he marched the 240 miles from his ashram at Ahmedabad to the salt pans at Dandi on the seashore near Bombay, where he and his followers made salt from sea-water in defiance of the salt monopoly. Its symbolism epitomised Gandhi's genius as showman and artist and was more potent than its effect.[40] The ensuing satyagraha at the Dharsana salt depot, where the obtruders suffered passively as the police beat them with *lathis*, was a triumphant witness of the Gandhian theory. Salt tax became an icon for oppression, and rebellion against oppression a virtuous action.

The viceroy and the rebel met as equals, but the Congress left believed Gandhi had been duped into attending a conference that was bound to founder on Indian differences, for which it would be blamed. Though civil disobedience had been as much a rural as an urban phenomenon, though it had united protest across the country, it was largely a Hindu effort. The Muslims in Bengal and the Panjab had, by and large, been lukewarm. Moreover Indian entrepreneurs and business men, particularly Parsis in Bombay, were worried about where the protest was going. More might be gained from cooperation than disobedience and gaols full of political activists were not contributing towards escape from economic crisis. At its meeting in Karachi, Congress endorsed the pact but instructed its delegates to accept only a constitution which put elected Indian representatives in control of the armed forces, and of foreign and economic policy. Churchill fulminated about handing power to a party bent on the humiliation of Muslims and the ruin of Lancashire, and which was also resolved to walk out of the British empire.[41]

The world economic crisis did not help the government meet a nation-wide challenge from a people who saw a new virtue in breaking laws. Unemployment put protesters onto the streets and parts of Bombay were given over to processions and pickets. Trouble in Peshawar invited marauding tribes down from the mountains in search of loot. In his day, Winston Churchill was not slow to affirm loudly, 'intruding Afridi tribesmen' would have been 'destroyed or hunted back to their mountains with heavy losses'.[42] Over the summer of 1930 some 60,000 people were imprisoned, including Gandhi and the Nehrus, father and son. This was the whirlwind Ramsay Macdonald was reaping from his promise of dominion status.

Simon's report, when it came in June 1930 was 'like a prehistoric monster moving in the wrong geological age'.[43] There was no mention of dominion status, no proposal to transfer power into Indian hands. The Round Table Conference, opened in London by George V on 12 November 1930, barely mentioned it. Gandhi, listening to his Inner Voices while in confinement, counselled Congress that nothing was to be gained by attending it.[44] Congress leaders from their gaols reiterated their demand for the immediate transfer of all powers to an independent Indian government, and the delegates attending it (58 politicians of various affiliations and 16 representatives of princely states) could do no other than to echo it. From the side-lines, Churchill fulminated against the prospect of a Gandhi Raj. The British government was feeding the tiger with cat's meat.[45] The one fruit of the conference was an agreement that both British and princely India should be incorporated into the new dominion, attractive to conservatives because, in a central executive responsible to an elected legislature, the princes would provide a built-in bulwark against radicalism. Safeguards for the minorities remained to baffle the constitution-makers.

Irwin, anxious that Congress leaders should be round the next table when it convened, released Gandhi on 25 January 1931. It was a brave decision, attacked for kow-towing to terror, but both sides had reached stalemate. On 17 February the die-hard imperialist in Winston Churchill was nauseated by the humiliating spectacle of 'this one-time Inner Temple lawyer, now seditious fakir, striding half-naked up the steps of the viceroy's palace, to negotiate and parley on equal terms with the representative of the King-Emperor'.[46] The eight meetings of the two Mahatmas concluded in a pact that was finally agreed on 4 March. Civil Disobedience ended and Congress agreed to be represented at the next sessions of the Round Table. There were concessions on both sides. Peaceful picketing of merchants selling British imported goods was to be allowed. All those detained in the Civil Disobedience protest who had not actually committed crimes of violence were to be released. The salt monopoly was relaxed.

Irwin's critics might accuse him of taking tea with treason, of favouring a Hindu raj, of failing to understand Muslim suspicions, on which the Round Table was ultimately to break, but he never lost his confidence that India must take her place among the self-governing dominions. It was to be another 16 years before he saw its consummation. His successor, Lord Willingdon, had been captain of cricket at Cambridge, and the *I Zingari* and Sussex blazers had wafted him from Parliament and tennis partnership with George V to the land of Ranjitsinhji, as governor of Bombay from 1913 to 1918, and of Madras from 1919 to 1924. Now in 1931, at the age of 65, he returned as viceroy. He did not share Irwin's sanguine view of Gandhi, who was to join the second session of the Round Table as the sole representative of Congress, 'one of the most astute politically-minded and bargaining little gentlemen I ever came across'.[47] If Gandhi could have taken with him an agreed Hindu-Muslim brief, self-government might have come earlier. But try as he would, he could not get the agreement of his own party to the concessions that the Muslims demanded, and he was bound by Congress's claim that it alone represented the voice of India and its refusal to concede separate communal electorates. Negotiations over federation with the princes gagged on Congress insistence that they must be elected, not nominated to the central parliament. Had democracy been a precondition of federation they would never have supported it. As the sessions ground their weary way into November it was clear that Gandhi would veto every agreement. Meanwhile, back in India, though the Gandhi pact held, there was trouble in the frontier province, in Bengal and in the United Provinces. If the Mahatma failed to denounce the unrest, Willingdon would arrest him.[48] Gandhi was soon back in prison and, though civil disobedience continued, it was headless. The Mahatma held court in Yeravda gaol, where he enjoyed all the privileges and comforts consistent with the demands of his austere life-style, but civil disobedience was dying on its feet and working the political system became more attractive to many Congress activists. In January 1934, a catastrophic earthquake in Bihar reminded the comfortable political classes of the precarious nature of life for the poorest, and showed that government and Congress could collaborate. By the end of the year it began to look as if there might be a future in partnership.

Stanley Baldwin's India Act of 1935 provided a halfway house to self-rule. If half the princely states consented to join, India – without Burma which was to be governed separately – was to become a federative union under the rule of the viceroy. By 1937, responsibility for most matters that affected the ordinary citizen passed to elected members of assemblies in the eleven provinces, which became virtually self-governing states, independent of both London and New Delhi. At the centre, the viceroy presided over an executive council of seven nominated members, four of them Indian, pretty much as he had since 1919, influenced by but not answerable to a bi-cameral central legislature of largely elected members, and responsible for defence and external affairs. Property ownership still determined the size of the electorate which represented about one sixth of the adult population of British India. The changes neither satisfied the majority of Congress members, nor pleased the 'die-hard' wing of the Tory party, led by Churchill, who called it 'a gigantic quilt of jumbled crochet work, a monstrous monument of shame built by pigmies'.[49]

After initial doubts, Congress contested the elections, and won enough seats to form governments without coalition in five provinces, and disconcerted the princes by demanding the installation of representative institutions in their states. That old cricketing warrior, Ranji, Jam Saheb of Nawanagar, after a campaign to alert British opinion in the Princes' favour, organised by another cricketing hero, CB Fry, warned the Chamber of Princes in 1940 that British indifference and Congress subversion had not created 'the basis which is essential for a close union between British India and the states'.[50] They declined by a two-thirds majority to join a federation. Congress also failed to overcome Muslim suspicion of a Hindu raj. While the Muslim League demanded a federation in which Muslim-ruled majority states enjoyed the same rights as Hindu majority and princely states, Nehru saw it as an unrepresentative union of Muslim landlords and aristocrats, having little contact with or understanding of the Muslim masses and even of the Muslim lower-middle class.[51] To win the popular Muslim vote, which had not turned out to support it en masse in 1937, the League organised a highly publicised campaign to prove that the Muslim community in India suffered cultural, racial and religious discrimination at the hands of Hindus. Lord Linlithgow (1935–43) was at a loss what to do. A cold, unsmiling, and proud Scottish grandee, of great height and partly maimed from a childhood attack of polio, he found it physically as well as emotionally difficult to unbend. His instincts were certainly Tory, but not die-hard Tory, and he had come to India determined to make federation work. His declaration of war on Germany in 1939, however, without so much as consulting the members of his own central legislature, was a blunder. If India was to be a dominion, she should be treated like one. The allies had taken up arms in defence of freedom and democracy for small nations, and those rights could not be denied to India. With an unequivocal offer of independence, the nation would address itself to war. On 17 October 1939, Linlithgow declared that any advance on the 1935 act must wait until the war was won. For Congress, such studied prevarication proved that the war was being fought for imperial ends, and the continued exploitation of India. It called on all provincial Congress ministries to resign.

The chance to capture power in Muslim-majority provinces (Bengal, Panjab, Sind and the North West Frontier Province) was too seductive for the Muslim League; Muslim ministers were invited to stay at their posts, and the government was relieved to find Muslims prepared to cooperate in those provinces where many of the sinews of war were being manufactured and from which Indian troops were largely recruited. On 7 November 1939, the secretary of state informed the House of Lords that Hindu-Muslim agreement must be a condition of any further constitutional advance. The winter was spent in fruitless talks between League and Congress until, in March 1940, Congress threatened civil disobedience unless the viceroy agreed to the appointment of a provisional national government with full sovereign powers. Three days later the League rejected federation as envisaged in the 1935 act and demanded that any constitution should recognise 'autonomous and sovereign' states where Muslims were in the majority.[52] In August, the coalition government authorised Linlithgow to promise dominion status at the end of the war and, in the meantime, to co-opt a larger number of Indians onto his executive council and to set up a war advisory council on which princes could serve. But Britain 'would not transfer power to any system of government where authority is directly denied by large and powerful elements in India's national life'. The Muslim League was handed a virtual veto on constitutional advance.[53]

For the next two years, there was impasse. War industries developed to make India more self-sufficient, spawning lucrative contracts and creating jobs, so that Congress denunciation commanded little support among all those who were doing well out of them. Opposition was silenced. But no one could conceal that the war was going badly for the allies, dramatically badly after the entry of Japan. The Americans felt that British immobility on the constitutional position was making India an uncertain ally. The expected fall of Burma made horribly possible a Napoleonic nightmare, of Japanese troops streaming across north India to join up with Germans pouring through Turkey and Persia from the Balkans and southern Russia, cutting off the supply routes to Chiang Kai-shek's China. Labour members of the British cabinet convinced a reluctant Churchill that another effort should be made to persuade Congress to cooperate in waging war. In March 1942 Stafford Cripps, fresh from his embassy in beleaguered Moscow, arrived with a great flourish to confirm that there would be an elected assembly after the war with powers to frame a constitution. But he had not established exactly what he could promise. Churchill had agreed to his mission to keep the Americans quiet, and Linlithgow was suspicious of his partiality for Congress. He returned to London empty-handed, leaving one promise in the air, that any province which was unhappy about union with an independent India could opt out.

To Congress the Cripps mission was a desperate throw by the British government. Gandhi urged it to acknowledge defeat and leave India to God and, 'if that is too much, then leave her to anarchy'.[54] As tyrants went, there was little to choose between Britain and Japan, and tyrants could be overcome by moral force. He offered to go to Hitler and impress upon him the virtues of non-violence; he suggested that the British people themselves should lay down their arms and oppose him non-violently, even if it meant the loss of home, independence, even life. For India to become a battlefield was an outrage to the Indian people, who had no quarrel with another Asian power, especially one whose new order promised liberation from colonial overlords. With the British gone, Japan would have no cause to invade India; if she did, then she should be opposed by non-violence.[55] How India defended herself, or whether she defended herself at all, was a matter for free Indians to decide.

In August 1942 the All India Congress Committee approved a 'Quit India' campaign, though it also promised that India would join the allies, if the British actually quitted. Congress was declared once more a prohibited association, and its working committee members were arrested. Britain ruled over a sullen, uncooperative but, despite Gandhi's statement that they were in 'open rebellion', mainly quiescent people, while she fought for survival.[56] In 1943 Linlithgow, who had borne the burden of office for just over eight years, the longest serving viceroy since Dalhousie, handed over to the supreme commander of allied forces in southeast Asia, Archibald Wavell, who had been in Delhi since 1941. The appointment came as a surprise, for he thought it was going to Anthony Eden. Churchill had no great opinion of Wavell as a military tactician, and thought he would be more useful as viceroy than supreme commander. At cabinet attended by the viceroy-designate, he showed that he knew 'as much of the Indian problems as George III did of the American colonies', by haranguing it for nearly an hour and a half on the scandalous fact that Britain owed India £800 million and that British workmen in rags were struggling to pay rich Indian mill-owners for the privilege of defending them from the Japanese.[57] Wavell was 'wafted to India on a wave of hot air', with instructions to utter only vague promises of constitutional advance when the war was won.[58]

By the end of the war, India had some two and a half million men under arms, all volunteers. They had fought in Malaya and Burma, in North and East Africa, in the Middle East, Italy, Greece and Indochina, and 180,000 had been killed, wounded and taken prisoner. Twenty of the 27 Victoria Crosses of the Burma campaign were awarded to Indians, 700,000 of whom formed the largest single unit army (one million strong) operating in the war. India herself was a massive base, aircraft carrier and provider of the sinews of war, and many Indians had been content to abandon political activism for the pleasures of making money.[59] With the war's end, the promises of Montagu, Irwin, Linlithgow and Cripps would come home to roost, Indian politicians would be released from gaol, British troops would insist on going home and the Indian army might well be mutinous if some constitutional progress were not made. There were already fewer Britons than Indians in the ICS and unless Britain were to remain in India for another 15 years, those who remained would safeguard retirement by trimming their sails to the wind of their future Indian masters.[60] Wavell already felt the want of good senior Britons in the administration, and suitable replacements were not likely to come from Britain.[61] His administration was already too tightly stretched dealing with famine. Civil unrest could snap it. The army might be sound but the police had already shown themselves unsteady while, simmering at the bottom of the pot, was the threat of communal violence, likely to destabilise both. Jinnah and Gandhi were far apart as ever on what the Muslims could expect from an independent India and Britain could not go on putting off decisions on the grounds that an independent India would never work. By the end of 1944, Wavell doubted his own capacity to persuade India to become a nation.[62]

Churchill, with a general election in sight, was in no mood to discuss India with his viceroy, who realised that, with the demands of social reconstruction at home, neither a conservative nor a labour government would spare resources to keep India subject. In June 1945, Wavell released all members of the Congress working committee still in gaol and called a conference at Simla to discuss constitutional change. Any hope that the Muslim League might be persuaded to forget its separatist ambitions was to be disappointed.[63] No working arrangement could be agreed between League and Congress on who represented Muslims at a national level. The viceroy saw no 'solution till the three intransigent, obstinate and uncompromising principals are out of the way; Gandhi (just on 75), Jinnah (68) and Winston (nearing 70)'.[64]

On 26 July, two weeks after the break-up of the Simla conference, Labour swept to power in Westminster. Attlee was now able to act on the experience he had gained as a member of the Simon mission. The Simla conference had failed because Wavell had offered too little. Congress had made it repeatedly clear that it would accept nothing short of dominion status with a cabinet responsible to an elected assembly, and the League, not to be outdone, demanded the same for those provinces where the Muslims were in a clear majority. Attlee thought the League perverse and pinned his hopes on a democratic Congress finding the solution. Wavell, summoned to London for consultations, was positive that no constitutional progress could be made until the Muslim issue was solved, but the prime minister seemed to him more anxious to conciliate the left wing of his own party and the USA and the Cabinet 'bent on handing over India to their Congress friends as soon as possible'.[65] The offer he carried back with him (largely the Cripps plan, modified by an executive body to be selected after the autumn elections) was rejected summarily by Congress as inadequate and by the League as providing no commitment to an 'autonomous and sovereign' Muslim state or states.

Any hopes that elections to the provincial assemblies might modify attitudes were dashed. Though the League could only form administrations in Bengal and Sind, it won 75 per cent of Muslim votes. Compared to the 4.4 per cent it had won in 1937, that was good enough for Jinnah. A cabinet mission, consisting of Cripps himself, now President of the Board of Trade, the Secretary of State, Lord Pethick Lawrence, and the First Lord of the Admiralty, AV Alexander, came to find out what would be acceptable to all parties. It spent seven bootless weeks in India, until on 16 May Attlee, to break the deadlock, repeated the offer of the Cripps plan with important additions: a separate Muslim state was rejected but there would be a union government, with an executive and legislature recruited from British and Princely India, responsible for foreign affairs, defence and communications. The 11 provincial governments, grouped so that predominantly Hindu and Muslim areas could enjoy virtual self-government, would control everything else. Any province which disliked the arrangements could opt out after ten years. A constituent assembly would then be called to decide on the Union constitution. Everyone now knew the British meant business, but nobody liked the plan. Congress wanted to secure a strong centre before the autonomous provinces went on their possibly separate ways, while Jinnah was disappointed that it ruled out an independent Muslim state. The Sikhs, for their part, expressed alarm at being incorporated into a Muslim-ruled province.

At Simla in June, Congress and League failed to agree on which Muslims, Congress or League, could serve in the interim government. Wavell feared that Cripps and Pethick Lawrence were far too ready to give way to Congress (their behaviour during the cabinet mission had been almost scandalous in this regard), and told Nehru that Britain could not hand power to a central legislature with a Hindu majority, without safeguards for the Muslims. Such a move would not lead to the united India which he assumed they both wanted.[66] The cabinet mission returned to London without securing agreement and Wavell set up a nominated interim government, in which Hindu and Muslim officials in equal numbers constituted the executive council, until he could persuade the parties to form a constituent assembly. Jinnah declared that the only tribunal to which he would submit would be a Muslim one. He had now forged his pistol and would use it. The League formally resolved upon an independent Pakistan in July 1946.[67]

For Attlee, and his American counterparts, who believed that it would not be viable, and would provide only a weak defence against Russian ambitions in the area, a Congress government for all-India was the preferred option. Attlee. moreover, suspected that Wavell was too dependent on tired, traditional advice from civil servants who had been in India too long.[68] Wavell believed that he understood the situation much better than the elderly Hussar subaltern of 1895, who was now leader of the opposition, and the veteran of the Simon Commission who was now prime minister. Congress was resolved on independence now, and would deal with the Muslims and Princes when they had it. The Muslims would never accept independence under a Hindu-dominated Congress, so that Britain could either hang onto India until there was a just settlement (this, in his view, was improbable), or surrender to the largest and most vociferous party (this would be dishonourable). Britain should put a date to her withdrawal and hope that the shock would bring the warring parties to an agreement.[69] He had some support for this view. Gandhi asserted that the communal mayhem that convulsed Calcutta in August and left something like 4,000 dead, mainly Muslims, was due to the presence of British troops which encouraged the Muslims and Hindus to fight it out, knowing that the police would not antagonise the communities by intervening impartially and that British tommies had no desire to die in a civil war between Hindu and Muslim in which they had no interest. Wavell, who claimed to have heard the pacifist Gandhi announce that 'if India wants her bloodbath, she shall have it', now produced his 'breakdown plan', for a phased abandonment of India.[70] The British would immediately evacuate, and Congress would be handed, 'Congress India' to rule, (Bombay, Madras, Orissa, the Central Provinces); the viceroy would retain control of the rest, thus securing India's defence and blocking the creation of Pakistan. Within a year, the 'rest' would either accede to 'Congress India' or constitute independent states, and the British would leave them too. British rule in India would effectively cease by the middle of 1948. Attlee would not hear of it. India must be handed over to a single successor government, which, despite the odds, the viceroy must try to achieve.

Wavell did his best. In October 1946 Jinnah agreed to join an interim government led by Nehru, but it was not a coalition, more an uneasy assemblage of opposed opinions. Communal violence assumed increasingly dramatic proportions, and at least 7,000 people died in two months after the interim government had been installed in September. In November, talks in London between Nehru and Jinnah achieved nothing, and Attlee now began to understand what Wavell had been telling him all along. The 'breakdown plan' was discussed in cabinet. However desirable it might be to leave the two snarling parties to solve their difficulties in their own way, Attlee could not countenance a policy of scuttle, leaving India in chaos with no guarantees for minorities. George VI showed a surprising understanding of the situation. 'We have plans to evacuate India,' he noted in his diary 'but we cannot do so without leaving India with a workable constitution. The Indian leaders have got to learn that the responsibility is theirs and that they must learn how to govern.'[71]

Attlee decided that Wavell must go. His 'breakdown plan' was too ignominious an end to 200 years of British involvement in India. Power must be honourably and peacefully transferred as soon as possible to one successor state or, if the worst came to the worst, to two. Mountbatten's choice as viceroy was largely conditioned by his advice to Attlee when, as Supreme Allied Commander in Southeast Asia, he had backed the former communist and collaborator with the Japanese, Aung Sang, as the man to lead Burma to independence. Mountbatten had been right in Burma. He was now required to be right in India. To remove any suspicion that the British would, by encouraging divisions between Congress and League, somehow wriggle out of a commitment to go, he would be given a deadline for British withdrawal. Congress in this way must either find an accommodation with the Muslims or accept an independent Pakistan which, Attlee was now convinced, was Jinnah's unalterable object.[72]

On 17 January 1947, Wavell was told that Churchill had appointed him for the duration of the war and the war was over. He was given one instead of the usual six month's notice that his time was up. It was, he remarked to his diary, 'discourteously done'.[73] Sixteen days before, Mountbatten, knowing what Wavell had suffered from back-seat driving in London, told the prime minister that he could not have Whitehall ministers breathing down his neck. Attlee was surprised. 'You are asking for plenipotentiary powers above His Majesty's government... You can't mean this?' When Mountbatten insisted that he did, Attlee gave him the powers and the job.[74] The announcement that British rule would end in mid-1948 was made to the Commons on 20 February, and despite enfilades from Churchill about 'operation scuttle' and his prophetic utterance that 'it was a melancholy and disastrous transaction whose consequence will darken, aye, redden the coming years' it received cross party support, much assisted by the former Lord Irwin, now Lord Halifax, who urged that, as no better solution had been proposed, the message to India from the House (of Lords) should not be one 'of failure, frustration and foreboding.'[75] Attlee told the Commons that the decision was not a betrayal of trust but the fulfilment of the British mission in India, as forecast by Macaulay, 'the placing of responsibility for their own lives in Indian hands'.[76]

Mountbatten reached India on 20 March 1947. By 19 April, convinced that civil war was in the making, he prepared for partition. On 4 June the viceroy told a press conference that the transfer to two new dominions could be effected at midnight on 14/15 August. Despite consternation in Whitehall, Attlee accepted the date. All the Parliamentary procedures were completed in time for royal assent on 18 July and of the events on 15 August he was able to write to his brother, 'at least we have come out with honour instead, as at one time seemed likely, of being pushed out ignominiously with the whole country in a state of confusion'.[77] British rule had suddenly come to an end.

15. 'CRUSHED BY ENGLISH POETRY'

> Every schoolboy knows who imprisoned Montezuma and
> who strangled Atahualpa. But we doubt whether one in
> ten, even among English gentlemen of highly cultivated
> minds, can tell who won the battle of Buxar, who
> perpetrated the massacre of Patna, whether Suja Dowla
> ruled in Oude or Travancore, or whether Holkar was a
> Hindoo or a Mussalman.
>
> Thomas Macaulay, *Essay on Clive*, 1836

> Crushed by English poetry, our freedom has been
> destroyed, under their laws, we have become bankrupt.
>
> VK Chiplumkar, 1881

> Lord Chesterton [filled] his carriage with red boxes
> containing minutes about... the wrongs of Dedarkhan
> Bux in the well-known cause of the Jaghire of
> Moneydumdum.
>
> Emily Eden, *The Semi-Detached House*, 1860

INDEPENDENCE WAS HANDED TO India and Pakistan because Britain feared a
communal civil war, which she could not control, not because she was beaten at
the barricades. Apart from the Mutiny, very few Europeans lost their lives at the
hands of Indians, whether criminals or 'freedom fighters'. The dissolution of
the British Indian empire was due less to anti-colonial ideology than to a
calculation that independent dominions within the Commonwealth would serve
what was left of Britain's imperial strategy better than a discontented nation in
thrall for a further fifteen years. At the end of empire, too, as one 'chota sahib'
remarked, the British still remained 'a little community of aliens'.[1] How alien
some felt was recalled by Hector Munro (Saki), last of a long line of India servants, one of whom had been assailed by a tiger while duck shooting on the
island of Saugar in 1792, and was the model for the European being mauled by
Tipoo's Tiger. Munro spent his alien time in the Military Police in Burma, until,
like Eric Blair, he was sent home after seven fevers in 13 months. His creation,
Comus Bassington, 'was a lost, soulless body in this great uncaring land; if he
died another would take his place, his few effects would be inventoried and sent
down to the coast, someone else would finish off any tea or whisky that he left
behind – that would be all'.[2] Because the British were aliens, it was easier for
them go when they had to. Most of them went. It was harder for those imperialists
who had put down roots into inalienable land.

The speed of departure bewildered everyone, but undivided India had for many years been behaving like an independent state and there were competent authorities to whom to hand over. Though many questioned the wisdom of advancing the date of the transfer of power, regretted the desertion of the princes, deplored the haste in which the borders were drawn, there was never any doubt that the British were going to leave. India was lucky in its imperialists, and Gandhi paid his own tribute when he chose 'his weapons shrewdly in contest with an enemy who was not prepared to have easy recourse to the means of violence of which it possessed a monopoly'.[3] Had the British been less arrogant, less socially stand-offish, less racially contemptuous, more able to take up the hand of friendship, would the parting have been delayed, or more violent? But the triumvirate of Stalky, M'Turk and Beatle had been formed in the lower fourth at Westward Ho, and one of the offspins of empire was the growth of Britain's public schools (and their export to India), whose emphasis on self-reliance, responsibility and team-spirit were the necessary experience of any young man about to embark 'armed with a ticket for a place called Amingaon'.[4] His relationship with Indians was, as a result, 'too much that of the prefects with the lower fourth, and hardly recommended itself to a people with an older culture than our own'.[5] Besides, prefects always leave school. For George Orwell's Flory, the timber merchant, the *pax britannica* was the *pox britannica* and keeping the peace and law and order boiled down to more banks and more prisons, which the British would chuck if it did not pay. But for 'an Unknown Indian', Nirad Chaudhuri, the gadfly of post-independence India, it deserved a better chit, and, in 1947, he dedicated his *Autobiography* 'to the memory of the British empire in India which conferred subjecthood on us but withheld citizenship; to which yet every one of us threw out the challenge "Civis Britannicus Sum", because all that was good and living within us was made, shaped and quickened by the same British rule'.[6]

From the dissolution of the Company it had been commonly held, even among educated Indians, that Britain held India in trust for the good of its people, and most servants of the Raj, both British and Indian, gave unstinted service in return for their privileged way of life. Gladstone, wishing to improve public service in Britain, turned to the model of what was the first service dedicated, not to a monarchy or a class, but to a whole people, entrusted to it by God and secured by a native army. The criticism of that service was that it held in place a country for Britain to exploit materially, to drain off its surplus and to preserve its primarily peasant economy, underdeveloped and in perpetual poverty. Agricultural output per capita did decline under the British land settlement and industrial development was from time to time slowed down by executive decisions in favour of British production. But India arrived at independence with one of the largest cotton goods industries in the world, mostly in Indian hands, structures for the exploitation of her mineral wealth and internal and external communications serving a thriving export trade. India overall did quite well materially out of British investment and could have done better if her rulers had been less afraid of rural unrest and less protective of inefficient farmers.

India was certainly exploited for the purposes of prestige. She helped a smallish off-shore island weigh in the balance with continental empires, but she also encouraged the myth of that weight to persist long after India had become a net burden on the British economy. Winston Churchill, while complaining about the fiscal debt to India which had converted imperial profit to deficit, nevertheless believed that her loss would be an irretrievable blow to Britain's place in the world. This powerful myth, more than any other consideration, deterred the British government from naming a date for dominion status or independence before the 1939–45 war. The extravagant claim that India was the jewel in the crown made the refusal to extend full citizenship to its inhabitants all the more galling.

'British rule', Chaudhuri affirmed, 50 years after his 1947 dedication, 'by bringing European cultural influences to bear on Indian life, created what was virtually a new culture.'[7] At its best this culture is summed up in Tagore's mission statement for Visva Bharati: to acknowledge India's obligation to offer to others the hospitality of her best culture and India's right to accept from others their best. It hurt him 'deeply when the cry of rejection rings loud with the clamour that Western education can only injure us'.[8] Books and pamphlets in Indian languages in the late nineteenth century expatiated on the benefits of British rule, unity, public safety, fair-play, dedication to the welfare of the peoples of India, but went on to ask questions like: 'How come, as human beings, we became slaves and they kings?' and 'How long will you suffer these sorrows as slaves?' If a royal personage were to come and reside in India, that might show that England loved India, as the queen did, but England did not rule by love, but by fear. It was a theme Gandhi was to develop with devastating eloquence.[9] Among the best that Britain had to offer was parliamentary democracy, which Congress accepted as the model for the future. Penderell Moon, a first-hand observer of the partition of India, believed that this was an inappropriate recipe for a land where millions were illiterate, communications were weak and populist policies could command too many votes. The last had brought about Pakistan.[10] Once that genie was out of the bottle, there was no returning it, for religion proved a more potent stimulus to nationalism than secular politics, and it was 'through quasi religious societies (like the *Brahmo Samaj*, the *Arya Samaj* and, most surprisingly, the Theosophical Society) that educated Indians first fell into the habit of thinking and organising on a national scale'.[11] The Macaulayan reforms meant that they thought and organised in English. The British Indian empire did not fall but was given away to new imperia, drunk on the resonances of the English tongue in court and parliament.

Despite India's embrace of socialism and secularism, *khaddar* and the Gandhi cap, Congress was never a grass-roots party. The peasantry for the most part had been indifferent to the result of the 'independence struggle', if not actually partial to the ruling power, having neither the language nor the education to understand the debate. The occasional *jacqueries* that so disturbed Gandhi were more the result of social misery than political dissent, and terrorism was an urban, middle-class phenomenon. The sons of peasants rallied to the flag in war as they always had, and successive viceroys had genuinely, if perhaps too wishfully, wondered what would be done for the toiling masses, whom they were pledged to protect, under a Congress government. The truth was: not much. The Raj was dead, long live the Raj. The governmental machine merely experienced a change of driver, as the latter-day pride of the British, the Indian Civil Service, changed colour, and the army, nurtured on bands and battle honours and its massed ranks of holders of the Victoria Cross, remained wedded to blanco, drill and the caste of rank. The new constitution of 1950 was remarkably close to the 1935 Government of India Act, the provinces becoming states with their own elected assemblies, governor and chief minister. A president, with a role remarkably similar to that of the British crown, lived in Lutyens' palace and a prime minister, variously called the last viceroy or the last Mughal, struggled to thwart his own autocratic impatience for reform by a commitment to democratic principles that themselves, dependent on majority decisions, inhibited change.

Jawaharlal Nehru had been in his lifetime the privileged son of a successful and prosperous lawyer, an English public schoolboy, a prodigal and inattentive Cambridge undergraduate, a dilettante intellectual, a Gandhian convert, a radical firebrand, a political prisoner, a best selling author, an uxorious husband and fond father and, latterly, prime minister 'accidentally', thrust into politics by force of circumstances and remaining there because the circumstances continued.[12] Though Gandhi was his lodestar, he did not share the Mahatma's belief that India and, through India, the world would only find true freedom in the Gandhian village, sustained by its own inner dynamic and social cohesion. Such an ideal did not appeal to the urban socialist, who believed in the power of legislation to change society and of planning to create wealth. Nehru could only see the 'actual villages with their depressing poverty, squalor, disease and superstitions. Was this what the master wanted to build the new India upon?'[13] The village was a backwater intellectually, and the Indian intelligentsia had learned a larger vision from the west, of educated masses, emancipated women, casteless citizens and satisfied consumers. The village epitomised what in 1885 one Indian writer had identified as the reason why there was no word for patriotism in any Indian language. 'The people simply cannot conceive of the kind of freedom for which Englishmen removed the Stuarts from the throne. Nor can they think of the happiness that the Italians derived from becoming self-dependent.'[14] If any freedom was crushed by English poetry, it was the arcadian fantasy of the Mahatma. The poetry of Tagore, for its part, embraced Shelley and Blake and the Promethean ambitions of the late Romantics, and was translated into socialising manifestos.

To create a free and just society and to tackle the endemic problems of development were more far-reaching ambitions than anything the British had professed. Conscious that they ruled by sufferance from a very narrow pinnacle of power, the British had been essentially conservative, and the paradoxical effect of the their attempt to bring Indian society out of what they saw as oriental bondage was that it helped to preserve it. The recruitment of Brahmans as the educated and literate class to fill the lower orders of administration had put power into the hands of a caste often resistant to change; the gelding of princes into complacent allies created a new status quo, while the need to recruit soldiers from the martial classes meant that the preservation of a society of peasants in the recruiting provinces, as guaranteed by the Lawrence stable, positively discouraged social or political development. Above all, the huge standing army, to sustain which meant that taxation bore hard on the cultivator, inhibited investment in the land and helped to sustain India as a 'cantonment of peasants'.

One oriental despotism had been replaced by another. The Mutiny had demonstrated the perils of accelerated change and Indians themselves were divided in their vision of the future: was India to be an efficient modern western state, or a 'glorious, unchanging, and distinctively Oriental Indian past.'[15]

In the mid 1920s, Malcolm Muggeridge, teaching English at the Unida Christian College in the princely state of Travancore, began dimly to recognise that a people could be laid waste culturally as well as physically, not their lands but their inner life, as if sown with salt. An alien culture, itself exhausted, trivial and shallow, had been imposed on India. It left behind railways, schools (not nearly enough) and universities, statues of Queen Victoria, industries, administrators, a legal system and much more, set in a spiritual wasteland. 'We had drained the country of its life and creativity, making it a place of echoes and mimicry'.[16] In drab 1948 England, which George Orwell had taken for his model of *1984*, the imperial experience at its apogee seemed not to compare with the glory that was Rome, worthy of the pen of a Gibbon or a Macaulay, but the squalid exploitation of a nation in bondage to the pursuit of wealth and the phantasm of world power.

In fact, the Roman occupation of Britain was the conscious paradigm of British rule in India, comprehensible to schoolboys who were still required to offer Latin to enter Haileybury and the Indian civil service. It lasted barely four hundred years and the settlement of Roman legionaries was never extensive. A small Romanised élite held power with the assistance of Roman arms, backed by the terror of the eagles, and enriched by membership of a large commodities market, dominated by good roads and waterways. The Roman empire was 'a highly mobile society with a high rate of migration and a lot of people trying to establish themselves, wanting to turn into Romans... The massive commitment of resources to their houses in decoration [was] a powerful way of playing this game'.[17] In nineteenth and twentieth-century India, migrants from the antipodes to the centre, from the Rann of Kutch, Cape Comorin and Chittagong to Calcutta, Bombay and New Delhi, turned into imperial Britons by mastery of their tongue and technology, filling their houses with European and American books, furniture, art, glass, china, drink, wearing western-style clothes, reading English-language newspapers and listening to English medium broadcasts. The successors to the proconsuls were... proconsuls, 'India's Westernised middle classes, the last remnants anywhere of the Edwardian English gentry'.[18]

In India's babel of tongues, English needed no Convention of Iona to obstruct the use of mother tongues but became the preferred medium of communication. Gandhi went to England to master it and even wrote a handbook on living in London. Nehru confessed that one never really escaped from the English, 'and the worse trouble is that you never really want to'.[19] Jinnah knew no other language in which to express himself clearly. Macaulay may have under-estimated the literary value of Indian writing, but he never intended that English should be taught as a simple communicative skill. It was to provide access to a treasure trove of wonder and a force for understanding, in a tongue of which he, too, was a master.

Indians, however, were uncomfortably aware that there was no one ready or even able to converse with them. They might go to Oxford, Cambridge and the

Inns of Court to drink of the Pierian spring and be intoxicated by a language in one of its great periods of expressiveness, only to return to an India of silence. For the British, unlike the Romans, and their Latin successors as colonial powers, had recoiled from cultural proselytisation by miscegenation or social mixing. They ridiculed the image of the westernised Indian in the columns of Punch, where the creator of Vice Versa and Mr Bultitude pilloried Mr Hurry Bungshoo Jabberjee, BA 'of a respectable Indian University, now in this country for purposes of being crammed through Inns of Court'.[20] All the British wanted an Indian to have was enough English to do his job, understand the requirement of his supervisors and keep his place. His place was not to converse on equal terms with his European colleagues, or to exchange ideas and principles.

Social recognition did not follow education. It was rare for educated Indians to mix with Britons and many Britons were too uneducated to mix with anyone. The Nehrus, the uncrowned lords of Allahabad, were refused admission to the Allahabad Club. Nirad Chaudhuri decided that the books selected for the Delhi Gymkhana Club library demonstrated a culture that put the deracinated, short-term residents from Britain beneath notice.[21] How does one express oneself to an intellectual, even social, inferior who believes he has a God-given superiority? Those Europeans who did not share the sense of intellectual apartheid were seen as eccentrics or as subversives, and the heights were surrendered with such gracelessness that the first Indian entrants to the civil service, the first barristers to plead in court, the first professors to teach in the universities were treated as spurious imitations of the European. Even Kipling shared in the dilemma. How could an Oxford educated babu, talking of bump-suppers, hold the mutinous affection of India's warlike tribes?[22]

The failure of the British to understand and harness the subtle Hindu mind, forsaking it for mercenaries from the Panjab and Rajputana who were faithful to any overlord who offered them a good scrap, and the conservative, even reactionary support of Muslims, was the ultimate failure of British rule. The move of the capital to Delhi was to escape from that mind, 'its deviousness, slipperiness, its nimbleness and... the loquacity which covered its workings'.[23] The capacity of the learned Indian to live in two cultures, sometimes three, put him in an intellectual class outside the normal experience of the ruling British, never wholly comfortable with ideas. Tagore lamented that 'our modern schoolmasters are Englishmen; and they, of all the western nations, are the least susceptible to ideas... They have vigorous excess of animal spirits, which seek for exercise in racing, fox-hunting, boxing etc. and they offer stubborn resistance to all contagion of ideas'.[24] Administrators and soldiers from a fox-hunting class were more at ease with the jackal-hunting farmers of the northern plains and deserts, whence India's warriors were latterly recruited. Even the poetry-loving Wavell had a lurking sympathy for the idea of Jinnah's Muslim state.

Despite that patronising attitude, a young Indian university teacher could say in 1992 that 'perhaps the most important legacy of British rule to contemporary India is the English-educated class'. Fifty years after independence, the search for English, the language and the values represented in its literature, both classic and modern, is more intense than ever.[25] She cited the example of an English medium school in Bihar which advertised itself as St Sanyal, using a common

Bihari name with the Christian prefix to suggest that it was run by a religious order and managed by Anglo-Indians (a statutory minority community of modern India, who are the dedicated custodians of the English language in Indian schools). Malcolm Muggeridge, for his part, rejected his aids to teaching 'an alien literature in an alien tongue', the 'little Dowden', a brief history of English literature by a Victorian clergyman, and the 'Made-Easies' which were to help him unlock the treasures of *Sesame and Lilies*, *Macbeth* and *Wuthering Heights*. Today the only international review solely dedicated to *Hamlet* studies is produced from an Indian university.[26] Paradoxically it was the British who provoked the revival of Hindu studies in the early nineteenth century, a riposte to the seductive sounds emanating from Macaulay's minute; but it was a revival based on western modes of textual criticism, historical chronology and philosophic realism. The key to the creaking doors of a civilisation, held to be impossibly ancient by its revered pundits, was oiled by English.

In 1961 the British Council mounted an exhibition in India of books by British hands on India, an Aladdin's cave of works to rival the imperial source books of the earlier empire of Rome. In ordinary life their authors were sappers, hydraulists, meteorologists, surgeons, surveyors, infantrymen, gazetteers, watercolourists, administrators, tax collectors, wives, missionaries and game hunters. On that broad basis has been erected an edifice of knowledge, in the English language, that is overwhelming. Charles Trevelyan saw English as the provider of 'a common science, common standards of taste, a common nomenclature' with the aim of leaving 'an enlightened nation where we found a people broken up into sections... and depressed by literary systems, designed much more with a view to check the progress, than to promote the advance, of the human mind.'[27] Like the British tribunes who quoted Thucydides, Virgil, Horace and Tacitus in the Houses of Parliament, Indian MPs illuminate debates in Indian assemblies by quotations from Shakespeare, Shelley and even Rudyard Kipling. The *Statesman* carries the *Times* crossword every day which forms the first daily task of civil servants and intellectuals from Bombay railway station to the rickshaws in Calcutta. British Council libraries are besieged for the latest novels coming out of Britain. English, which remains one of the constitutional languages of the republic, is virtually mother tongue to communicators who wish to address the world. Meetings are punctuated by commentaries, in English, on test matches and there are three stumps, a bat and a ball on every maidan in the land. International cricketers and the rules of the game, in English, are known to every urchin who has no word otherwise of the alien tongue.

These are indigenous phenomena, appealing to the Indian love of tradition, ritual and correct procedure, and hallowed by the mass media, vastly encouraged by the emergence of English as the language of America and the *lingua franca* of the modern world. To those who see, in the successor state, only brown colonialism, a colonialism of the mind, a society divided by a caste of language, the government in Delhi looks like Theodoric the Goth imitating Caesar in Ravenna. An English-speaking middle class, which has become more prosperous and more entrenched than ever, has, through its education, control of power. Critics of the new India find this oppressive. It sustains the legal system which the British imposed, and which, by introducing an essentially literary thing, the law of evidence, into justice, protracted cases beyond the means of the poor, licensing an army of paid perjurers and benefiting the plaintiff or defendant who could afford them, and forcing a reliance on police brutality to extort confessions. It impedes the extension of mass education and the elimination of illiteracy, as the fruits of power go to those who pass through the proliferating Indian universities and have more than a passing acquaintance with the ways of the western world.

The missionary certainties of Macaulay and Trevelyan are only beginning to be modified 150 years later. 'Writers in Hindi, as surely in most other Indian languages, have... made the most searching, fertile and creative use of English literature and then in due course gone on to liberate themselves from their historically necessary but now also historically exhausted stimuli.'[28] Jawaharlal Nehru, no mean historian himself in the language of Gibbon and Macaulay, admitted to André Malraux that the greatest difficulty, after 1947, was to create a secular state in a religious country, by which means he felt confident that India's cultural and religious diversity would be preserved. 'The fate of India is largely tied up with the Hindu outlook.' That Hindu outlook, of all communal outlooks in the sub-continent, took most readily to the ideas of political democracy.[29] Now, its critics say, it has learned how to use it. 'Imperial authority... merely turned into Central authority... Democracy in action at best consisted of the question: Who should reign?'[30] The English language still dominates education, decides the law and conveys the messages. The Indian without English is the spectre at the feast. No one knows accurately how many Indians use English as a constant means of communication. Some have put it as high as 12 million. Those who use a demotic form of the language in which all the trigger words are English may be 50 million. If India is to be the Asian power her wealth of talent gives her the qualifications to be, it will be by penetrating the industries to which English is the key, especially information technology, the new world order to which the imperial experience, according to Nirad Chaudhuri, introduced India. Social critics may lament that this élite has too readily continued in its own interests the collaboration it wandered into with the British: to create a society with power structures it could inherit. The Booker prize winner, Arundhati Roy, could say on a radio broadcast that 'the empire has interfered with my deepest thoughts, with everything about me', but the world supremacy of English means that she has become an international bestseller.[31]

Macaulay did not live to write his history of India but he did speculate correctly 'that by good government we may educate our subjects into a capacity for better government; that, having become instructed in European knowledge, they may, in some future age, demand European institutions'.[32] That they have, and India is today the eighth industrial power in the world, a regional, now nuclear, superpower, a major centre of scientific research and, through the diaspora of her citizens, has an influential voice in centres of administration, learning and business throughout the English-speaking world. But in 1999 she also ranked 138th in the list of 179 countries in the Development Programme of the United Nations. Over 400 million of her citizens were illiterate and lived in the direst poverty, and 200 million had no access to safe drinking water.[33] Infant malnutrition is as bad as, if not worse than, sub-Saharan Africa. Infant mortality is still 75 per 1,000 births and only 52 per cent of the population can read and write.[34] The successor government in Pakistan now rules a garrison state buffeted between militant Islam and the desire of its English-educated élite to preserve its secular gains. In India it is a shifting panorama of political parties among which some 100 out of 535 members of the lower house have criminal records for bribery, rape and attempted murder.[35] The decline in standards of honesty in the public services, the support for a return to a primitive form of Hindu dominance, now challenge the Nehruvian principles of the secular state, parliamentary democracy, a free press and an incorruptible civil service. The sad truth is that very few people in Britain today care very much which wins.

Access to India demanded the transfer of the Cape provinces, leading inexorably to the Boer War, preoccupation with her security induced Disraeli to acquire a majority of shares in the Suez canal, leading inexorably to a protectorate over Egypt and Sudan, while fear of Russia and a revived Turkey led to acquisitions in the Gulf and the Red Sea, leading inexorably to the emergence of Arab nationalism. India's need to sustain an export trade to the markets of the east led to the Straits Settlement, and rivalry in south central Asia left its bones in the Khyber pass. In 1930, the former hussar, historian, polo-player and lepidopterist, Winston Churchill, prophesied that 'the loss of India would mark and consummate the downfall of the British empire. That great organism would pass at a stroke out of life into history.'[36] In 1936 Baldwin's government was too obsessed by Mussolini's invasion of Ethiopia, and a possible threat to the Suez canal and approaches to India, to see the menace in Hitler's repudiation of the Locarno Treaty and his annexation of the demilitarised Rhineland. There was always the danger that anxiety over India would distract Britain from understanding what was actually happening in Europe. Yet, despite the 'astounding phenomenon' of Britain's acquisition of India, she was never of much interest to the common Briton.

To John Bloke, India had been for nearly two centuries a source of wealthy uncle figures and of employment for younger sons. Their preoccupations were largely obscure when not figures of fun. Thackeray's ancestral memories kept popping up to amuse him (and us) in Josh Sedley's district of Bogglywollah, implying a place of mind-boggling boredom, Emily Eden invented the jaghire of Moneydumdum (in a passing reference to Clive), Edward Lear's coast of Coromandel suggested a place of pearly fantasy, Wilkie Collins bemused his readers with prestidigitators in pursuit of a moonstone, Sherlock Holmes puzzled over the Indian rope trick, Hurree Singh was an exotic school fellow of Harry Wharton (good with the bat, like Ranji) and of Billy Bunter (good for a bit of ready cash), but India was peripheral to ordinary life. From the 'nabobs' on, service in India did not enjoy the reputation of being a particularly worthwhile activity, unless it was 'biffing' tribals in the northwest frontier, so loved of the *Boys Own Paper*. It was well rewarded and that was enough. 'When I was in Poona' was the comic prelude to an anecdote bound to bore its listeners. India debates in the House of Commons were sure to empty it. Only after the Mutiny had brought home to the British that their rule was not universally admired, did a cult of power emerge. 'Have ye served us for a hundred years / And yet ye know not why? / We brook no doubt of our mastery, / We rule until we die.'

'When the strong command, obedience is best.'[37] India was best left to strong men on the spot.

India's influence on Britain's cultural life was slight: in food and clothing it was benign but in the way ordinary sahibs and memsahibs acquired gentility in a single generation, and let it be known on their retirement, it was not. Clive Newcome was as excited by Orme's *History* 'containing the exploits of Clive and Lawrence', as his twentieth-century cousin was by Dan Dare or the captain of the starship *Enterprise*. India was an exotic other place for the intrepid or desperate. It gave them visions of a larger world than that their daily life normally encompassed, provided politicians with the delusion of greatness, and allowed the Queen-Empress Victoria to play her part as the grandmother of Europe. What was undivided India is now two irreconcilable nations, brothers under the skin, divided by history and now by the 'Muslim' and 'Hindu' bombs. An unpleasant nationalism takes on the ideology of religion, and Hindu politicians speak openly of Muslims as did Pertab Singh to Curzon's secretary (see page 191). Yet India ranks only after Indonesia and Pakistan as a home to Muslims. The efficacy of the Macaulayan legacies of law and language and the disinterested civil service of his brother in law, Charles Trevelyan, as instruments to keep a secular ruling class in power, are being critically challenged. Can they continue to be the cement holding together what is left of a divided continent in loyalty to a concept that was Hindostan, a Hindu nation of immense antiquity, and ancient tolerance of refugees and conquerors? Whatever the judgement of history, the British performance in India remains astounding, and deserves to be remembered with the legacies of Alexander of Macedon and Julius Caesar of Rome, whose ghosts still haunt the world stage.

NOTES

1. 'To Agra and Lahore of Great Mogul'

1. Parry, pp 301–2.
2. Gibbon, cap. xxxi.
3. The Portuguese established autonomous trading posts in Sofala and Moçambique (1505 and 1507), Goa (1510), Malacca (1511), and Hormuz (1515). Factories were permitted at Galle in Ceylon (1507), Hooghly in Bengal (1537), Mylapore, near Madras (1547), and Macau (1557).
4. Cipolla, pp 109–116.
5. Boxer, *The Portuguese Seaborne Empire*, p 50.
6. Bayly, *Indian Society*, p 45.
7. Hakluyt, *Voyages*, vol iii, pp 266–7.
8. Harrison, p 341.
9. Hakluyt, iii, pp 287–8.
10. Ibid., p 288.
11. Pulo Run in the Banda islands was one of the few indigenous homes of nutmeg. It changed hands during almost every Anglo-Dutch confrontation but was returned finally to the Company in 1665, whereupon, two years later, the directors exchanged it for another small island, off the North American coast called New Amsterdam. It is now Manhattan.
12. Boxer, *The Dutch Seaborne Empire*, p 24.
13. Pepper, from about 1650 to 1680, was the principal import, and accounted for about one third of the total sales revenue of both the Dutch and English companies. It shipped easily as ballast; indeed without it, it could have been difficult to stabilise the ships returning from the east. As a result, more was shipped than could easily be sold so that, to bring the price down, traders looked for cheaper sources of supply. The Dutch solution was to control the means of production and to exclude and/or eject rivals from the pepper-growing lands. KN Chaudhuri, pp 313–16.
14. Strachan, 'India', in Quinn, I, p 209, quoting Sir Humfrey Gilbert's *A Discourse of a discoverie for a new passage to Cataia* (1576).
15. Boxer, *Dutch Seaborne Empire*, p 200.
16. Schweinitz, p 73.
17. Keay, *Company*, p 77.
18. Ibid., p 83.
19. Foster, *Roe*, p 121: Roe to James I, 29 January 1615.
20. Strachan, *Roe*, p 145. *Negotiation of Sir Thomas Roe* (London 1740) pp 21, 37.
21. Strachan, *Roe*, p 85; Foster, p 155n.
22. Strachan, *Roe*, pp 90–91.
23. Foster, ed., *Middleton*, p xiii: Letter of 5 November 1601.
24. Hakluyt, iii, p 204: 'The Narrative of Caesar Fredericke', 1563.
25. The name Madraspatanam seems first to have been used in 1640 by the Surat factors, but the origin of this name is mired in doubt. Yule believed that it may have been supplied by the Nayak; the settlement was known as Fort St George, and the use of Madras to describe the 'black town' only became general in the early 18th century.

The Indians have renamed the city Chennai, as the Tamil name given to the settlement was Chennaipatanam, or Chinapatam. Yule, *Hobson-Jobson*, entries for Chinapatam and Madras.

26. Macaulay, *History*, iii, p 19. Saltpetre, like pepper, was good ballast for returning Indiamen, and because of its weight could most easily be transported by water. A 'sensitive barometre' of relations with Indian princes was the amount shipped to them by the Company. European saltpetre was running out and the Company agreed in 1664 to sell all its shipments to the British government. Between 1664 and 1682 the volume sold rose from 500 to 1500 tons. As the Company had to meet the demand, so saltpetre 'barons' moved into the market and stored it, selling at good prices when demand rose. Two of the biggest entrepreneurs were Amin Chand (Omichand) and his brother Deep, who were ruined after Plassey, when saltpetre became a Company monopoly in Bengal and Bihar. KN Chaudhuri, pp 336–9.

27. Sir Josiah Child, 'New Discourse of Trade', written in 1669, published in 1692, in Fox Bourne, pp 238–9.

28. Evelyn, 18 December 1682.

29. Keay, *Company*, p 134.

30. Foster, *Company*, p 101.

31. Losty, p 11.

32. Marshall, *Fortunes*, p 5.

33. Ibid., p 33.

34. Yule, ed., *Hedges*, ii, p li: Secret Committee to Bengal, 14 January 1686.

35. The story that the grant originated with Aurangzeb whose carbuncle had been lanced by a surgeon sent by Charnock cannot be substantiated.

36. Losty, p 15, quoting Charnock, 22 March 1689.

2. 'A Field Left Open for Adventurers'

1. Alam, p 44.

2. Ibid., p 21.

3. Bayly, *Indian Society etc*, p 7.

4. Ibid., p 1.

5. Alam, pp 40–41.

6. Wilks, i, p 302.

7. SN Sen, *The Military System*, p xiii.

8. Sardesai, i, p 146–7.

9. Macaulay, *History*, iii, p 20.

10. Spear, *India*, p 7. Child made his first fortune by supplying American timber to His Majesty's dockyards and was MP for Portsmouth in 1659. A second fortune was made as a supplier of beer and victuals to the navy, so that by 1683 he was worth, according to John Evelyn, £200,000. With capital like that, it was easy for him to become chairman of the Court of Proprietors.

11. Mill (1858), i, p 87. In March 1693, bribes worth £80,000 passed through the *Company*'s books. Keay, *Company*, p 181.

12. Quoted from White, 'Account of the Trade to the East Indies', in Fox Bourne, pp 243–4.

13. Macaulay, *History*, iii, p 25.

14. Ibid., p 29: resolution of the Directors of the East India Company, 1689.

15. Léon Deschamps, 'Un Colonisateur au temps de Richelieu' in *Revue de Géographie*, xix, 460, December 1886. Boullaye la Gouz to Colbert, 1 April 1666, quoted in SP Sen, p 45.

16. The success of 'medical diplomacy' was remarkable. The governor of Bengal allowed the English a factory at Hooghly because a Company surgeon healed his daughter, while Charnock, to support his request to settle Sutanati, sent his personal physician to lance Aurangzeb's boil. Primitive though it was, European surgery depended more on the knife than on the stars – the Mysorean ruler, Haidar Ali, died in 1782 as a result of holding off Surgeon Noel's knife on a lethal carbuncle until the stars were propitious. Keeping a surgeon at the court of a powerful potentate became almost as important as having a political agent there, though European surgical practice was only marginally superior at that time to Indian.

17. H Froideaux, 'The French Factories in India' in *The Cambridge History of India*, v, p 69. Caron's anxiety to avoid a clash with his former employers was to lead to accusations that he was still in Dutch pay. SP Sen, pp 178–9.

18. *Mémoires de Bellanger de l'Espinay sur son Voyage aux Indes Orientales* (Vendôme 1895), p 204.

19. Alexander Pope, *Moral Essays*: epistle iii, lines 361–5, originally wrote:

    Asleep and naked as an Indian lay

    An honest factor stole a gem away

    He pledged it to the Knight, the Knight had witt,

    So kept the diamond and was rich as Pitt.

    He thus suggested that Pitt had come by the stone dishonestly. When challenged he altered the fourth line.

20. Losty, p 20, quoting Alexander Hamilton, *A New Account of the East Indies* (Edinburgh 1727).

21. Marshall, *Fortunes*, p 26.

22. Ibid., p 10, quoting Directors to Fort St George, 20 November 1668.

23. Ibid., pp 218–9.

24. Ibid., p 10, quoting Directors to Fort William, 23 January 1751.

25. Ibid., p 15, quoting Barwell to Beaumont, 1 September 1774.

26. Woodruff, *Founders* (London 1955), p 66.

27. Woolf, *Growing* (London 1961), pp 16–17.

28. Muggeridge, *Grove*, p 26.

29. Losty, p 14. India was acknowledged a land of marvels, in which a money-baring tree, like the Gilded Man of South America, was a popular chimera. The pagoda was actually a Portuguese coin, bearing the image of a temple and reckoned the equivalent of $2^1/_2$ rupees. *Hobson-Jobson*, pp 367–9.

30. Hickey, i, p 121.

31. Ibid., pp 118–9.

32. N Chaudhuri, *Clive*, p 347.

33. *Hobson-Jobson*, pp 652–7.

34. Marshall, *Fortunes*, p 79.

35. Ibid., p 75, quoting *Parliamentary History of England*, xvii, p 338.

36. Losty, p 19, quoting Hamilton.

37. The Armenian diaspora to India probably began with the deportation of several thousands by Shah Abbas to his new capital at Isfahan in 1604. Sharing a fate similar to that of the Jews, they had seen their land conquered by Turkomen nomads, Osmanli Turks and Shia Iranians. Tribes of Arabs and Kurds had settled their lands. Their monophysite faith, the assertion of one nature in Christ, separated them from those other heterodox Christians of the east, the Nestorians, who held that in Christ there were not only two natures but two persons – Nestorius being unable to contemplate God as an infant. Permanent refugees and lukewarm heretics, the Armenians had developed considerable commercial gifts and, readily accepting the tenets of Roman

Catholicism from the Portuguese, they settled in nearly every port controlled by the nation. Their Asian personality, ambivalent religious allegiance and knowledge of tongues made them indispensable interpreters and middlemen. An Armenian accompanied the first French expedition to seek a foothold on the Coromandel coast; another, Khwaja Wajid, was banker and suspected – by the British – to be the evil counsellor of nawab Siraj-ud-daula. Their church of the Holy Nazareth is still the oldest place of worship in Calcutta.

3. 'That Man not Born for a Desk'

1. Sardesai, ii, p 92.
2. Ibid., ii, 106.
3. A Martineau, 'Dupleix & Bussy', in *Cambridge History of India*, v, p 139, Bussy to Dupleix, 26 February 1754.
4. Bence-Jones, p 78.
5. N Chaudhuri, *Clive*, p 23.
6. Panikkar, p 78.
7. Bence-Jones, p 56, quoting an English sergeant at Arcot, that the sepoys fought with 'a bravery uncommon to blacks'. The general opinion of topasses, who formed a considerable part of the presidency army, was that they were 'a black, degenerate, wretched race of the ancient Portuguese, as proud and bigoted as their ancestors, lazy, idle and vicious withal, and for the most part as weak and feeble in body as base in mind'. Keay, *Company*, p 278.
8. Meadows Taylor, in his novel *Ralph Darnell* (1865), p 207. This was consistent with the standard demonology, but Taylor goes on to describe a not unendearing young man, a creature of caprice, occasional benevolence and loyalty to his concubine. Even Indian sources accept that Siraj-ud-daula could make no distinction between right and wrong and carried defilement wherever he went, even into the homes of men and women of distinction. N Chaudhuri, *Clive*, p 153.
9. Keay, *Company*, p 311.
10. Marshall, *Fortunes*, p 44.
11. The casualties at Plassey, 500 or so of Siraj's soldiers, 4 Europeans and 14 Company sepoys, indicate the nature of the encounter. The story that an indirect casualty was Amin Chand who, confronted with the news that he was to get nothing for his treachery, suffered a debilitating stroke and died soon after, cannot be accepted. He swallowed his disappointment and was later successful in negotiating a salt contract. But he was finished as an arbiter of events, though his chiding spirit was to brood over the squalid events that were now to follow. N Chaudhuri, *Clive*, pp 242–3.
12. Moon, *Hastings*, p 49.
13. Bence-Jones, p 100, Clive to Pigot.
14. Ibid., p 37.
15. The Chief and Council in Dacca, 1763, quoted in *Hobson-Jobson* under 'Dustuck'.
16. Vansittart, iii, pp 13–4.
17. Richard Burton, *Explorations of the Highlands of the Brazils* (London 1869), vol 1, p 217. Burton did not invent this aphorism which was current as early as 1689. John Ovington, *A Voyage to Surat in 1689* (ed. HG Rawlinson, Oxford 1929), p 30.
18. Moon, *Hastings*, p 51.
19. Marshall, *Fortunes*, p 126: R Leycester to J Carnac, 10 January 1763.
20. Malleson, pp 204–5.
21. N Chaudhuri, *Clive*, p 331.
22. SN Sen, *Military*, p xv.

23. Ibid., pp 62–3; also Bayly, *Indian Society*, p 22; and *Rulers Townsmen & Bazaars*, p 14.
24. Keay, *Company*, p 322.
25. Ibid., p 324.
26. Srinivasachari, the Court of Directors to the President & Council at Fort William, 26 April 1765, p 98.
27. Ibid., comment by the editor, p xxiii.
28. Verelst, Appendix I, letter to the Court of Directors 30 September 1765. See also Marshall, *Fortunes*, p 174.
29. Marshall, *Fortunes*, p 205: Sykes to Warren Hastings, 28 January 1773.
30. Ibid., p 179.
31. Srinivisachari, pp 193–4: Clive to Directors, 17 May 1766.
32. N Chaudhuri, *Clive*, p 36: 31 January 1766.
33. Forrest, *Clive*, ii, p 256.
34. KK Datta, pp 39–40.
35. Forrest, *Clive*, ii, p 289.
36. Srinivisachari, p 337. Clive calculated that with military expenses at 60 lakhs of rupees, the nawab's allowance of 42 lakhs and the pension to Shah Alam II of 26 lakhs, the Company would have a clear £1,650,900 to defray the expenses of the investment, furnish the whole of the China trade, provide for the needs of the other settlements and still leave a healthy balance.
37. Ibid., p 330.
38. Ibid., pp 331–2.
39. Ibid., p 340.
40. Ibid., editor's comment, p xxxv.
41. KK Datta, p 45: Richard Becher to the Secret Committee of the Court of Directors, 24 May 1769.
42. Sutherland, p 137: quoting Charles Jenkinson, Secretary to the Treasury.

4. 'The Mind that Grasps at Such Wealth Must be Vicious'

1. Feiling, p 70.
2. Sinha, p 9: quoting the diary of Ananda Ranga Pillai.
3. Ibid., p 53: Select Committee Proceedings, 16 June 1767.
4. Ibid., p 69: Court of Directors to Fort St George, 13 May 1768.
5. Ibid., p 91.
6. Sheik Ali, p 144: Directors to Madras, 23 March 1770.
7. Sutherland, p 148: Luke Scrafton to Clive, 12 April 1766.
8. Ibid., p 222: quoting *The Last Journals of Horace Walpole*, vol I, p 72.
9. Macaulay, *Clive*, ii, p 120.
10. Marshall, *Fortunes*, p 156, quotation attributed to Mir Qasim.
11. Hotblack, p 96.
12. In 1760 there were as many soldiers as civilians in Madras, many of them belonging to king's regiments who had been sent out to reduce the army's reliance on sepoys.
13. Hotblack, p 87.
14. Sheik Ali, p 63: Directors to Fort St George, 13 May 1768.
15. Edwardes, p 58.
16. Sutherland, p 257: Sykes to Warren Hastings, 8 November 1773.
17. Edwardes, pp 63–4.
18. Feiling, p 57.
19. Ibid., p 75.

20. Moon, *Hastings*, p 115.
21. Feiling, p 103.
22. Moon, p 103.
23. Feiling, p 99. The governor-general to be was Sir John Shore.
24. Moon, p 105.
25. Guha, pp 60–89.
26. For an assessment of Francis and his opposition to Hastings, see Feiling, p 131.
27. Ibid., p 133.
28. SN Sen, *Relations*, p 48: Francis to Charles d'Oyley, 12 January 1775.
29. Feiling, pp 134, 138.
30. Moon, p 91.
31. Feiling, p 152: *Hastings* to Francis Sykes, 7 August 1775.
32. Guha, pp 17–19.
33. Moon, p 198.
34. 'Memoir Relative to the State of India, 1786' in Forrest, *State Papers*, ii, p 58.
35. KK Datta, p 65.
36. Gleig, i, pp 507–10: Memoir of 26 February 1775.
37. KK Datta, p 71: Hastings to Sir Alexander Eliot, 12 January 1772.
38. Sarkar, Jadunath: 'James Browne at the Delhi Court, 1783–5', in *Bengal Past & Present*, April-June, 1937.
39. He lived until 1806, once again an English pensioner after General Lake had delivered the death-blow to Maratha power at Delhi on 11 September 1803.
40. Spear, *Nabobs*, p 68, quoting T Grose, *A Voyage to the East Indies, 1774*, i, p 33. Even after the fish manure was banned in 1720, the fevers continued.
41. Graham, p 23.
42. Spear, *Nabobs*, p 71, quoting from *Representation of the Maratha Invasion of Portuguese Territory and the State of Bombay relating thereto*, para 42.
43. Parsons, p 216.
44. Kochhar, pp 39–45. The first Indian to be elected a Fellow of the Royal Society was Ardaseer Cursetjee, 1808–1877, son of a master builder in the Bombay dockyard. He played a prominent part in converting Bombay built ships to steam and became chief engineer and machine inspector in the Company's steam factory and foundry, a position that gave him an international reputation. He also pioneered the introduction of gas lighting to Bombay.
45. SN Sen, *Relations*, p 51: Supreme Council to the Council of Bombay, 31 May 1775.
46. Ibid., p 66: Upton to the Supreme Council, 2 February 1776.
47. Ibid., p 89: Mostyn to Hastings, 22 May 1778.
48. Moon, *Hastings*, p 205.

5. 'A Storm of Universal Fire'

1. Sheik Ali, p 4.
2. Sutherland, p 323.
3. Feiling, p 71.
4. Ibid., p 205.
5. Gleig, ii, pp 311–12: 27 August 1780.
6. SN Sen, p 153, *Relations*, quoting letter 1416.
7. Feiling, p 229, quoting Elijah Impey, 27 August 1779.
8. Sinha, p 191, from a French account of *The Campaign of Nabob Hyder Ali Khan*, 1780.
9. Ibid., p 191, quoting Philip Francis.

10. Shepherd, p 128.
11. Forrest, *State Papers*, ii, p 746.
12. Sinha, pp 194–5: Coote to Hastings, 25 January 1781.
13. Wilks, ii, p 373.
14. Barras, i, p 40.
15. SN Sen, *Relations*, p 196.
16. Feiling, p 230.
17. Richard Sheridan, completing his case for the Begums of Oudh in June 1780.
18. Colley, pp 102–3.
19. Edwardes, p 13.
20. Ibid., p 14.
21. Bearce, p 17, quoting Burke, *Works*, vol ix, p 362.
22. Colley, p 130.
23. Moon, *Hastings*, p 273.
24. Feiling, p 360.
25. Marshall, *Fortunes*, p 207: Hastings to S Droz, June 1782.
26. Sardesai, iii, pp 86–7.
27. Feiling, p 331.
28. Bayly, *Indian Society*, pp 42–3.
29. Sinha, pp 240–1: Munro's 'Report on The System of British Statesmanship in India', *Records of the Bellary District*, 10 April 1806.
30. Moon, *Hastings*, p 349.
31. Schweinitz, p 165.
32. Saletore, p 254. On 21 September 1785, the directors questioned possible double-payments to the families Clerici and Sperra, spinners of raw silk.
33. G Smith, pp 67–8.
34. Bayly, *Indian Society*, pp 124–5. Also KN Chaudhuri, pp 331–3, and Schweinitz, pp 157–9.
35. Bayly, *Rulers*, pp 108–9.
36. Marshall, *Fortunes*, p 147: Francis Sykes to Clive, 12 September 1768.
37. Ibid., 148: D Lillican to G Graham, 30 November 1775.
38. Spear, *Nabobs*, p 87.
39. Marshall, *Fortunes*, p 180.
40. Saletore, p 225: Council of Directors to Governor-General etc, 21 September 1785, para 6.
41. Ibid., p 257, para 13.
42. Ibid., p 208, para 32; Peers, p 47.
43. Ibid., p 251, para 25.
44. Marshall, *Fortunes*, pp 235–8. Fisher, p 14.

6. 'English Man, Very Good Man'

1. Heber, pp 31–2, 11 & 12 October 1823, makes the comparison with St Petersburg.
2. Roberts, i, p 8.
3. Spear, *Nabobs*, p 20.
4. Spence, pp 121, 129–31.
5. Keay, *Company*, p 349.
6. Bayly, *Indian Society*, p 116. Thereafter the China trade was through Hong Kong.
7. Fay, p 181: letter of 29 August 1780.
8. Eden, p 208: Ferozepur, 3 December 1838.
9. Roberts, i, p 60.

10. Eden, p 16: Dinapore, 9 November 1837.
11. Roberts, i, pp 31–41.
12. Lawrence & Woodiwiss, p 42.
13. Spear, *Nabobs*, pp 53, 73; Burton, pp 46–7. The slave trade but not slavery continued in India until abolition in 1824. Slaves who entered the country as slaves remained slaves. Arab traders from the Red Sea ports did a good line in black boys for pages or catamites, sometimes both, and girls for service in the zenana. The first Baptist missionaries reckoned there were as many as 9 million slaves in India in the first decade of the nineteenth century. G Smith, p 215. The Company in 1783 sought by decree to suppress the kidnapping of low caste children for sale as slaves outside India. Saletore, p 128: Directors to Governor-general, 10 September 1783, para 32.
14. Fay, p 180: letter from Calcutta, 29 August 1780.
15. *Hobson-Jobson*, entry for 'mehtar'.
16. Eden, p 253: Camp Soonair (Sanawar), 25 January 1839.
17. Sleeman, p 2.
18. Eden, p 93: Meerut, 12 February 1837.
19. Roberts, i, pp 102–3.
20. Ibid., p 55.
21. Mukherjee, p 8.
22. N Chaudhuri, *Clive*, p 119.
23. Forbes, ii, p 457.
24. Kindersley, p 132.
25. Sardesai, iii, p 148.
26. Sinha, p 215.
27. Longford, p 50: Letter to Richard Wellesley, 12 July 1797.
28. N Chaudhuri, *Clive*, p 335, quoting from Scrafton's *Reflections of the Government of Indostan*, 1763.
29. Mornay Williams, *Serampore Letters* (Calcutta 1892), 15 February 1794.
30. PC Gupta, p 185, quoting J Briggs, *Autobiographical Memoirs of the Early Life of Nana Phadnis*, p 52.
31. AW Lawrence, p 46, from *A Narrative of the Sufferings of James Bristow* (London 1794).
32. Fay, introduction by EM Forster, p 10 and p 110: letter of 12 February 1780.
33. Ibid., p 166–6: letter of 17 April 1780.
34. Marshall, *Hinduism*, 8, quoting Oeuvres Complètes de Voltaire (Paris 1877–85), vol xxix, p 166.
35. Mukherjee, p 15.
36. Marshall, *Hinduism*, p 29.
37. Feiling, p 236.
38. Ibid., p 236.
39. Gibbon, iii, footnote to Chapter xliv, on the Justinian Code, Section III.
40. Cannon, p 122, quoting from a pamphlet, *The Best Practicable System of Judicature*, that William Jones sent to Burke shortly after his arrival in Bengal.
41. Mukherjee, p 74.
42. Cannon, p 146.
43. Jones, ii, p 110: letter to Marquis Cornwallis, 19 March 1788.
44. Mukherjee, p 140.
45. Jones, ii, p 102: Letter to Thomas Caldicott, 27 September 1778; p 66: letter to John Macpherson, 1786.
46. Mukherjee, p 116: letter to Lord Althorp, 23 August 1787.
47. Though the works of William Jones were in University College library, Shelley and Southey more probably took their Indian inspiration from two popular works: *The*

Missionary, an Indian Tale, by Miss Owenson (Lady Morgan), 1811, and *Hindu Pantheon*, by Edward Moore, 1810, which were both much more accessible. The influence of both has been traced in Southey's *The Curse of Kehama* and in Shelley's *The Zucca*, and of Miss Owenson on Shelley's *Alastor*, *Epipsychidion*, *Prometheus Unbound* and *The Sensitive Plant*. SR Swaminathan, 'Possible Indian Influence on Shelley', in the *Bulletin of the Keats-Shelley Memorial Association*, no 9, 1958, pp 30–45. Leask, pp 102–3, analyses the effect of *The Missionary* on Shelley – he called it a 'divine thing' – as Lady Morgan propounded through her heroine, the Princess Luxima (closely based on Jones's translation of *Shakuntala*), a pure pantheistic Hinduism, freed from Brahmans, as a worthy companion to a Christianity, freed from Jesuits. For Leask, p 95, *Kehama* is steeped in the work of Jones.

48. Leask, pp 18, 70.
49. Jones, ii, p 126: letter to Lord Monboddo, 24 September 1783.
50. Mukherjee, p 120: letter to Robert Orme, 12 October 1786.
51. Jones, ii, p 41: letter to Lord Ashburton, 27 April 1783.
52. Chatterji, p 82.
53. See Shelley's preface to *Hellas*.
54. S Lane-Poole, 'Colebrooke', in the *Dictionary of National Biography* (Oxford 1975 ed.).
55. Colebrooke, ii, p 2.
56. G Smith, p 64, quoting Carey.
57. Srinivasachari, p 121: Directors to Governor in Council, 24 December 1776.
58. G Smith, p 55.
59. Morris, p 111.
60. *Life of the Rev. Thomas Coke LLD* (Leeds 1815), p 201.
61. Marshman, i, p 29.
62. G Smith, p 41.
63. Ibid., pp 52–3, quoting W Ward, *Farewell Letters on Returning to Bengal in 1821*.
64. Ibid., p 63.
65. Ibid. pp 96–7.
66. Page, p 17.
67. G Smith, p 275: Letter to the American Baptist General Convention, 25 January 1816.
68. Ibid., p 212.
69. VN Datta, *Sati*, pp 24–5, quoting the advice of the Acting Registrar of the Nizamat Adalat to the Secretary to Government, 5 December 1812, *Parliamentary Papers 1821*, xviii, pp 27–8.
70. Sydney Smith, pp 132, 137: *Indian Missions*.
71. G Smith, p 245, quoting the *Missionary Magazine of Edinburgh*, 1797.
72. Sydney Smith, p 135: *Indian Missions*.
73. G Smith, pp 253–5.
74. Stokes, p 31, from Wilberforce's address to the Commons, 22 June 1813.
75. Buchanan, *Works*, p 86.
76. Buchanan, *Establishments*, p 1.
77. Taylor, *Story of My Life*, pp 258–9.
78. Sleeman, p 337.
79. Bayly, *British Orientalism*, p 4.

7. 'We Must Go to the Orient'

1. Henry Dundas in the House of Commons, 14 April 1783.

2. Marshall, *Fortunes*, p 185. The Lord Lieutenant earned £30,000 a year but his personal expenses were greater than those of the governor-general.
3. Bayly, *Indian Society etc*, p 78, quoting WK Firminger, *Fifth Report from the Select Committee... on the Affairs of the East India Company* (Calcutta 1917) i, p 80.
4. Ray, pp 516–7. In 1799, Wellesley was able to raise ten million rupees for the war against Tipu at reasonable rates of interest because the lenders were sure of being repaid, p 518.
5. Mill, ed. Thomas, p 483, extracted from book vi, chapter 5.
6. Bayly, *Indian Society*, p 77.
7. Ehrmann, pp 455, 463.
8. Ibid., p 437, quoting from *Considerations on the Subject of a Treaty between Great Britain and Holland relative to the Interest in India*, October 1787.
9. Kincaid, p 133.
10. Woodruff, *Founders*, p 149.
11. His elevation in 1800 to the Marquisate of Wellesley, still in the peerage of Ireland, upset him greatly and even, he claimed, affected his health. The King could have done better for the man who had rid India of Tipu and the menace of the French. Ingram, *Two Views*, p 306: Wellesley to Dundas, 12 November 1800.
12. Words attributed to Napoleon Buonaparte by Fauvelet de Bourrienne, *Mémoires*, iv, p 236.
13. Losty, p 76, quoting Valentia, *Voyages and Travels in India*.
14. Hickey, iv, p 236.
15. Losty, p 75, quoting Tom Raw.
16. Heber, i, p 34: 22 October 1824.
17. Pearce, i, p 15: Parliamentary debate on Irish Affairs, 1787.
18. Ingram, *Two Views*, p 201: Mornington to Dundas, 26 October 1799.
19. Ibid., p 282: Wellesley to Dundas, 10 August 1800.
20. Ibid., p 287: Dundas to Wellesley, 4 September 1800.
21. Ibid., pp 315–6: Dundas to Wellesley, 30 December 1800.
22. Ibid., p 282: Wellesley to Dundas, 10 August 1800.
23. Ibid., p 287: Dundas to Wellesley, 4 September 1800.
24. Ibid., pp 315–6: Dundas to Wellesley, 30 December 1800.
25. Malleson, *French Struggles*, p 244.
26. SP Sen, *1763–1816*, p 553: Wellesley to the Secret Department, 12 August 1797.
27. Herold, p 16, quoting *La Corréspondance de l'Armée Française en Egypte* (Paris, Year VII, XXIX), p 430.
28. *Memoirs of the Late War in Asia* were published in 1794, being the accounts of a private in the Bengal army, and of an officer in the Madras army. In 1929 these were republished as *Captives of Tipu*, ed. AW Lawrence, to which was added the account of James Scurry, an ordinary seaman on *HMS Hannibal*, handed over to Haidar by Suffren, aged 14. He was nine years in captivity, 'Mahommedanised', compulsorily married to another 'Mahommedanised' captive, a child bride from Arcot, by whom he had two children and was so considered to have exempted himself from the exchange of prisoners in 1784. Another and possibly truer view of their treatment and the disposition of Tipu can be found in Hassan, pp 392–5.
29. Misra, p 41: J Duncan to the Secret Committee, Bombay, 21 June 1799, quoting Napoleon's promise to Tipu.
30. The words are those of John Keats. He saw the tiger on display in Leadenhall Street and wove the image into his faery poem, *Cap and Bells*. The tiger was an obsession with Tipu. His father's name meant tiger, the tiger motif was constant in his furniture and design, and his troops were dressed in a tiger-striped uniform. Archer, p 5.

31. SP Sen, *1763–1816*, p 43: Wellesley to General Lake, 8 July 1803.
32. Misra, p 85: Loustanau's plan for an invasion of India, 3 August 1803.
33. S Smith, p 251, quoting TD Broughton, 'Letters written in a Maratha Camp during the Year 1809', in *Edinburgh Review*, 1813.
34. Sardesai, iii, p 384.
35. Kaye, *Malcolm*, i, p 305.
36. Mill (1858), vi, p 465.
37. Sardesai, iii, p 424.
38. Hinde, p 110.
39. Ibid., p 114: Castlereagh to Wellesley, 21 May 1804.
40. Ibid., p 115: Wellesley to Lord Grenville, 30 June 1806.
41. Ingram, *Wellington*, p 12. Ingram holds that it was Wellington's preoccupation with India's security as an Asian power which led to the 'Great Game', in which Russia and British India played for influence and trade in central Asia.
42. Gupta, p 83.
43. TE Colebrook, ii, p 41.
44. Sardesai, iii, p 514.
45. Ray, p 517.
46. Gupta, p 94.
47. Bayly, *Imperial Meridian*, p 4.
48. Ingram, *Two Views*, p 312: Wellesley to Dundas 12 November 1800.
49. Ibid., p 322: Dundas to Wellesley, 30 December 1800.
50. Rosselli, p 168: 12 May 1812.
51. Philips, *Bentinck*, i, p 311; Rosselli, p 182: Macaulay to Margaret Cropper, 27 June 1834.
52. Peers, pp 54, 65.
53. Stokes, p 11. After storming Gawilgarh during Wellington's Assaye campaign, Mounstuart Elphinstone spent the evening discussing these poets in his tent.
54. Heber, ii, pp 385, 499.
55. Beaglehole, p 96, quoting Robert Rickards to the House of Commons, 2 June 1813, during the debate on the renewal of the Company's charter.
56. Ibid., p 76: Munro to William Petrie, 22 May 1805.
57. Ibid., p 8: Munro to the Board of Revenue, 15 August 1807.
58. Sleeman, p 3.
59. Bearce, p 125: quoting Munro's evidence to the Parliamentary Commission on the Charter, 12 April 1813.
60. Gleig, *Munro*, ii, p 87: Munro to Canning, 20 June 1821.
61. TE Colebrooke, ii, p 124.
62. Ibid., ii, p 68.
63. Peers, pp 53, 11.
64. Ibid., p 31, quoting Strachey to Elphinstone, 13 November 1823.
65. Mill, ed. Thomas, p 224, from Book 2, chapter 9.
66. Ibid., p 33, from Book 2, chapter 1.
67. Ibid., p 48, from Book 2, chapter 2.
68. Ibid., p 200, from Book 2, chapter 9.
69. Ibid., p 163, from Book 2, chapter 65.
70. Ibid., pp 225, 236, from Book 2, chapter 10.
71. Ibid., p xxxix, W Thomas from the introduction.
72. Ibid., p 248, from Book 2, chapter 10. Colebrook's claim was made in a discourse to the Royal Asiatick Society of Great Britain & Ireland, published in *Miscellaneous Essays* (London, 2 vols, 1837) i, p 1.
73. HH Wilson, introduction to his edition of Mill's *History* (London 1858), pp viii–xx.

74. VN Datta, *Elphinstone*, asserts that Elphinstone realised that he could not write narrative history to rival Macaulay whose essays on Clive and Hastings discouraged him from taking his *The Rise of British Power in the East* beyond the grant of the diwani of Bengal. He had started it with the intention of presenting a different version from Mill's but, in the end, he had to agree with Mill's general criticisms of Clive and Hastings. In his *History of India (The Hindu and Muhammedan Periods)* he was able to correct some of Mill's grosser errors and moderate some of his more contemptuous judgements.

8. 'Our Empire seems Destined to be Short-lived'

1. McCulloch, p 365.
2. Macaulay, *Works*, 8 (London 1897), viii, p 141. See also Stokes, p 43.
3. Sleeman, pp 413–4.
4. Rosselli, pp 196–7, quoting a minute of 30 May 1829.
5. Law, ii, p 51: 17 June 1829. Ellenborough was then Lord Privy Seal in the Wellington administration; in 1830 he was President of the Board of Control.
6. Ibid., i, p 273: 11 December 1825.
7. Losty, p 105, quoting Jacquemont.
8. Rosselli, pp 105–6.
9. *Hansard*, xix, pp 523–6: Macaulay's speech to the House of Commons, 10 July 1833.
10. VN Datta, *Sati*, pp 91–2: Bentinck to William Astell, 12 January 1829.
11. Ibid., p 249. Bentinck's minute on suttee.
12. Rosselli, p 202.
13. Ibid., p 193.
14. GO Trevelyan, *Macaulay*, i, p 237: Letter to Hannah and Margaret Macaulay, Bath, 10 June 1832.
15. Ibid., i, p 343: Macaulay to Thomas Flower Ellis, Ootacamund, 1 July 1834.
16. Mill, ed. Thomas, pp 539, 549.
17. Macaulay, *Works*, vol viii, p 139: Speech to the House of Commons, 10 July 1833.
18. Macaulay, *Works*, vol vii, pp 502, 514; 'The Indian Penal Code, On Offenses against the Body'; p 519 'On Offences against Property'. GO Trevelyan, *Macaulay*, i, p 384.
19. Stokes, p 199: Macaulay's minute of 2 May 1835.
20. Rosselli, p 222.
21. GO Trevelyan, *Macaulay*, i, pp 385–6.
22. Rosselli, p 216.
23. Serampore College, founded in 1821, was licensed by Frederick VI of Denmark to award degrees, and offered courses in Hebrew, Greek, Latin, Bengali, Mathematics, Chemistry, Mental Philosophy, and Ancient and Ecclesiastical History. In 1834, the year of Carey's death, the student body comprised 34 Brahmans, 48 native Christians and 10 of mixed race. G Smith, p 288.
24. GO Trevelyan, i, pp 371–2: Minute on Education, 2 February 1835.
25. Kopf, p 248: Resolution in Council, 7 March 1835.
26. Ibid., p 352, quoting Brian Hodgson, former resident in Nepal, *The Pre-eminence of the Vernaculars – the Anglicists Answered*, Serampore Papers 1847, vol xxx, p 4.
27. Ibid., p 238.
28. *General Proceedings of the Governor-General in Council*, xiii, 11 October 1853, p 101. In 1805 George Canning, as President of the Board of Control, had approved plans for the establishment of a preparatory college at Haileybury where aspirant civil servants would spend two years, before topping up their language proficiency at Fort William College. Wellesley's university of the east was demoted to a language school.

29. Viswanathan, p 75, quoting the evidence of the Rev W Keane to Parliament in 1852.
30. Ghose, p 434.
31. As described by a Company servant in *The Friend of India*, Calcutta, 22 August 1839.
32. Sleeman, p 321.
33. VN Datta, *Sati*, p 97, quoting WH McNaghten, then Registrar of the Sadr Diwani Adalat, West Bengal.
34. Peers, p 111, quoting, first, Henry Spry, 20 January 1830, and, second, JC Marshman in the *Calcutta Review*, 1844.
35. From the inscription on the statue of Bentinck originally in the grounds of the Victoria Memorial, Calcutta.
36. Mahajan, *Grand India Tour*, p 23.
37. Mahajan, *Picturesque India*, p 27, quoting the Daniells's description of 'The View on the Ram-Gunga between Buddell and Bilkate' in *Oriental Scenery*. Also Pal & Dehejia, pp 42–4.
38. Mahajan, *Picturesque India*, p 133.
39. Johnson, ii, pp 1025, 1070.
40. Mahajan, *Picturesque India*, pp 127–8.
41. Keay, *India Discovered*, pp 43–4.
42. VN Datta, *Sati*, pp 121, 127.
43. ST Coleridge, *The Collected Letters* (ed. C Coburn, New York/London 1976), vol 4, p 97. Kopf, pp 196–202.
44. Ray, p 524.
45. Rosselli, p 224. Cf Kopf, p 27.
46. E Roberts, i, pp 296–323.
47. Eden, p 59: Cawnpore, 28 December 1837.
48. *Hobson-Jobson*, pp 915–6.
49. Bayly, *Information*, pp 173–6, takes the view that 'thuggee' was simple crime, dressed up to be something sinister and oriental by its suppressors.
50. Tuker, p 89.
51. Ibid., p 108.
52. Ibid., p 120.
53. Metcalf, *Land*, pp 32–7.
54. Tuker, p 174.
55. Sleeman, p 186.
56. Taylor, *Seeta*, chapter 50.
57. Taylor, *My Life*, p 127.
58. Ibid., p 138.
59. Ibid., p 292.
60. Ibid., p 370, from the Maratha address to Taylor, Darassao District, 27 August 1857.
61. Ibid., p 464.
62. Heber, ii, p 344.
63. Bayly, *Imperial Meridian*, pp 209–210.
64. Mill (1858), v, p 466, quoting Sir Henry Strachey: 'The crime of dacoity has, I believe, increased greatly since the British administration of justice'.
65. Sleeman, p 280.

9. 'Why... Deprive Me of my Poor & Barren Country?'

1. Peers, p 64, quoting a report of 1820/1.
2. Sleeman, pp 615–20.
3. Peers, p 95, quoting from WD Arnold, *Oakfield or Fellowship in the East* (1854).

4. Jacquemont (Philips), p 26: to M de Melay, October 1829.
5. Ram, p 37.
6. Sleeman, p 639.
7. Trotter, *Hodson*, p 82, on the battle of Chilianwala, 13 January 1849.
8. Vibart, p 154. Also Collister, p 5.
9. Bingle, p 145.
10. Boulger, p 177: minute of 12 March 1835.
11. VN Datta, *Sati*, p 85. Also Bayly, *Imperial Meridian*, p10.
12. Malcolm, ii, p 76.
13. Trotter, *Hodson*, p 140: William to the Rev George Hodson, April 1857.
14. Ram, pp 49–50.
15. Trotter, *Hodson*, p 194.
16. GO Trevelyan, *Macaulay*, i, p 336.
17. Warner, p 1.
18. Eden, pp 293–4: letter of 25 May 1839.
19. Ram, p 115.
20. Lambrick, p 60.
21. C Napier, ii, p 188.
22. Ibid., ii, p 297.
23. P Napier, p 268.
24. Lambrick, p 21.
25. Eden, pp 198, 209: letters of 28 November and 3 December 1838.
26. Jacquemont, ii, p 179: Letters of 8 October and 26 December 1831 to his father and of 15 December to Prosper Merimée. Ranjit Singh received Lord Auckland with both feet stockinged, but he soon removed one so that he could cradle his bare foot in his hand most comfortably.
27. Cunningham, p 185: Captain Wade to government, 11 January 1837.
28. Eden, p 209: letter of 6 December 1838.
29. Jacquemont, ii, p 222: letter of 15 December 1831 to Prosper Merimée.
30. Of the 96,000 British troops committed to the Crimea between 1854 and 1856, 2,755 were killed in action and 11,848 died of their wounds. A Ramm, 'The Crimean War' in *The New Cambridge Modern History*, vol x (Cambridge 1960), p 485. British killed in the battles of the first Sikh war were: Mukdi, 18 December 1845, 215; Ferozeshah, 22 December, 694; Aliwal, 28 January 1846, 151; Sobraon, 10 February 1846, 320. Cunningham, pp 265, 268, 277, 285. The losses at Chilianwala were nearly the equal to those killed in battle in the whole Crimean War.
31. Ram, p 143.
32. George Meredith, *Chilllianwalla*, opening verse.
33. Bearce, p 202.
34. HB Smith, p 130.
35. Stokes, p 257.
36. Cunningham, p 279.
37. Ibid., pp 291–4.
38. Heber, pp 30, 310: 31 December 1824.
39. Eden, pp 97–8: 20 February 1838.
40. Sleeman, p 307.
41. Stokes, p 153, quoting an undated minute of 1831/2.
42. Sleeman, pp 545–50.
43. Bearce, p 209, quoting a private letter of 4 December 1852.
44. James Thomason (1804–53) had come to India from Haileybury in 1822, and was appointed Lieutenant Governor of the North-West Province in 1843, holding the

post until his death. His rule was remarkable for the clarity and thoroughness of his instructions to his settlement officers and collectors, which combined care for the farmer with the interests of government and persisted as a model to field officers through the post-Mutiny years. He was the strongest advocate of the Ganges canal project, which Ellenborough, who appointed him, resisted and which was only carried out, to the immense benefit of the Panjab, after his death.

45. Metcalf, *Land*, pp 169–70. A total of 9,000 out of 23,000 villages were removed from taluqdari control.
46. Ibid., p 176: 31 March 1858.
47. Henry and Honoria Lawrence did not neglect secular literature and tried to keep to a language learning schedule of Hindostani and Italian, the latter by reading Ariosto. Lawrence & Woodiwiss, p 100. The Rev Thomas Malthus was appointed Professor of Political Economy at Haileybury in 1805.
48. HB Smith, p 39, quoting his assistant, Charles Raikes.
49. Ibid., p 43.
50. Ibid., p 40.
51. Lady Edwardes, i, p 58.
52. VN Datta, *Sati*, p 169.
53. Smith, p 313.
54. Ibid., pp 313–4.
55. Ibid., pp 351–2.
56. Trotter, *Nicholson*, p 344.
57. Jacquemont, (Philips), p 102: letter to his father, Simla, 21 June 1830.
58. Trotter, *Hodson*, p 36.
59. The fracas in which Shelley, Byron, Trelawny and Taaffe were involved outside Pisa on 24 March 1822, was an example of English racial superiority coming into conflict with Italian resentment. The behaviour of the two poets was instinctive, but at the time Shelley's cousin, Tom Medwin, late of the East India Company, had just joined Shelley's Paradise of Exiles and Retreat of Pariahs. R Holmes, *Shelley, the Pursuit* (London 1974), pp 706–8.
60. GO Trevelyan, *Cawnpore*, p 31.
61. Stokes, 252.
62. Ibid., p 253: evidence to Parliament, 7 July 1853.
63. Lawrence & Woodiwiss, p 220.
64. Stokes, p 240, quoting the *Edinburgh Review*, 1841.

10. 'Europeans Cannot Retreat'

1. Bright, pp 1–17: 3 June 1853.
2. Kaye, *Mutiny*, iii, p 99.
3. Ahmad Khan, p 6.
4. SN Sen, *Eighteen Fifty Seven*, pp 92–3.
5. Kaye, *Mutiny*, iii, p 289.
6. *Aunt Liza's Story as told to Anne Parnis*, printed privately, Ibadan, 1958. I owe this story to Miss Elizabeth Parnis.
7. The chapatties which mysteriously appeared in the villages of northern India may have been antidotes to cholera of which there were increasingly frequent outbreaks. SN Sen, *Eighteen Fifty Seven*, pp 398–9. An alternative explanation was that they carried the message that all regiments were to mutiny on the same day, but the Meerut garrison jumped the gun. Kaye, *Mutiny*, ii, p 418.
8. Duff, p 587.

9. Viswanathan, p 53.
10. Ahmad Khan, p 25; SN Sen, *Eighteen Fifty Seven*, pp 9–10. Many government schools were staffed by missionaries who were identified as government servants. School inspectors, many of whom were Christians, were also believed to be native clergymen.
11. Ahmad Khan, p 11.
12. Ibid., p 18.
13. Ibid., pp 51–4.
14. For the 'passing and groundless panic', Kaye, *Mutiny*, i, p 418 and iii, p 235.
15. Ahmad Khan, p 9; SN Sen, *Eighteen Fifty Seven*, pp 13–4.
16. Taylor, *Life*, pp 345–7.
17. Ahmad Khan, pp 79–83, was confident that the fatwah was a forgery and the jihad therefore invalid. Muslims, moreover, tended to be less dedicated to their military career, more open to dissipation and impiety. Peers, p 90. They had fewer ideological grievances.
18. HB Smith, p 360: to Adjutant-General Norman, 24 July 1857.
19. SN Sen, *Eighteen Fifty Seven*, p 413.
20. The larger figure is almost certainly exaggerated. SN Sen, p 406, reckons that 70,000 troops were mutinous in North India and 30,000 loyal. Sickness and sunstroke were much the biggest killer. In 1858, of over 1,000 soldiers who died, only 100 died in battle. FS Roberts, p 226.
21. FS Roberts, p 132. The generals were George Anson, 60, died 27 May; Sir Henry Barnard, 58, died 5 July, both of cholera; Sir Thomas Reed, 61, retired 17 July, after handing over to Archdale Wilson. Barnard had come from the Crimea, 'no more fit' for his post than 'to be Pope of Rome'. Young, p 80.
22. SN Sen, *1857*, p 101. Flora Annie Steel's mutiny novel, *On the Face of the Water* (London 1896), describes the fortunes of a British spy within the sepoy-held city and the fate of an English woman in hiding.
23. HB Smith, p 318. Blowing from a gun was the usual penalty for mutiny. The mutineer's chest was secured to the muzzle of a light artillery piece and he was blown to pieces with a blank charge. Mutineers taken in battle were hanged. Among the more enthusiastic executioners were the 'villainous Afridis, Mohmunds and Eusofzies, men who had spent their lives in robbing and killing our subjects... delighted to pay off old scores upon the sepoys'. Ibid., p 313. To Lawrence's credit he counselled a relatively merciful approach, suggesting that no more than a third of the mutineers should be killed.
24. Kaye, *Mutiny*, ii, pp 216–26.
25. Forbes-Mitchell, p 100.
26. GO Trevelyan, *Cawnpore*, p 27. Charlotte Canning, writing to the queen on 9 April 1857, referred to the rumour that her husband, the governor-general, had signed a bond to make all Indians Christians within three years. Surtees, p 229. Robinson, p 142, suggests that 'every memsahib, in her more patriotic moments, conceived herself to be... Queen Victoria's ambassadress in India'.
27. Bayly, *Raj*, p 241, commentary by B Allen.
28. Robinson, pp 125–152, on the 'Cawnpore survivors'.
29. GO Trevelyan, *Cawnpore*, pp 20–21.
30. Forrest, *Mutiny*, ii, p 333: Colin Campbell to Lord Canning, 24 March 1858.
31. Yelland, p 10.
32. Bearce, pp 223–5.
33. Bright, p 28: 24 June 1858.
34. Yelland, p 39: report of Captain Herbert Bruce to James Outram, 12 September 1857.

35. Bearce, p 239, quoting *Parliamentary Papers*, 1857–8.
36. Ahmad Khan, p 14.
37. Quoted Metcalf, *Ideologies*, p 48.
38. Trevelyan, *Competition-Wallah*, Letter 10: 'Christianity in India', p 204. For numbers of converts, pp 186–7.
39. Surtees, p 172.
40. John Alexander Pitt, the author's great grandfather, in an unpublished letter from Calcutta to his grandmother, 25 September 1857, in the possession of the family.
41. GO Trevelyan, *Competition-Wallah*, Letter 9: 'British Temper Towards India', p 158.
42. Surtees, p 231.
43. Ibid., p 271: Queen to Charlotte Canning, 9 December 1859.
44. GO Trevelyan, *Competition-Wallah*, p 229, Letter 11: 'Education in India'.
45. St Aubyn, p 506.
46. Gopal, *Policy*, p 121: Lord Mayo to Sir Henry Durand, 29 April 1870.
47. Fisher, p 16. Muslims constituted about half of the officer rank of the native troops in the Bengal army and a third of the sepoys, a number which did not reflect their proportion of the general population. The British wished to replace the traditional purbiah with members of the 'more warlike tribes'.
48. Beames, pp 102–3.
49. Ibid., p 105.
50. GO Trevelyan, *Competition-Wallah*, Letter 9, p 168.
51. Gopal, *Policy*, p 55: Lawrence to Wood, 1 August 1865.
52. Lutyens, p 124: Lytton to General Strachey, 30 April 1878.
53. GO Trevelyan, *Competition-Wallah*, Letter 7: 'About Calcutta', 12 April 1863, p 109. HB Smith, *Lawrence*, p 482.
54. Buckland, i, p 281, quoting Sir John Strachey.
55. HB Smith, p 481.
56. Blunt, p xvii.
57. Morley, i, p 84.
58. Gopal, *Policy*, p 27: Lord Stanley to Sir Charles Wood, 8 December 1860.
59. Ibid., p 33: Sir Charles Wood to Sir Henry Maine, 19 February 1866.

11. 'The Great Chiefs and Landlords of India'

1. Maclagan, pp 180–91, for Canning's Oudh proclamation.
2. Metcalf, *Land*, p 221.
3. Ibid., p 296.
4. Ibid., p 228, quoting Sir Harcourt Butler, Deputy Commissioner of Lucknow, 6 July 1907.
5. Ibid., pp 229, quoting JP Hewett, Lieutenant-Governor of Oudh, 3 October 1907.
6. John Beames was suspended from his post in Bihar for imprisoning an old zamindar who was managing a gang of dacoits in Bihar, *Memoirs*, p 185. For contemporary goonda-ism, Peter Popham in the *Independent*, 14 February 1998.
7. HB Smith, p 487.
8. Valentia, i, p 137: 3 March 1803. The Company was esteemed an old lady with many grandsons, who came to India to be governor-general.
9. Ibid., i, p 100.
10. Ibid., i, pp 399, 359.
11. Macdonald, p 81.
12. Maclagan, p 271.

13. Nath, p 112.
14. Surtees, p 187: letter to Lady Canning from Windsor, 25 January 1865.
15. Nath, pp 108–9. Lutyens, pp 75–8, 105.
16. Prinsep, chapter 3. The significance of this sham mediaevalism in imposing a foreign monarch on a native gentry is discussed in Metcalf, *Ideologies*, pp 75–80.
17. Hurtig, p 28.
18. Nath, pp 112–6. WR Lawrence, pp 213–4.
19. Ross, p 28.
20. Lutyens, p 168.
21. Metcalf, *Land*, p 327, quoting an opinion in 1904 of the taluqdars' sons who attended Colvin College, Lucknow, founded to give a practical education and equip them to be good landlords and administrators.
22. EM Forster, *A Passage to India*, chapter 5.
23. WR Lawrence, p 200. Not all the princely minders were progressive. 'In the course of their twenty five years expatriation, members of the ICS (seconded to the service of princes) lost touch with the culture of change and became unduly concerned for stability at he expense of innovation.' Moore, p 430.
24. Wakefield, p 160.
25. Montagu, p 235: 31 January 1918.
26. Furbank, ii, p 77: Salisbury to Lytton, 7 June 1876.
27. Visram, pp 172–3.
28. Ibid., p 175: Curzon to Lord George Hamilton, 27 August 1902.
29. Gopal, *Policy*, p 253: Curzon to Governor of Madras, 14 July 1900.
30. Aldous Huxley, *Jesting Pilate* (Phoenix Library edition, London 1930), pp 141–2.
31. Wakefield, pp 208–18. By independence, all but three princes had settled their immediate future with one or other of the successor dominions. Only Junagadh, Hyderabad and Kashmir had not, the two first ruled by Muslim princes with a majority Hindu population and the third by a Hindu prince ruling a predominantly Muslim population. Pakistan eventual absorbed Janagadh, the Nizam of Hyderabad was frustrated from joining a state nearly a thousand miles distant, by a police action of doubtful legality, while the vale of Kashmir was secured by a military force, flown in by Nehru, when the Maharajah decided to adhere to India, an action with fateful consequences to this day.
32. HB Smith, p 532.
33. Gopal, *Policy*, p 70: Mayo to the British ambassador in St Petersburg, 14 December 1870.
34. Lutyens, p 11: Lytton to Lord Morley, 9 January 1876.
35. HB Smith, p 549.
36. Gopal, *Policy*, p 80: Lytton to Salisbury, 23 June 1877; Lutyens, p 169.
37. Magnus, p 264.
38. Gopal, *Policy*, p 137: Dufferin to Kimberley, 5 April.
39. Newton, p 106: to his mother, 19 January 1993.
40. Hunter, pp 145–6.
41. EF Knox, 'Border Manners'; Edmund Candler, 'Going North', two tales from *Blackwood Magazine*, in *Tales of the Outposts, Tales of the Border* (ed. Col. LA Bethell, Blackwood, Edinburgh 1936), pp 1–2, 53.
42. Webb, p 130: Peshawar, 4–6 March 1912.
43. Dunsterville, p 161.
44. R Kipling, 'The Head of the District' from *Life's Handicap*.
45. "Pousse Cailloux", 'Retaliation', in *Tales of the Border*, pp 173–4.
46. Beaton, p 23.

47. Dunsterville, pp 255–6.
48. Ibid., pp 288–9.

12. 'Worth Three Hundred a Year – Dead or Alive'

1. Gopal, *Policy*, p 35: Sir Charles Wood to Lord Elgin, 28 August 1862.
2. Beames, pp 63–4.
3. Woodruff, *Guardians*, p 28.
4. Beveridge, p 36.
5. Woodruff, *Guardians*, pp 156–8. Of the three, one, Romesh Chander Dutt, from 1871 to 1892, rose from Assistant Magistrate in Alipur to Commissioner for Orissa, and member of the Bengal Legislative Council. Of the other two, one was dismissed the service for allegedly deceiving his collector. In 1857 there were 163 covenanted civil servants in Bengal to 402 uncovenanted, and in the North West Province, 102 to 363.
6. Gopal, *Policy*, p 117: Salisbury to Lytton, 13 April 1877.
7. Brown, *Modern India*, p 146.
8. Crick, p 77.
9. Duncan, pp 134–5.
10. Bright, pp 48–50, addressing the House of Commons, 1 August 1959.
11. WR Lawrence, p 152.
12. Woolf, *Growing*, p 230.
13. Woolf, *Letters*, p 72: to Lytton Strachey, 8 January 1905.
14. Ibid., p 80: to Desmond MacCarthy, 26 February 1905.
15. Ibid., p 74: to Lytton Strachey, 23 January 1905.
16. Ibid., pp 76–6: to GE Moore, 5 February 1905.
17. Ibid., p 83: to Lytton Strachey, 14 March 1905.
18. Beames, p 225.
19. Woolf, *Letters*, p 73: to Lytton Strachey, Thai Pongal Day, January 1905.
20. Crick, p 88; G Orwell, *The Road to Wigan Pier*, pp 149, 143.
21. 'Shooting an Elephant', 1936, para 1. It appeared in *New Writing*, No 2, Autumn 1936.
22. Shelden, p 100.
23. 'Shooting an Elephant', para 2.
24. *The Listener*, 9 March 1938, reviewing Maurice Collis, *Trials in Burma*.
25. Orwell, *Essays*, ii, p 23.
26. Dewey, p 216, from *The Report of Commissioners [on] Certain Colleges & Schools*.
27. 7 May 1876, quoted by M Lutyens, *Lyttons*, p 44.
28. Maclagan, p 296.
29. Gopal, *Policy*, p 124: Chief of the Intelligence Department, 9 October 1876.
30. Philips, *Select Documents*, pp 105, 111: Robert Knight, editor the *Scotsman*, to Major Owen Burne, Lytton's private secretary, 31 July 1876; Lytton to Northbrook, 25 April 1878.
31. Ibid., p 169: Dufferin to the Queen, 31 March 1887.
32. Kipling, 'A Real Live City', 2 March 1888 in *From Sea to Sea* (London, 1910 ed., 2 vols), ii, p 205.
33. J Strachey, pp 58, 188.
34. Longford, *Blunt*, pp 203–4.
35. EM Forster, *A Passage to India*, chapter 3.
36. Gopal, *Policy*, p 167: Lord Cross to Dufferin, 3 February 1887.
37. Steevens, p 89.

38. Elliot, p 108, entry for 7 September 1915.
39. Wakefield, p 160.
40. Bingle, pp 143–163.
41. Hastings, p 67.
42. *Scinde, the Unhappy Valley* is sprinkled with words like 'catalepsed', 'graveolent', 'agnomen', 'confabulate', 'succedaneum', 'cachinatory' and 'vellication' in the very first chapters. In the *Kamasutra* he uses 'yoni' and 'lingam' to describe the receiving and received organs of congress. FM Brodie, pp 76, 296–8.
43. Francis Watson, 'Must we Burn Vatsayana?' *Encounter*, March 1964, p 70.
44. R Churchill: Exile in India, to his mother, 4 August 1896, p 288; on Anglo-Indians, to ditto, 4 October, p 297; on acquiring knowledge, to ditto, 14 April 1897, p 298; his political programme, to ditto 6 April 1897, p 318; on being prime minister, p 352; review of *Malakand Field Force* in the *Athenaeum*, p 381.
45. Ibid., p 422. Churchill was on home leave from the Nile campaign, before returning to finish his military service in India.
46. Throughout the Great War, Churchill's name continued to figure as a possible Viceroy when it was all over, and he was considered as a serious candidate to follow Hardinge, except that he found waging war from Whitehall too exciting to leave it.
47. WR Lawrence, p 178.
48. Dewey, p 43.
49. Ibid., pp 61–6: the Gurgaon experiment.
50. Forster, *Dickinson*, p 141: Letter to HO Meredith.
51. Furbank, ii, p 92n.
52. Dewey, p 151: letter to Arthur Cole, 9 January 1908.
53. Wakefield, p 19.
54. WR Lawrence, pp 39, 70.
55. Furbank, ii, pp 126–30.
56. Dewey, p 151.
57. Maclagan, p 292.
58. N Gupta, p 179, quoting Hardinge to Sir Malcolm Hailey, 28 July 1913.
59. Emily Lutyens, p 34.
60. M Lutyens, *Edwin Lutyens*, p 129.
61. Ibid., p 123.
62. Edwin Lutyens, p 251: 4 June 1912.
63. M Lutyens, *Edwin Lutyens*, p 199. Sir Swinton Jacob's *Portfolio of Indian Architectural Details*, appeared in 1890 was intended to be a cornucopia of designs for architects and patrons who wished to have a building in the 'Indo-Saracenic' mode. TR Metcalf, *Ideologies*, pp 158–9.
64. Edwin Lutyens, p 256.
65. Hussey, p 280.
66. Robert Byron, *Architectural Review*, 1931.
67. Byron, 'New Delhi', from *Country Life*, vol lxix (6 June 1931), p 710.
68. Elliot, p 133: 25 December 1915.
69. Ibid., p 162: 22 February 1916.
70. Kiernan, p 49, quoting a native of Bombay, *A Voice from India. An Appeal... by the Khojas of Bombay.*
71. A remark attributed by Neville Cardus to Ted Wainwright, *The Wisden Anthology*, ed. Benny Green (London 1979), p 5.
72. While preparing for entry to Cambridge, he was reputed to have scored three centuries in a single day's cricket on Parker's Piece, two for his own side, and the third in quite another game, in which one side was a man short. Ross, p 39.

73. Ibid., p 17, quoting *The World*.
74. Ibid., p 75.
75. Steevens, pp 264–5.
76. Montagu, p 4: 10 November 1917.
77. Judd, *Reading*, p 228.
78. E Roberts, i, p 103.
79. Montagu, p 204: 19 January 1918.
80. WR Lawrence, pp 75–6. A host who engaged to provide a cold weather tiger for a guest, like the viceroy, to shoot, spent considerably more, in the 1880s, than the usual £100 for every tiger 'brought to table'.
81. Dyson, p 121.
82. Duncan, p 40.
83. Ibid., p 186.
84. Ibid., p 198.
85. Newton, p 59: Lansdowne to his mother, 10 December 1888.
86. R Strachey, p 21.
87. Macmillan, p 122.
88. Ballhatchet, pp 96–8.
89. R Kipling, *Something of Myself* (1937 ed.) p 56. A Roberts, p 731. At the time that the Boer war was brewing, about half of the 72,000 British troops in India had had treatment for sexually transmitted diseases and there were seldom less than 3,000 under treatment at any one time and thus hors de combat.
90. Ballhatchet, p 139.
91. Ashby, p 49.
92. R Strachey, p 53.
93. Quoted by Vernède, p 103 from FA Steel's *Complete Indian Housekeeper and Cook*, (London 1988).
94. Jacob, pp 130, 150: Diary 4 July, 29 December 1898.
95. Macmillan, p 159. Lady Hailey, wife of the governor of the United Provinces of Agra and Oudh in the 1920s.
96. Dewey, p 214.
97. Jacob, p 103: Diary, 25 December 1897.
98. Webb, p 193: Poona 8/10 April 1912. It was a sentiment they shared with a later intellectual pilgrim in his own country, Nirad Chaudhuri, whose whole oeuvre is really a statement of this fact.
99. Ibid., p 222, *On the Homeward Sea*, 16–25 April 1912.
100. Beveridge, p 89: Annette to Fanny Ackroyd, 27 March 1873.
101. Ibid., p 91.
102. Ibid., p 248.
103. Gilbert, p 243.
104. Catherine Mayo and Moyca Newell claimed to have come to India to establish the truth for her American readers about British rule in India. Were 'the soulful, spiritual Indian people... being oppressed and bullied by the unimaginative, brutal beef-eating British, as was commonly believed in America, or were they not? They were afforded 'all courtesies' by the government machine, and the result clearly pleased the die-hard school of British imperialists. Garbett, p 12.

13. 'We Are pledged to India'

1. Alberigh-Mackay, p 3.
2. Gopal, *Policy*, p 147: Gladstone to Ripon, 24 November 1881.

3. Annette Beveridge, in Beveridge, p 228, quoting from her letter of 3 March 1883 to the *Englishman*.
4. Gopal, *Policy*, p 115: Salisbury to Lytton, 30 August 1876.
5. R Kipling, *Something of Myself* (London 1937 ed.), p 51.
6. On the Constitution of Local Boards, 18 May 1882 in Philips, *Select Documents*, p 41.
7. Sir James Fitzjames Stephen, Letter to *The Times*, 1 March 1883. He was merely echoing Lord Salisbury in June 1875 when he asserted to the governor of Bombay that 'India is held by the sword'. A Roberts, p 139.
8. Naoroji, pp 650–1. The Parsi Dadabhai Naoroji some time professor of Gujerati at University College, London, and director of his own cotton company in London, financed young Indians to take the civil service examinations in London. In 1875 he was elected to the municipal council of Bombay and in 1885 was appointed a member of the governor's legislative council. Three times president of the National Congress, he was a strong critic of British government, estimating that India annually remitted £30–40,000,000 to Britain, for the benefit of the poor of neither country but for the enrichment of the already rich.
9. Philips, *Select Documents*, p 41: Wood to Bartle Frere, member of Supreme Council, 18 August 1861.
10. R Kipling, 'The Sending of Dana Da', *The Week's News*, 11 February 1888.
11. Webb, p 20: 20 January 1912.
12. Steevens, p 21.
13. Brown, *Modern India*, p 80.
14. Mujeeb, p 531. Also Ray, pp 526–7.
15. Sadiq, p 2.
16. *The Times of India*, vol lxxix, No 14, 6 October 1906: Address by the Aga Khan to Lord Minto, 1 October 1906.
17. Hunter, p 183.
18. Webb, pp 28, 33: Allahabad, 11–16 January 1912.
19. Ibid., p 141: Lahore, 9 to 12 March 1912.
20. Gopal, *Policy*, pp 194–5: Crosthwaite to Lansdowne, 1 September 1993.
21. WR Lawrence, p 209.
22. Brown, *Modern India*, pp 101–2.
23. Judd, *Empire*, p 77.
24. Dilks, *Curzon*, i, pp 27–8.
25. D Gilmour, p 68, quoting from his diary.
26. Ibid., p 137: Queen Victoria to Lord Salisbury, 25 May 1898.
27. Ronaldshay, ii, p 27: Curzon to Sir Anthony Godley, India Office, 26 January 1899.
28. Gilmour, pp 156–7: Curzon on Sir Frederick Fryer, governor of Burma, and on Sir Anthony Macdonnell, governor of North West Provinces and Oudh, in a letter to Lord George Hastings, 18 July 1900.
29. Gopal, *Policy*, p 226: Curzon to Hamilton, 9 April 1902.
30. Curzon, *India*, i, pp 488–9.
31. Gilmour, p 168: Curzon to Hamilton, 11 June 1900. William Beveridge's father, who shared few of the British social attitudes of the day shared Curzon's dismissive attitude to Bengali babus. 'If they could only act half as well as they talk, there would be no need for us westerners to rule over them.' The lying witnesses and interminable pleaders sat 'like a nightmare on our souls'. Beveridge, pp 6, 175: letters to his future wife, Annette Ackroyd, 13 March 1873, 26 August 1979.
32. Goradia, pp 103, 156.
33. Visram, pp 174–5: Curzon to Hamilton, Secretary of State for India, 18 July 1900. The prince was the Rajah of Kapurthala.

34. Goradia, p 156: Curzon to Hamilton 29 August 1990.
35. Gilmour, p 135.
36. Gopal, *Policy*, p 225: Curzon to Balfour, 31 March 1901; Curzon, *Persia*, i, p 4.
37. Goradia, pp 85, 100.
38. Banerjea, p 161.
39. Gilmour, p 218: Curzon to Mary Curzon, 2 September 1901.
40. By 1905 Curzon had spent £120,000 an India's architectural heritage, half of it on Fatehpur Sikri and the Taj, and the annual budget for archaeology had risen by six times. He laid out the gardens that surround the latter, based on the original Mughal plans, so that the whole environs were returned to what they had been when Shahjahan ordered his wife's tomb. Dilks, *Achievement*, p 246.
41. Gilmour, p 245: Curzon to his wife, 5 April 1902.
42. The dress is now on display at Kedleston Hall.
43. Ibid., p 285: Curzon to Selborne, 23 January 1900. Between 1857 and 1914 there was nearly always a famine somewhere in India, some more serious than others. In 1876–8, it was estimated that half a million people died in famines and in Curzon's viceroyalty there were two major famines. Famine relief got more sophisticated as the century progressed but it was often defeated by the fatalism of Indians and their strict dietary laws. See Kipling's two part famine tale, *William the Conqueror*, 'The Gentlewoman', 1895/6.
44. Dilks, *Curzon*, i, pp 34–5.
45. Bipin Chander Pal, quoted by Goradia, p 184.
46. Gilmour, pp 342–3: Curzon's valedictory speech to the Bombay Byculla Club in 1905.
47. Dilks, *Curzon*, i, pp 64–5.
48. Dilks, *Curzon*, ii, pp 125–6, 182–4.
49. Esher, ii, p 124: entry for 6 December 1905.
50. Gopal, *Policy*, p 259: Curzon to the Lieut-Governor of the NW Province, 1 June 1900.
51. Since the Mutiny only two Europeans had been hanged for the murder of Indians, of whom some 84 had been unlawfully killed between 1880 and 1900. Dilks, *Curzon*, i, p 211.
52. Ibid., p 270: Curzon to Ampthill, 5 January 1904.
53. Kripalani, p 104.
54. Dilks, *Frustration*, p 257.
55. Gopal, *Policy*, p 395–6: 17 February 1904.
56. Ibid., p 297: Curzon to Godley, 9 April 1901.
57. WR Lawrence, p 234.
58. Dilks, *Curzon*, i, p 97.
59. Ibid., p 107: Curzon to Hamilton, 7 March 1901.
60. Ibid., p 261.
61. Jenkins, p 164.
62. Dilks, *Curzon*, ii, p 255. Moore, p 441.
63. Dilks, *Curzon*, i, p 255: Curzon to Edward VII, 10 September 1902.
64. Steevens, pp 368–9.
65. Dilks, *Curzon*, i, p 101: Queen Victoria to Curzon, 12 April, 1900.
66. Sir Henry Ponsonby, Queen's secretary, quoted in Queen Victoria, *Journal*, p 217.
67. Victoria, *Darling Child*, p 106.
68. St Aubyn, p 502.
69. Victoria, *Darling Child*, p 163.
70. Longford, *Victoria*, p 536.

71. Newton, p 90. The Secretary of State, Lord Cross, was convinced that 'Munshi tells her that there is in India the greatest devotion to herself, ... but at the same time distrust and dislike of the Government, and that the native chiefs think that the Residents are rude and overbearing.' To Lansdowne, 15 October 1991.
72. St Aubyn, p 506.
73. Gilmour, p 266.
74. Steevens, p 88.
75. Philips, *Select Documents*, pp 151–6: Reports of the Indian National Congress, 1885–1905.
76. R Elliot, *Journal*: 17 November 1905.
77. Ibid., entry for 17 November 1905.
78. Philips, *Select Documents*, p 75: J Morley to Minto, 15 June 1906.
79. Minto, p 147.
80. Philips, *Select Documents*, pp 76–9: Minto to Morley, 11 July and 4 November 1906.
81. Ibid., p 80. This opinion was certainly Morley's own, as he confessed to WR Lawrence, pp 293–4.
82. Lawrence, p 286.

14. 'We Are Marching to an Impossible Solution'

1. Ross, p 161.
2. Visram, p 119, quoting from *The Times History of the War*, p 350.
3. Asquith, p 360: 5 January 1915.
4. Visram, pp 129–30.
5. Asquith, p 423. Edwin Montagu, moreover, was dead against it.
6. Kitchener had hoped to succeed Hardinge while still in Egypt, before the Great War broke out. In 1915, when Lloyd George, disenchanted with his military competence, was demanding his removal, Asquith toyed with the idea of making him Viceroy of the East, with both India and Egypt in his belt. Magnus, *Kitchener*, p 451. Gilbert, p 602, quotes Curzon's belief that Kitchener's days as secretary of state for war were numbered and that he wished to save face by going to India as viceroy.
7. Philips, *Select Documents*, p 203: Report of the 32nd Indian National Congress, 26 December 1917.
8. Ibid., pp 264–5: Montagu's announcement, 20 August 1917.
9. Montagu, p 135: 22 December; p 123: 20 December 1917.
10. Charmley, p 94: Lloyd, Governor of Bombay, to Montagu, 30 April 1920.
11. Montagu, p 62: 27 November; p 66: 29 November and p 71: 30 November 1917.
12. Datta & Mittal, pp 116–7: Edwin Montagu on the disturbances in India, 22 May 1919.
13. Philips, *Select Documents*, p 208: from the Sedition Committee Report, Calcutta, 1918.
14. Rowland's colleagues on the Commission were the British Chief Justice of the Bombay High Court and an Indian judge of the Madras High Court, but no one representing the Calcutta High Court. As Bengal was where most of the unrest had been, this was immediately seized on as weakening the force of the report.
15. Datta & Mittal, p 98: report on the disturbances in Madras, 20 April 1919, by the Chief Secretary of the Madras Government to the Secretary of the Government of India in Delhi.
16. Montagu, p 207: 21 January 1918.
17. Brown, *Gandhi*, p 74.
18. Philips, *Select Documents*, p 216, quoting from *Young India*, November 1919. Shirer, pp 30–1.

19. Draper, p 187: evidence of JP Thompson to the Hunter Committee.
20. Datta & Mittal, i, p 18: Gandhi's satyagraha vow of 2 March 1919.
21. Nehru, p 386.
22. Montagu, p 136: 23 December 1917.
23. Webb, p 11: 4 January 1912, had found both the Member for Education in the Viceroy's Council, Sir Harcourt Butler, and the member for Agriculture agreed that more Indians must be admitted into the higher reaches of the Civil Service and the army, 'but they were not keen on it and they objected to any particular way of doing it'.
24. Charmley, p 82: Chelmsford to Montagu, 30 April 1920.
25. Judd, *Reading*, p 206: Reading to Montagu, 19 May 1921.
26. Ibid., p 208.
27. Ibid., p 223: Reading to Montagu, 24 November 1921.
28. Charmley, p 95: Lloyd to TE Lawrence, 26 August 1920. The legions appeared to be withdrawing from Egypt when, in August 1920, the British government was prepared to offer Egypt her independence.
29. Ibid., p 80: Blanche Lloyd's diary, 16 January 1919.
30. Ibid., p 81: Lloyd to ES Montagu, 26 February 1919.
31. Ibid., p 101: Reading to Montagu, 5 January 1922. Gandhi was genuinely appalled by the behaviour of his Bengal audience, who at the hartal in November 1921 to mark the arrival of the Prince of Wales, listened to his impassioned plea for non-violence but before the end of the day had erupted into riot.
32. Judd, *Reading*, p 207: Reading to Lloyd George, 4 May 1922, describing a meeting about a year earlier.
33. Montagu, p 315.
34. Waley, p 235.
35. Webb, pp 61–2: 4 February 1912.
36. Harris, pp 77, 83: Speech in the Commons, 2 December 1931.
37. Birkenhead, p 245.
38. Gilbert, p 356: *Daily Mail*, 16 November 1929.
39. Colonel George Lane-Fox, MP for Barkston Ash.
40. Fischer, p 293.
41. Gilbert, p 368: from a speech to a Conservative party meeting in the house of Lord Carson, 20 August 1930.
42. Birkenhead, p 286.
43. Gopal, *Irwin*, p 54, quoting a letter to Srinivas Sastri of 12 January 1930.
44. Gilbert, p 377: Speech to the Indian Empire Society at the Cannon Street Hotel, 12 December 1930.
45. Ibid., p 390: Speech to the West Essex Conservative Association, 23 February 1931.
46. Ibid., pp 398–9: Speech to the India Empire Society, 18 March 1931.
47. Brown, *Gandhi*, p 255: Willingdon to Samuel Hoare, 28 August 1931.
48. Ibid., p 262.
49. Quoted by Hodson, p 48.
50. Rizvi, p 73; Wilton, pp 339–40.
51. Nehru Papers, 10 January 1937 in Chopra, i, p 26; Rizvi, pp 93–4.
52. Philips, pp 370–1. Also Datta, *Azad*, p 165.
53. The resolution of the Muslim League at Lahore on 24 March 1940 referred to '"independent states" in which the constituent units shall be autonomous and sovereign'. At this stage it would accept a unified state whose constitution provided for these.
54. Gandhi, writing in *Harijan*, 24 May 1942.

55. Brown, *Gandhi*, p 322.
56. Datta, *Azad*, p 169.
57. Wavell, p 12: 27 July 1943.
58. Ibid., p 23: 8 October 1943. The words were Amery's.
59. Dilks, *Wider World, 1939–45*, p 5. Despite Churchill's claim to President Roosevelt in 1942 that 75 per cent of Indian troops were Muslims, they actually accounted for about 35 per cent of the total, Hindus being 41 per cent, Sikhs 10 per cent, Gurkhas $8^1/_2$ per cent and Others $5^1/_2$ per cent. Rizvi, p 176.
60. Brown, *Modern India*, p 326.
61. Wavell, pp 97–8: letter to Churchill, 24 October 1944.
62. Ibid., pp 107–8: 31 December 1944.
63. Brown, *Modern India*, p 354.
64. Wavell, p 79: 11 July 1944.
65. Harris, p 366: record of Wavell's conversation with the prime minister, 4 September 1945. Also Wavell, pp 169–70.
66. Wavell, p 279: 26 May 1946.
67. Datta, *Azad*, p 174.
68. Wavell, pp 453–4. Wavell believed that Krishna Menon in London and Congress politicians in India had been assiduous in accusing him of this to the secretary of state.
69. Ibid., p 387. Wavell's analysis was handed to Attlee on 3 December 1946.
70. Ibid., p 341: 27 August 1946, meeting with Nehru and Gandhi; p 347: 5 September, meeting with Sardar Patel.
71. Harris, p 372.
72. Harris, p 374, insists that the idea of a deadline was not Mountbatten's, as his entourage had seemed to imply. Cabinet had already decided on this before the post of viceroy was offered to Mountbatten on 18 December 1946. Wavell, p 417: 4 February 1947. Indeed Congress had already begun to see that a Jinnah-run constituent state within the union could only distract the government of India from its task of social reconstruction and reform, and was prepared to let it go. Moon, *Divide and Quit*, p 64.
73. Ibid., p 378.
74. Harris, p 378: Mountbatten's record of the meeting with Attlee and Stafford Cripps.
75. Ibid., p 380: Lords debate, 25/6 February 1947.
76. The House of Commons debate on 6 March.
77. Harris, p 385.

15. 'Crushed by English Poetry'

1. Rowntree, p 30.
2. HC Munro ("Saki"), *The Unbearable Bassington*, chapter xvi. Comus was dying in West Africa, where Munro never served.
3. Gopal, *Irwin*, p 5.
4. Rowntree, p 7.
5. Ibid., p 30.
6. *Burmese Days* (1949 ed.), p 41 and NC Chaudhuri, *Autobiography* dedicatory page.
7. NC Chaudhuri, *Thy Hand*, p xx.
8. Quoted by Amartya Sen, 'Tagore and his India', in Silvers & Epstein, p 105.
9. Chandra, pp 29–30, quoting a public lecture by Bharatendu Harishchandra (1850–1885), a rich banian's son from the North West Provinces in 1877; pp 52–3 quoting NL Dave (1833–6), architect of Gujerati literature.

10. Moon, *Divide and Quit*, pp 284–5.
11. Seal, p 249.
12. Brown, *Nehru*, quoting a speech in Chicago, 27 October 1949.
13. Chandra, p 7.
14. Ibid., p 163.
15. Washbrook, pp 412–5.
16. Muggeridge, *The Green Stick*, p 116.
17. A quotation taken from an article in *The Times*, 31 May 1994, by Professor A Wallace-Hadrill, Director of the British School at Rome.
18. Ashis Nandy, 'The Last Englishman to Rule India', from a review of *Nehru: A Trust with Destiny* by Stanley Wolpert, in the *London Review of Books*, 21 May 1998, p 14.
19. Recorded by James Cameron, in 'The Land of Chota Pegs and Tiffin' in the *Daily Telegraph Magazine*, 18 August 1967.
20. Anstey, p ix.
21. Chaudhuri, *Thy Hand*, p 731.
22. Kipling, 'The Head of the District', from *Life's Handicap* (London 1891).
23. Chaudhuri, *Thy Hand*, p 727.
24. Quoted by Thompson, p 265.
25. Mahasweta Sengupta, 'Liberating English Literature in a Post-Colonial Society', in Malik and Robb, pp 275, 283.
26. Muggeridge, *The Green Stick*, pp 106–7.
27. C Trevelyan, p 124.
28. Harish Trivedi, 'Reading English: Writing Hindi', in Joshi, pp 202–3.
29. Quoted by Premen Addy, 'A Hall of Mirrors', in Malik & Robb, pp 247, 253.
30. Pankaj Mishra, 'A New Nuclear India', in Silvers & Epstein, p 240, quoting a former Indian (Congress) prime minister, Narasimha Rao.
31. Quoted by Minette Marrin in the *Daily Telegraph*, 17 June 1999, from a BBC broadcast discussion on 15 June.
32. Speech on the India Bill to the House of Commons, 10 July 1833. Macaulay, *Works*, viii, p 143.
33. A Roy, in Silvers & Epstein, p xxiv.
34. R MacFarquhar, 'The Imprint of Empire', in Silvers & Epstein, pp 174–5.
35. Tharoor, *India*, p 266.
36. Jog, p 7. Indeed, over 50 years after Independence, Norman Davies, in his huge book on Europe (Oxford, 1996), deals with Britain's involvement with India in a few lines, representing in his judgement its importance in the scale of things European at the time.
37. Henry Newbolt, *A Ballad of John Nicholson*, verse 15, and last two lines.

BIBLIOGRAPHY

(All titles listed here are sources of quotations or judgements in the text)

Alberigh-Mackay, GR: *Twenty One Days in India* (London 1880)
Alam, Muzaffar: *The Crisis of Empire in Mughal and North India: Awadh and the Punjab, 1707–48* (Delhi 1986)
Anstey, F: *Baboo Jabberbee BA* (London nd *c*.1920)
Archer, M: *Tippoo's Tiger* (London 1959)
Ashby, Lilian: *My India* (London 1938)
Asquith, HH: *Letters to Venetia Stanley* (Oxford 1985)
Ballhatchet, K: *Race, Sex and Class under the Raj: Imperial Attitudes and Policies and their Critics, 1793–1905* (London 1980)
Banerjea, SN: *A Nation in the Making* (Oxford 1925)
Barras, Paul de: *Memoires* (trans. CE Roche, 2 vols, London 1895)
Bayly, CA: 'British Orientalism and the Indian "National Tradition", *c*1780–1820', in *South Asia Research*, vol 14, no 1, Spring 1994
— *Empire and Information: Intelligence Gathering and Social Communication in India, 1780–1870* (Cambridge 1996)
— *Imperial Meridian* (London 1989)
— *Indian Society and the Making of the British Empire* (Cambridge 1988)
— *Rulers, Townsmen and Bazaars* (Cambridge 1983)
— ed., *The Raj: India and the British, 1600–1947* (London 1950)
Beaglehole, TH: *Thomas Munro and the Development of Administrative Policy in Madras, 1792–1818* (Cambridge 1966)
Beames, J: *Memoirs of a Bengal Civilian* (London 1961)
Bearce, G: *British Attitudes towards India, 1784–1858* (Cambridge 1961)
Beaton, C: *Indian Diary and Album* (Oxford 1991)
Bence-Jones, M: *Clive of India* (London 1953)
Beveridge,WH: *India Called Them* (London 1947)
Bingle, RJ: 'Henry Yule' in *Compassing the Vaste Globe of the Earth, Studies in the History of the Hakluyt Society, 1846–1996* (Cambridge 1996)
Birkenhead, The Earl of: *Halifax* (London 1965)
Blunt, WS: *Ideas on India* (London 1885)
Boulger, D: *Lord William Bentinck* (London 1897)
Boxer, CR: *The Dutch Seaborne Empire, 1600–1800* (London 1965)
— *The Portuguese Seaborne Empire, 1415–1825* (London 1969)
Bright, John: *Speeches on Questions of Public Policy* (London 1869)
Brodie, FM: *The Devil Drives, a Life of Sir Richard Burton* (New York 1967)
Brown, JM: *Gandhi, Prisoner of Hope* (London and Yale 1989)
— *Modern India* (London 1994)
— *Nehru* (London 1999)
Buchanan, C: *Works* (Boston 1811)
— *Colonial Ecclesiastical Establishments* (London 1813)
Buckland, CE: *Bengal under the Lieutenant-Governors* (2 vols, London 1901)

Burton, D: *The Raj at Table* (London 1993)

Cannon, G: *Oriental Jones* (New Delhi 1964)

Chandra, S: *The Oppressive Present: Literature and Social Consciousness in Colonial India* (Oxford and India 1992)

Charmley, J: *Lord Lloyd and the Decline of the British Empire* (London 1987)

Chatterji, SK: *Sir William Jones* (Calcutta 1948)

Chaudhuri, KN: *The Trading World of Asia and the English East India Company, 1660–1770* (Cambridge 1978)

Chaudhuri, Nirad C: *Autobiography of an Unknown Indian* (London 1951)

— *Clive of India* (London 1975)

— *Thy Hand, Great Anarch! India 1921–52* (London 1987)

Chopra, PN: ed., *Towards Freedom 1937–47* (New Delhi 1985)

Churchill, Randolph S: *Winston Churchill: Youth, 1874–1900* (London 1966)

Cipolla, C: *Guns and Sails in the Early Phase of European Expansion, 1400–1700* (London 1965)

Colebrooke, HT: *Miscellaneous Essays* (2 vols, London 1837)

Colebrook, TE: *The Life of the Honourable Mountstuart Elphinstone* (2 vols, London 1824)

Colley, L: *Britons, Forging the Nation, 1707–37* (Yale 1992)

Collister, P: *Hellfire Jack VC: General Sir William Olpherts, 1822–1902* (London 1989)

Crick, B: *George Orwell, a Life* (London 1980)

Cunningham, JD: *The History of the Sikhs* (ed. HLO Garret, 1915 ed., New Delhi 1966)

Curzon, GN: *Persia and the Persian Question* (2 vols, London 1889)

— *Lord Curzon in India* (London 1906)

Datta, KK: *Shah Alam II and the East India Company* (Calcutta 1965)

Datta, VN: *Maulana Azad* (New Delhi 1990)

— *Sati: Widow Burning in India* (New Delhi 1988)

— and Mittal, SC: *Sources on the Indian National Movement*, vol 1 (New Delhi 1985)

— 'Elphinstone', in *Sonderdruck aus Kunwar Mohammad Ashraf: an Indian Scholar and Revolutionary, 1903–1962* (Berlin 1969) pp 182–4

Dewey, C: *Anglo-Indian Attitudes* (London 1993)

Dilks, D: *Curzon in India*, Volume I: 'Achievement' (London 1969)

— *Curzon in India*, Volume II: 'Frustration' (London 1970)

— *Great Britain, the Commonwealth and the Wider World, 1939–45* (University of Hull 1998)

Draper, A: *Amritsar* (London 1981)

Duff, A: *India and the Indian Missions* (Edinburgh 1839)

Duncan, Sara Jeanette: *The Simple Adventures of a Memsahib* (London 1893)

Dunsterville, LC: *Stalkey's Reminiscences* (London 1928)

Dyson, CC: *From a Punjaub Pomegranate Grove* (London 1913)

Eden, E: *Up the Country* (Oxford 1930)

Edwardes, Lady: *Memorial of the Life of Sir Herbert Edwardes* (2 vols, London 1886)

Edwardes, M: *The Nabobs at Home* (London 1991)

Ehrmann, J: *The Younger Pitt: The Years of Acclaim* (London 1969)

Elliot, Ruby: *Letters and Second Indian Journal, 1886–1961* (Privately published, York 1995)

— *Indian Journal, 1905–1906* (ed. M Walker, privately printed, nd)

Esher, Lord: *Journals and Letters* (2 vols, London 1934)

Evelyn, J: *Diaries* (Everyman Edition)

Fay, E: *Original Letters from India, 1779–1815* (ed. EM Forster, London 1980)

Feiling, K: *Warren Hastings* (London 1954)

Fischer, L: *The Life of Mahatma Gandhi* (London 1957)

Fisher, H: *The Travels of Dean Mahomet: an 18th Century Journey through India* (Berkeley 1997)

Forbes, J: *Oriental Memoirs* (4 vols, London 1813–5)

Forbes-Mitchell, W: *The Relief of Lucknow* (ed. M Edwardes, London 1962)

Forrest, GW: *The Life of Lord Clive* (2 vols, London 1910)

— *A History of the Indian Mutiny* (2 vols, Edinburgh 1904–12)

— *Selections from the State Papers of the Governors-general of India: Warren Hastings* (2 vols, Oxford 1910)

Forster, EM: *Goldsworthy Lowes Dickinson* (London 1934, ed. of 1962)

Foster, Sir W: ed., *The Embassy of Sir Thomas Roe to the Court of the Great Mogul, 1615–19* (London, for the Hakluyt Society, 1899, 1926 reissue)

— ed., *The Voyage of Sir Henry Middleton to the Moluccas, 1604–6* (Cambridge, for the Hakluyt Society, second series, vol 88, 1943)

— 'The East India Company, 1600–1740' in *The Cambridge History of India* (New Delhi ed. 1963)

Fox Bourne, HR: *English Merchants* (London 1886)

Furbank, PN: *EM Forster, a Life* (2 vols, London 1978)

Garbett, C: *Friend of Friend* (Oxford 1943)

Ghose, GC: *They Hate us Youth: Selections from his Writings* (ed. MK Ghose, Calcutta 1912)

Gibbon, E: *The Decline and Fall of the Roman Empire* (Everyman Edition)

Gilbert, M: *Winston S Churchill, 1922–1939* (London 1976)

Gilmour, D: *Lord Curzon* (London 1994)

Gleig, GR: *Memoirs of Warren Hastings* (3 vols, London 1841)

— *Life of Munro* (3 vols, London 1830)

Gopal, S: *British Policy in India, 1858–1905* (Cambridge 1965)

— *The Viceroyalty of Lord Irwin, 1926–31* (Oxford 1957)

Goradia, N: *Lord Curzon, the Last of the British Moghuls* (Delhi 1993)

Graham, M: *Journal of a Residence in India, 1809–1811* (London 1813)

Guha, R: *A Rule of Property for Bengal: an Essay on the Idea of the Permanent Settlement* (New Delhi 1981)

Gupta, N: *Delhi between Two Empires, 1803–1931* (Oxford and India 1998)

Gupta, PC: *Bajirao II and the East India Company, 1776–1818* (Bombay 1964)

Hakluyt, R: *Voyages* (Everyman Edition)

Harris, K: *Attlee* (London 1982)

Harrison, JB: *India in the Muslim Period* (Oxford History of India, 1958 ed.)

Hassan, M: *History of Tipu Sultan* (Calcutta 1971)

Hastings, M: *Sir Richard Burton* (London 1978)

Heber, R: *Indian Journal* (2 vols, London 1844)

Herold, JC: *Bonaparte in Egypt* (London 1963)

Hickey, William: *Memoirs, 1749–75* (ed. A Spencer, ninth ed., 4 vols, London nd)

Hinde, W: *Castlereagh* (London 1981)

Hodson, HV: *The Great Divide, Britain – India – Pakistan* (London 1969)

Hotblack, K: *Chatham's Colonial Policy* (London 1917, reprinted 1980)

Hunter, WW: *The Indian Mussalmans* (London 1871)

Hurtig, C: *Les Maharajahs et la politique dans l'Inde Contemporaine* (Paris 1988)

Hussey, C: *Edwin Lutyens* (London 1950)

Ingram, E: ed., *Two Views of British India: the Private Correspondence of Mr Dundas and Lord Wellesley, 1798–1801* (Bath 1969)

— 'Wellington and India' in *Wellington, Studies in the Military and Political Career of the First Duke of Wellington*, ed. N Gash (Manchester 1990)

Jacob, V: *Diaries and Letters from India, 1895–1900* (Edinburgh 1990)

Jacquemont, V: *Voyage dans l'Inde pendant les années 1828–32* (Paris 1841/4)

— *Letters from India... during the Years 1828–1831* (2 vols, Oxford and Karachi 1979)
— *Letters from India, 1829–32* (trans. CH Phillips, London 1936)
Jenkins, R: *Gladstone* (London and New York 1996)
Jog, NG: *Churchill's Blind-spot: India* (Bombay 1944)
Johnson, E: *Sir Walter Scott, The Great Unknown* (2 vols, London 1970)
Jones, Sir William: *Letters... from Lord Teignmouth's Collection* (2 vols, London 1819–21)
Joshi, S: ed., *Rethinking English, The Cultural Politics of Literature, Language and Pedagogy in India* (New Delhi 1991)
Judd, D: *Empire: the British Imperial Experience from 1765 to the Present* (London 1996)
— *Lord Reading* (London 1982)
Kaye, J: *The Life of Malcolm* (2 vols, London 1856)
— *The History of the Indian Mutiny* (ed. GB Malleson, 3 vols, London 1897)
Keay, J: *The Honourable Company* (London 1991)
— *India Discovered* (London 1988)
Khan, Ahmad: *The Causes of the Indian Revolt, 1857* (Lahore 1873 ed.)
Kiernan, VG: *The Lords of Human Kind: European Attitudes to the Outside World in the Imperial Age* (London 1969)
Kincaid, D: *British Social Life in India, 1608–1937* (London 1973)
Kindersley, NE: *Letters from the East Indies* (London 1777)
Kochhar, RK: *Ardaseer Cursetjee, 1808–1877* (Notes and Records of the Royal Society of London 1993)
Kopf, D: *British Orientalism and the Bengali Renaissance* (California 1969)
Kripalani, K: *Tagore, A Life* (New Delhi 1961)
Lambrick, HT: *Sir Charles Napier and Sind* (Oxford 1952)
Law, Edward, Lord Ellenborough: *A Political Diary* (2 vols, London 1881)
Lawrence, AW: ed., *Captives of Tipu* (London 1929)
Lawrence, J and A Woodiwiss: eds, *The Journals of Honoria Lawrence: India Observed, 1837–54* (London 1980)
Lawrence, WR: *The India We Served* (London 1928)
Leask, N: *British Romantic Writers and the East* (Cambridge 1992)
Longford, E: *Wellington, The Years of the Sword* (London 1969)
— *A Pilgrimage of Passion: The Life of Wilfrid Scawen Blunt* (London 1979)
— *Queen Victoria* (London 1964)
Losty, JP: *Calcutta, City of Palaces* (London 1990)
Lutyens, Edwin: *Letters to his wife, Lady Emily* (ed. C Percy and J Ridley, London 1985)
Lutyens, Emily: *Candles in the Sun* (London 1957)
Lutyens, M: *The Lyttons in India* (London 1979)
— *Edwin Lutyens* (London revised edition 1971)
Macaulay, TB: *History of England* (London, Everyman ed.)
— *The Life and Works*, vols 7 and 8 (London 1897)
— 'Robert Clive' in *Critical and Historical Essay* (2 vols, London 1866)
Macdonald, B: *India... Sunshine and Shadows* (London 1989)
Macmillan, M: *Women of the Raj* (London 1988)
Magnus, P: *Gladstone* (London 1954)
— *Kitchener* (London 1958)
Mahajan, J: *The Grand India Tour* (New Delhi 1996)
— *Picturesque India: Sketches and Travels of Thomas and William Daniell* (New Delhi 1983)
Malcolm, J: *Sketch of the Political History of India since 1784* (2 vols, London 1826)
Malik, KM and P Robb: *India and Britain*, proceedings of a seminar at the School of Oriental and African Studies, London University (New Delhi 1994)

Malleson, GB: *Decisive Battles of India* (London 1914)
— *Final French Struggles in India and on the Indian Sea* (London 1878)
Marshall, PJ: *East India Fortunes, the British in Bengal in the Eighteenth Century* (Oxford 1976)
— *The British Discovery of Hinduism in the Eighteenth Century* (Cambridge 1970)
Marshman, C: *The Life and Times of Carey, Marshman and Ward* (2 vols, London 1859)
McCulloch, JR: 'Indian Revenues' from the *Edinburgh Review*, 45 (1827)
Metcalf, TR: *Land, Landlords and the British Raj* (Berkeley 1979)
— *Ideologies of the Raj* (Cambridge 1995)
Mill, James: *The History of British India* (3 vols, London 1817/8; 9 v., 1848, 10 v., 1858)
— *The History of British India* (ed. in 1 vol by W Thomas, Chicago 1975)
Minto, Mary: *India, Minto and Morley, 1905–10* (London 1934)
Misra, GS: *British Foreign Policy and Indian Affairs, 1783–1815* (Bombay 1963)
Montagu, ES: *My Indian Diary* (London 1930)
Moon, P: *Divide and Quit* (Oxford and India 1998)
— *Warren Hastings and British India* (London 1947)
Moore, Robin J: *Imperial India, 1858–1914* (Oxford History of the British Empire, vol iii, 1999)
Morley, J: *The Life of William Ewart Gladstone* (2 vols, London 1908)
Morris, H: *The Life of Charles Grant* (London 1904)
Muggeridge, M: *Chronicles of Wasted Time: The Green Stick* (London 1972)
— *Chronicles of Wasted Time: The Infernal Grove* (London 1975)
Mujeeb, M: *Indian Muslims* (London 1966)
Mukherjee, SN: *Sir William Jones* (Cambridge 1968)
Naoroji, D: *Poverty and Un-British Rule* (London 1901)
Napier, C: *The Life and Opinions of General Charles Napier* (4 vols, London 1857)
Napier P: *I Have Sind: Charles Napier in India, 1841–1844* (London 1990)
Nath, Aman: *Jaipure: The Last Destination* (Bombay 1993)
Nehru, J: *The Discovery of India* (Calcutta 1946)
Newton, Lord: *Lord Lansdowne, a Biography* (London 1929)
Orwell, G: *Collected Essays, Journalism and Letters* (4 vols, London 1968)
Page, J: *Swartz of Tanjore* (London 1912)
Pal, P and V Dehejia: *From Merchants to Emperors, British Artists and India, 1757–1930* (Ithaca and London 1986)
Panikkar, KM: *Asia and Western Dominance* (London 1953)
Parry, JH: *The Discovery of the Sea* (London 1974)
Parsons, A: *Travels in Asia and Africa* (London 1808)
Pearce, R: *Wellesley Papers* (2 vols, London 1914)
Peers, DM: *Between Mars and Mammon: Colonial Armies and the Garrison State in Early Nineteenth Century India* (London 1995)
Philips, CH: ed., *The Correspondence of Lord William Bentinck* (2 vols, London 1977)
— *The Evolution of India and Pakistan, 1858–1947, Select Documents* (Oxford 1965 ed.)
Prinsep, Val C: *Imperial India* (London 1878)
Quinn, DB: ed., *The Hakluyt Handbook* (2 vols, Cambridge 1974)
Ram, Sita: *From Sepoy to Subedar* (ed. J Lunt, London 1988)
Ray, RK: *Indian Society and the Establishment of British Supremacy, 1765–1818*, in *The Oxford History of the British Empire*, vol 2 (Oxford 1998)
Rizvi, G: *Linlithgow and India, a Study of British Policy and the Political Impasse in India, 1936–43* (London 1978)
Roberts, A: *Salisbury, Victorian Titan* (London 1999)
Roberts, E: *Scenes and Characteristics of Hindostan* (3 vols, London 1835)

Roberts, FS: *Forty One Years in India* (London 1900)

Robinson, J: *Angels of Albion: Women of the Indian Mutiny* (London 1996)

Ronaldshay, Lord: *The Life of Lord Curzon* (3 vols, London 1928)

Ross, A: *Ranji, Prince of Cricketers* (London 1983)

Rosselli, J: *Lord William Bentinck, the Making of a Liberal Imperialist* (London and Sussex 1974)

Rowntree, J: *A Chota Sahib, Memoirs of a Forest Officer* (Padstow 1981)

Sadiq, M: *The Founder of Aligarh: the Story of Sayyid Ahmad Khan* (Karachi 1968)

St Aubyn, G: *Queen Victoria* (London 1977)

Saletore, BA: ed., *Fort William – India House Correspondence, 1782–5*, vol ix (New Delhi 1959)

Sardesai, GS: *A New History of the Marathas* (3 vols, Bombay 1957)

Sarkar, Jadunath: 'James Browne at the Delhi Court, 1783–5', in *Bengal, Past and Present*, April–June 1937

Schweinitz, K de: *The Rise and Fall of British India, Imperialism as Inequality* (London 1983)

Seal, A: *The Emergence of Indian Nationalism* (Cambridge 1971)

Sen, SN: *The Military System of the Marathas* (Calcutta 1958)

— *Anglo-Maratha Relations during the Administration of Warren Hastings, 1772–1785* (Calcutta 1961)

— *Eighteen Fifty Seven* (Calcutta 1958)

Sen, SP: *The French in India, First Establishment and Struggle* (Calcutta 1947)

— *The French in India, 1763–1816* (Calcutta 1958)

Sheik Ali, B: *British Relations with Haidar Ali* (Mysore 1963)

Shelden, M: *Orwell* (London 1991)

Shepherd, EW: *Coote Bahadur* (London 1956)

Shirer, WL: *Gandhi, a Memoir* (London 1981 ed.)

Silvers, RB and B Epstein: *India: A Mosaic* (New York 2000)

Sinha, NK: *Haidar Ali* (Calcutta 1941)

Sleeman, WH: *Rambles and Recollections of an Indian Official* (London 1844, ed. V Smith, reprinted Karachi 1973)

Smith, G: *William Carey, Shoemaker and Missionary* (London 1884)

Smith, HB: *Life of Lord Lawrence* (London 1885)

Smith, Sydney: *Works* (London 1869)

Spear, P: *A History of India* (Harmondsworth 1965)

— *The Nabobs, A Study of the Social Life of the English in 18th Century India* (Oxford 1932, 1963 ed.)

Spence, J: *The Search for Modern China* (London 1990)

Srinivasachari, CS: ed., *Fort William – India House Correspondence 1764–1776*, vol iv (Delhi 1962)

Steevens, GW: *In India* (London 1899)

Stokes, E: *English Utilitarians and India* (Oxford and New Delhi ed. 1982)

Strachan, MF: *Sir Thomas Roe, 1581–1644, a Life* (Salisbury UK 1989)

Strachey, J: *India* (London 1888)

Strachey, R: *A Strachey Child* (Oxford 1979)

Surtees, V: *Charlotte Canning* (London 1976)

Sutherland, L: *The East India Company in 18th Century Politics* (Oxford 1952)

Taylor, Meadows: *Story of My Life* (Edinburgh 1878)

— *Ralph Darnell* (London 1865)

— *Seeta* (London 1872)

Temple, R: *Oriental Experiences* (London 1883)

Tharoor, S: *India: From Midnight to the Millennium* (New York 1998)

Thompson, E: *Rabindranath Tagore, Poet and Dramatist* (ed. H Trivedi, Oxford and Delhi 1989)

Trevelyan, C: *On the Education of the People of India* (London 1838)

Trevelyan, GO: *The Life and Letters of Lord Macaulay* (2 vols, Oxford 1932 ed.)

— *Cawnpore* (London 1885, New Delhi reprint 1992)

— *The Competition-Wallah* (London 1886, reprint New Delhi 1992)

Trotter, LJ: *The Life of Hodson of Hodson's Horse* (London 1901, Everyman ed. 1927)

— *The Life of John Nicholson* (London 1897)

Tuker, F: *The Yellow Scarf: an Account of Thuggee and its Suppression* (London 1961)

Valentia, George: *Voyages and Travels to India, Ceylon, the Red Sea, Abyssinia and Egypt* (3 vols, London 1806)

Vansittart, H: *A Narrative of the Transactions in Bengal* (London 1761)

Verelst, Henry: *A View of the English Government in Bengal* (London 1772)

Vernède, RV: *British Life in India* (Oxford and India 1997)

Vibart, HM: *Addiscombe, Its Heroes and Men of Note* (London 1984)

Victoria, Queen: *Highland Journal* (ed. D Duff, London 1980)

— *Beloved and Darling Child: the last letters between Queen Victoria and her Eldest Daughter, 1886–1901* (ed. A Ram, Stroud, Glos. 1990)

Visram, R: *Ayahs, Lascars and Princes: Indians in Britain 1700–1947* (London 1986)

Viswanathan, G: *Masks of Conquest: Literary Study and British Rule in India* (London 1990)

Wakefield, E: *Past Imperative* (London 1966)

Waley, SD: *Edwin Montagu* (London 1964)

Warner, WL: *Protected States of India* (London 1910)

Washbrook, DA: *India, 1818–1860: The Two Faces of Colonialism* (Oxford History of the British Empire 1999 vol iii)

Wavell, A: *The Viceroy's Journal* (ed. P Moon, Oxford 1973)

Webb, Sydney and Beatrice: *Indian Diary* (Oxford and New Delhi 1987)

Wilks, Colonel M: *Historical Sketches of South India in an Attempt to trace the History of Mysore* (2 vols, London 1810–17)

Wilton, Iain: *Fry: an English Hero* (London 1999)

Woodruff, P: *The Men Who Ruled India: The Founders* (London 1953)

— *The Men Who Ruled. India, The Guardians* (London 1954)

Woolf, L: *Growing* (London 1961)

— *Selected Letters* (ed. F Spotts, London 1989)

Yelland, Z: *Boxwallahs: the British in Cawnpore, 1857–1901* (Norwich 1994)

Young, K: *Delhi 1857* (London 1902 ed.)

Yule, H: ed., *The Diary of William Hedges* (London, for the Hakluyt Society, first series, 2 vols, 1888)

— and AC Burnell: *Hobson-Jobson* (London 1886, ed. W Crooke 1903)

Glossary

ahimsa	avoidance of all violence
akali	Sikh zealot, self appointed censor of the community
almirah	a cupboard
amir	a local Muslim chieftain or territorial ruler (also Mir), deriving his title originally from Istanbul
awadhi	a native of Oudh
babu	an honorific for an educated Bengali, but used by the British to denote a clerk
badmash	a bad hat
banian (banyan)	businessman or merchant who, in Calcutta, often managed a Company officer's affairs as well as his own
bashi-bazouk	irregular troops employed by the Ottoman Turks to quell the Balkan risings
batta	allowance given to European officers and men of the Indian army when on active service in cantonment, barracks or permanent encampment
bhoosa-box	a 'hay box', the husks and stalks of straw left by the oxen after being trodden for corn
Brahmo-samaj	a movement founded by Rammohan Roy for the 'modernisation' of Hinduism
chhatrapathi	title of the consecrated Maratha ruler of Satara
chauth	tribute levied by Marathas on conquered people
chobdar	a staff denoting office
chowkidar	night watchman
chunam	a finely polished plaster made of crushed lime which could be made to resemble marble
chuprassi	an office messenger
circar	name given to territory in the north part of the Coromandel coast separating the areas controlled by Forts William and St George and ruled by the Nizam of Hyderabad
coffre	mixed race (usually Dutch/Bantu) native of Southern Africa and Mauritius
competition-wallah	European civil servant who had entered the service by competition
dacoit	member of a gang given to rural crime
darzi	a tailor
Dassehra	Hindu festival at the end of the wet season, in October; known in Bengal as Durga-Puja
dastak (dustuk)	pass issued by the Company, exempting Company goods from taxes and duties otherwise levied on goods in transit in the nawabi of Bengal
dastar, dastur	any procedure sanctified by custom
Deccan	the name given to the table land between the Eastern and Western Ghats (q.v.)
diwali	the festival of lights in honour of Lakshmi in October-November when Hindus decorate their houses with little clay lamps

diwan, diwani   Mughal viceroy, area of rule assigned to diwan. Also used of the seat of oriental government (e.g. divan)

doab   the land between the confluence of two rivers, mainly used of that between the Ganges and Jumna

dorbar   full gathering or levée of an Indian prince's or vice-regal court

dubash   'man of two languages', interpreter or business manager, mainly in south India, corresponding to banian (q.v.)

Eurasian   mixed race (Indian/European) used in the nineteenth and early twentieth centuries to describe the children of mixed marriages. After Independence the term Anglo-Indian, formerly used to denote long term British residents in India, is used instead

factory   trading establishment, usually European, established in major African and Asian ports

fakir   mendicant religious, usually Muslim, but often applied inaccurately to Hindus

firman   a permissive document deriving from the Mughal emperor in Delhi

foujdari   local Mughal military officer responsible for law and order

gadi   cushion denoting a throne

Gaekwad   title of the ruler of Baroda

gardi   Indian soldier trained in western drill

Ghats   chain of mountains to west and east of the Indian cone, leading to the Deccan (q.v.); a burning ground usually place of cremation of the dead adjacent to a river

gomastah   a native agent or factor

haj, hajji   the Muslim pilgrimage; individual pilgrim

hartal   a strike

Hobson-Jobson   a glossary of Indian terms, called after the English corruption of the Moharram ejaculation of 'Ya Hasan'

jacquerie   (French) rural unrest taking the form of attacks on property

jagir   an assignment of land to a subject by a native ruler, usually for a year, at most for life

jats   race of peasant farmers and warriors mainly in Panjab and United Provinces

khaddar   Indian home-spun cloth

Khalifat   a Muslim movement dedicated to the cause of retaining the Caliphate in the person of the Ottoman ruler in Istanbul

Khalsa   technically meaning pure, applied to the religious and collective community of Sikhs, used sometimes to refer to Sikhs under arms, an army of the pure

khitmutgar   Bengal only, the servant who waited at table

koss   a unit of distance measurement, generally held to be about 2-miles

lathi   long metal tipped bamboo cane used for crowd control

mahajan   usually a banker or moneylender

mahatma   literally great soul, used by theosophists for master spirits in Tibet; a title applied popularly to Gandhi

maidan   open space separating blocks of houses

masnad   ceremonial cushion used as a throne

maulvi   a Muslim lawyer

mela   a fair, usually associated with a religious festival

mir   a chieftain of Sind (q.v. amir)

mofussil   up the country, away from Presidency cities

munshi	variously, a teacher or scribe, a native secretary
mutasaddi	native accountant
nabob	term given to any Briton who returned home with an ostentatious fortune made in India
naik, nayak	a title of honour in the Deccan; noncommissioned sepoy officer
nawab, nawabi	a title conferred on an Indian governor by the Mughal emperor; the land under a nawab's control, corrupted by the British to nabob
nawab-wazir	used of the semi-independent ruler of Oudh
nautch	song and dance, frequently lascivious, more often tedious, performed by women as an entertainment
nizam, nizamat	title of the ruler of the Deccan (q.v.); the territory under his command, conferred by the Mughal emperor
nizam adalat	Muslim civil court
nuzzer	a ceremonial gift, usually from an inferior to a superior
padishah	a title for the Great Mughal
padishah-ghazi	commander in chief of Muslim faithful, literally Sword of the Faith
pagoda	south Indian temple giving its name to a coin in south India bearing the image of one
pandit	a learned man, usually in Sanskrit law
pargana	a district, like a county. The 24 Parganas were the 'counties' round Calcutta that formed Clive's jagir (q.v.)
patel	village headman
patwari	an officer accounting for the collection of revenue from villages
pentiti	(Italian) a criminal turning King's evidence
Peshwa	formerly chief minister, later elected ruler of the Maratha confederacy
pindari	a band of marauders, usually of paid-off Indian mercenaries
purbiah	the 'poor bloody infantry' of the Bengal army, recruited from Oudh, Benares and Bihar
qanungo	a revenue officer, usually collecting from village headmen
romal	the scarf used by ritual stranglers (q.v. thuggee)
ryot, raiyat	peasant, any 'tenant of the soil' who worked the land
saddhu	a Hindu holy man
satyagraha	policy of passive resistance, developed by Gandhi
schruyver	the Dutch term that corresponded to a Company writer (see below)
sepoy	a native soldier trained in the European style
serai	building for the accommodation of travellers
shastra	lawbooks and sacred writings of the Hindus
shroff	Indian banker, money-changer
sicca rupee	the rupee coin minted by the Company as opposed to a native ruler
sirdar (sardar)	an officer in charge of military or civilian operations, extended first to the Company, then to the British Indian government
sowar	member of a mounted camel corps, used for ceremonial attendance and to patrol the dry lands of north India
stupa	(Buddhist) a solid dome covering a sacred building
subha, subahdar	a Mughal governor or viceroy; later a native officer commanding a company of sepoys
suttee (sati)	the immolation of a surviving Hindu wife or wives with the dead husband
swadeshi	home spun cloth or any home, not imported, Indian product
swaraj	self-government
taluqdar	minor nobility and landowner in Oudh

thanadar	a native police constable
thuggee (thagi)	ritual killing, usually by strangulation, a manifestation of rural crime, by gangs of 'thugs'
topass	mixed race descendant of a Portuguese and Indian union, usually a Christian
wazir	vizier, or royal minister
writer	junior Company clerk responsible for the writing of bills of lading and other commercial documents (q.v. schruyver)
zamindar	under Mughal rule a landholder, a temporary assignee of land from the throne, with powers of raising money to meet his dues to the emperor or viceroy; a practice adopted by the Company
zenana	the women's quarters

INDEX

Ackroyd, Annette (see Beveridge)
Addiscombe, 126, 135, 174
Afghanistan, 4, 37, 55, 100, 102, 105,
    120, 122, 145, 152, 154, 158, 166,
    193–4, 207; British wars with, 125,
    127–30, 162–4; defeat Marathas, 40–
    41; mercenaries, 35; sack Delhi, 31–2
Africa, 2–3, 19, 26, 28, 150, 226; African
    slaves, 26, 75; South Africa, 174,
    178, 198, 204–5
Agra, 7–8, 10, 21, 89, 98, 113, 118, 137,
    150, 155–6
Ahmad Khan, Syed, 147, 176, 187
Ahmedabad, 7, 10, 29, 60, 210; prison, 205
Ahmed Shah Abdali (Durrani), 40–41
Akbar ('Zelabdin Echebar'), 4–6, 8, 161,
    172
Aleppo, 4, 21
Alexander, AV, 205; James, 115
Aligarh, 98; Muslim University of, 190
Alipur, 51, 80
Alivardi Khan, nawab of Bengal, 32, 36,
    38, 54
Allahabad, 67, 93, 181, 189, 234, 224;
    club, 224; Treaty of, 44
Alwar, HH of, 181
Ambala, 143
Ambon (Amboina), 7, 11
America, South, 123; United States of,
    62–64, 67, 91, 146, 189, 213–6, 225
Amherst, Lord, 134
Amin Chand ('Omichand'), 37, 230n, 232n
Amritsar, 143, 201, 203–4 (see also
    Jallianwalabagh)
Amsterdam, 1, 10, 48
'Anglicists', 117–8
Angria, house of, 19, 32
Anwar-ud-din, nawab of Carnatic, 32
Arabian sea, 3, 5, 8,
Archaeological Survey of India, 116, 133
Arcot, 32, 34, 60–1; nawabi of, 32 (see
    also Muhammad Ali)
Argaon, battle of, 99–100

Armagaum, 7, 11
Armenians, 13–4, 77, 231–2n; in
    Calcutta, 14, 24–25, 30, 54
armies in India: abolition of flogging in
    Company army, 110 127;
    adjustments to size of British army
    in India after 1857, 150–1, 171; after
    1947, 222–3; Bengal a., 39, 44, 72,
    96, 125–6, 134, 141–3, 147–51, 245n;
    Bombay a., 151; Company a., 125–7;
    effect of European warfare, 69–70;
    European a., 151, 168; Indian a.s, 34,
    41, 125–7, 151; in two World Wars,
    151, 201, 213–4; Madras a., 33, 72,
    88, 151, 233n; Maratha a., 103;
    morals of British army in India,
    182–3; Mughal, Maratha and
    Company a.s compared, 41–2, 96
Arya Samaj, 221
Asaf Jah Chinqilich Khan, Nizam of
    Hyerabad, 31, 33
Asaf-ud-daula, nawab-wazir of Oudh, 74,
    100, 120
Ashoka, 116
Asiatick Society, 81–3, 85, 106, 115–7;
    Asiatick Researches, 81; Journal, 172
Asquith, Herbert, 202, 252n
Assam, 74, 127, 175
Assaye, battle of, 99–100
Attlee, Clement, 201, 209, 215–7
Auckland, Lord (see Eden)
Aungier, Gerald, Governor of Bombay, 13
Aung-Sang, Burmese leader, 217
Aurangabad, 31, 33
Aurangzeb, Emperor, 16–7, 19, 21, 32,
    41, 101, 115, 230–1n
Awadh, Awadhi (see Oudh)

Babur (Zajir-ud-din Muhammad), 4–6,
    17, 35, 41
Baghdad, 2, 4
Bahadur Shah of Gujerat, 3; King of
    Delhi, 134, 141